World-renowned researcher and lecturer on UFOs and encounters with non-human intelligences, Mary Rodwell, has provided an intellectual analysis of a real phenomenon. She presents some of the most fascinating individual cases ever published on this topic, which should give second thoughts to even the most hardened skeptic. Her scholarly examination of the evidence provides a thought provoking and required foundation to help better understand the nature of our reality within a multidimensional universe. Highly recommended!

Robert Davis, PhD Neuroscience.

When I grew up I had no one to turn to and no one understood what I was talking about or why I acted and behaved the way I did, that I was an Experiencer and a Contactee. If my mother and other family members would have been able to listen to Mary Rodwell and to read her books maybe my childhood would have been totally different, more balanced and loving. I´m coming out of the "space closet" as Mary calls it. I do that as a private person/Experiencer but also with all the knowledge I've collected through the years as a scientist and a therapist. I´m coming out so that people like me, and especially children like I was, can connect and feel they are not alone. Through Mary, many others in this book are also coming out. I hope all people that read this book understand that we might be different in many ways, but that different in this context is a good thing and is likely the next step in evolution. Our new set of skills are not frightening but are partly the result of evolution and society's development.

Lena Ohlson, PhD Molecular Toxicology,
BSc Molecular Biology, and Biochemistry.

The New Human is all about our evolution. We are evolving and we need to evolve for the survival of the human species and the planet. This evolution is also necessary for our planet to maintain its position in the universe.

The New Human is an extraordinary book. It holds vital information and keys for this process of evolution; this book is a catalyst. Not only does it expand our awareness and enhance our understanding of the most significant process happening on the planet today, but the actual words, the stories and the information, hold frequencies by which, reading them, a person will be activated. *The New Human* is a book that has the ability, on many levels, to wake people up and change the course of history.

By intelligently presenting extensive evidence and research, a subject that has been met with ridicule and discrimination has now been given the platform it deserves.

We need to listen and understand, take our heads out of the sand and embrace what is happening to our species.

I would recommend this book to anyone who sees a world in need of change. To any person who wants to understand what is actually taking place on the planet and to humanity. To anyone who is feeling the effects of our planet's current state and to anyone who has sensed something big is going on.

In particular, teachers, leaders, politicians, doctors, scientists, lawyers and those in any position of authority need to become aware of this information to help guide and ensure the necessary evolution of the species.

The New Human is a book that will help heal and propel us towards a better future. This information is leading edge.

I congratulate Mary for her years of dedication to this field and on producing this valuable work.

Dr. Maree Batchelor, MBBS Hons, FRACGP, Dip RACOG.

The New Human is a timely book, if we view the current chaos on our planet and the need for radical change. Mary has interviewed hundreds of people world-wide and she gives us an extraordinary, hopeful message for the future. Our species is evolving with the help of advanced, benevolent extraterrestrials. New children are being born with incredible gifts and insights into who they are and where they come from. They are highly intelligent, highly aware and many offer healing gifts for our planet and talk about bringing in new frequencies through their art, music and through light languages. While the Transhumanist agenda advocates a more controllable, more robotic human, better suited to a hive mentality, Mary, in contrast, reveals through *The New Human* that a kinder, wiser, more loving species is being introduced to our planet to wake us up and to remind us of our true destiny.

The New Human contains confirmation from a molecular biologist and astrophysicist that changes are occurring to human DNA. While our news media focuses on war and political and economic chaos everywhere, this subtle change in the human species is occurring, unobserved by the general public or our leaders. Covert disinformation and debunking agendas over decades have made sure that the UFO and ET subjects are ridiculed and dismissed. Thank goodness this is changing, due to the overwhelming evidence available now. These new children report on their star origins and what they are taught on extraterrestrial craft. The need for a new education system becomes apparent since these children do not fit into the old, limiting system. They are not programmable robots. They know who they are. *The New Human* reveals a more honest, ethical and compassionate human being, highly attuned to Mother Earth and all species, both animal and human. They are true Galactic humans. I applaud Mary for her groundbreaking work over the past twenty years in bringing this information out. The revelations in this book could be the catalyst for a better future for humanity and I cannot wait to see it unfold.

Mariana Flynn, President of UFO Research NSW Inc/Exopolitics Sydney,
Clinical Hypnotherapist.

It was back in the 1960s that I started my serious research into the subject of UFOs, and very quickly came to the realization that the scientific community followed a status quo that opened no doors into the possibility of other realities. Fifty-five years on and nothing has changed. In a review of a book about the hidden history of the human race, one man of science writes: "Your book is pure humbug and does not deserve to be taken seriously by anyone but a fool."

Mary Rodwell's exciting new book, *The New Human: Awakening to our Cosmic Heritage*, is of staggering importance in understanding the future of mankind. As Mary states, this is a book about the new kids on the block; children who have a different genetic makeup.

According to Mary's meticulous research of this global phenomenon, these children have been upgraded and numerous genes have recently been added to the human genome. These children are essential to the survival of the human race. The first wave (of the modern era) happened over sixty years ago and there have been continuous improvements ever since. Once these children find themselves in positions to make real change: in politics, environment, health, healing and education, all life on Earth will move forward in Light and Love, as it was always destined to do. If you seriously want to discover what is truly happening to mankind at this important point in our evolution, you must read this book.

Or, you may want to follow that sacred path of science: "Your book is pure humbug and does not deserve to be taken seriously by anyone but a fool." However, as Amber Jayanti says, in her book about the Tarot cards: "The fool appears to be walking off a cliff into the great beyond, denoting both a trusting attitude and life's infinite possibilities." This is a brave book and well done Mary Rodwell.

Mike Oram, author of *Does It Rain In Other Dimensions?*

The New Human: Awakening to Our Cosmic Heritage is an evolutionary leap toward preparing us for the inevitable: the exciting moment when our collective human spirit (re)connects with the greater extraterrestrial reality. Our cosmic family is indeed awaiting us on the new frontiers of higher consciousness! Author, Mary Rodwell, a long-time expert on the expansive and emerging ET phenomenon, has written a stunning masterpiece that boldly synthesizes a huge array of extraordinary experiences. DNA decoding, hybrid children, parallel universes, soul connections, time machines, teleportation, pyramid technology, Mars bases, AI, off-planet agendas, and many other fascinating subjects are amazingly sourced from first-hand Contact experiences. *The New Human* takes you on an adventurous ride down the rabbit hole and is destined to rock the planet. Thank you, Mary, for all you are doing to enlighten and educate the world!

Tonia Madenford, Executive Producer, Screen Addiction
UFO Greatest Story Ever Denied, Solar (R)evolution, Packing For Mars, and
Klaus Dona Chronicles.

THE
NEW HUMAN

Awakening to our Cosmic Heritage

Mary Rodwell

Published by New Mind Publishers

Publisher's Note

First published 2016
Re-printed in Australia
by New Mind Publishers, 2017

www.newmindpublishers.com

Copyright © Mary Rodwell 2016, 2017

ISBN: 978-0-9807555-1-0

Cover Artwork by Lloyd Canning © Lloyd Canning
Graphic Design by Danielle Rodwell
Edited by Fran Pickering and Janelle Brunckhorst

This book, *The New Human*, is dedicated to my beautiful and very special grandchildren, Bodhi, Eden, Haevan, Scout and India.

These children, just like so many other souls incarnating now, are creating a new future for humanity. The new children are humanity's hope for an enlightened future, and I hope that in some small way this book will support them so that with their help we can heal our beautiful planet and create a new, loving, caring, and evolved mature humanity.

About the Author

Mary Rodwell is the author of *Awakening: How Extraterrestrial Contact Can Transform Your Life*. Mother of three and grandmother, Mary migrated from the UK to Australia in 1991. A former nurse-midwife, Health Educator, and counselor, Mary was employed in several counseling agencies in Australia before branching out into private practice as a professional counselor, hypnotherapist, metaphysical teacher, Reiki healer, researcher, and writer. Mary has produced a 5-CD series of metaphysical meditations and is co-director of New Mind Records.

www.newmindrecords.com

Mary became involved in the UFO encounter phenomenon whilst studying for an Advanced Diploma in Counseling. The lack of professional support for the Contact experiences was instrumental in her forming the first professional support network in Australia: the Australian Close Encounter Resource Network (ACERN). To date, over 3,000 individuals across the globe have resourced ACERN.

www.acern.com.au

Mary has also worked with various groups and organizations internationally. Recently, she became one of the co-founders and Directors of the Dr. Edgar Mitchell Foundation for Research into Extraterrestrial Encounters (FREE).

www.experiencer.org

Mary has produced two EBE-Award-winning films: *Expressions of ET Contact: A Visual Blueprint?* and *Expressions of ET Contact: A Communication and Healing Blueprint?*

Organizer and presenter of the international conference 'Hidden Truths', in Perth, Mary has also appeared in several documentaries, including the *OZ Files*, *My Mum Talks to Aliens* (SBS, 2010), the *Paranormal Files* and *Animal X*.

As an international speaker, Mary has given presentations in Europe, France, Malta, Scandinavia, Denmark, Norway, Sweden, UK, Ireland, USA, Canada, Hong Kong, New Zealand and Australia.

Awakening: How Extraterrestrial Contact Can Transform Your Life, is a resource book to support the Experiencers through the process of their awakening.

The New Human: Awakening to Our Cosmic Heritage is Mary's second book and takes this awakening to the level of real disclosure as the recent generations of starseeds have different needs and more conscious awareness of who they are and their mission to assist with this evolutionary shift in human consciousness.

Contents

Foreword

It is my pleasure, Dear Reader, to provide a foreword to this book, *The New Human*, by author Mary Rodwell.

The author presented, earlier, the book *Awakening*, in which she used her unique skills to offer a positive perspective on Encounters with Extraterrestrial entities (ETs).

The earlier book was described by Dr. Roger Leir, M.D. as "The Bible of the Alien Abduction Phenomenon." The author showed her professional skills (from Educational, Medical, and Psychological Sciences) in her research, and her personal skills in her writing, psychological counseling, hypnotherapeutic interactions, and her consultations with patients/clients/families/colleagues, et al. She found that many Participants changed their viewpoint about these encounters: They were not abducted (taken away from Earth); they were adducted (taken toward the Stars). Thus, from a multidisciplinary perspective, many Participants viewed themselves as developing a multidimensional perspective about their encounters with ETs. These encounters were viewed as physical/biological/psychological/spiritual events, and the effect was to develop a purpose or personal "mission" to assist Earth and Humanity.

In this book, *The New Human*, Mary Rodwell continues her multidisciplinary approach, and she increases her contributions to the multidimensional perspective. Emphasizing the written and oral statements, from children and their families, she provides both data and direction of these New Humans.

She analyzes the names – and labels – that have been applied to these "new kids": Crystal, Indigo, Millennials, Star Children, etc., as well as the behaviors that can be viewed as abnormal or dysfunctional, e.g., Autism, Attention-deficit/hyperactivity disorder (ADHD), Post-traumatic stress disorder (PTSD), etc. She quotes children who not only describe their memories of past lifetimes but also state their missions in this lifetime. Sometimes, a child describes a special school on Mars, where she/he receives further instruction about her/his mission. Sometimes, a child shares her or his knowledge through unusual messages, as in art, dreams, music, etc. Sometimes, a child presents a prediction, e.g., something important is going to occur before the year 2017.

These children are able to talk about the physical spacecraft; the biological aspects of surgical interventions and 'implants'; the psychological aspects of their interactions with ETs and military personnel and the spiritual aspects of their HSA (Higher Sense Abilities): psychic abilities as well as their purpose or mission. Not only are they New Humans, but they view themselves as working with other humans and ETs to build a New Earth as to develop a New Humanity.

I can recall, some years ago, sitting in my office and listening to a boy in the eighth grade. He knew that he was in contact with ETs and he knew that as an adult he would be working with others in terraforming Earth: modifying the soil of Earth to improve agricultural and meteorological results. His younger sister knew that she would become a teacher in a planetary educational system. These children were very bright according to IQ test results and they were very psychic in their awareness and our discussions. I enjoyed talking with them and I viewed them as "planetary persons" and also as "cosmic citizens." (Sprinkle, 1999, 2009).

Author Mary Rodwell provides you, Dear Reader, not only with the results of thousands of case studies; she also provides you with a summary of writings from many scientists. The Old Science was based on the theme that Matter and Spirit are separate. The New Science is based upon the thesis that Matter and Consciousness are not only connected – they are One. All is Energy.

As mystics have claimed for thousands of years, everything is connected and every event is energy. Whatever label is applied: God, Spirit, Consciousness, Energy, etc., the New Science, based upon Quantum Physics, gives us the knowledge that ESP is no longer paranormal; it is normal. Reincarnation of the Soul into another body and a new life is an ongoing process. Our Sun rises and sets in the eyes of an earthling. However, from a Galactic perspective the Sun continues to shine.

And yes, Dear Reader, every section of *The New Human*, by Mary Rodwell, allows her to Shine and to Share! Enjoy! May we all share Love and Light.

R. Leo Sprinkle, PhD.
Professor Emeritus, Counseling Services, University of Wyoming.

References:

Sprinkle, R. Leo. *Soul Samples: Personal Explorations in Reincarnation and UFO Experiences.* Columbus, NC: Granite Publishing, 1999.

Sprinkle, R. Leo. *ET Experiencers: From Planetary Persons to Cosmic Citizens?* A Galactic Gathering, Denver, Colorado. 25/27 Sept. 2009.

Acknowledgments

I want to express my deep gratitude to all the beautiful souls, individuals, families, and children who have courageously and generously shared their stories in this book. Your contributions are priceless and will offer healing, validation, and understanding to others who have trodden a similar path.

A huge thank you for the courage of Dr. Lena Ohlson, Dr. Maree Batchelor, Rev. Michael Carter, Minister Jeff Schulte, Lea Kapiteli, Antonio, Zachariah, Leonie Appelt, Samantha Mowat, Debbie Malone, Julliena Okah, Julia Sellers, Mike Oram and the others who have identified themselves and shared their stories with such bravery in coming out of the 'space closet' so that others may find the courage to do the same. Special thanks to artist and Experiencer, Tracey Taylor, for continued contribution to this phenomenon both in *Awakening* and *The New Human*.

Words cannot express how enormously grateful and thankful I am to the angels who helped me to edit and compile this book. Janelle Brunckhorst, Fran Pickering, Melinda Staunton, Callista Summerfield, who have given their invaluable help and precious time in this endeavor. I could not have done this without you.

Danielle Rodwell, my talented and very loved daughter-in-law, for her support and expertise to get this book ready for publishing.

Dr. Leo Sprinkle, for his generosity and kindness in writing the foreword; with special thanks to his daughter, Kristen, for all her assistance.

Lloyd Canning, for creating the stunning cover art. I love it and it was more than I had hoped for; the images, colors and bright energy. Brilliant! Thank you.

My dearest friends and colleagues within FREE – co-founder, Rey Hernandez, Dr. Rudy Schild, the late Dr. Edgar Mitchell, Dr. Bob Davis, for their contributions to this book and for allowing me to share the FREE survey data.

Barbara Lamb and Miguel Mendonca for their support and contributions from their complementary research with ET-human hybrids.

Dr. William Brown: Exopolitics.

To my wonderful colleagues and friends within the Ufological Community: UFOR President, Marianna Flynn, PRSA /UFO Campbelltown, Larraine Cilia, and Dominic McNamara, UFORQ Queensland, Sheryl Gottshall, T.A.L.K. Group, Leigh Kerr and Mick Harrison. To my other special friends and colleagues, you know who you are, thank you for your support, enthusiasm and dedication. Nicole Bartlett, for her love and support via ACERN web site, and Jacinta Goerke, a dear friend, who created the new site (www.maryrodwell.com.au). Thank you.

Dr. Carol Rosin, you are an inspiration.

Gary Heseltine, Editor, UFO Truth Magazine and AJ Gevaerd, Revista UFO (UFO Magazine), Brazil; Sharon Rowland, Oddities Magazine, and Alexis Brooks, Higher Journeys Radio; Duncan Roads, Nexus Magazine, and his team, who have helped get this information to the public.

My adult children – Christopher, Michaela and Tim, and their partners, Danielle, Scott, and Sharnie, for their continued love and support, and for the gift of my beautiful grandchildren – Bodhi, Eden, Haevan, Scout and India, who fill my life with such joy and hope.

To everyone who has contributed to my understanding and research over the many years I have been involved in this phenomenon, you know who you are. Thank you on behalf of all those who have been helped by your generosity.

A special mention for the support of a dear friend who passed away in 2014; a very special soul and one passionate about the truth, Graeme Bartlett. I am sure you are doing all you can on the other side, dear friend, to help as you did when you were on this planet.

To all my seen and unseen support, grateful thanks.

My Real Parents are in Space

"Mum, you are my parents as far as bringing me onto this planet, but my REAL parents are in Space. I come from somewhere out there. Something of great importance is going to happen on this Earth. Not in your lifetime, but in mine. It will affect all units of consciousness, whether they are mineral, vegetable, animal or man. It is to do with global consciousness; a vast change of consciousness and that is why I am here at this time, to experience this change."

Mike Oram (UK) at four years old.

"The 'Light-beings' told me that energy was heading our way and the essence of that energy was Light and this light would be of a frequency that would repair our DNA. They said it would make us more complete and who we really are. This would enable us to have a different reality by moving frequency. When this is, I do not know – but if I go with my feelings, then I would have to say it is just around the corner."

Does it Rain in Other Dimensions? Mike Oram (UK).

Introduction

DISCLOSURE FROM THE GROUND UP

Astronomers tell us that there could be as many as five hundred billion galaxies in our Universe and possibly one hundred billion habitable Earth-like planets in the Milky Way Galaxy alone.

Human logic declares we cannot be the only intelligent life in this vast cosmic soup, even if we consider the denials by individuals who choose to believe that *Homo sapiens* are the pinnacle of the intelligence pyramid. Human arrogance aside, the debate regarding extraterrestrial reality centers on this question: Has intelligent life advanced enough to become space faring and has it visited planet Earth?

I believe there is an abundance of tangible evidence, both anthropological and archaeological, to confirm that advanced civilizations visited our planet over millennia i.e., the 'gods' (with a lower-case 'g') modern man interprets as 'extraterrestrial intelligences'. Anomalies in human DNA suggest these intelligences have actively participated in human evolution, by manipulating human DNA, and continuing to this day through what is known as extraterrestrial encounters.

DNA research by whistleblower geneticists confirms human DNA has been spliced and altered. Former Ufologist researcher, Lloyd Pye, researched the so-called 'Star Child' skull, which was discovered in a cave in Mexico. It displayed numerous anomalies to suggest it was not of human origin. Pye also researched the nature of the anomalies in human DNA in his last book, *The Intervention Theory*. In this book, a geneticist whistleblower states:

"By certain methods of DNA dating, one can tell that numerous genes have been recently added to the human genome. If workers in my field were to say such things openly we would be ostracized and forced to live in a tent. Any work along these lines would be rejected without any form of appeal. So what can we do?"

DNA Deep Throat.

Excerpt from a letter to Lloyd Pye, author *Intervention Theory*.

Homo sapiens have an unexplained, sideways insertion of two hundred and twenty-three genes, which are unique to our species. Ancient artwork and sculptures have images of these 'star visitors' and their spacecraft. Giant skeletons and unusual skulls have been found globally. Indigenous tribes have known through their oral language and on-going extraterrestrial encounters, that 'they' (the extraterrestrials) added their DNA to the existing indigenous species on this planet to create humans.

Conspiracy or the Truth

The myriad of books on UFO and extraterrestrial reality has become abundant in recent years and explores evidence from many differing perspectives. The 'nuts and bolts' of Ufological research explored the scientific evidence such as credible witness accounts, footage of craft and trace evidence, with the corroborative testimony of 'whistleblowers' from both the military and other secret organizations. It became clear to diligent researchers that Black operations and other intelligence organizations have deliberately and criminally covered up this truth. I personally have spoken to many individuals within these organizations who have admitted that they have been part of the intimidation of witnesses as part of the truth embargo on extraterrestrial reality. However, the majority of the public remains uninformed, due to this deliberate program of propaganda, disinformation, and outright denial. There are many books on this subject to explain the reasons why this unwholesome, deceitful strategy still exists. Historian and researcher Richard Dolan, the author of *UFOs and the National Security State*, offers an excellent overview of how and why the denial of UFOs and the extraterrestrial presence is still operating today.

This book, however, is not written to prove evidence of the extraterrestrial reality because I believe it becomes obvious to anyone who is truly interested, open-minded and seeks the truth. It is impossible to dismiss the evidence of thousands of credible witnesses from astronauts, scientists, pilots, to police, lawyers, and medical personnel, who have shared their experiences with much to lose (particularly professionally) but have still done so.

Military personnel, researchers and former politicians, including Canada's previous Minister of National Defense, the Hon. Paul Hellyer, (author of *Light at the End of the Tunnel*), testified at the Citizen Hearing on Disclosure in Washington, D.C. (2013), that aliens are living amongst us and that it is likely at least two of them are working with the US government.

Hellyer Stated

"At least four species of aliens have been visiting Earth for thousands of years. Some of the aliens hail from the Zeta Reticuli, Pleiades, Orion, Andromeda and Altair star systems and may have different agendas."

(*Huffington Post*, Canada, 30 October, 2015.)

Former Professor of Psychiatry, Dr. John Mack, and Pulitzer Prize winner, author of *Abduction/Encounter Phenomenon*, a must read for those who seek to understand from a therapeutic and psychological perspective, had worked extensively with 'Experiencers' (i.e., individuals having extraterrestrial encounters). Dr. Mack's credentials alone must give pause for thought. As a psychiatrist, he examined the mental health of those individuals he worked with via rigorous psychological testing and his conclusions were clear.

"Alien encounters and Contact: it's both literally and physically happening."

> The late Dr. John Mack, former Professor of Psychiatry,
> Harvard University, author of *Abduction and Passport to the Cosmos*.

After twenty years of research and working with Experiencers, my conclusions are identical to his: extraterrestrial encounters are both physical and multi-dimensional in nature.

The organization I founded in 1997, the Australian Close Encounter Resource Network (ACERN), was created to offer professional support to those with encounter experiences, and since that time I have worked with over three thousand individuals and families. Due to my research, I have no doubt non-human intelligences are visiting our planet and interacting with humanity on multiple levels of human consciousness. This suggests to me that we may be connected to them, not only through our genetics but also spiritually. It begs the question, What does this mean for us as a species?

It is hard to know the implications when we have a truth embargo, which suggests these answers are unlikely to come from governments who are already hiding information about this phenomenon from the public. However, there is another vital source of information, which stems from individuals experiencing ongoing Contacts[1] and communication with extraterrestrial intelligences. The information the Experiencers receive is multifaceted and complex, and it suggests a far different agenda to the very negative and polarized version the popular media and covert agencies seek to promote, i.e., that humans are victims being used by extraterrestrial intelligences for their own dark agendas, with the possibility of an invasion at some future date. Although if the reports are accurate, it suggests some of these intelligences do have some self-serving agendas.

President Eisenhower warned of the threat of the military-industrial complex when he became aware of the 'truth embargo', and the realization that even Presidents were not privy to this information, let alone the general public. Dr. Carol Rosin worked with rocket scientist Werner Von Braun, who, due to his top-secret clearance, anticipated such a program. He warned that covert agendas of shadow governments would create a false flag event so that the public would believe an invasion by extraterrestrials was possible/imminent, as an excuse to weaponize space. For over thirty years, Dr. Carol Rosin has been campaigning against this false flag operation.

Note: http://www.peaceinspace.com

The Experiencers information gained through their encounters, combined with whistleblower information and other sources of alternate knowledge, paint a different picture. One that is the antitheses of the negative, fear-based scenarios portrayed by such agencies, and even through fiction, e.g. films such as *Independence Day* and *Signs*, etc. However, the public is waking up to the fact they cannot rely on governments to tell them the truth in any sphere of government. The nonsense the public has been fed: that we are too far away from life-bearing stars to be visited, assumes an arrogant, myopic view of human intelligence and technology, when many civilizations could be far more advanced (socially, technologically and spiritually), mastering space travel when we have not. The latest scientific, factual information indicates there are numerous life-bearing worlds, and we almost certainly share a cosmos teeming with life. One of the more recent Roper polls, as well as Reuters, suggests that over one and a half billion of the world's population believe that extraterrestrial visitation is a reality, and eighty-five percent believe the government is not telling the truth. The public at large, despite strategies to convey the opposite information, is waking up to how they are being manipulated, and that governments only disseminate propaganda which suits their latest economic or political agenda and reinforces the current fear agenda.

However, I believe that humanity is being helped to perceive the truth through encounters with extraterrestrial intelligences and that this is also occurring through an upgrading of the new generations of humans, born 'aware' and more intuitive than before. I share accounts from these children who already know more of the truth. The children speak of an intimate and profound connection with these 'beings' as well as what they learn from them, including information about the darker agendas propagated by those on this planet who wish to retain the status quo. Covert agencies are fully aware that those having Contacts are being taught a different perspective and these agencies have tried to counter this with propaganda and ridicule to portray them as mentally ill or 'fantasy prone'.

However, these intelligences are fully aware of such agendas and have bypassed current corrupt systems to go directly to the people themselves through their encounters. It is those individuals who will ultimately convey the truth to the general public, and why I believe disclosure of this phenomenon will come from the ground up.

Disclosure from the Ground Up

The extraterrestrial reality is coming into the public consciousness more than ever before, with sightings of craft, credible footage emerging from around the globe – although, for some, it has come at a cost in terms of credibility for many individuals. The ridicule factor has been so effective in denigrating their sightings and experiences. It appears, though, that despite these obstacles, many are being inspired to 'come out' and share their stories; some triggered to do so by a powerful and dramatic incident, such as told by molecular biologist Dr. Ohlson, below.

Coming Out of the Space Closet

Dr. Ohlson resides in a country where disclosure of Contact is viewed akin to professional suicide. However, recently she experienced a dramatic instant healing after she asked the beings with whom she is in Contact if it was time to share her story; the immediate healing was the response. Dr. Ohlson believes that this was indeed the answer to her question about whether to share publicly (See: *Now is the Time, My Story*, published in *UFO Truth Magazine*, 2015). Dr. Ohlson has gone one step further and in Chapter Fourteen shares her understanding of the changes in human DNA and the new programs for humanity.

I applaud all those who have taken this hugely difficult and challenging road to come out of what I call the 'space closet', especially when professional and personal reputations are at stake. So many have faced tremendous judgment from the uninformed public. In this book are several brave souls 'coming out' publicly for the first time – such as members of the clergy who have faced personal challenges to share how their experiences have changed how they interpret their religious beliefs. A GP, Dr. Batchelor, bravely and honestly shares her process of awakening to this reality and how that has led to her healing her patients holistically and multi-dimensionally. These courageous pioneers, sharing their understanding and experiences, I know will empower others to honor their truth, so we can no longer ignore the extraterrestrial 'elephant in the room'.

Why is Disclosure of Extraterrestrial Reality so Important Now?

Human society is at a point in its evolution where I believe it not only has the right to know the truth of its origins, but it needs to know, especially now that we have the capacity to become a space-faring species. We have covert groups/shadow governments making decisions on behalf of humanity, and the general public has little or no input in those decisions that could ultimately be catastrophic for our species. Decisions which only demonstrate to galactic civilizations the baser instincts of our species. Experiencers in communication with these 'intelligences', are shown how dangerous this is. Technologies that have the power to destroy, not only Earth's ecology, but also affect other dimensional ecologies. It is limited understanding similar to handing a small child a loaded gun without the child having the maturity to understand how dangerous the weapon may be and how fatal its effects. Humanity is already destroying the Earth's ecology, even though there are cleaner, non-polluting energy systems/technology available. These intelligences make it clear that we cannot bring such destructive, infantile behaviors to the Galactic community. If we want to be part of this community, we must clean up our act and evolve into a mature, responsible species emotionally, psychologically and spiritually.

Call to Action

However, I also believe it is the responsibility of all of us to be prepared to own our truth, i.e., to take responsibility for our behavior on this planet, whether we are part of a subtle or not so subtle 'awakening' program.

How can we:

- Not be deeply concerned regarding our future, when we are destroying the very habitat our future generations of children will rely upon to survive.
- Not be deeply concerned that there are organizations and governments on this planet who ignore the welfare of the very people they were elected to serve.
- Not be horrified that despite advances in technology, health, and farming, much of the population of this planet continues to die in wars and through starvation and disease.
- Not be disgusted that governments are spending trillions of taxpayers' dollars on destructive technologies to kill and maim their own species, rather than on health, education, and food.
- Not be appalled that destructive technologies are being moved into space, with the aim of destroying galactic communities.
- Not be shocked by man's inhumanity to man. The deliberate program to ridicule ET reality, so that individuals believe they are psychologically unsound. This is compounded by pseudo-abductions, which appear to be extraterrestrial, but are, for the most, part human orchestrated abductions by covert military agencies (MILAB). Individuals are programmed to believe all their trauma stems from 'evil aliens'. This has resulted in untold pain and conflict for those having such experiences.

I address this darker aspect of the cover-up, which is explored through the eyes of children and young adults aware of these covert programs. Their information is supported by research and whistleblower testimony.

The Shift in Human Consciousness

I believe that a shift in human consciousness is occurring, which alerts the individual to their previous, and indeed collective, 'sleep state' of conditioned reality. For some, this shift occurs through a sighting of a UFO or extraterrestrial encounter, a 'near-death experience' (NDE), out-of-body experience (OBE), a profound grief event, kundalini awakening, a shamanic journey or even a hypnotic regression. There are some, however, born consciously awake, appearing in ever growing numbers, most often in the new generations of children. For example, the young child who announces to his/her parents that they 'do not come from here' their 'real family' is in space. However this shift occurs, it inspires the individual to seek truth and is ultimately transformative.

The 'Dr. Edgar Mitchell Foundation for Research into Extraterrestrial Encounters' (FREE) has recently initiated in-depth surveys. This organization has facilitated the very first complex and in-depth surveys into those who have experienced Contact with nonhuman intelligent beings. This academic study is co-chaired by Dr. Jon Klimo, retired professor of Psychology and Dr. Bob Davis, a retired professor of

Neuroscience, coupled with an advisory committee of experienced researchers and therapists. It is a comprehensive, multilingual, academic research study on individuals who claim to have had UFO-related Contact experiences, inclusive of how they are interpreted. This research has several thousand people participating and has already highlighted some amazing outcomes from those experiencing encounters. Much of what was believed about the negative outcomes of Contact phenomenon to date, has been contradicted by these surveys. These surveys discovered that eighty-five percent of those who experienced such Contact experienced a major transformation in their lives, incorporating positive, spiritual change. This negates much of what the public has been fed by the popular media and the fiction of the abusive nature of such experiences.

Ref: www.experiencer.org

What these surveys have conclusively demonstrated is that, contrary to popular belief, sensationalized victimization is not true for a high percentage of those having encounters. For the most part, the results of such interactions are ultimately transformative. It has also highlighted that for many, such experiences are a catalyst for awakening, exposing the individual to the truth of what is really happening on this planet. The individuals become more aware of human inequality, the damage to the environment, darker agendas and corruption and the inaccuracy of much that is taught. This 'lifting of the veil' and shift into a higher state of awareness means they are able to discern truth more accurately, perceive other realities and connect to other intelligences from both the physical and non-physical Omniverse. No longer self-absorbed and materialistic, they become aware of the deeper connection and develop respect for all life without the boundaries of judgment and fear.

This new research indicates that a consciousness shift can be facilitated by non-human intelligences interacting with humanity on multiple levels, such as human biological systems, and multidimensional education. It appears that there are complex programs for humanity. Some of these programs are discussed. It suggests that when we reach a level of awareness and spiritual maturity required by our cosmic neighbors, we will then be allowed to journey into the stars, and connect and interact with the galactic community of life forms.

Awakening to Our Cosmic Heritage:

It appears that this Awakening is for all of us, if we desire it and when we become conscious of our programming and conditioning it enables us to explore the matrix with greater freedom and perhaps to reclaim what we have lost. This is a theme shared by the many of the accounts in this book.

The new generations of children, however, do not appear to have these limitations and appear to be born in such a way that they are less likely to succumb to the old programs and 3D conditioning. It suggests they can retain their multidimensional understanding and awareness for longer. They appear to intuitively KNOW they are here to help humanity shift in consciousness. Although their parents' Contact journey may have been fraught with fear or self-doubt due to their 3D programming, the children, for the most part, are at peace with their experiences, integrated in ways which astonish their parents. These children I call the New Humans because they are conscious, different, and multi-dimensionally aware. It also means they can be misunderstood and given labels, mostly because they often struggle to understand the limited 3D reality (e.g. ADHD). I explore this concept of 'labels' in depth in the following chapters because the reader will notice how relevant these labels are to so many of the new ones. I believe the labels actually highlight crucial 'differences' which are vital to understanding for the future of our species.

The Earth Mission

It is through the new generations of children and young people that much of the data in this book has been sourced. It is information that will surprise many (due to its complexity and depth) because it is conveyed by children far too young, in most cases, to have access to such data or understand its content. Parents struggle, as they have no idea where their child has obtained such information other than how the child has explained its source. Some information appears to be conscious under-standing, but some, they say, comes from beings, or special non-human friends.

These children do not need governments to tell them that we are not alone in the universe because they already know. They know that the planet is in dire shape, both ecologically and spiritually. They know we are lied to and manipulated. They know that we are educated and programmed into limiting and a limited third-dimensional reality. They know about covert technologies which control the public and its fear based mindset. They know there are many species visiting our planet because they are in communication with them and that some are considered 'family'.

I was told about these new children some years ago by a young woman, Tracey Taylor, who came to me in her early twenties with her story about her Contact with non-human intelligences. The proof of her encounters evidenced by amazingly complex, geometric artwork, which she said was downloaded from her Contacts with extraterrestrial intelligences. She also articulated unusual languages and wrote unusual scripts.

Tracey wrote about her experiences in Chapter Eight of my first book *Awakening*, and has kindly written an update to her continuing story. It was with courage and determination, she shared her story with a panel of psychiatrists who, surprisingly, did not label her as unwell. Tracey shared her story and understanding with a balance and authenticity. In this book, she adds more information on her understanding. The statement below was written ten years prior to similar data by two molecular biologists, Dr. William Brown and Dr. Lena Ohlson (previously mentioned), which I share in this book, confirming much of what Tracey told me all those years ago.

The Bringers of Light

"There is a race of beings upon the planet, increasing in number, although visually and physically indistinguishable to most humans. They are the 'bringers of light', and are here to guide the awakening of terrestrial consciousness. The New Children are born without programs and will bring about a Global Awakening."

Tracey Taylor, Artist/Experiencer.

The New Human

The 'New Humans' are new generations of children and young adults consciously and intimately connected to galactic intelligences. They contend that they have come from star origins to bring about change and spread the truth of who we really are. They tell us that the star visitors are the ancestors of humanity, and created us. They say most of our species are still asleep and need to be awakened to our true heritage, and that they have come here to help, particularly with new ecologically and spiritually based technologies. Through their awareness and knowledge, they believe they can help older generations understand their heritage.

My first book, *Awakening*, was written primarily as a resource to meet the needs of earlier generations of Experiencers; to help them understand and integrate the reality of their encounters, through the process of acceptance and integration. However, the new generations of starseeds have different requirements. Far less fearful, and most often they have embraced their experiences and encounters because they perceive reality through a far broader multidimensional lens. This means their human struggle is the difficulty to fit into the 3D box and be understood.

The New Humans – New Programs: 'Letter People'

The new programs of humanity can be embodied in human labels, such as Attention Deficit Hyperactivity Disorder (ADHD), Asperger syndrome (Asperger's) and other forms of autism and dyslexia, conventionally believed to be the result of faulty genes, poor diet, vaccinations, poor parenting, and pollution, etc. Although some of these may be contributing factors, it cannot explain why these children are so dramatically different in terms of perception and behavior. Is it possible these apparent dysfunctions are part of a new evolving human? Molecular biologist Dr. Lena Ohlson believes this is not a dysfunction, but they are fundamentally different, and has coined the term 'Letter People'. Dr. Ohlson believes she is a 'letter person'. This understanding has been due to her research into the differences both as a scientist and because of her own personal experiences. Dr. Ohlson explains that there are qualities these children/people have, which are not being understood because they are fundamentally different.

Metaphysical communities have long noted these differences in children and interpreted them as an evolving shift in human consciousness, defining them as Crystal Children, Indigos, Children of Light, Golden Children, or Rainbow Children, as they recognize their heightened awareness sensitivities. These terms, however, are dependent upon the behaviors observed and although this has validity, in my view it doesn't tell the complete story. The missing link, which is crucial in their understanding of the evolving human. This 'missing link' is the part that extraterrestrial

9

intelligences play in our metaphysical and physical reality. Their involvement with human DNA is a significant factor in our continuing evolution as a species. This particularly relates to the new programs for humanity we are observing right now.

The Physical Reality – Modification in Human DNA

The reader will observe that throughout this book I place great emphasis on human DNA. I believe this is an important key to understanding what I believe is happening now. Research has demonstrated the indisputable link to extraterrestrial encounters, and their on-going focus with human DNA. I believe, as do many other researchers, that this indicates these intelligences have been involved in changes and modification of human DNA throughout our genesis. The late Dr. Roger Leir agreed and was convinced humanity was being 'upgraded' through their interactions with extraterrestrial beings.

He stated:

"I have come to the conclusion that not only are there Star Children amongst us, but the entire human race has been advanced forward at a rate that is unlikely to be due to slow evolutionary forces, but far more likely that this rapid advancement of the human species is due to alien intervention of our bodies and minds."

Dr. Roger Leir, author of *The Aliens and the Scalpel.*

Nonhuman intelligences regularly collect genetic material during encounters. Research and witness testimony suggests they also have programs for altering human DNA, even at conception. This information offers a relevant and logical explanation as to why there are so many important and dramatic changes in human abilities and behavior in the newest generations of humans. Molecular biologist, Dr. William Brown, also believes we are changing as a species.

"I believe genetic modification is occurring right now in utero and is actually producing 'New Humans'."

Molecular biologist and Experiencer, Dr. Ohlson, agrees and has a name for the New Humans: Aquantum Letter People.

"Letter people bring different multidimensional skills to humanity."

Dr. Ohlson comments on how this shift in human consciousness should be explored from a physical and multidimensional perspective, as well as soul level:

"It is not as simple as foreign DNA. It's a combination of genetically improved bodies in combination with souls from different places in our Universe, incarnating in these "improved" bodies. The souls have different frequencies/vibrations, depending on their evolutionary status, and that plays a role in activation of the DNA in that particular body. I believe we also have to take into account the collective soul of *Homo sapiens.*"

Dr. Ohlson (In correspondence with the author, 2014).

"Humanity has been at this point three times, but has been knocked off course. This time, there is a ninety-five percent chance we will make it, and possibly a hundred percent chance we are headed to a higher level. It's slow, but they are getting more in tune with things, and that's due to the shift that's affecting everyone. It's the Starseeds and Indigos of the planet Gaia cherishes because they help the vibration of the planet more than any others."

Peter, twelve years old.

New Humans – Qualities and Abilities

The ADHD, Asperger's, etc., individual may have some, but not all abilities listed below:

- Superior mental and analytical capabilities, which allows them to connect more multi-dimensionally with the unseen world.
- Enhanced DNA.
- Photographic memories.
- Non-verbal communication.
- Ability to manipulate time and space.
- The perception of reality with various parts of their body, not just through the eyes.
- Abilities to communicate and interact with intelligences in many forms, both physically and in astral forms (i.e., 'Out-of-body' state).
- Extreme empathy for the emotions and feelings of their parents' as well as other humans.
- The perception of a broader spectrum of reality than older human generations, including heightened sensitivities in all five senses.
- Ability to sense or perceive 'presences/energies'. These can include non-corporeal entities such as spirits, inter-dimensional presences, and extraterrestrial beings.
- Telekinetic abilities (moving objects with the mind).
- Remote influencing skills.
- Mind meld skills (awareness through other consciousness, human and animal)
- Interspecies communication (i.e., animals and plants).
- Ability to access information/recall of past lives, both on Earth and other planets and star systems.
- Universal spirituality, not limited to religions.
- An innate understanding of the multidimensional nature of reality.
- An innate awareness of healing energies and how to utilize them.
- Ability to sense what a truth is and the ability to access individuals through their frequency and very essence.
- Conscious astral traveling.
- Some display a full awareness of terrestrial consciousness, and can override the dominant conditioning and programming that occurs from birth.
- Ability to bypass unsubstantiated clutter, and link directly to the subconscious

(also called the higher self or super-conscious) with greater clarity.
- Non-linear thinking.
- Naturally born with universal wisdom and awareness.
- Gifted creatively – music, art, etc.
- Connected to nature and all life forms.
- Precognition (foresee future events).
- The manifestation of unusual symbols or scripts.
- Able to articulate non-human languages.
- Perception of more of the visual spectrum than normal (i.e., Kirlian photography shows this as energy fields or auras).

Note: Scientist Dr. Harry Oldfield is able to demonstrate energy fields through his invention of PIP (Polycontrast Interference Photography) software.

"PIP instrumentation can distinguish between many different grades or qualities of light. The innovation is in the computer program and the end result is an image on the computer screen shown as pulsating bands of color and light. PIP imaging shows variations in energy fields."

Harry Oldfield's Invisible Universe by Jane and Grant Solomon.

Extra-high-functioning children (See: *China's Super Psychics* by Paul Dong and Thomas E. Raffill, 1997) demonstrated the teleportation of objects at the Institute of High Energy Physics.

Such children are often identified in many cultures as 'super psychics'. This phenomenon is perceived and interpreted based upon cultural, scientific and spiritual beliefs.

The Children and Young Adults
These upgraded new generations do not appear to have the same challenges as their parents or struggle with their multidimensional experiences.

They:
- Have conscious recall of their experiences.
- Have minimal fears or concerns about beings encountered.
- Accept their encounters and feel quite comfortable with them.
- Acknowledge their 'star family' as their real family and miss them.
- Struggle with the density of Earth.
- Have difficulty understanding a materialistic society.
- Feel human behavior is primitive.
- Feel very different.
- Feel like they have been adopted.
- Feel more connected to the stars than Earth.
- Have a sense of mission and purpose.
- Feel connected to specific star systems.

- Feel quite alien on this planet.
- Have access to knowledge they have not consciously learned through 'down loads', conscious connections to past lives, or from their star family.
- View objects with a multidimensional perspective and have difficulty under standing our third-dimensional view of what is 'solid'.
- Are aware they can levitate, change frequency and move through solid objects.
- Have many abilities outside of what is considered the norm.
- Have an understanding of many complex fields of knowledge, such as physics, spirituality, the nature of reality, manipulation of space-time, the true origin of the species, and perceive the truth despite deception.
- Are aware of inaccurate educational programs on this planet and the harm they do.
- Are aware of the manipulation of certain unhealthy energies and frequencies.
- Are aware of mind control technologies.
- Are aware of negative self-serving beings.

The New Humans struggle to operate and function when their awareness and understanding is not understood. This may manifest in them as arrogance or frustration, but most often confusion or sadness. They can feel they have been 'dumped' by their star family and struggle to stay on this planet. It can be overwhelming and lead to a conscious or unconscious desire to dumb themselves down with alcohol or drugs, or vacate through suicide.

They Have Come to Help

The New Human is integrated and accepting of their multidimensional reality and extraterrestrial heritage. In this book, we explore their stories, and what is being highlighted to us as a species as we take a quantum leap into the future of human consciousness.

It Incorporates

- Information, both from an experiential and scientific perspective.
- Strategies to help the children who have encounters cope emotionally, psycho logically and spiritually.
- The importance of past lives in this phenomenon and how everything is connected.
- Exploring multidimensional awareness and abilities, and what this means.
- The abilities of the letter people; a perceived dysfunction, or a sign of a multidimensional gift?
- Beliefs and religious understandings of God: how do extraterrestrial encounters affect religious beliefs?
- Information on covert agendas on this planet and other locations of interference.
- A NEW way to educate - the adults listen. How do we help the children to help us?

- Hybrids – what does this mean, and does it apply to you?
- Expressions of ET Contact: symbols, scripts, and star languages. What does all this mean?
- Frequencies, and their importance in the awakening of human consciousness.
- How to explore human consciousness from a 3D reality.
- Deprogramming from the matrix.
- Shamanic healing.
- Humanity and its future.

"Adults have small ears, they don't want to hear the messages we try to tell them. Adults don't want to hear what the Star Kids have to say; they are too stressed out and it interferes with the reality that the adults live in."

"Mary has big ears because she listens, most adults don't."

Cathy, 9 years old, Europe.

Will We Listen?

These are real-life true stories recounted by individuals, families and children. A compilation of extraordinary accounts retelling of their multidimensional experiences. It illustrates how each successive generation interprets their encounter experiences with a different perspective. I hope it will provide a unique window of an expanded reality for those who are ready to explore the multiverse.

Throughout this book, I attempted to corroborate as much as possible with information from 3D, scientific perspective, as well as a multidimensional one. I do not pretend to have the answers to all the questions this book raises, especially information beyond our present level of science. However, this does not, in my opinion, preclude its veracity. It may just highlight that we have much to understand about ourselves and the nature of reality.

I hope it challenges beliefs. The challenge can highlight how much we may be entrenched in 3D conditioning and programming. I believe it is healthy to re-evaluate as we grow in understanding. The information raises some fascinating and intriguing questions. Do we need new ways of assessing what it is to be human? If we have the genetics of our extraterrestrial ancestors, what makes us different to them apart from the physical container? Are we really changing as a species? If so, how do we know and how will those changes manifest? Are we indeed just 'them' in human disguise, as some suggest?

It is a great pity that the truth embargo has meant that the public does not have access to the data held by covert agencies, which could qualify some of these important questions. I am certain they do know about the new children – and what they are capable of.

I have done my very best to do justice and honor the courage of those individuals who have 'come out' so bravely to share their truth in these pages; These stories are just the 'tip' of the proverbial iceberg, there are many more extraordinary experiences, that I was unable to include in this book. This can only be a snapshot of the broad range of Encounter experience. It is important to note; those who have contributed to this book have nothing to gain by sharing their stories, other than their desire to provide through their experiences information which can help and support others like themselves.

I have not altered, changed or edited any of the accounts that have been verbally spoken or written, except to make the text more easily understandable to the reader. This may occur when a child struggles to articulate their understanding or experiences clearly. However, in most cases, what is written is how they expressed it.

I make no judgment on the information, other than to state its origin and where this information can be explored more fully or corroborated. At no point do I state the information documented is irrefutable proof. It is up to you, the reader, to decide if any of the information resonates with you. However, if some information challenges your world view, I would ask you to pause and listen to your heart as well as your mind, as you explore what you may not presently know.

[1] Throughout this book, the capitalization of the word 'Contact' is used to specifically refer to the interaction between human beings and beings from elsewhere.

Chapter One

BEGINNING THE HUMAN JOURNEY

"The pre-birth soul connection."
Samantha Mowat

I have chosen to begin my book with a compelling story of a family from Canada, as it explores the concept not only of an intergenerational link to Contact with non-human intelligences, but the connection to their children prior to incarnation. In my research, it appears this is not so unusual because I have heard of other accounts where the mother had a similar 'soul to soul' relationship before their child's physical birth, which continued after their birth.

If what they believe is true, it confirms communication between a living human and the spirit world, which many clairvoyants and mediums believe they have on a regular basis. This concept or experience also appears to be a pattern for some of the new children incarnating now.

Samantha Mowat resides in Canada with her family. She has two children, a daughter, four years old and son three years old. Samantha is gifted intuitively and aware of her encounters with non-human intelligences. She acknowledges her children have similar multidimensional abilities.

Samantha became aware of my research regarding the New Human as the information was very relevant to her own children. Samantha describes her encounters with various groups of extraterrestrials, and shares some of the information they have imparted over the years.

Samantha recalled communication with the 'souls' of her children before they were born:

Samantha Wrote
"Prior to becoming pregnant with my children, I met them on the other side. They would often visit me through lucid dreaming and I have been very blessed to be in Contact with my children's guides."

Many individuals share this concept, as in the interview below with Dr. Edith Ubuntu Chan.

"My son started to visit me for months in my meditation and dreams. He showed me himself in different forms, from a toddler to a light being. He told me many things about the planet and to purify ourselves to be ready to receive him and how a mass of 'light beings' is getting ready to come to this planet."

Dr. Edith Ubuntu Chan L. Ac. on Indigo Crystal Children, in a video interview with Lilou Mace TV, 21 Dec, 2015.

Dr. Chan has a Doctoral Fellowship (specializing in Endocrinology and Neuromuscular Medicine), a graduate degree from American College of Traditional Chinese Medicine, and a Bachelors Degree in Applied Mathematics with Magna Cum Laude from Harvard University.

The Mission

Samantha's understanding of what her daughter's mission is in her human life:

Samantha: "My daughter's primary objectives in this life are Justice and Preservation. She is here to bring about a change in this world; one focused on bringing harmony through correcting the imbalance of power. This imbalance being the lack of personal power because: 'they believe they have no power,' 'they are a woman,' or 'they are poor,' or 'they are too young or too old.' That said, her perception of rights extends to animals, plants, ET beings, the deceased, stones and elements. She has a strong sense of what is right or wrong. When people are cruel, she has no tolerance for their lack of consideration and can often be seen standing up for other children, plants, insects and animals.

My daughter is also here to bring awareness of how we use our planet; she is highly focused towards how we treat animals. She has often told me that this cat is feeling 'sad' or that dog feels 'lonely.' She gets annoyed with people when they go to throw out food and has informed many adults that they are being wasteful. She then becomes highly upset if they proceed to put food waste in the garbage rather than the compost. She loves to heal, but she says that is not why she is here. She often puts stones around the houseplants to balance their energy.

My son has not yet shared his purpose, nor have his guides. In March I had a member of his soul family, a female Mantid (an insect-like being that resembles a praying mantis), visit me in a dream one night. At first, she appeared to me in human form, then she and I were revealing to various humans what their purpose on Earth is and how they can achieve their objective. Afterward, she and I were talking; I said to her, 'What do you really look like?' She then laughed and told me that if she were to reveal her true identity to me at this time, I would be scared and for now it is better this way. I asked her why she was visiting me and she told me that she was there for my son. He is a member of her family and she was allowing me to get to know her that way, so I could learn how to better manage/understand my son. She was incredibly kind and gentle.

I do feel his job is about changing what people eat, how they eat and securing the survival of higher vibrational foods to eat, that are not processed, not GMO and not animal based. The Mantids are vegan; they do not eat cooked food or processed food.

I do know that when I see my children playing at home, I often see sparks and beings of energy in amongst them, playing. The children look to these energies and interact with them."

The New Human

"In regards to the New Human, *Homo noeticus*, I found it incredibly fascinating and the information needs to be shared. I agree that there is an intergenerational link between those who have ET experiences. My family on both sides seem to be in Contact with the white beings and small browns. I agree with Dr. L. Ohlson when she discusses the sudden rise in Attention-deficit disorder (ADD), Attention-deficit/hyperactivity disorder (ADHD), Asperger's and other letter people being the human upgrade. I feel that is in part why the New World Order (NWO), through schools and the medical community, are often in such a rushed state to medicate these children - to medicate them away from their light.

I have come to notice about these children that their auras are very different from children in the general population; they are vibrant and brightly colored. Their auras are clear and extend further from the body than even in healthy, awake adults. However, the introduction of medication to the children alters their auric body, diminishing its vibrancy, bringing the aura closer to the body, and making it a slower frequency.

I believe that Dr. Ohlson and Tracey Taylor are correct in their belief that genetic modification is occurring while in utero. I have come to learn, through my work, that Star Children are often visiting their parents prior to incarnating on Earth. One way in which these children are getting to know their parents, and in part preparing their parents for their arrival, is through dream visitation.

I believe that all who volunteer to come here to Earth have a trigger. They can sense it from a very young age. I knew I had to, at some point in my life, go to a psychic. I knew that after that event, my life would begin to take shape, and it did. There is something that each of us feels deep within our being; something we feel we need to do. Mary, one thing that has been expressed to me time and time again by the ET beings - humans fear change. We fear change because we have been taught that what we do not know is scary, is dangerous and that we must remain as we are if we are to remain. Mary, as I read the articles you provided I can feel my 'little brown guy' radiating happiness and loving energy. The beings I work with did not tell me to stop at any point while I was reading. They expressed gratitude."

The ADD Link!

"I have found that a large percentage of the children that I encounter at the play-groups seem to have their minds working differently than those of typical children.

A girlfriend of mine has twin boys who have ADD, both of whom have an incredible amount of indigo and yellow radiating from their auras. These two boys are highly aware of the energetic frequencies in their environment as well as in their food. They live on a farm, and when the boys are outside, they are completely calm and rational, with the ability to think clearly, especially when they are barefoot. The boys have mentioned how it grounds them to be in a direct exchange with Earth energy. These boys are twelve years old.

I am not sure if I have discussed this component with you: with my children, I do not wish for them to go to preschool or the supermarket and tell the world about their ET experiences, so we call the beings who visit us 'our special friends.' I feel it is a safe term for our children to use in front of non-experiencers. It enables them to tell us exactly who they mean without revealing too much information in front of those whose intentions we are not aware."

Healing by the Extraterrestrials

"I feel grateful that my children are having these experiences. My children very seldom become ill, but when they do, the ETs have provided my children with healing. I have awakened on several occasions to sense beings in the room, only to be put back to sleep rather quickly. I have seen beings dropping symbols of energy into our bodies, and on one occasion, witnessed a small, black, triangular healing device upon the bed towards my son's side. I could sense the being altering his vibration to be invisible, but he had in his haste dropped (or momentarily forgotten) the device. I looked away for a moment to look at my daughter, and when my vision returned to where the device was, it was gone.

My son was born with many allergies: wheat, corn, shellfish, fish, lactose intolerance, grass, dust, and is asthmatic. The beings have explained to us that his body was unaccustomed to the vibration on this planet and the level of toxicity, and therefore was experiencing a shock to his system. They have come to him repeatedly, to align his body and alleviate his allergies. He now has a fraction of the allergies. I know that my children will always be protected, and that they came to this planet awake, and that it is my duty to ensure that they stay that way.

I love that my children know that they are not of this world. Better yet, I love that they know where their soul is from and that their soul family is looking out for them. My children understand and talk about energy, spirit guides/multidimensional beings and other worlds as easily as other children talk about Disney princesses.

Initially, my daughter and son seemed apprehensive towards the Tall Whites, the Grays and the Browns, but recently they seem quite comfortable with our special friends coming to visit. On one visit, several months back, my children and I were in a joined dream encounter. We were in a city. It was a bright, beautiful clear day and we were in a tall building. We noticed a craft approach the building beside us. The craft went quite low to the roof, then several ETs jumped out of the craft, wearing clown suits, and then they teleported us to them on top of the building.

They changed their vibrational structure to being human-like and we went to a fair/park. The ETs do this often with the kids, showing them the happy side and that they are safe in their company, then shift to being humanoid if the children seem uncomfortable."

Connecting with the Extraterrestrials

"At one time I had to take my husband to work. My daughter and I opened the blinds and were looking at the stars for a few minutes. She then pointed to a star that looked like it was part of a grand trine of stars and said 'Mommy, I am going to wish on that star and I am going to wish to see my special friends. I really miss our special friends.' I said 'Honey, that's a great wish. I will wish for that too.' Then, a moment later, the star started moving horizontally for a few moments, then down, then stopped again. She and I were so excited. She said, 'There they are, my wish came true.'

My daughter went through a phase earlier this summer where all she wanted to draw was craft. She was having frequent visitations at night, and would draw me where she had gone the night before. I asked her to tell me what the ships looked like and the description she gave sounded similar to the silver, mirror-like exterior, with a round shape."

Space School

"My children have begun to mention going to school on craft. My son complained to me earlier this week for that very reason. He said 'Mommy, I no go to school. I already went to school. I was at school with my special friends.' I asked him when he was at school. He said, 'Today, night time. I got back now.' I asked him what school looked like and he said he had 'a small class' and a boy was teaching them, but the boy had 'really big black eyes and white clothes.'

I have not taught my children how to access their psychic abilities, but both of my children are clairvoyant and are more psychic than several of my friends who work as professional psychics. They are aware of how the energy of other people affects them and they gave me the technique for my clients to use to protect, cleanse and ground their energy. On many occasions, we have been late because my children will not leave the house until they have their white light, golden bubble and grounding cord in place."

Connection to the Consciousness of Plants and Minerals and Healing Water

"My daughter is able to hold stones and identify which are good for healing the body or healing plants. She says that the stones have feelings and are not happy when they are alone and in the house. She holds her hands over the water jug before watering the plants because she says the water is not happy and needs to be healed. She performs Reiki on the plants and the animals she meets. When she meets new people she often tells them what their guides are and if their energy feels good or otherwise. My daughter has told me that I will have another child, a girl. She is adamant about this. My husband is fixed, but she has said with certainty that this child is coming. You cannot raise your voice to my daughter or throw your aura around if frustrated. She cowers and says the aura is 'scaring' her.

My son is clairsentient, empathic, a medium and clairvoyant. My father in law passed away this summer and my son kept pointing to various areas around the house saying, 'Papa, over there.' Unfortunately, being a medium is not my gift. All I was able to see in the areas he pointed was a large mass of washed-out energy. He knows which nights our special friends are coming. He often tells me at bedtime if he can hear their ship or feel it coming. He draws auras on the characters in the coloring books. My daughter is in the habit of educating her friends on animal rights, expressing how cow's milk is meant for baby cows - not humans. My son could live off fruit.

I feel as though these gifts have a correlation to our genetics and that Contact has activated the gene somehow. Both my children are telepathic. I do not have any pictures, but my children prefer to express things through song or telepathy rather than speech."

Precognitive Abilities; World Changes

"The children have been shown many of the same things I have been shown. They have described it as: 'everyone fighting; police not being nice to people; people taking each other's food, and the cities not being safe.' My daughter has told me that she does not want to get any vaccines, and so I am respecting that and not giving them any. She says they will make her sick and make her tummy hurt.

The ETs have shown me several trajectories for this event. Each time, they have placed focus upon one very important factor: 'get out of the city; go into the woods; we will find you; you are safe; you will come home.' They showed roadblocks, UN vehicles, no snow on the ground, people in long sleeves and jeans (so either fall or spring), and people being rounded up like cattle. Each time they show the children being with me, but they have shown my husband being amongst those who are caught in the snare. I have asked them what can be done to prevent this from happening. Time and time again, they tell me that we must 'wake everyone up.' They must develop their psychic abilities, remember who they are and raise their vibration."

Past Life on Another Planet

"My daughter has talked about this more than my son. He was quiet for the first two years and really only started talking in sentences in the last few months. However, my daughter has talked to me about her life in the 'crystal kingdom' that is far away from here and no one is ever hungry or sad. She said it is wonderful and our 'special friends' are there, but they aren't really special there because everyone is a 'special friend' there. I think it is her way of saying that everyone is an ET She said that everyone lived in a giant crystal building and it was clear like quartz. She picked up quartz to show me what she meant. She has described living in a jungle world with other cat people, but she said that they didn't live in houses like we do; she said they

21

were round and smaller. She says she has not lived here before. I believe her when she says it.

My daughter's soul family is from Lyra. She is a cat person and she has told me this several times. She highly identifies with cats. Her primary guide is a Lyrian female, who comes to her in two ways: as a tiger and as a woman/tiger mix. My daughter calls her 'Sapphire.' She has never been afraid of Sapphire and is happiest when Sapphire brings the babies with her. My daughter does not assign names to many of these beings; she just calls them her 'special friends.' She says Sapphire is white with stripes, but she asked Sapphire to make her stripes rainbow and she did. She says that she and Sapphire talk with their minds and not with their mouths.

My children have seen the white beings with crystal blue eyes that often come to me. They know that the one I have drawn is my brother and they accept that as part of life. My daughter has drawn him on many occasions and is saddened when he visits me but not her. She knows that sometimes they come to see just one of us or some of us, but she likes it best when they come to see her. She believes that they are there to keep us healthy, to remind us to play games and to teach us. I just asked her and she describes him as 'tall, skinny, big head, no hair.' She says they have 'witch's fingers' because their fingers are so long. 'No clothes (he likes to be naked); blue eyes (like her brother).' She seems a little bored describing him, as though it is no more interesting than the weather. She seems more excited when we go onto the craft and change our vibration to being in our true form.

My son has described the Mantis as the 'big bugs.' He thinks they are really funny looking. He also describes a lion being that comes to him, who he calls 'Baby Lion.' I have seen this energy mass around him and it is not as big as Sapphire. I feel it could be either a young Lyrian or a smaller one. He describes it as 'cute.' He says the baby lion is there to keep him safe and is his best friend. He says the baby lion is here to make him brave and make everyone better. My children believe that everyone has 'special friends', but some people aren't nice to their special friends and then their special friends don't visit anymore because people empty their (the ETs) bucket, when they (the people) are mean or scared, or try to hurt our friends.

My children have a beautiful understanding of our ET friends. They are aware that they are taken aboard craft and have a sense of loving familiarity with the beings that visit them."

The Contact Begins

Mantid and Clicking Language

"It was at two years of age when the beings who are involved with my family seem to have made their primary entrance. That said, perhaps they were there all along and that is just the age that my children were able to make it known to the rest of us.

When my son turned two he would awaken in the night and I would sense someone in their room, but it was as though they had shifted their vibration to invisible. Early this year, my son started making a clicking noise as a form of speech, when referring to things he liked. For instance, he would point to a favorite book or snack and then click his tongue in his mouth. At first, I thought he was regressing, until I had a Manta female appear to me in a dream as a human, then explain to me that my son was not regressing, rather he is from her family group. She would appear to me later as her true self when I was ready. She made the same clicking sound.

Now my son seems to see them in the house all the time; he often refers to them as 'ghosts' but his sister corrects him and says 'They're not ghosts, they are our friends, ghosts don't look like that.' I began to see sections of beings moving around my house, sometimes as an invisible outline of a being moving about, or as a section of a body - like part of a chest or arm movement.

My four-year-old daughter loves being visited by our special friends. They began visiting her when she was a little over two years of age. She started waking up in the middle of the night, saying 'Mommy, aliens.' It did not occur to me at the time that my daughter could be being visited. I assumed that my daughter was seeing her spirit guides and was interpreting their visitations as scary. I told her it was all right and that it was just her spirit guides visiting. It does not seem to matter where my children and I are, whether we are at our house or someone else's house or in a hotel, or if we move, our ET friends seem to know precisely where we are and are able to visit us easily. I do not find fear in that thought, but I do find immense comfort in knowing that we are being looked out for."

Special Friends

"I was making breakfast one morning, after a night of ET Contact, and my daughter came up to me and told me she was mad at our special friends. When I asked her why she was mad, she told me that last night one of her special friends came at night and told her that they were only taking mommy tonight and that she had to stay home. She told me that she loves going on the space ships and looking at the stars. She tells me that she loves them and often wants to go home. She speaks as casually about her special friends as she does about anything else. When I ask my daughter to tell me about her friends, this is what she says: 'They come at nighttime. They look gray I guess; some are shorter than me; some are taller than me. They use their mind to talk to us. Friends are really tickly, really tickly on their body. They play with me and take me places.' She often talks of Sapphire. Sapphire has been with my daughter since she was born. I first Contacted her spirit guide when she was less than a year old, to create a communication link between us for my daughter's benefit.

I was unaware at the time that we can have ETs as guides (angels, ancestors, council – whatever you wish to call it), and she had projected herself as a white tiger, but now I feel Sapphire and I are more comfortable and she comes to us as a tiger/human-like being."

The New Earth

Samantha was given information regarding the future of humanity: a false flag, to make people believe in an invasion of extraterrestrials and the New Earth.

Samantha

"Massive riots around the false flag invasion will occur world-wide. I was shown people believing that we truly were being invaded by a group of extraterrestrials and yet they did not seem to sense it being orchestrated by humans.

They showed me thousands of people leaving every city and most of them appeared to be leaving by foot. I do not recall a lot of vehicle traffic. I have been told there is some form of electromagnetic propulsion device used to destroy the circuitry of vehicles in motion/use at the time of its firing. This was previously displayed to the public in the movie *War of the Worlds* as a means of embedding in the human mind that if/when this was to happen, life will be at risk. They (ETs) have expressed deep concern for this event occurring and are trying to initiate as much peaceful Contact as possible to prevent this event.

I looked around for any indication of a day, month and year, but I did not see any. The style of clothing looked very similar to now, as did the vehicles. I did not figure out a day but I will try to remember to ask the next time I am visited.

I have noticed a surge in the number of ET groups attempting to make Contact at this time. This year I have had:

- The Grays
- The Browns (smaller and larger)
- The Tall Whites
- Mantids
- Pleiadians
- Coneheads
- Reptilians
- Light Beings
- Ascended Masters
- Lyrians

All are trying to make Contact with me. I do not understand why or what it means. If you have any idea, please let me know. My readings have shifted; people are being taught about their star origin and where their soul is from. They are highly understanding of having ET spirit guides and it resonates with everyone who has had the information brought forward. In past life regressions, my clients are being taken off-world rather than staying on Earth. They feel relieved and have a greater sense of purpose and understanding after they encounter these experiences.

My information comes from several groups: the Mantids (insect, praying-mantis-like beings), the Tall Whites with blue eyes, the small brownish Grays, the Pleiadians and Light Beings, as well as others. They teach me on a one-on-one personal way of initiating Contact. I believe this is to allow for the standard person of the world to invite Contact without being in a highly exposed setting. They placed emphasis upon the insecurity of humans and our fear of scrutiny. They wish to help prevent the mass fear and panic of an alleged invasion, orchestrated by the shadow governments and wish to meet directly with the people of Earth, to go around the current blocks in play.

In an interview on 'www.holisticadvocate.com', which hosted you, you mentioned a man showing his four-year-old daughter a paper which contained an ET language, and the little girl mentioned to her father that it was about the New Earth in a different universe. This correlated with information I was given by one of the groups in Contact with me.

They have shown me massive riots and protests occurring around the false flag invasion. As a means of safety for those who have been in Contact and are here to help, I have been shown this in a highly lucid dream for my family. I was told to go back home and get the kids, then to leave. I got my children in the back seat and I remember driving through the night away from the city. A couple of hours before dawn, I approached two mountains that the road ran between. I look up to the sky because I can feel the familiar vibration of multiple craft approaching. Behind the mountain, on the right, comes a series of stars in a row, ten in total. As they emerge from behind the mountain, they form a circle, then change into ten individual black craft with red lights, followed by the creation of one large craft from the ten. Then my children and I are instantly boarded up. I look around and see several people, none of whom I know consciously, but all of whom I know on a deeper level. They are familiar. Then we change properties somehow from being in our human form to be long, thin, brownish colored beings who look similar to the Grays, but taller and kind. The first thing to cross my mind after I change is 'I forgot how uncomfortable being in human form was.' I knew we were being taken home.

I had communication about the New Earth. This is a paraphrased version of what was said: The New Earth is in a different dimension. In order to go from this dimension to the next, we must change our vibration from low, heavy, dense and slow pulsating, to be higher, faster and lighter. In shifting from vibrations, we experience changes to our preferences, lifestyle, and attitude towards 'what is and isn't' acceptable for others, animals, the environment and ourselves.

We will:

- Become environmentally more conscious.
- Adopt a vegetarian or a vegan, raw diet with an inability to handle highly processed foods and animal products.
- Be aware of the energetic vibration being emitted by other people and how it affects us, as well as how our energy affects others.
- Have increased psychic abilities.
- Be more accepting of all beliefs, preferences, appearance.
- Not desire addictive substances, such as caffeine, alcohol, tobacco and drugs.
- Have increased telepathic ability.
- Be happier, more loving and calm.

- Not resonate to material lifestyles.
- Sense when others are not being truthful.
- Be strongly empathic.
- Function on less sleep.
- Not accept or handle abuse, neglect or unfair treatment towards children, women, men, animals, plants, resources or weather.
- Age slowly and have optimum physical functioning.
- Succumb less to diseases – slowly diseases will be abolished.
- Have the ability to change the molecular structure of things, e.g. infusing Source energy (God energy) into water to heal and restore it to original properties.
- Communicate with plants, Earth and animals."

Samantha Mowat, speaking at the *Countdown to Contact 2014*, conference.
https://www.youtube.com/watch?v=_Nscg8DH7VI

Note: Samantha has encapsulated an awareness of the intergenerational, human genetic links to her children, as well as her connection to them on a soul level.

Chapter Two

THE GRANDKIDS
Out of the Mouths of Babes

The ADD Connection

Grandmother, Leonie Appelt, Queensland.

This is a communication from a wonderful lady in Queensland. Leonie Appelt came to one of my presentations at the Nexus International Conference on the Star Children. Leonie has children and grandchildren she believes are part of these new upgraded programs, and shares from two perspectives: as a mother and grandmother.

Leonie: "I feel compelled to write to you because I wanted to tell you that when I saw you at the Nexus conference, I just wanted to thank you from the bottom of my heart, and let you know that you have changed my world and that of my whole family. After having seen you, I was at last able to connect the dots in my life in a profound way. I must say, from a small child I had 'awareness' but it was always surrounded by a fog. Since our meeting. I have had a flow of connecting information, or I should say 'form and feeling,' because that's the way it comes to me, which can be difficult to put into words sometimes. I have always found it hard being here on Earth. I feel that, like most so-called ADD people, it is the way we take in information and it is difficult to translate, and vice versa.

This information applied so much to my son, who is now twenty-eight, but previously battled with his very existence here on this planet, from the moment he was born. Now he has absolutely transformed dramatically in so many ways; it is hard to recognize him in the last twelve months. He has changed from someone who lived in the dark and hated the world, covering himself with tattoos, with a negative agenda and seeing everyone as mindless sheep, into someone who now has the sun on his face and is opening his heart to all possibilities. He now spends a lot of his time nurturing the spiritual growth of his children.

My grandson I have always known to be switched on and he is absolutely angelic and displaying more and more of his Star-Child abilities. He describes the balls of light that fly around his room at night. They move so fast that they have tails; we almost have no need to speak to communicate with them. He radiates pure light and affects everyone around him.

My granddaughter is two and is always pointing out the spirits of other 'people' in the room. She is displaying ADHD behavior and is finding it hard to adjust."

Update from Leonie

"I want to go home."

"I'd like to give you an update on the grandkids. My little granddaughter is now three and has an invisible friend for the last couple of years, which she says is about two-foot tall, whom she calls 'Margar'. She has Contact experiences on an almost nightly basis with what she calls the 'big mozzies', who take her up into the black holes, into a place where she plays with other kids and has a good time. She told her mother that when this happens she asks the big 'mozzies' (which I assume are Mantids); she wants to go home, and when her mum says that all she has to do is ask them to return her to her home, she is most indignant and says 'No, not this home Mummy.' I realize that she is not the only one saying this but thought it was worth a mention."

The Problems of Knowing and Being Different!

"My little grandson, who is now six, is finding it increasingly hard to integrate at school. He is a very honest little boy and wears his heart on his sleeve. He is frustrated with other kids when they don't understand what he says and accuse him of lying when he tells them about reincarnation and alien life on other planets. He is absolutely perplexed that they don't know about such things."

The Soul Connection on Many Planets with Granny!

"The other day my grandson sweetly buried a Christmas beetle, placing three evenly spaced sticks on the little grave, and announced that this would allow the beetle to leave and travel into space, and reincarnate into another animal of its choosing. I asked him how he knew this; he screwed up his face and said to me that he doesn't know how he knows, he just knows things. I asked him to repeat what he had said on camera and the second time he said that his 'angel' told him. Just yesterday, he said to me that we had been on heaps of planets together and when I commented on the fact that I wasn't sure if I like the one that we picked this time, he told me 'Oh no, Granny, this is a great planet. It's the only one that has mixed species on it!' "

The New Earth

"He has also told his mum and dad that he might not be coming with them to the New Earth, as he has work to do here."

Leonie had this 'download' recently, which I felt was valuable information. It explores how Awakening can occur on multiple levels of human awareness as an energetic signature:

The Empathic Component of Contact

Leonie A: "I just wanted to share or expand on some information I received through a download the other day, about why and how the mechanics of the empathic component of Contact works on an ascension level.

I was shown in simple terms that the empathic makeup of the vibrational upgrade of the New Human, is programmed in such a way that is ever evolving, due to personal experience on an individual level, as well as connected to the collective consciousness.

I was shown energetic key points that are created through experience that manifest as active components we carry in our energy field. They almost have their own intelligence in a sense because even though they are in our energetic makeup they can only be recognized on a subtle level.

Greg Doyle struck a cord with me when, in his book on Astral Travel: *Awakening the Giant Within*, he went into detail about why symbols and symbolism (e.g. Reiki symbols for instance) have such a significant effect. He put it into very simple terms: anything that is repeated on any level (as we know), is manifested in this reality and creates an energetic signature that can activate other energies.

So when I was told that so many of us are here just to 'be' and hold the space for vibration, I wanted to understand the mechanics of this. I know when I am amongst people in any way; I can feel that a connection is taking place and that energetic key points are being established (even on passing). Some kind of activation takes place that has been agreed upon on a soul level giving permission for vibrational upgrades. So everything we experience empathically builds a library of vibration that is in service to others.

Even now I have the flu, which is something I normally never get; I am told that I am being inoculated with an energetic key point that will be of service somehow to others. We are carrying a hidden armory to sabotage the actions of the 'powers that be' who are trying to keep the vibration of humanity down.

I especially feel this is true with the new kids; they carry with them this energetic defense system that pre-empts any situation that is set up to sabotage the very reason why they are coming in. It's a bit as if these intelligent key points are an accumulation of individual experience on every vibrational level (and from any timeline) and know exactly how to transform events before they come into contact with their (the person's) energy field, defusing any threat that is disruptive. On some level, they only allow in energetic upgrades that they have given permission for, to enhance their vibration in service to others. All of it is being put into place to achieve a collective consciousness.

Recently, April 2016, Alfred Lambremont Webre, in his interview with Rey Hernandez (FREE), talked about density ascension, and the hypothesis that we are connected to spiritual dimensions, and that in the fourth density of love we all are one.

I feel the mechanics of the empathic contact is an essential component to pull in vibrations working towards collective consciousness, as Alfred says, 'from service to self to service to others'.

Dr. Robert Davis, Neuroscientist – also a director of FREE – (in the same interview) said that our brains have the capacity to interpret frequencies from other dimensions and that everything is connected.

I think that when people work on a higher vibrational level with any event, feeling or any interaction they have, there is a key point that attracts truth like a magnet because it holds the exact vibrational qualities that identify with the vibration of truth which has been manifested through time, over and over again, and it assumes a pure collective identity.

So when people are asked 'How do you know?' and they say, 'I just know', it just resonates with me. We are connecting with that very key point. I have been encouraged to pass it on."

Ref: https://newsinsideout.com/2015/07/free-experiencers-of-ets

The Intergenerational Connection – The New Earth

I am constantly amazed at the deep concepts articulated by young children and this is one shared by a mother from Turkey. The mother is an Experiencer, and her five-year-old daughter speaks about a New Earth!

Ozlem is a resident of Turkey, who wrote to me about her intergenerational link with encounters via her five-year-old daughter, as well as her seventy-seven-year-old mother. The generations from grandmother to grandchild have witnessed UFOs and been Contacted.

Ozlem: "Attached (see overleaf) is a picture of my five-year-old daughter's writing/ script, similar to what is in Dolores Cannon's books. Do you think there could be more to it?

My daughter said it was about the New Earth. I asked my daughter about this before, but she doesn't like to speak about it and says that people don't know about this. I had been keeping that paper and when I gave it to her; she right away turned it around and said that I was holding it upside down!"

This was our conversation:

O = Ozlem

D = Daughter

O: "What was it that you wrote here?"

D: "I don't remember, let me have a look at it (turns it right side up). It's about the New Earth."

O: "What does it say?"

D: "When we die, we're going to go to a New Earth, and it's in a different galaxy, not this galaxy. It's similar to Earth, but not exactly."

Instant Space Travel and God

Ozlem's daughter covers the topic of space travel, God and 'anomalous lights in clouds.'

O: "This was a conversation with my daughter over breakfast. It was just the two of us. I had my phone beside me and managed to record some of it with translation. Here it is":

O: "You mean there is no such thing as time there?"

D: "No there isn't."

O: "How does that work because I can never understand that, really?"

D: "Because the person who invented time isn't there."

O: "Hmmm. How do you travel from one 'world' to another?"

D: "They are very close to each other. You can go in two seconds. Like this...one, two!"

O: "Wow! How do you know all this?"

D: "Because I went before you all were born."

O: "Well, were you born before we were born?"

D: "Yup, but I got old and died, then came back to life. Actually, there is no such thing as getting old."

O: "You never get old there?"

D: "No, you are always young. There is no such thing as dying."

O: "Well, how can it be that you came to this lifetime?"

D: "I just came."

O: "When do you see God?"

D: "I had to wait till you all were born (interrupted by my question). " You can see God very easily there?"

O: "What does God look like?"

D: "It has no shape...and is side by side by side...like water." (She had a hard time explaining this).

(I have to say I felt this deep energy was present at this time. It felt like the energy of love, I leaned over and kissed my daughter).

D: "God has beautiful eyes; when It's winter It changes to blue and when It's near the sea It's brown. It can change the colors whenever It wants to."

O: "How did you feel when you saw God?"

D: "It was so beautiful."

O: "Really?"

D: "It has a very different shape."

O: "How did that make you feel?"

D: "Very good."

O: "Can you talk to God?"

D: "Yes you can, but sometimes God sleeps. Then we can't talk to it."

"When I asked her before (and I asked her again) why she chose me as a mother, she told me there were others, but 'you and my aunt' (this is my sister) 'were the only white ones.' That's why she chose me. Mary, this is twice she has told me this. Can a child remember what she 'made up' and keep going on with it?"

Anomalous Balls of Lights in the Clouds?

"We were watching a children's movie when my daughter saw some beautiful white clouds and said the following":

D: "There are angels in those clouds just like the ones I saw the other day."

O: "What did you see?"

D: "I saw balls of light between clouds."

O: "When?"

D: "When I was in the car on the way to school."

O: "Maybe it was the sun?"

D: "It was raining, Mom!"

O: "Did anyone else see them?"

D: "No, nobody else knows about it."

O: "Were they moving or were they still?"

D: "They were not moving."

O: "She said they were balls of light that were orange, yellow and a bit of blue.

She drew it, and she made sure to draw squiggly lines around the ball of light indicating that it wasn't smooth. By the way she explained it, they were glowing."

Note: This is an example (as previously mentioned) from my research of the depth of 'knowing' the children have.

Synchronicity

At a similar time as receiving Ozlem's correspondence, I received a letter from another parent, about a conversation he had with his daughter when she was approximately five years old - also about the New Earth. They reside in Sydney. The father, David, has encounters, and has written about his experiences. His daughter is now seven.

David: "Yes, my daughter told me that all the kids would be taken to another Earth. I asked her which planet. 'Maybe we can see where it is on a map of the stars?' I started naming stars, and she stopped me and she said 'We don't call them those names.' I wanted to play into her imagination and suggested I would visit. My daughter said no, it was only children being taken there from Earth!"

I Am Not From Here!

David: "Since our last email, my daughter has not spoken a word about 'her world' until recently. I felt the need to write and share this information with you again. Whether it will sound familiar or might help with anything (?).

While playing in the swimming pool she said to her mother 'Mom, this water is exactly like where we used to live before. Remember how we used to live in the water? I am different anyway; I am not like you guys. I don't belong here and I am going to leave!' "

Mother: "Where will you go?"

Daughter: "Back home. I have a mother there too, and a sister. We are very rich."

David: "How will you go there?"

Daughter: "With a jet plane – but it's not like the planes you go on here. This plane goes from one place to another in the blink of an eye!"

David: "So this is a plane?"

Daughter: "It's a ship-like plane."

David: "And who drives it?"

Daughter: "We all do. There are pictures of where we can go, and we press on the picture and we go there, very quickly (closes her eyes and opens them). These planes don't leave from an airport. You have to go to a village and that's where they leave from, but it's far."

David: "When she is telling me these things Mary, she never thinks about her answers. There is never an 'ummm or hmmmm.' I sometimes ask her tricky questions or repeat my questions, like Do you just visualize where you want to go and you're there?"

Daughter: "No, there are pictures and we pick where and press on it like a button."

Past-life connections can be extremely powerful when it is a present conscious recall. I have had numerous conversations with Paul and his family. Paul's mother and her husband have both experienced encounters and this has led to an understanding that Paul is also having similar experiences, as follows.

The Mantid Are My Family

Paul was eight when I first met him. He lives with his family in Queensland Australia. Paul's mother can recall her encounters as a six-year-old child. When she reached adulthood, she discovered her sibling, and possibly her father, were also involved. As a child, however, she was not allowed to speak about her experiences. Because of her background, she realized something was going on with her son Paul. He started drawing spacecraft and 'beings' from a very young age and she felt strongly that this indicated something more profound than just his imagination.

As a small child, Paul said to his mother:

"There is no end to the Universe and nothing is impossible."

My conversation with Paul:

P = Paul

M = Mary

M: "What made you want to do such drawings?"

P: "I have been drawing what I have been seeing, and some just pop into my head. Sometimes it's planets, what I see on the ships, also the beings I see when I am down here (on Earth). They are walking around and I see them but others (other people) don't. Sometimes I see them in my head, and they talk in my head."

M: "When they talk with you, what do they say?"

P: "My purpose, what I should do, and about things that are good or bad."

M: "What do they tell you about your purpose?"

P: "My purpose is to help animals, make sure people don't mistreat them."

M: "How do you know what animals are feeling?"

P: "I see pictures in my head or hear it. I can feel their response."

M: "Anything else?"

P: "Some things I can't tell you about because it's too complex."

M: "Too complex for me to understand?"

P: "Yes."

M: "What do you see?"

P: "Shapes and forms of beings?"

M: "Such as?"

P: "The mantis, the lion, and this one (he points to a drawing of a being he has done). He's my uncle; he is an angel."

M: "Does that one look like you or me?"

P: "No."

Note: Paul made chirping/trilling noises he told me were made by the Manta/Mantid beings, who are his family.

Paul also mentioned that while on board the spacecraft he 'evaporated' into Mantid form for a while!

P: "I didn't feel I was in a human-like body."

M: "What does it feel like when you are in the other shape? Do you feel comfortable or strange?"

P: "I feel strange."

Note: Paul is not the only Experiencer who has shared that, for a time, his 'soul essence' moved into another form. Simon Parkes (politician in the UK) also reported moving into Mantid form to help with humans on board spacecraft.

Hidden Knowledge –The Pyramids

"People built the sphinx to tell people in the future that they are real, to let them know that there were ET life forms and all life forms."

Paul.

M: "Ancient Egyptians, what were they like?"

P: "The ordinary people were humans, but the rulers were not human, they were like Cat beings."

A number of Experiencers have also mentioned that they believe the Sphinx was built to tell humans that there are other life forms.

The 'Big Bang'

P: "The dinosaurs were around before the Big Bang."

M: "What do you know about the Big Bang?"

P: "They exploded ... I don't know how I know?"

Note: Paul mentioned that starships went inter-stellar and that there were artificial gates/portals all over the planet Earth, and also in space. He mentioned that in other Universes there was seeding of other planets by many of these non-human intelligences and that they travel through these artificial gateways.

The Manta/Mantid 'Soul Transfer' on Spacecraft

M: "When you are on the spacecraft you separate out of your physical body and go into a Manta body, or does it change into a Manta body?"

P: "It can be either – sometimes on the craft there is a Manta body to go into and I leave my physical body and evaporate from my human form and evaporate into my Manta body."

M: "A bit like steam? Is that how it happens?"

P: "You just think it and it happens!"

"The Mantid beings are 'my family'. I am also visited by Lion Beings, who also protect me."

Paul.

"The Mantid Are my Family"

A Mantid being told Simon as a child 'I am your real mother.' What is compelling is that this is exactly what Paul was told. Below are some very specific comparisons of their accounts: Simon Parkes, a town councilor in the UK, has spoken publicly about his encounters with both Praying Mantis beings, a soul connection to Lion Beings and Reptilians.

Simon Parkes and Paul mention the 'trilling/chirping' sounds the Mantids make when they are happy with them. They both said, independently, that when they were held above a Mantid's head the 'trilling' sound was heard.

Soul Transfer

Simon Parkes and Paul have mentioned that their 'consciousness' or 'soul essence' is transferred into the Mantid form when on the spacecraft.

Note: It has been compelling that a number of Experiencers mention their 'soul consciousness' being transferred into another lifeform for a short time; e.g. Their 'essence' migrating into a Gray/Zeta being, or another life form on board craft.

Note: Simon Parkes and Paul have not communicated. However, both articulated some unique specific behaviors of the Mantids during their encounters with these beings.

The Yearly Medical

Paul told me he has often gone up onto the craft with two of his school friends and described that they were all in 'pods', including himself.

P: "I could see the Blue ones and equipment on their hands, technology."

M: "Why were you in the pods?"

P: "Checking me out, they kept me still by the liquid."

M: "What did you feel?"

P: "Just checking me out. Once a year they check us out."

M: "Did it hurt?"

P: "No."

The Space Education

P: "I was in a circle. They learned with me, my school friends and other children that were different."

M: "How were they different?"

P: "Their eyes were different; a bigger shape."

Note: This statement is suggestive of Hybrid children.

M: "What were you learning?"

P: "Maths and something; our brainwaves. It was in the air and we were all learning."

M: "Do you get told anything in your mind?"

P: "Yes – why we are here."

M: "What is the craft like?"

P: "I think I levitated last night. I was in a bubble (orb) when I traveled."

M: "Do you think they are spirits or extraterrestrials?"

P: "I see ET or spirits that are people I have known (Paul becomes teary, emotional). My ancestors say that I go back to my planet when I die. The Great Ancestor is from somewhere else, a Manta."

M: "They sound really important to you?"

P: "Yes, the brother Manta is someone I see on the spaceship. Sometimes I see him human, sometimes he is Manta."

M: "You see him here where you live?"

P: "At school. Sometimes he is a child and sometimes in adult form. I have grown up with him."

Note/Corroboration: Hybrid children are often seen on board spacecraft. Human children also recognize them as not human. I mention accounts of the 'Missing

Pregnancy Syndrome' in my book *Awakening* – Chapter Ten.

Paul and his family are all Experiencers. Though I was impressed by the complex scientific concepts Paul mentioned, what was even more compelling was the unique understanding he showed about his connection to the Mantid beings. This was corroborated by Simon Parkes, who has similarly referred to a 'soul transfer' (into Mantid form) in prior accounts. In Paul's case, such a concept is extremely profound for an eight-year-old child.

As mentioned previously, neither Paul nor Simon has communicated, yet both have very compelling and unique similarities in their accounts of experiences with the Mantid beings.

The Mission

"I Can Heal Water"

In 2013, I received the following email about a nine-year-old from Northern Europe who speaks about her ability to 'heal' water through star languages. She also gives her perspective on God and her Mission:

"Poor us. Poor kids who come to volunteer; we have such a difficult time ahead of us, a real fight. I am here to help my family 'wake up', EVERYONE is sleeping."

Cathy's Mother

"My nine-year-old daughter speaks 'star languages' to heal water. I live in Northern Europe and have four children. At the time of my first pregnancy, a 'voice' told me my children were not mine. They would only come through me. These children belong to no one. It wasn't until recently that I was aware there were such things as extraterrestrials.

My nine-year-old daughter is a special girl who finds the conventional world and rules difficult. She asks me why isn't she allowed to do things her own way. Cathy has healing abilities and dictated some healing words in an ET language to purify water. I noticed the water actually tasted different afterward. She says that star languages are from a place outside of the Universe.

Cathy receives messages in ET languages and understands what they are saying to her. She says that they are important. I showed her your presentation, where a woman does healing and writes several ET languages. My daughter responded with joy and excitement, 'She knows what I have written'."

Astounding as Cathy's claim may be, a scientist from Northern Europe is research-ing ways to energize water and explains how this could be possible. Dr. Ohlson (PhD) is a Swedish scientist referred to previously as coining the term letter people. She is also studying water and its properties.

Dr. Ohlson States

"As a scientist, the spiral formations I've been working with in my water research, such as loading energy back in water, helps healing, recharges and strengthens the energy field, the aura. Healing works on a cellular level, whether you believe it or not. The healing from my hands affected the protein binding to a gene P53, which plays a role in turning genes on and off. Rightly used, it could be bliss for humanity in rebuilding our Earth."

Masaru Emoto, the former Japanese scientist, demonstrated in numerous scientific tests, the crystalline nature of water and how it can be programmed, purified and changed by frequencies through certain types of music, prayer, and human intent.

Note: For studies that have demonstrated how frequency and intent can alter the crystalline nature of water see:

(a) Masaru Emoto and *The Messages in Water Information* and

(b) *Secret Code in Water* by Karin Halbritter, translated from German into English by Bernard Robinson.

God: A Different Perspective

Cathy's mother continues:

"Cathy doesn't use the word God as she says it's misused. She calls It a 'BEING' who resides in the 'DAY LIGHT.' It is an 'OVER TERRESTRIAL'. Day Light is where we all originate. God is not a man or woman. It has no gender. This Being sowed the seed of Light and Love, and it's where the light and angels live.

Everything is divided into three parts: Day Land, Evening Land, Night Land. The Day Land is where the light lives. Evening Land is blue and where they fuse together; that's where her 'friends' are from. The other side of this is the Black Night land, where we are now.

Cathy has 'helpers' who guide and teach her. One of the beings is called 'Emenoke', a female and is blue, has no hair or ears; her eyes are like human eyes, only bigger. The green guide is male. She has a helper from Day Land (dimensions), who helps her understand what her guides tell her. She says 'my friends are here all the time.'

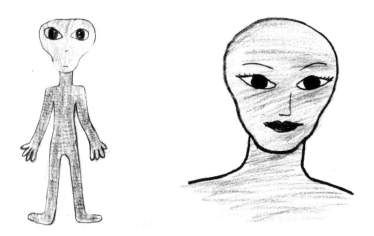

Cathy's drawings of the beings.

The Knowledge

"Cathy's spirit ET friends have given her information in seven books (not real books, but this is the best way she can describe them).

- The red book is about creation and our origins.
- The brown one is about different planets and the life there.
- The light green one is about nature, and how we can make contact with plants and animals and understand nature.
- The dark green one is about the body, how it really works and how we get it to evolve.
- The blue book is about light and truth.
- The red-brown book she can't open yet because 'a dragon took the key' from her sometime in the 1700s.
- The black book explains about darkness and evil and is dangerous.

All the books contain important information."

The New Programs

Cathy's mother added some insight into the 'multidimensional awareness' of a young autistic boy in the same school as Cathy. This young boy spontaneously told her he saw beings. Cathy's mother asked him why he didn't tell his parents? He answered: 'I have chosen to tell you. It's because of energy in your face'."

Note: It appears that these intuitive children can read our frequency and it tells them when it's safe to share and when it isn't. I was considered safe to speak to because of my frequency.

During an interview with another child in the USA (nine years of age), I was similarly told that because of my frequency the child felt comfortable in speaking with me about their story.

Autistic boy told Cathy's mother he 'is affected by frequencies':

"There is a bubble that protects me, but when I get close to wireless internet my 'bubble' bursts."

"He said it's devastating how it affects our bodies. There are five children like my daughter at the school." As a parent, Cathy's mother is concerned because Cathy doesn't fit in at school, and is bored.

Schools, Educational Systems – What is Wrong

Cathy spoke via an interpreter on Skype:

"What they teach in schools is inaccurate. They program you like computers and shut out your light. There is nothing good about this system. The children are programmed, the teachers just push the keys. The children already contain the learning we need, but they don't allow the children to expand on it and finish because we have to stop and do something else.

The information is set and rigid at school. The school programs are like a virus, it destroys what we have inside us and when we are like the computer, which is old, and we grow up, we will be finished. We lose access to information we had at the beginning.

But education is only one of the ways this happens. Our inner core can be destroyed by too much stress, facing multiple tasks, less sleep and more anxiety. We are deliberately destroyed."

Note: Cathy was clear this is a deliberate strategy.

"The same is happening to animals and nature; everything is being stressed out. It is important to care for nature and treat animals well. Adults have small ears, they don't hear the messages we try to tell them. ADULTS DON'T WANT TO HEAR WHAT STAR KIDS HAVE TO SAY. They are too stressed out; it interferes with the reality the adults live in."

The Potential of Humanity, Imagination and Making Something a Reality

"Everything is possible."

"People need to know we can do anything we desire. When children play by using their imagination, it's not just imagination. When we stop them by saying they can't do this or that, it stops them making it a reality. What they are imagining can be a reality. What at this time we call imagination can be reality. We say it's not possible, but everything is possible. We need to believe it, then we will have this capacity. When we rediscover what we can do, we can achieve our full potential."

Humanity Has to Believe in Itself

"It is difficult because first of all, we don't believe it, then if we believe but still have doubts, this prevents us from reaching this potential. We have to be at a point within ourselves to get in touch with our REAL truth in order to achieve this. There is a certain time we will achieve it, and if one person does, it will spread to other people, and this is the way it will start. But at what time I can't tell you."

Cathy shares why the Star Kids have come to this planet at this time:

"The Star Kids have come to show us the way. They are the ones to start the process, helping the rest of humanity to wake up."

Cathy says she is from Evening Land, to help us evolve. When her purpose is accomplished, she will go to the Day Light. We have already been in Day Land, but because we wanted to have more experiences, we came to this planet. The beings in Contact with her, like Emenoke, do not live on another planet. They are located at the 'edge of the universe' in the White Light. "The 'light orb' is sent to protect us. My little brother has a blue orb that protects him."

C = Cathy

M = Mary

M: "You said he will also be a teacher – in what way?"

C: "He will be my teacher, as I will be, and he will be home schooled so he will retain true knowledge."

M: "What do your guides teach you?"

C: "They are teaching me different knowledge so I can teach adults. The danger is that it can be changed and then the true information is lost. Then people get confused and lost by making fun of the Star Children, or not believing them. Many Star Kids are destroyed by education."

M: "How many Star Kids are there?"

C: "Forty or fifty percent of people of a hundred, but many get lost and only twenty percent will remember who they are."

"We Have to Wake Up"

"The beings want us to wake up and see reality as it is, to understand how powerful we really are. Some individuals from Day Land and Evening Land have come here to help humanity with the Awakening. It's very dangerous to come here to help because our past life memories can be deleted at birth and some of this is destroyed by society and education, drink and drugs. Those who come here are aware of the dangers and still want to come and help. We are not awake yet."

M: "How can we wake up?"

C: "We have to increase our energy as we don't have the energy required; it's stolen from us."

M: "How can we protect our energy?"

C: "At present, we only have point five percent of our energy. We need to have one point five percent.

- Don't get angry about small things.
- Don't speak on mobile phones for a long time.
- Don't eat white sugar.
- Don't watch TV.
- Don't use microwaves.
- Don't have wireless internet."

The Next Five Years: 2012-2017

"Something important will happen in the next five years on this planet. The parents have to listen to us. We need to educate the parents."

Cathy told me that her purpose here on Earth is to get her family to wake up and to protect her little brother because he is important for humanity. By this, she means he will become her teacher when he grows up, as he will, in turn, help humanity wake up.

"Mary has BIG ears, she listens – most adults don't."

Chapter Three

INTER-CULTURAL ENCOUNTERS AND HYBRID CHILDREN

"My children and fiancé are ex-Ojibwe/Anishinaabe Indian. I am Native American as well as English, Scottish, and Irish. I want to help others like me. I feel that I was sent here to help people."

In this chapter, we explore a family with a rich cultural heritage and their understanding of the star 'visitors', and also from an intergenerational perspective. (Names have been changed to protect identity.)

Grandma with 'big' eyes
The Children's Encounters

Children can share their encounters quite spontaneously with their parents. It happened this way for 'Sarah' with her five-year-old daughter and took her completely by surprise when her daughter suddenly spoke to her about her experiences with extraterrestrials.

S = Sarah (Mother)

S: "It was very late, around midnight, and I was driving back to Duluth from Grand Portage Reservation. Out of the blue, my five-year-old daughter said 'Mama, I want to talk about the aliens who take us'."

She went into great details that were so overwhelming that to tell you verbatim would be too difficult. This is what I got out of it:

She told me that they take us often and that they carry her. She can't move, but is not scared and can see everything that is happening. They take all of us together, with different aliens of different sexes and in different groups for each one of us. They think daddy's snoring is funny and they laugh at him. I know they have a sense of humor and that further confirmed that for me. She told me that when they take daddy they make sure he is asleep because they are afraid of him. He is too strong for them and he might hurt them. He is six foot two inches and two hundred and fifty pounds. He has similar scars and implants as mine but has no recollection of anything. So what she says makes sense to me.

She said that they don't ever hurt us, but they take us to a doctor's office to make sure that we are okay. She told me that I am afraid of them sometimes and they will make me go to sleep. She started telling me that there are two girl aliens that come for her and I asked if they had pretty brown hair like her. She said condescendingly 'Mama, they don't have hair.' My response was, 'Did you know they were girls because of their pretty blue or green eyes?' Again she replied 'Mama, they have BLACK eyes.' I said 'Were they wearing dresses?' 'No mama, they look old and were not wearing anything.'

I asked how she knew they were girls, and she said, 'I just know, Mom.' She was unable to tell me how she could hear them, she just can. I did as best as I could, not to lead her. What was so surprising was she shared this spontaneously."

M: "Does she know why you are taken?"

S: "She said that they help us, and do doctor check-ups. I listened and did not pry. I wanted to see what she would say. She talked mostly about being carried through the house and why they make Daddy sleep so hard. I have a feeling that she will spontaneously offer more details soon. She is like that. She sees these things all the time as she has described them to me out of the blue.

She is also sharing more stories about 'Grandma' with big huge eyes and no eyebrows making me fall asleep, and turning into animals and all kinds of bizarre things, which I know is similar to many other encounter stories. What is your opinion on what I should do with/for her? At this point, I just listen when she wants to talk to me about it.

She has also begun to tell me more about the aliens in much more detail. She did not learn this from me. I am quite careful. The details blow my mind, including how they take us, why they do it, when it happens, and how many aliens are involved, including their genders, what they look like, etc. She is very matter of fact without any symptoms of being afraid or having been traumatized.

Regarding the visitors, I look at them as 'little people.' It is the initial Contact: I am asleep and become abruptly aware that I am being paralyzed and separated. Right after my hypnotic regression, they came for me but seemed different. They did not send someone in after me. It was more like they were taking me from the outside, using technology. It started as a gentle vibration on my bed, and then I could feel it getting stronger and stronger. It woke me up with a jump and I looked around and then at the clock. Everyone else was sound asleep. The clock said 2:30 a.m. I said out loud 'If it is you, you can take me and I will not resist, but if it is someone else, I will not go without a fight.'

I lay back down, looked around again, and felt no familiar presence and gave permission to the one that I know to proceed. The vibrations proceeded, but only for about ten minutes. I sat up in bed wondering if they had given up. The clock now read 4:15 a.m. I was afraid at first that either they would not come for me again or that they would be upset or disappointed that I 'told' about them. I am not actually afraid of them in my memories of being with them."

Implant, but from Humans?

"I have a new implant now. I discovered it two nights ago because it was itching. That is how I discovered the others too. It is like a bug bite, itchy but huge, and I don't think this one is alien but from humans because of its size and location. I will wait until I am taken again and ask them to remove it if it is human."

Note: My research indicates that most solid implants are more likely to be placed by our own species. See information on MILAB (Military Pseudo Abductions – see *Contact* by Dr. S. Greer).

S: "A few weeks before that, I asked my eldest daughter if she ever had anyone in her bedroom at night that she knew or was afraid of. She said 'No.' I asked her if she ever woke up and could not move. She said 'Yes, quite often', but it does not scare her. I told her that if she starts being scared she could come and talk to me about it. I did not offer her more details and she dropped it at that as well. My eldest daughter is the one who can see spirits of the deceased. She has seen many spirits in her room and has told me about them. She knew before I did that my grandfather had died. She told me that he was standing at the bottom of her bed. She saw her grandfather's dog after he died. He (the dog) took her outside and told her, after making a motion to the sky, that they are coming. She told me that he meant 'Star People' – those were her words.

S: "Did I send you a copy of my regression? It was very strange, not at all what I expected."

M: "What was the main understanding you gained from the regression?"

S: "I think the main thing I got was confirmation that something is happening. I was dreadfully afraid that I am going crazy. I did not see too much more than what I had consciously recalled. The stuff that was new was rather surprising, and I also had a hard time conveying some of it to my husband. I could feel his frustration. Then, I would be blocked. I am still reflecting upon some of the memories that I saw flooding in, that I did not mention to him. Not only were they bizarre, but also many similar memories came at once and from several different perspectives. He did not let me explore the memory that I had of the little Gray that I love."

M: "Can you tell me more about this?"

S: "When I was a child, about three or four, my sister, who was two years younger than me, and I were playing in the creek by my grandparents' house. The men were out putting up hay and so it was only the women and children at home.

45

We knew that they would not allow us to go to the creek, but we knew that no one would notice we were missing. My sister started putting her head under the water and I was afraid that she would drown. I was not strong enough to lift her and so I started screaming. No one came. I decided to run into the house to get my mom, my aunt or my grandmother, but I could not find anyone. I freaked out. I ran back out to my sister and then she came out of the creek.

Under hypnosis, I could see the craft hovering above my grandparents' house. I did not want to see it as it was new to my memory. I realized that the females in my family had been taken and then I knew that was why we went down to the creek. When my dad and granddad came home, I told them about not being able to find anyone when the incident happened. I was very articulate at this age and they could perfectly understand what I was talking about. My grandma and my mom got into trouble, but swore that they were there the whole time."

Lately, I feel they are doing something else. They (the beings) came before my hypnosis session. I saw writing of some sort. It reminded me of hieroglyphics in a way."

Scripts and Past Life?

"This brings me to another topic and that is, that my eldest daughter is fascinated by Egyptian history. We went to the King Tut exhibit at the Science Museum, and that is where I saw the writing that was similar to what I had seen with the 'visitor.' At the exhibit, my daughter was correcting the lady doing the tour about who and what the gods were, what they stood for and what was done with certain body parts. She just knows these things. The lady asked another person on the tour about what my daughter was saying and he did not disagree. He said that he had heard some of what she had said before, but no one really knows for sure. My children never cease to amaze me."

Is My Child Being Monitored?

"I am writing to tell you about some more strangeness and an 'ah-ha' moment I had while browsing the ACERN website. I was reading the article where you had a link to the guy who did my regression, and it hit me when I read about the baby that could lift his head at two weeks. When my eldest daughter was born, we filmed everything. When she came out of my body they laid her on my chest; she lifted her head and grabbed my chin. They then put her on the scales which had a see-through side, and she rolled over and grabbed the side of it while having her little leg hang over the side as well. She did this within minutes of being born, and I had it on tape. She was walking (on tape) at nine months; she never crawled. She also did many other things early that were on that tape. One day we came home and our house had been broken into. The only thing stolen was the camcorder and the tape of her that was in it. I feel 'they' were taking the proof that she was doing this."

The Gifted Child

"Before I became pregnant with my (now) ten-week-old son, a tall, wispy, long-fingered ET told me that the male child in my body would be gifted. Here are my experiences with my gifted child, and so far he says complete words when he is hungry. He has said the word hungry perfectly on several occasions and startled my daughters who were holding him at the time. He could hold up his head from birth, or at least after we were released from the hospital. I have people comment on his strength all the time.

I had an experience with him a couple weeks ago that nearly scared the daylights out of me. I knew something was going to happen, as I had seen one of 'them' out of the corner of my eyes, but they disappeared when I looked straight on. Later that evening, I was in a hypnogogic state (trance). I hate when they do that to me. I would wake up and they would try to make me go back to sleep. I would scream 'You cannot have her. Why her?' I was under the impression that something made me think it was my daughter, but it wasn't, but I distinctly remember my baby son floating out of my arms and towards the window. I was frantic. I was screaming and they could not make me sleep through it. I kept grabbing him and pulling him back. When they were finally done I woke up and he was sleeping soundly beside me and the 'moon' was shining like a spotlight into my room. Then it disappeared behind the clouds. I must have made enough racket that I woke up my daughter because she wanted to know what was wrong.

I believe they also took me because later on, I was looking at my C-section scar as my physician sutured it, and it had been reopened in a couple of spots. I knew how and why when I saw that and it relieved me of my fear that 'they' would be upset with me for getting my tubes tied."

Note: Sarah has been involved in the hybrid program – see Chapter 15 on hybrids.

Sarah Discusses Her Other Son Who is Six Years Old

"Here's the kicker, my son (six years old) discussed with me something I could have never put into his head. He started a conversation about the 'real' aliens after we were playing with his mean alien action figures, not Gray-looking and just ugly monster types. He said, 'That is not what the real aliens look like, right Mom?' I asked what they looked like and he said 'You know, skinny,' and sucked in his belly and made an upward motion with his arms. Then he said that the arms and legs were 'real' skinny. I asked how tall they are and he made a motion to a size just about his head. He is forty-seven inches tall. Then he said 'Momma they like you because you are nice.' I asked how he knew that. He said that he tried to wake me up when he was with them, and even stated that there were three of them in the room with us, but they kept his mouth quiet so it could not talk. They stood beside my bed and looked into my brain through my eyes. He said that they could see everything in there. They knew I was nice.

Then my son started laughing hysterically. I said 'Honey, what is so funny?' He said it was the look on the man's face. I was confused, and I said 'What man?' He explained they took him (my son) on their ship, which was right outside our window, and he saw people on it and 'they' were working on them. The guy he was watching was screaming and my son said that 'they' told him without words that they were saving the man's life. They were not hurting him, but he was afraid. I asked him if he knew anyone on there and he said he did not. I also asked how he got on the ship and he said 'We went through the window.' His last statement before going off to play outside, 'Mom, the aliens are nice, but their eyes creep me out.' Then he showed me with his hands how the eyes are big and wrap around the head. I did not ask him to elaborate, as I knew exactly what he meant. What is it with them and windows?

My son has always been able to see them and would tell me that he would see aliens creeping around the house and hiding in the bathroom. He used to be afraid of them but now says they take him with them and show him stuff. He said that he gets to watch them work on people to help them and save them, but the people are scared. As you know, I try not to talk about any of this in front of my children and most of my conversations occur online with people like you. I feel that their stories are genuine and do not come from me; although my children know they can talk to me about anything. My son has always described the big-eyed gray beings, but not any others at this time."

M: "Does he say what he does with them?"

S: "He mostly says that he watches and they keep his mouth quiet – that he cannot talk from his mouth, which I find to be interesting. They tend to narrate what is happening, or perhaps he can hear them conversing and figure it out. He was not specific and I wanted to listen more than pry."

Orbs

"Both my daughters see orbs all the time. One daughter sees them and even feels them enter her. She was watching one as we were driving one day and all of a sudden she jumped. She said 'I saw a dark ball and it came right through the car and into my leg.' She told me it did not hurt, but startled her, and that she sees so many orbs at times and they look like multicolored raindrops. I think they may be similar to orbs I see on a daily basis. She has mentioned she can see emotions as colors when people speak. It comes out of their mouths. She said that when I am angry it is a different color than when I am happy, even when I try to hide it in my voice. My daughter asked me what orbs are. I told her that I thought they were spirits; both my daughters agreed.

She can also see colors around people in their aura. I can too. My daughter's aura is pink/red, then it goes further out to a rich gold color. She also told me she could hear voices in her head and one day she told me she could hear what I was thinking, and was correct. I am careful when I am around her that I do not let random thoughts pervade my mind. All kinds of stuff are going on here, and I am so glad to have you to talk to about it."

Past Life Soul Groups?

Sarah: "My son made an interesting comment recently. He asked me if we would be together in every life. Then he asked me: 'Mama, why did you want to be a girl this time?' I was caught off guard and I asked what he was talking about. He said that he is with me in all of his lives and that he was a boy every time except a couple of lives when he was a girl. I told him that I don't remember choosing my lives. He said that he does and remembers all of them and that he has been here many times. He told me that I am his mama in most of them. He also asked how many times he would come back and be with me. I told him that I thought it had to do with lessons that are being learned. He did not fully understand (or perhaps I am wrong), as he is only six. I had never mentioned multiple lives to any of my kids prior to this.

My six-year-old son is the one son that could walk at six months, speak complete proper sentences at eighteen months, and he could write his entire name (in capital letters) by two-years-old. His preschool teacher asked me if he was a super genius when she first met him. I said he just likes to write and draw. One daughter and my son are both off the charts on standardized tests. He tests at the third-grade level and he just graduated from Kindergarten. My daughter was testing at the fourth-grade level and able to do algebra, and she just completed first grade. These kids blow my mind sometimes."

Hybrids?

"I thought of another thing that my six-year-old son has mentioned. He used to tell me all the time about his brothers and sisters who are dead. I asked him why he thinks they are dead and he said they look dead. I asked if they are my kids and he said no, they are all Daddy's. I asked how he knows them and he said that they come and play with him at night. I also asked where they play and he said somewhere else, and that he is not sure, but he thinks it's at their house. I speculated that he was playing with sickly-looking hybrids and that they may indeed be his father's. I know that they take him too as they took his mother."

M: "So you think they are maybe his father's hybrid children? This would make sense, but I wonder why he would think they are dead?"

S: "It is my opinion that he thought they were dead because they may have floated or walked through a solid object in front of him. Also, because they usually look so sickly. That is just how he described it.

His father's mother (paternal grandmother) was a very traditional Ojibwe Indian. She was born in a wigwam and did not speak English very well, not having actually seen a White person until her teens. She described a typical abduction to me one evening when I asked her about the 'little people' – that is one of the terms that the Native Americans call the ETs. I have talked at length with elders and medicine people about the little people. There is apparently more than one type. Her reaction was initially, 'Phish, the little people, just kick them.' She did speak some Ojibwe, but then went on to say that they want to look inside the body. She said that they had her on a table and they looked in her and made a motion to her bottom. Then she said they tried to scare her, but could not. I asked what they did and she told me that one got right in her face and looked in her eyes. She laughed at him. Then she said he grew bigger and did it again. Again she said she laughed at him. I asked how she escaped. She said she kicked him and ran, but did not recall how she got home. My assumption on this is that a smaller one initially looked in her eyes, and then a taller one looked in her eyes. She described typical Gray-type beings to me. I have heard others describe the little people as 'little Indians' and I do not think they are authentically talking about someone real. She also had extensive Contact with Bigfoot, and had witnesses that saw her and Bigfoot communicating."

M: "So she said she communicated with a Bigfoot? I believe they communicate telepathically and are connected to UFOs as well?"

Bigfoot

S: "I asked her how she talked to them. She said they understand both English and Ojibwe. She called them 'old time Indians' and said they are ancestors to the Anishinabeg. Where European people believe they came from a monkey, she believed Indians came from Bigfoot. She said that one came up to her at a powwow in Canada and some people were frightened. She went right up to him, offered him tobacco and started talking to him. She said that most of the replies were nods, but could not specify how he talked. Most Anishinabeg consider Bigfoot to be a trans-dimensional being and that you are never to look in his eyes, out of respect. She also met with Bigfoot at a landfill. They were dropping off garbage and he was just standing there. Everyone with her stayed back and she went right up to him and started talking and offered tobacco. Her youngest son was with her and is still alive as a witness to this."

Trees and Consciousness

"I just thought of another incident with my six-year-old son, although I may have mentioned it to you before. One day last summer, we were driving home and there were some tree cutters cutting down trees. My son became quite upset and then asked me why people don't love trees. Why don't they care if they are alive or not? I have an affinity for trees, and seeing them being cut makes me terribly upset, but I usually just say people are dumb. I wish they wouldn't chop down trees that are where our oxygen comes from. He did not say this. He went into details about the trees hurting and seeing them bleed. I do not see them bleed. I can feel them and hear them scream, but I have never seen one bleed."

Life Jumping?

"One daughter has been doing my thing now. She does the 'life jumping' while sleeping. One day she woke up scared and confused. She told me that she must have dreamed that she woke up and lived out a whole day, only to wake up in the morning at her regular time. She asked if that ever happened to me, and if I was scared? I told her that I get confused and that it happens all the time. I advised her not to be scared since her body is grounded in this life and therefore anything that happens in the one she is 'visiting' she will be safe from any harm. I told her that she is most likely helping the one she is visiting or learning lessons that this life cannot offer at this time, in a safe but very real way.

'Life jumping' is actually my term and we both do this while sleeping. I have many stories about my own experiences, but it amounts to being able to either access past lives or being able to visit parallel or other lives in the present. I do not know which it actually is since it has been explained to me that time is not linear like we understand, but circular. This would explain why I could visit other lives that are past, but not 'actually' past. It is confusing to me, but I am able to do it. Now, my oldest daughter can and my oldest son can remember his lives consciously but does not have to visit them.

Native elders told me that my daughter would remember her past lives when she receives her pipe. She is supposed to be a pipe carrier. The woman that has her pipe will not give it up, and since the vibration of the instrument is no longer fitting to this woman, she is becoming very sick. That is her choice. I was told that she (daughter) would keep coming back to help her people. Her Great Grandma was a medicine woman. My daughter is/has her spirit. Funny thing, the day before she was born, I told my husband that I wanted to name the baby girl what was his grandma's English name."

M: "So she has experienced time anomalies?"

S: "For her, yes. She said she lived out a whole day in the other life, while she had not even awakened in this one for the day."

Communicating with Animal Spirits

"My daughter also sees animal spirits as if they were still alive. She watched a wolf spirit run alongside our vehicle for miles and then follow us around town and into a store. It apparently did not want her to cut her hair. She said it growled at the lady that cut her hair, and then it disappeared. Native American people have a firm belief that people are not supposed to touch your hair, especially strangers. Getting it cut is also a no-no, and should be done as seldom as possible since hair helps our senses be acuter. Just think of the difference in how your legs sense before and after shaving. They are almost numb to the touch after a good shave.

Note: Many Experiencers share that they can communicate with animals that are still alive, and some report a heightened awareness of those in spirit form/deceased.

This family combines the cultural awareness of a North American Indian family with a Western understanding of encounters. Fortunately, Sarah is very informed and was able to support her children with listening and openness as they articulated their experiences and multidimensional abilities. She is also aware that not all experiences are extraterrestrial but that one can be picked up by covert agencies and monitored.

For those who feel this has happened to them, an excellent reference is:

MILABS – Military Mind Control and Abduction by Dr. Helmut Lammer and Marion Lammer, 1999.

Chapter Four

THE INTERGENERATIONAL-EXTRATERRESTRIAL CONNECTION

Edward lives with his partner, Jenny, and children, seven-year-old Alice, and twelve-year-old Peter. The children are not genetically related to Edward but they all experience extraterrestrial Contact.

Note: Research suggests individuals often find themselves attracted to partners with similar experiences.

Note: Names have been changed to protect identity.

Edward is an engineer. The family resides in Texas. His partner Jenny discovered they were both having encounter experiences and so it appeared, were Jenny's children. In this case, the adult encounters were experienced and corroborated by her children. The children appeared to have not only conscious recall but a complex understanding of what this meant.

In the series of communications with Edward, over many months, it became very clear there were intergenerational links via the mother. Ufological Research shows that this is a common pattern with the encounter phenomenon. This intergenerational link demonstrates a marked upgrade in awareness with each successive generation. This includes expanded psi abilities and a more conscious knowledge of their encounters. In this case, it certainly demonstrated how the children might assist the parents to understand what is going on.

Note: The intergenerational link, in this case, is through the mother.

Edward contacted ACERN primarily due to his own numerous sightings of anomalous lights and Out-of-body experiences (OBEs). He felt he was almost a magnet for the UFOs and felt the activity had been increasing. He believed he had seen more UFOs per week than most people see in a lifetime.

Edward wrote:

"They always come at night and they keep getting closer and more vivid each time. I believe they are good beings of some kind because they interact with my emotions. Last night, I was aware that I would be visited long before it happened. At nine o'clock in the evening, a huge yellowish light faded in and got brighter as it was headed my way. It was descending and I just knew it was going to land in my yard. The very second I felt fear kick in, the light dimmed and started to go in the other direction. Even after the light was gone, I could still see the craft in the dark. It was very close."

Alice is just seven; she had dreams about meeting with Gray aliens. She told Edward that some of the Grays were small and some tall and they put something in her leg so they will know where she is. He told me her dreams are very vivid and seem very real to her.

Note: The detail of sizes of the beings and her sense of having an implant is not something a child would be aware of, and its purpose, is very compelling.

Edward wrote:

"I am by profession an electrical engineer. I feel as if I have learned much about energy from 'them'. My creative outlet is building concept electrical motors in my garage. In my motors, I use specially designed coils. To me, it's an art. The coils look like many of the designs you see in crop circles and sacred geometry. I believe energy naturally flows in these patterns. I'll spare you the technical details, but it works well.

Jenny, my partner, has Contact in the form of dreams. Alice, her daughter, has the same dreams, and I have both conscious and unconscious Contact in many forms. All of our experiences seem to line up with each other.

"I've seen the craft from one hundred feet or so. Alice called the craft the 'big one'. She said the others on the drawing were smaller. The big one is actually only about thirty feet across and twenty-five feet tall. Check out the picture and see what you think.

I enjoy writing about my strange, secret life but I am also nervous that certain people could find out about me and cause issues. The ETs are coming and no one can stop them but someone or some agency could make it more difficult for me. Do you know if that is an issue in the USA?

Since you want to use some of this info in your book, I thought I might write the story of all of us. I feel as if I have experienced a lot but I've spent hours watching videos and reading as well. I figured out real quickly, the UFO community in the US is infiltrated with disinformation and people watching what's going on. It's a mess. All of us have validated aspects of our experiences without knowing what the others have seen. If I put this in chronological order, many things will line up.

When I was six or seven, I saw a UFO that I called a 'car in the sky'. During that time I started to experience sleep paralysis often and felt a presence in the room during that. I am sure things went on that I can't remember. I never put the UFO and aliens together back then, but I was terrified of aliens because my very religious mother told me they were demons and that aliens do not exist. To this day, I have many out-of-body experiences. In the astral, I've seen ships and been to many places. I also have a telepathic connection at times, although I have not had any meaningful communication in words. Sometimes I will hear my name called and feel a 'download', as some people call it. I also receive downloads that take hours or days to understand.

At age twenty, I started to research ways to make a technology that would reduce energy bills. That continues to this day. The ETs have inspired me to think about new designs and I feel compelled to keep testing and trying new things. Basically, I have received concepts with a lack of details as to how it's done.

Jenny, my partner, told me that when she was eleven years old, she saw many UFOs on one night while camping with friends in the woods. They were high in the sky. She said it looked like a war going on and scared them to the point that they went home. Jenny and I were strong believers in Christianity through our twenties. We have both adopted a much broader spiritual understanding in the last five years or so. In the last few years, the first major event was with me on the lake at dusk and something with seven to ten red lights. The size of an eighteen-wheeler, it flew up off the water by some power lines. Another person confirmed that, and the guy was visibly shaken. The timing was amazing because I had just begun to understand that ETs might be active in many people's lives. This was because I had seen some of your lectures around that time.

Jenny and I spent many nights on the lake fishing, and we started to watch the skies. We would see anomalous lights most days, but nothing major at the time. One night, Jenny, Alice and I went to the lake. We saw a yellow light in the sky, which appeared to be a planet, but it was out of place. As a plane got near it, it took off at an amazing rate of speed. Alice got so excited, she said (over and over), 'I want to go on a spaceship and meet the aliens!'

Jenny drew a picture of the craft and it was exactly like the one I saw. It was more of a bell shape than a typical saucer. I've never seen this craft on YouTube video so it was very odd for her to have drawn that shape. She gave fine details that I had seen in person, like where all the lights were and how the top looked like two-way glass. When Alice saw the picture, she said 'Hey! That's the big one.' Meaning that was a larger craft that she saw, with the smaller craft the one she was on. Alice was dead on with the actual size and color of the craft as well (thirty feet, aluminum). Although she doesn't know it, we actually call the craft I see The Big Guy. Jenny said she knew there was something in the bottom of the craft. The drop shape is what we see.

One night, Alice told me that the craft that I saw up close would have landed if I had stayed calm. I never told anyone that I didn't stay calm, but it was true, I was shaken a little. She also said they take her to Mars to teach their children about Earth people. They treat her like a queen."

Note: Boriska, a Russian boy, who said that in his past life he came from Mars. See Project Camelot, http://projectcamelot.org/boriska.html.

There have been a number of whistleblowers from Military Super Soldier Black Ops that have said that we have jump gates to Mars and also the Moon. Andrew Basiago, a lawyer by profession, and participant in Project Pegasus, speaks of his time as a child when he was trained with these technologies.

Alice – Her Trips to Mars and Space School (Seven Years Old)

"Alice and I went fishing, and, that's where she told me about her 'dream' with aliens. She dreams that she is levitated out of bed, to a spaceship with three legs, where she meets with Gray Aliens. Some are small and some seven feet tall. She saw the kids on planet Mars. She said it was very dusty. The little boys were darker in color than the girls. They once put something on, or in, her leg so they will know where she is at all times. The aliens got her from her bed and she woke up as they were picking her up. Jenny and I were asleep and they did something to keep us that way. They said to her that I was a big guy and they are smaller, and I needed to stay asleep. Jenny and I have no recollection of this happening but I am aware of the ETs abilities to screen out memories."

Note: It is well documented that those not taken onto the craft will be kept in a deep sleep. For Alice to mention this concept at seven years old is unlikely in normal circumstances.

"Alice said the aliens took her to Mars and on the way they fed her. She says they are very nice to her. She says she meets alien kids that were scared at first but now they play together. The aliens fed her something which, she said, made her feel more love in her heart.

On Mars, she told me she went to a school where she learned some paranormal skills. One was looking through walls (she claims she still can do this at times, although I have not tested her). She didn't remember that part of the trip well, but she remembered what the aliens looked like. She said the boys were dark gray or black and the girls were pink. She interacted with a teen alien in school and learned the most from her. She also saw babies in a crib. They showed her aliens of various ages. From what I gather, the beings were somewhat like the typical Grays. They spoke telepathically, and also whispered out loud to each other but she says they were very quiet with the verbal language. When she returned we were looking for her, and the aliens did something to cloak their craft so the neighborhood could not see them as they were. When they dropped her off, we spent a few minutes meeting them and they left on good terms. She talked about this for over two hours.

Below is a picture Alice drew of what she saw on Mars. She drew the people as examples of what they looked like at different ages. The adult was her teacher. The teen was her friend. The kid was her helper, and she says there were two babies in a crib. She says the school was on Mars. She says she doesn't remember much about

Alice's drawing is of her time on Mars. She described it as a desert.

what she learned, but she said, 'They don't learn anything we learn here (on Earth).'

I've spoken to her several times in the last few weeks, to jog her memory. She has since told me that the ship I saw had a smaller craft in the bottom.

To answer your questions, Mary:

Alice said the Martians she sees look like the typical Grays but slightly more human than the Hollywood version. They are like Grays but with slightly larger heads than humans, and large eyes, although I showed her some pictures of Grays and she picked those that were dark in color; six-foot tall adults. She is very aware how much hoaxing there is on the Internet when it comes to aliens. I didn't tell her if any of the photos were real, but she knew the ones that were most likely real."

Note: What is fascinating is that Alice, at just 7 years old, could apparently discern the real from the fake.

"As I'm sure you know with kids, they don't think anything about all this. It's just no big deal to them, so I've had a hard time getting all the details from them. She says those photographs are real but the ones she sees are darker in color. Like an African person. I could not find the exact picture she originally pointed out but those are close. While we were looking through the pictures, she was also pointing out the ones she felt were real. The photographs that she said were real were also photographs that I felt had the highest potential of being real. I recognized most of the ones she picked and there was usually a believable story behind them. One was the alien autopsy photo. She said those were a different race of gray beings. Overall, she chooses two to five percent of the pictures to be real out of hundreds we searched on Bing and Google images. In my opinion, that's probably the accurate number of photos that even look real to me, and I've spent countless hours researching this. She was just going by how she felt."

Link: http://www.bing.com/images/search?q=alien+pics+greys&view=detail&id=111078CB1AF86BD0A594037B38DB57CAC6A18351&first=26

"Alice explained how there is time dilation when they come get her. She said that it's only a minute in our time but seems much longer in real time. I have a hard time to believe she made that up! After that incident, I started to watch the skies at home occasionally and never saw more than a few odd lights at first. One night, I was feeling emotionally warm and fuzzy after successfully working out an issue with someone. I felt compelled to watch the skies that night and an hour after dark it happened! In a burst of light, a craft powered up as it was descending out of the sky, and appeared to be coming to my front yard. I live on one acre and it would be a good landing pad. After a few seconds, I felt the fear kicking in and it dimmed the light at that exact moment. The light seems to be more than just light and comes with a download of information at times. There is no other light like it. It does not glare like a star or plane. Even after the craft dimmed its light, I could still see the shape of it. From that night on, they are here most nights and will show up wherever I am."

Healing Abilities

"After that first night, we watched them each night and they would show up for a few minutes then leave. They appear to be able to hear your thoughts and often show up immediately after asking (in my head) 'Where are you guys?' A few weeks went by and one night they showed up two hundred yards away with no lights on, but I could still see them. That night I lost time from eleven thirty to six in the morning. The next day, when I touched Jenny on the head I noticed my hand got hot and I felt a wonderful sensation. I later found that experience is similar to a Reiki healer does. Recently I went to see a friend in the hospital, who had gallbladder issues. She was going to have emergency surgery. When I put my hand on her, my hand got hot again and I felt that same wonderful feeling. I don't know that I healed her, but she never suffered any more pain after that, to my knowledge. She was released a few days later, and her surgery was postponed."

UFO Landing – Telepathic Communications and Black Helicopters

"I had one other very close sighting, where the craft came about one hundred feet from me and I was able to get a good look. That's also when the black helicopters started to show up. They are very quiet for a helicopter and make a low thumping sound that is similar to traffic noise. There is a helicopter that flies by every night and looks military. Today, about noon, we had three Apache helicopters fly about one hundred and twenty feet above our house. It was so loud, everyone came out to look. The noise shook our insides. I don't know if that is related. One more thing: I saw a truck, on two occasions, pull into an empty parking lot and wait at night.

When one of the ships flew over, the driver got out and watched with binoculars as it flew by at ten thousand feet or so. I was watching from a dark field where I go to meditate at night. He never knew I was there. Apparently, I'm not the only one that knows they are here.

Shortly after that, Jenny had a dream where she met the alien, after he landed in the exact spot I always thought he would land. He spoke telepathically and she described it as 'Hearing with your whole body.' He answered all her questions and put her at ease about taking a trip with him. She was concerned about the time she would be gone and he said something like 'The time you are actually gone will only be minutes in Earth time.' She also said his personality was warm and it was like meeting an old family member. When they first met, she yelled out to him 'I'm not armed,' and he answered back like 'Stop worrying, all is well.' She said she felt like he was smirking at her, like 'Stop being ridiculous.' In the end, he said he would be back soon to take us for a ride. He looked something like a Gray in appearance. I get the impression they show up in the form you are ok with. I've had similar dreams but I don't remember all that has been said between us. I will say they are amazingly caring in my dreams."

Note: Screen memories are common where the extraterrestrial being will 'disguise' its form so that there is less fear.

"I am from Andromeda" – The ADHD link

Peter, twelve years old.

"When Peter was five, I discovered he knew everything there was to know about Andromeda. From the day he could read, he read all he could about space. He's twelve now and asked me to hypnotize him and do a past life regression. He wants to know why he is so interested in space and the Andromeda galaxy. As I said in the last email, he's ADHD, and he's probably the eighth or tenth ADHD person I've been close to. I can tell you much about ADHD, but overall these people are struggling. They need a different world to function normally. Thanks for your efforts to change the world."

Note: Letter people such as ADHD have different programs.

"Peter is a video-game-playing pre-teenager and extremely sensitive. He is very afraid of this world. I'd say he's scared of his own shadow, although he has gotten better in the last year. But before that, even a knock at the door was too much for him to handle. Peter stated that if reincarnation is true, this is his first life on Earth because he does not fit in at all. He gets bored very easily and, even though he's seen a few real UFOs, it's not exciting to him. He acts as if it's all normal, and wonders why people are surprised about all this. He claims to be able to see through other people's eyes at times and he will even ask me to explain what I was doing at work because he couldn't understand the computer code I was writing. He also feels he can read people's minds. That is something I relate to also and I teach him that he has to learn how to turn off his radar at times. Other people's thoughts are not always something a person wants to know. It can be scary."

Note: The ability to access another consciousness, read minds and access their visual focus is another ability of the New Human, *Homo noeticus*.

"Amazing things are happening to Peter now. He has always been drawn to Andromeda, so I had a conversation with him where I suggested maybe he was from there. A week later he couldn't get it off his mind. So I spent a few minutes trying to jog his memory. During the conversation, he went into a trance (I didn't hypnotize him) where he saw a vision. While he was in the trance he said 'I can do great things. Something amazing happened before I died. I had a peaceful death. We left something on the moon to help Earth, I was sent to help.'

He took a big gasp of air and said: 'I'm back. What did I just say?' I told him, and he said about the object on the moon, he wasn't sure if it was biological or mechanical.

The next day I listened to the Andromedan channel, and it was said they put a portal on the moon that would have been a machine, which worked with consciousness as well, so it was both biological and mechanical. I asked Peter if that was accurate, and he immediately said 'Yes! That's it!' Since then, Peter says the portal used magnetic energy to physically move people or ships around, and could also work as a time machine, although, as a time machine, it would only send your consciousness to a different time. I think that's because the future is based on potentials, and not nailed down yet.

As for me, I'm learning fast! After this interaction with Peter, I was surprised how I knew just what to say to remind him who he was. Now, if you ask him he says he's from Andromeda. He's currently trying to contact old friends and guides. Who knows what's coming next."

Increased Psychic Perceptions

"Peter says he sees through other people's eyes when he wants to but really can't explain how he does it. I've seen him do it, and it appears he can induce a trance at any time. In that altered state, he can focus on someone and see through his or her eyes. Peter knows he's getting in tune with his higher self. He's starting to pay attention now. He says I increase his ability to remember with my presence and I ask the right questions. I know the answers to many things, but I don't lead him. I let him give me his way of seeing it. When I write to you, I put it in words that the UFO and metaphysical communities would understand because Peter doesn't always have the vocabulary to express everything like he wants. Yes, I would say Peter has some visual telepathy ability. He seems to be in touch with a voice such as his higher self or past self, maybe other beings. He says all his experiences include voices of some kind. He doesn't recall everything in his past life as of today but he's remembering pieces regularly. He didn't say the moon itself was artificial, but he gets the impression it's full of artificial things, and possibly hollowed out.

I played some of the star languages to Peter six months ago and he said they sound familiar, but his language was more thought forms with telepathy. They must have traveled often because he talks about several places. He said a lot of things like 'There is something special about the triangle galaxy.' I'm sure all this comes by what you call 'downloads'. It's nonlinear information that's usually easier to get than understand. I've recently found that with my downloads the key is asking them to repeat the download. Each time, you can get more out as long as you can hold the connection. I personally believe it is we using our higher self as a portal to speak with any entity that has the same ability. There's information across the universe as well as across the veil.

Peter is remembering daily, and today he remembered an Andromedan mother named Star Fire. A blue-skinned female with possibly gold braided hair. He was in the mood to talk, so we discussed many things. He says he feels wiser than ever. About the moon, he says the Grays/bad ETs have an agenda to destroy the stargate on the moon, but because of the rise in consciousness they are having a hard time doing that. I suggested the moon may be hollow or have tunnels and he said, 'That's probable,' but he feels 'Luna' has a consciousness as 'Gaia' does. He remembered a planet consciousness's name. He said Lasurus is the name of that planet, and it's far away. He mentioned several facts about several subjects that he will have to work on. He didn't have details yet. He spoke of Mars and Venus. Mars had a bad race that died out somehow, and Venus has a thriving planet with red rivers and plant life, along with people. He says the people are further along than us in consciousness, but not like Andromedans or Pleiadians. They are learning also. He says that somehow the people have gone against the consciousness of the planet and Venus is having a hard time with the people right now."

Note: A whistleblower, John Lear, also mentions that Venus has life, and that the public has been lied to about this. See his interview with George Noory on 'Coast to Coast' radio via the links below.

http://www.coasttocoastam.com/shows/2006/05/11
https://www.youtube.com/watch?v=ZpCpziLsRb0

Religion and God

"During this time, Peter explained how God works, and how we are all one mind and that he, Peter, is accessing this one mind. Regarding religion, Jesus and others are Masters sent on purpose to Earth to start a religion so there would be a record of high consciousness in the collective consciousness of the planet. It wasn't for the religion; it was for the coming of higher consciousness people (Indigo, Starseeds) who would be born later. It was to give the whole planet a reference point when these new people start to show who they really are. He also says these beings incarnate wherever needed all over.

Peter said that bad ETs backed off recently because of the rise in our consciousness during the galactic alignment in the last three years. He says that Gaia will cleanse herself now they are gone. He says the great flood was also a cleansing. He said the flood was to get rid of genetically-engineered, bad ETs who were huge (fallen angels). I told him there was a small ice age being talked about. Peter said that was the cleansing. He mentioned how planetary consciousness works. We are the children of the planet but if the children get too low in consciousness, then a plague may occur to cleanse the bad energy. Only the strong survive. You can look back at the history of Gaia and see she has cleansed herself many times from various issues. Peter says they can all go that way and that's why you see barren planets or lost civilizations on planets. This 'being,' said that not all planets are divine like Gaia. The current cleanse is to fix pollution, some bad energy and so on. It's not extremely life threatening. He says there are different levels of cleansing a planet. He says, there is something really special just past our view. He thinks it's several galaxies together, but is not sure. I thought it was fascinating that Gaia can target low consciousness and cleanse it.

I asked Peter if he had any friends who were like him. He said he had one friend but that friend's parents were very religious and he wouldn't be able to accept anything about ET or spiritual paranormal things. Peter invited him over and I never spoke with this twelve-year-old kid but I watched closely and I'd say he's exactly like so many of the letter kids (ADHD, Asperger's), but an extremely nice young man. I'm sure he has his own stories, if I can find a way to talk to him appropriately. The reason I'm saying this is because it tells me how common this is in my area."

Encounter and Healing

"In the year before this event, I had been on pain relief drugs but the doctor had just released me as his patient, due to a new law that went into effect. They didn't have room for me because there were other people with more serious conditions. I was distraught because I was in constant pain. After the night where I lost time, my pain has not returned. Yes, I feel I was healed, and I am not sure if I can heal, but it appears so. I've awakened on so many levels. In my opinion, all of this is about human awakening."

Note: Missing time is a classic pattern accompanying an encounter, and many people with encounters also can experience healings. See: *UFO Healings* by Preston Dennet.

"The whole family has had strange things happen in general. Jenny and I were once arguing one time about why she feels she has to turn off all the lights in the house every night. I turned them off that night, just to make her happy. However in the morning, all the lights were on, and all the doors that had been locked were unlocked. These guys have a sense of humor, apparently. We have had arguments outside at night and they always show up, as if to say, 'Is that really important?' It disarms us and we calm down because we remember we are affecting the collective consciousness and ourselves. I feel as if much of this is going on in most households all over the world but people are programmed to disregard it. Recently, we have seen some kind of light orbs that make me think of a fairy. Both Jenny and I have seen them. They hang out by the door and fly away when we open it. Interesting, but strange. They seem nice but shy."

The Shift

"It continues to this day; every day is exciting. I can't wait to see what will happen next, although it's difficult to 'play dumb' with my coworkers, as I listen to them talk about things they think they know, and they are constantly trying to uphold a fundamentalist viewpoint of the world. In all honesty, they are struggling to hold on to their old ways of thinking. It's not working for them anymore. I wish I could talk to them, but they live in a box. I've made a few comments to them, alluding to the fact we are not alone. Some of them tremble at the thought of it because, on some level, they know I'm right."

Downloads, the Shift, and Understanding

"So what do we do with all this? The downloads have brought me up to speed quickly. I've learned so fast that I can hardly process all the information that comes in, given the rate it is hitting me. Why are we not further along? When is this shift? How I understand it: the closed minds are slowing the process. Education, religion, etc., are putting their minds in boxes and giving people beliefs that stop the learning process. They teach in absolutes by making statements like 'This is how the world works,' rather than saying 'This is what we think, but we hope to discover more soon.' Some are starting to wake up, but many don't know what to do with it. When there are enough open minds, the shift will happen, and the open-minded people will be able to help the others understand what's happening.

From what I understand, the ETs are here to inspire us to evolve because we are at a point where we are a danger to them and ourselves. They have rules to some degree. They can interact, but not too quickly or dramatically because it would disrupt the natural learning process we must go through. There are many people on the verge of having experiences. Those people can have their own experience in a matter of days, with the right mindset. The good ETs know how much you can handle, and they won't push you too far. In this field, like attracts like. So if you ask the universe to show you with love, you will receive a loving being. Open your hearts and your eyes. Push away all your beliefs for a time. Spend a few minutes in nature (outside) when you can and tell them in your mind 'If you are there, I want to see you.' They will show as they did for all of us. They start far away but depending on your reaction, they will come closer and interact physically and spiritually. They are out there listening to the consciousness of the planet. When they hear a sincere person who needs inspiration, they will show in whatever form you are ok with.

I've had several dreams and felt telepathic communication where I don't really understand what is being said. Their craft will come within one hundred feet or so at times. I am still waiting for a face-to-face visit. I may have had one but don't remember. I'm convinced they are good in nature. Yes, I do feel led to build technology. I'm working as an engineer, but I've thought about this long before I ever engineered anything.

I have a question. I had a dream a few months ago in which I heard an electronic voice say 'The Vedic Five' twice. There was a very powerful energy in the room and I felt it even after I woke up. I was up for hours after that. I've researched all kinds of Vedic things to find the answer, but the best I could find was Vedic numerology for the number five. I mentioned this to Peter and when I said, 'The Vedic Five', he said, 'Oh yeah, Nevadic Five! It's a massive control center for their section of space. Like a planet that has biological drones that roam on their own.' Peter said this place is a higher consciousness than most. He said the Nevadic Five seems to have consciousness like the ten or so masters that move around planets (including Jesus). That being said, he told me he had no idea why he knew that, and it was a little far out there for even him.

The thing is, in my dream, I thought I heard 'The Vedic Five', but I remembered it was actually 'Nevadic Five', just like Peter said. Do you know anything about this? If not, I'll shelve it for now and keep listening for someone to mention it. There are so many ET groups out there, it's hard to say if that was valid or not. Most of our info can be validated by other sources.

In my past, when I have had a vivid dream or even a vision, there was always a link somewhere. Just this week, I saw a woman's house fall down in this dream. The house foundations were rotten but it was repairable. I wondered who it was so, I asked my ex-wife if she was ok and she replied 'I feel like my world is falling apart.' She was diagnosed with some variety of feminine cancer and was upset because no one around her can pick up on her issues. She was surprised I could tune in to her at such a distance. Distance doesn't matter. It's a non-linear form of communication similar to quantum entanglement, and anytime I have these dreams there is a connection on some level."

Peter Asks the Questions

"Last night Peter was asking if I knew why Nevadic Five was Contacting me because super-high-conscious beings don't just pick random people. He said I must have a strong connection for them to speak to someone twenty thousand light years away. (He also said it could be twenty million light years). All I know is the voice I heard sounded pre-recorded or like an electronic device, and it gave me the impression it was trying to make me remember something in my past. Things seem to be showing up, right as I am open to them.

I feel it is valid, especially because I even said the word wrong and Peter knew what I meant (I said *The Vedic* and Peter said *Novadic*). I'm sure there is something to it. I'm just looking for more information that resonates with me. Also, I'm used to living in a society that needs years of hard evidence to prove the reality of a subject. That being said, people are more open than ever, and you are in perfect position to report all the wonderful things that are going to happen in the next few years."

The Orbs

"I assume you know about the orb phenomenon. Some say they are consciousness without a body. Some think they are divas or fairies. I'm not sure, but I can tell you they are everywhere here, and I just started seeing them in the last year or so. They are intelligent because they scatter when you get too close. I can see them without a camera, but they move very quickly, so it's easier with a camera. I'd be glad to hear your take on this.

Knowledge and understanding make a difference. One point worth making: it's about how this is affecting our everyday lives. I've been asked several times, 'How does this knowledge help you in any way?' I noticed that Peter has matured abnormally fast. A month ago, he had no confidence and he was awkward around people. After learning who he is, he woke up one morning and said he felt wiser than ever. Since then, he has excelled in his robotics class and is on his way to a competition for the school. Night and day difference! For me, the ETs triggered me to search further in my understanding of consciousness. Now, I'm applying it to my life every chance I get. We lost our dog last night and were afraid she had been hit by a car until I decided to remote view her. She was safe in a neighbor's house. The neighbor brought her home in the morning.

ETs are becoming a very interesting part of the collective consciousness of humanity, although the real benefit is the rise in human awareness. It is giving our children wisdom and our adults more understanding of the big picture.

I was talking to Peter and asking him what he could remember about Andromeda. I asked if he remembered a religion, and he fell into a trance. After five minutes, he started speaking as the Andromedan Council. I think the council was a council of people. We spoke for two hours! I asked every question I could think of and recorded some of it. We talked about DNA and quantum physics and everything you can imagine. It was great! The energy that came with them was very loving. They must be the nicest beings I've ever spoken to."

The Shift with Accelerated 'Intuitive' Abilities; Evolutionary Change in Human Consciousness

"I recently came to a conclusion, between downloads and research, that we are definitely shifting. It explains why Peter's and my abilities are enhancing, and the experiences are common. I've heard we reach this point in cycles and in the past we didn't make it. Tonight, Peter said we've been here at this level of consciousness at least three times before and fell, due to bad ETs knocking us off the course. In the past, we just didn't have the consciousness to push them away. He says they do it to every planet that reaches this level and it's almost like a religion for them (we are talking about some of the abductors and partner races). He says that this time there is a ninety-five percent chance we will make it, and possibly a one-hundred percent chance we are headed up to a higher level. It's slow over time, but he said the last three years he's been getting more and more in tune and it's due to the shift that's affecting everyone. He said it's the Starseeds and Indigos of the planet (like us), that Gaia cherishes because we can help the vibration of the planet more than any."

May 2015

"I have new info. If you remember, Alice (now eight) said the beings she encountered looked like Grays. Jenny saw Grays in her dreams and Peter met them once as well. He says they took him on a tour, but he doesn't have a good memory of it. I finally saw one in person. I woke up when they came to get me. I felt as if I had signed up for it and felt a calm energy that put me in almost a trance. I took his hand, and it had a texture of felt and was cool to the touch. I'm sure I've been on many rides but don't remember a lot. Jenny has also been on many rides with them where she remembers a lot. It's the typical abduction story. She's taken on a ship where they do medical procedures and leave triangle bruises.

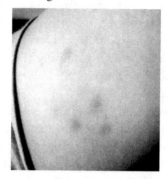

They do all kinds of tests, and we both feel we are being enhanced while also we are helping them in some way. Last night she said she asked them to leave her alone for a while because they came to get her several nights in a row. She always feels a peace and calm. One of them rubs her head while she is being worked on. There's no pain. We now see a new kind of ship. It's a triangle with lights on the corners and a red light in the center. You can see these very ships if you search 'easttexasufo' on YouTube. I have met the guy that runs that channel. The videos are shot ten miles from me. The craft appear to be like planes but they are not. In person, there is no doubt what they are. I went out-of-body and flew right up to one. It looks like something from a batman movie. When they fly over, they are not hiding. They fly low and slow, and seem to show up when you ask them to. In the videos, you can see he has some footage where they circle for thirty to forty-five minutes. There was a famous picture on the Web of a triangle craft from Belgium. These are identical. The 'easttexasufo' guy says they are benevolent Reptilians, and I would agree, although they don't look all that scary. Alice has all kinds of symbols in her mind that she has never seen, including the Merkaba (pyramid in a pyramid), sacred geometry, and the eye of Horus."

Edward: "Peter wrote this on his hand. He is not sure what it means, but he feels it's something important? Have you seen anything like it?"

Note: I have a number of cases where children have written symbols on their arms and hands, and also say the symbols are important.

Support the Children

In all honesty, it's anyone that's contributing. No matter if you heal the sick, speak star languages, or spread the word and bring these light workers to the attention of the world. If the older generations can teach and encourage these kids that it's ok to talk about it. Help them develop their skills and this planet will develop in no time. Every day is exciting!

Mars Connection and Schools on Mars

(See Chapter Five)

I received a symbol (image) from a mother in the USA whose seven-year-old daughter drew the symbol below.

"My seven-year-old daughter recently told me that she's had experiences with ETs. In addition, she's seen a symbol repeatedly, but she's not quite sure what it means. She saw it going along her wall one day, and then a couple more times after, in different locations. I've attached the drawing that C made of it. I would love to know if you've seen this symbol before, and/or any thoughts you may have on it."

Note: I sent this symbol to Edward to see if his children recognized the Symbol, as his daughter said she had been to Mars as well.

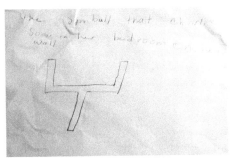

Edward: "I asked everyone in my family about this symbol, and Alice (eight years) said she didn't know exactly what it meant, but she saw the (ET) teacher write it on the board when she was on Mars. She said it means, 'We found you and we are tracking you, and we will continue to come get you,' but then said, 'I'm not sure exactly what it means though.' In other words, if a person sees this, it is a sign you have made Contact although there is a higher meaning.

The way I take it, it would be like if I went to Mars and left an American flag. If ET found it, he could say, 'An American was here and wanted us to know it,' but the meaning of the flag itself is different. Also, keep in mind that I did not tell her where the picture was from or why I was asking her what it meant. At the very least, it is surprising that she knew instantly that it was about ET Contact."

L answered: "Wow, that's amazing! I asked my daughter the things you wanted to know and when I asked her how the symbol makes her feel she said it makes her feel like she's being watched by the aliens. In addition, the experiences she can remember, the very first one was a dream. In the dream she was somewhere she didn't recognize, but then she saw two ETs. She walked over to them and asked where she was. Their answer was that she was on Mars and that they'd brought her there."

Note: Both families were unaware of each other, and their stories of going to Mars. At that time, I received another account in Australia of a young girl of seven years old, who said to her father she had been to Mars on spacecraft.

Chapter Five

SPACE SCHOOLS ON MARS
Communication with Non-Biological Matter

"Rocks seem like they are actually living."

Max, at eight years.

Note: To protect identity, all names have been changed.

Amy resides in the USA with her family of three children: her son Max aged eleven years, and two daughters, Clementine (twelve) and Fern (eight). All the children appear to be highly intuitive and aware of their multidimensional abilities. Fern can heal and describes her interactions with non-human intelligences (extraterrestrials), and Max was just eight years old when he shared with Amy he could communicate with rocks. However, I begin this chapter with Amy's story of her experiences and childhood.

Amy received her Bachelor degree in Psychology and later worked as a counselor, with plans to gain a PhD. In time, however, she decided to become a 'stay at home' mother and focus her attention on learning Reiki healing and regression hypnosis. Amy is claircognizant (the ability to acquire psychic knowledge without knowing how or why it occurs). She is also an empath and can sense the emotions and feelings of others.

Amy has experienced extraterrestrial encounters throughout her life. It began with interactions with spirits and as she grew older, she gained a greater understanding of her experiences. She has interacted with various intelligences such as Mantids, Reptilians, small Grays and Energy Beings. Amy has become very comfortable with her experiences and this lack of fear has enabled her to help and support her children through their own experiences. This has meant that her daughter Fern perceives her own encounters as wonder-filled and amazing.

The Military Connection

Amy was raised in a military household with her siblings. Her father had a significant position in the US Air Force, and Amy grew up on the Air Force base.

Amy: "I now believe my father knew much more than he was letting on. I clearly remember one day, completely out of the blue, he asked if I believed in aliens. He and I had many philosophical conversations so this didn't seem strange. I told him that yes, of course I believed in them. I've never doubted it, even without proof. I'll never forget his response. He smiled and pointed up towards the sky and said, 'Just look at the night sky. Really look at all the stars out there. In a universe that big, how could we possibly be the only beings alive?' He then smiled and that was the end of the conversation. Now I wonder if perhaps he was trying to hint at something he may have known, or was simply just trying to get me to think about the subject. Either way, that has stuck with me for more than twenty years.

It would be impossible to say when my Contact experiences began. I believe I have been having them for as long as I can remember, even when I didn't realize what was going on. Even as a child I was very open to the idea of the paranormal, or anything outside the realm of what most people would deem normal. The earliest experience I can remember happened around the age of three or four. I saw the spirit of my great grandmother sitting on the edge of my bed before I discovered she had died. Once I started practicing Reiki it seemed my experiences moved to an entirely new level. It was during meditations I nearly always had some entity visit with me. Whether it was spirit guides, angels, elementals or ETs, someone was always there to teach me something new.

One important phase of my discoveries began with two very lucid dreams. The first I recalled was being on a ship while flying through space. It was as if I was on a tour of our galaxy and it was the most beautiful thing I'd ever seen. I didn't see my tour guide, but I knew he was there.

The second dream was very intense and I awoke sitting upright in bed. I remember looking around as if expecting someone to be there. I saw no one and I went back to sleep. The next morning, I couldn't remember much from this dream other than a particular scene. It was a scene which stayed in my head for about three days, before I thought to draw it. I wondered if, by putting it on paper, it would help my brain process it more clearly.

In this scene, I could see two short Gray aliens peeking up over the edge of the table I was on, just looking at me, and further back was standing a Mantid, wearing a burgundy-colored robe with gold details. For some reason, it was very important for me to draw the robe correctly. I had drawn it but received 'communication' that I had drawn it incorrectly, and was shown a close-up image in my mind's eye to give me a better perspective. I remembered this as a dream. I knew it wasn't one, and I can clearly remember the curious nature of the two Grays as they watched me, and the wisdom and kindness that radiated from the Mantid. It was this feeling that led me to look further into the idea of ET Contact. The more I understood, the more things in my life made sense."

The image Amy drew of the Grays and Mantid. Fern, her daughter, surprised Amy as she pointed to the Mantid and said she had also seen this being on the spaceship.

Amy: "As time went on, I came to understand through a series of synchronistic events that I have a lifetime (I prefer not to use the past tense as I believe these lives are currently happening) as an Arcturian.

One of the most definitive moments I've experienced with a UFO led me to recall this information. I was driving home from my daughter's orchestra concert. What appeared to be a large star (much bigger than a planet would appear) kept following me, and stayed in my view through the passenger side window. At one point during the drive home, I pulled over and using an infrared filter on my camera, I took a picture of it. As I drove home, through three towns this object stayed with me. When I arrived home, I was still able to see the object in the sky outside my kitchen window. I knew this meant something important, but I wasn't sure what. When I looked at the pictures I had taken, what I saw was a red orb with blue points coming out from it. Later that night, I fell asleep wondering exactly what this was. The next morning I did some research and looked at a sky map in my area from the night before and tried to rule out a planet or star. There was nothing large near that area of the sky, except for the star Arcturus. I'd never heard that name before but was struck with the idea that perhaps I should look into this further.

Recently I have made a new discovery. When in deep meditation, I received a visit from a large Reptilian. Of course, working with Experiencers as I do, I had heard of Reptilians. I found them fascinating and wanted to learn more. I had never had an experience with them myself, and I wasn't afraid of them. I felt that regardless of their negative reputation there was no way that all of one species could be bad. I knew there were also people who talk of positive encounters and perhaps this reinforced that belief.

I went into a meditation without any expectations, simply being happy to get to a place of deep inner quiet. I always go in with an open mind and this time was no exception. As I sat there, I heard and physically felt the vibrations from a series of booming footsteps. Suddenly a large, imposing figure began to appear. At first, I saw the feet which looked like something you would expect a dragon to have. The two huge feet with large talons supported an equally imposing body. The well-defined musculature was impressive. As I panned up, I could see a large head with a face that looked kind with chiseled features, though it was Reptilian in shape and form. However, perhaps the most noticeable feature of all was the spines that went from the top of his head all the way down to the tip of his massive tail.

As I sat there, silently watching this creature walk around me, I felt a loving feeling both welling up within myself and coming from him. I recognized instantaneously that I knew him. He went from an interesting creature to someone quite dear to me. He circled me, not out of intimidation but as a protective gesture. I knew that no one was going to get by him, physical or etheric. I heard a voice in my head telling me that he was always around me protecting me from harm. I soon learned that his name was *Kuma* and that he was my partner in a Reptilian lifetime. While this was quite surprising to learn, it also made sense. As a child I always loved reptiles and amphibians, having many pet snakes, lizards and turtles. From the earliest I can remember, I was always obsessed with dinosaurs. It amused my parents. They would tell me that I was the only five-year-old they'd ever met, who said she wanted to be a paleontologist when she grew up. As I grew up my love of dinosaurs stayed with me but I turned my focus more towards living animals and to this day my house is always full of them.

I know that I am far from understanding everything about the world around the multi-verse, our very existence and myself and me. I know for sure, the reason we are here on this planet is to learn. While our lessons may be different, I understand that we are still one, and the same. But the most important thing that I've learned, is that love is what truly matters. Whether I'm an energetic Arcturian, a Reptilian being, or a human, truly doesn't matter. What does matter and what's most important is that I know love.

Here's my two cents, use it, as you will: There may always be darkness and horrible events that happen in this lifetime. While it's important for us to acknowledge those things, and try to learn from them, it's also equally important not to get caught up in them and make them the main focus of our lives. Live your lives to the best of your ability, learn from the journey, and try to enjoy yourself in the process.

I think when I was younger I may have had a MILAB experience, going to school on an Air Force base. I remembered this a couple of weeks ago for some reason. I have a memory of this. However, my mother said I never went to school on a military base. Recently, for the first time, I had a hypnotic regression. It turned out I was part of the secret space program and my father was involved."

This Update on Amy's Story in a Recent Hypnosis Session, 2016

Regression – Feb 13, 2016.

"I was seven years old and at home; there was a knock at the front door. Neither my step-mom nor brother seemed to react so I opened it. Standing there were three or four men dressed in what looked like black military outfits and black helmets (black glass in front so I couldn't see their faces). They were so tall they had to bend down to go through the doorway. I saw three or four blue and purple feathers sticking out from underneath the back bottom of the helmets. My brother didn't seem to notice them.

They brought me outside and told me they needed to take me somewhere. Suddenly, we were surrounded by (what looked to me like) a bubble. We flew quickly up through the sky past the atmosphere into space, where we came upon a huge ship that to me looked like a tall building on its side. As we approached we entered into a docking area which was quite large. There were other ships of varying kinds docked there as well. I could see a man in the distance quickly walking towards us. As he got a bit closer, I noticed that he was my father. I immediately went from surprised to upset, repeating, 'I can't believe he lied to us, I can't believe he lied!' Tears began to form in my eyes. We were now standing just outside our bubble ship. The men dressed in black surrounded me, blocking me from my father's view, as if to give me a moment to gather myself. When asked why I was upset by the regressionist, my response was because my dad had always instilled in us how horrible it was to lie, and here he was on a spaceship, when he told us he was working on the Air Force base.

My father approached us; he motioned for me to follow him (men in black came too). They brought me to a room where there were other kids at tables, in pairs. My dad told me he needed to leave me here for a little bit but that some of the men would stay with me. I stood at the front of the room, not sure what to do. Soon a little boy came over to me, grabbed my hand and led me to a table with a glowing sphere, or what I called a globe, hovering just above it. It was light blue in color. He told me to place my hands, palms facing it, on either side of it and as I did the plasma went from blue to pink where my hands were touching it. Not sure how I knew it was plasma, but suddenly I did. He then made a joke (I believe since I called it a globe) that I now had the world 'in the palm of my hands.' This made me laugh and seemed to help me relax.

He told me that I needed to try and make the energy inside the sphere move, simply by thinking it so. I tried, and the energy started to slowly move. He then told me I could speed it up by thinking 'faster' repeatedly. The ball then filled with a bright pink energy and it started swirling around. All of a sudden, the lights in the room seemed to go out and it felt as if everyone was watching what I was doing. I didn't mind as I was enjoying this exercise. Next, the boy told me to keep my palms open but slowly move my hands out to the sides and try to pull the energy off the ball. I did and it stuck to my hands like bubble gum, stretching out with the movement of my hands.

Once this was done, the lights came back on in the room. Two of the tall men dressed in black came in to bring me somewhere. We walked along a walkway that seemed to run down the entire center of the ship. It was open in the center and I could see six floors on either side of the center open area. Each floor had a walkway like the one we were on. We walked past several doors to our right (the center open area was on our left). One seemed to be a phlebotomy lab, as it had a window and I could see someone getting what looked like blood taken. We turned down a hallway and went around several corners. It looked very much like an office building on Earth, but an older one, nothing too high tech in appearance.

We then arrived at my dad's office. He had me come in and sit down. He had a smile on his face and told me I had done really well and asked if I enjoyed it. I said, 'Yes, but what is this place?' He then told me that I would know more when I was older, and then also asked if I had liked the 'bubble ride'? I said that I had liked it very much! He replied that he had chosen that for me because he thought that I would enjoy it. He then told me that the men were going to bring me home now, but that we'd be going a different way, as they didn't usually use the bubble to travel. The men then brought me to a room with a circle on the floor. They had me stand in the center and the three men surrounded me. All of a sudden, there was a bright flash of light and I was in my living room. My step-mom and brother didn't react, and when I asked if she'd seen that flash of light she said she hadn't seen anything, that I had an over-active imagination, and to stop lying.

In the next part of the regression, we went to another point in my life. I was older, in my mid to late twenties. I was back on a ship (similar to the one I was on previously) and wearing some kind of lab coat. There were all kinds of alien creatures in glass enclosures of varying sizes. I knew that I worked here and that these animals were my responsibility to study and take care of. Suddenly one of the same tall men, dressed in black military clothing came in and told me that they urgently needed my help. He brought me to a room where there was a woman thrashing about on an exam table. I told them to give her a sedative. Once she was sedated I scanned her body with a machine. I saw that she had some sort of parasite in her lower abdomen. I used a laser to open her and carefully remove the parasite. It was near her uterus and had long tentacles that seemed to be entangled a bit, in her intestines. Once I was able to get it out, I placed it in a specimen jar and told them not to kill it.

I realized that I was a biologist of some sort, but that I was able to telepathically/empathically connect with these ET creatures/beings. I was on the ship to take care of and study them. I also taught any children on the ship about them, and tried to help them not immediately fear them. I had one animal in particular that I used with the kids. He looked like a large rabbit with a face that resembled a bat but with huge fangs. While he looked a bit scary at first, he was actually very gentle. He was great with the kids and they loved him.

I also helped when new extraterrestrials came onto the ship. I was used to 'interface' with them, and learn more about them. Then, if they were a higher-vibrational being, I would try to convince them to stay and interact with us for a bit. This was a military ship and had plenty of lower-vibrational beings on it. It was my way of trying to achieve more balance for those on the ship. However, I got the feeling that higher-vibrational beings didn't like to be on the ship for too long. I also tried to teach the people on the ship to appreciate other life forms. Don't 'shoot first, ask questions later.'

My favorite place on the ship, aside from my lab, was the garden area. It was very lush with trees, plants and all sorts of alien flora and fauna. There was a pond that was bioluminescent at night when the ship's lights were dimmed. Also, the roof of the ship above the garden area was clear, so that if you lay down next to the pond you could look up into space. This was my sanctuary amongst the military feel of the rest of the ship.

At one point, I also saw a grown woman, naked, floating in an egg-shaped container with some sort of liquid inside. She had what looked like an umbilical cord attached to her. When I tried to connect mentally to her I could tell that she was somewhat aware and was frightened, as she didn't know where she was, or what was happening to her.

I wanted to find out if my dad was also on this ship. I saw one of the men dressed in black walk by and asked him if he knew my father, and was he on this ship. He said that he did know him and offered to take me to his office. As I got there, I could see that my dad was sitting at his desk in his office. He motioned for me to come in and sit down on the chair directly across from him. I did so, but I felt strange, as if my brain was in a fog. I obviously knew him, but at the same time, he felt like a stranger that I didn't have anything to talk to about. I said this to him and he replied saying that he had put a block in my mind so no one would know I was his daughter, and that this was mutually beneficial for both of us. At first, I thought this might be because I was a pacifist and he was military but now I believe it was so that I could not be used as a bargaining chip in case of an attack against the ship."

April 11, 2016 – Second Regression

"I went back to the time when I was about seventeen or eighteen years old. The same men in black military outfits came as before into my house during the night and brought me to a small craft. The craft was wedged-shaped and could hold six people: two pilots and four passengers. I remember in the regression seeing an extraterrestrial female: light blue skin, and instead of hair she had these fleshy tentacles coming out of the top of her head (I believe there were three of these tentacles). However, the most noticeable aspect to her appearance was the large, BEAUTIFUL, violet-colored irises of her eyes. They seemed to sparkle, and were the first thing my eye was drawn to. She seemed to be a warrior of some kind and she explained to me that she was I in another lifetime. She told me not to fear my warrior side, as where we came from it was honorable to be a warrior, a protector. It was not power-hungry or aggression-driven like so much I am opposed to here on Earth. I don't know where she came from."

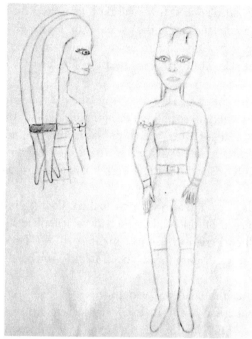

Amy's drawing of her warrior ET self.

Amy's Son Max

Amy: "My son Max was eight when he told me he could communicate with rocks. Max can also communicate with spirits, and says he can 'talk' to crystals and other stones. I had video footage where he talked about communicating with stones; he loves to make crystal grids."

Note: I was very interested in the way this eight-year-old explained his communication with a meteorite. Max said, he is not really sure how he can communicate with rocks but that he puts his finger on them and the words come into his head. It is interesting that I have heard similar experiences from others who are sensitive.

Max: "Rocks seem like they are actually living. This little meteor, well there are abilities they have. They do not breathe like we do, but they communicate through your mind. This little meteor told me:

1. They can communicate by you putting your finger on it and it can talk to you through your head. It's like your own voice, but it's really the rock.
2. They have feelings. This rock told me when it was crashing on Earth and people

were scared. It made it sad but it was happy in water.

3. The meteor told me it made friends with the puffer fish and the sharks. It also told me where it crashed, which was London and it also had likings and it likes space."

Amy: "I asked Max what he knows about himself. He said:

1. Communicate with rocks.
2. Communicate with spirits.
3. Sensitive to smells.
4. Feel others emotions, and if they are crying he will cry too and feel their sadness."

Can We Communicate with Solid Matter?

"As you focus closer and closer on the structure of the atom you would see nothing, you would see a physical void. The atom has no physical structure. Physical things have no physical structure. We have no physical structure and physical things really don't have physical structure. Atoms are made out of invisible energy, not tangible matter. We need to get over the inarguable conclusion. The Universe is immaterial-mental, spiritual."

R. C. Henry, Professor of Physics and Astronomy, Johns Hopkins University.

Amy: "I am not sure if this is related, but he has also been different than most kids socially. Up to recently in the school year, he really didn't play with other kids. He would play by himself and was not at all concerned about it. As a toddler, he was inside his own head a lot of the time. He could play by himself for an hour or more at a time (even at two years old). Recently he has developed more friendships, but he never noticed he didn't have the friendships the other kids seem to have. It doesn't come naturally to him, but he's got a few close friends now. He's still happy to be by himself. I feel that perhaps he was having more interaction with the unseen world, and didn't need to socialize. It worried me more than it did him."

Note: Communication with non-material objects:
Is this linking into the multidimensional ability to gain information, similar to the psychic ability to access information from a personal object known as psychometry? *Encyclopedia of Mystical and Paranormal Experiences* (p. 487) defines this as 'a psychic skill in which information is conveyed through connecting with objects called psychometrizing.'

Schools on Mars and Symbols

Amy sent me a drawing of an unusual symbol that Fern, her daughter, had drawn. Fern was seven years old at the time and drew this symbol after she told her mother she had an experience where she said she had been to Mars on a spacecraft.

Amy: "Fern recently told me that she's had experiences with ETs. In addition, she's seen a symbol repeatedly, but she's not quite sure what it means. She saw it going along her wall one day, and then a couple more times after that in different locations. I've attached the drawing. I would love to know if you've seen this symbol before, and/or any thoughts you may have on it."

Note: I had an astonishing response from the parent: I sent the symbol to Edward. (See Chapter 4, section – Mars Connection and Schools on Mars)

I asked Edward to ask his daughter Alice, who had also shared she had been to Mars on a space craft, if she recognized the symbol.

Edward: "I asked everyone in my family about this symbol and Alice (eight years) said she didn't know exactly what it meant, but she saw the (ET) teacher write it on the board when she was on Mars. She said it means, 'We found you and we are tracking you and we will continue to come get you' but then said, 'I'm not sure exactly what it means though.' In other words, if a person sees this, it is a sign you have made Contact although there is a higher meaning.

The way I take it, it would be like if I went to Mars and left an American flag. If ET found it, he could say 'An American was here and wanted us to know it', but the meaning of the flag itself is different.

Also, keep in mind that I did not tell her where the picture was from or why I was asking her what it meant. At the very least, it is surprising that she knew instantly that it was about ET Contact."

I forwarded this response to Amy

Amy: "Wow, that's amazing! I asked my Fern the things you wanted to know and when I asked her how the symbol makes her feel she said it makes her feel like she's being watched by the aliens. In addition, the experiences she can remember, the very first one was a dream. In the dream, she was somewhere she didn't recognize but then she saw two ETs. She walked over to them and asked where she was; their answer was that she was on Mars and that they'd brought her there."

Amy continues

"At one point, a while back, she said that at school one day, during class, she saw two aliens standing behind one of the students. When I asked her about that last night, she couldn't remember that happening. I also asked her how the Contact makes her feel and she said, 'Kind of weird; surprised. Like a mix of happy and surprised.' She said, she isn't scared of them. As I am a Reiki Master, it is wonderful to see how she's able to work with those same skills and her proficiency at it."

Fern: "I've had lots of experiences and I can help people with them."

Amy: "I can manipulate energy with my hands (feel it, direct it, etc.); she's still learning how to do it, but is a natural at it. I hope that answers your questions. She said she doesn't really know any star languages, but heard the word nasuna (pronounced 'na-soo-na'). She doesn't know what it means though. I suggested she repeat it often and perhaps she'll come to know the meaning. It's what I do when I get phrases (I'm Arcturian), so perhaps it'll work for her. I forgot to tell you in my last email, my daughter was horrified that I spelled the word wrong. Evidently, it's spelled 'nusuna'. It must mean something important to her, judging by her reaction. 'That's not how it's spelled!'

When Fern got out of her bath this evening, she said she thought she saw a star in the middle of her forehead while looking in the mirror, but then it was quickly gone. She also said that as she was wringing water out of a washcloth it reminded her of 'wringing water out of the stars.' Not sure what that one means. She says she knows that she is from a star, but doesn't know the name of it. All of this is recent, in the past six months or so. It seems to be coming to her more and more, so perhaps she'll come to know where she's from and why she's here. Fern is my youngest. The other two also have abilities, but haven't had any ET experiences. My oldest daughter, Clementine, is an extremely strong empath.

These are a couple of drawings Fern made regarding her Mars experience. She said she keeps remembering more details, which isn't too surprising. So she first told me she remembers seeing an 'arch with a door.' She said it was hard to describe, so she drew it for me. She said she saw this while she was on Mars and that she thought it was like a house. I found the shape fascinating, as she's never said anything about domes on Mars.

The second picture – she is in the ship. She described it as a teardrop shape. The bottom descriptions are (and she spelled them out phonetically, so I'll translate) exhaust pole thingys, fire (not sure if that's how she interpreted it that way or was actually fire), and obviously Earth is the very bottom. If you're able to, take a close look at how she drew the Earth. To me, it looks as the Earth would be if you were to look at the Pacific Ocean side! I just asked her if she recalls anything else, and she said two little aliens talked to her and they were giving her a tour of the Solar System, and Earth looked very tiny. I asked if she recalls anything else? They were pointing to other planets and other stars and they told her that a lot of people lived on them and they liked to go and visit. She said 'they' talked a lot and it was hard to remember it all. On the ship she remembers being in a room similar to a little apartment; there was canned food and astronaut ice cream, that she loves, and bottles of water."

Mantid on Mars

Fern told Amy: "This alien looks very important to the alien community because he wears a special-looking robe, and very different too! And he looks different from the little Gray aliens. Also, he has green shoes! The little Gray aliens don't need clothes because of their species of aliens. The green alien, I think, is rare because I have only seen one in my life and this is it on the right. I did the best I could possibly do! The Gray aliens talk a lot but this one does not talk at all!"

Note: *This Mantid drawn by Fern also has a purple robe, as in her mother's drawing.*

Alien Pig from Mars

Amy: "Fern said, 'These pigs live on Mars, on farms that aliens have. They are basically the same as pigs on Earth only that they have a mark on their forehead. The pigs on different planets have different marks on them'."

Mary: "So she knows these pigs are on other planets too, or just Mars?"

Amy: "Fern said these pigs are on other planets too."

Update: Conversation with Fern 2016

Mary: "What kinds of beings have you seen?"

Fern: "Praying Mantis beings, Grays, and horse-faced ones."

Fern had told her mother of a recent experience where she was taken to another planet which was surrounded by an artificial dome. I wanted to hear more. In this experience, Fern told me she was taken by spaceship to a planet with dog-like beings and human-like beings but didn't recognize them. I asked what the planet/star looked like.

Fern: "The grass was purple and light gray. There was oxygen because of the dome. The people were a lot smaller than the dog-like beings. Some of the dog-like beings were golden, and some were gray or brown, and taller than the human-like beings. The dog-like beings were six and a half feet tall (Fern was very specific). The people, had whitish color skin. The controllers had buttons to call spaceships and I could ask questions."

I asked Fern what the dome was made of as it was around the whole planet/star. Fern said that she was given directions to the location of this star because they needed her to have directions, so that she could visit again.

Mary: "Why was this important?"

Fern: "To have an experience on the dome; to try experiences. If I used dye on the dome, like paint, it would change color?"

Note: Fern said it was like she had to use her energy on the dome, to change the dome's frequency.

Mary: "So this was like an experiment?"

Fern: "The dome is made out of hardened oxygen/clay. The dome is all round the planet."

Mary: "Have there been other human children visit this star?"

Fern: "Yes, but with the other children the experiment did not work, but mine actually worked."

Mary: "How did you know what to do with the dome?"

Fern: "I just think with my brain like I had to do this."

Mary: "Like you knew what to do and they were happy with this? What difference did it make?"

Fern: "It's like something touched it and it would change color so they wanted to make it like a rainbow."

Mary: "To change the color or frequency?"

Fern: "Yes."

Creating Hybrid Species

Fern: "I went around to see another experiment with water, and they could change the species, as they need to survive on Earth. How they change them was they had a science lab on Earth. The hybrid would get the blood from that animal and they would combine it with a tall human; a formula in an egg which would hatch the hybrid out and then they would make the hybrid able to survive on that star."

Mary: "So it was a mix of the animals and humans and they created a being that would be useful to them."

Fern: "Yes, so that it would survive."

Mary: "Was this told to you, or were you able to see it?"

Fern: "I was able to see it."

Mary: "Who was doing this?"

Fern: "They look like human, but they were a human/alien hybrid mixed together. Like a normal human they bring back from Earth and mix it with the animal."

Mary: "What was the location?"

Fern: "They do this on this star as they have laboratories there."

Mary: "Why did they show you?"

Fern: "I don't know. On the space craft there were cows that produced different substances such as water, or if you wanted carrot, it would taste like carrot or different things. I was also shown alien skeletons on the space craft."

Mary: "The drawing of the dog beings; are they like the ones in Egypt – like Anubis?"

Fern: "I asked them and they said no, they are not like Anubis, but we know them, and the images of Anubis are not accurate."

Mary: "What color were the dog beings?"

Fern: "Golden/brown, gray and green ones, many colors."

Mary: "What did it feel like to communicate with them? Like a dog was speaking to you, or speaking in your mind?"

Fern: "Like normal speaking, but barks. They told me that they created the dome so people could come and have oxygen on the planet so they could survive, and it took two years to create the dome. Although they worked around the clock to do this, the only break was to eat and drink."

Mary: "Do you know where you are from?"

Fern: "All I know is that I am from a star."

Mary: "Do you have special abilities?"

Fern: "I can feel what people feel when they are emotional. I can feel that happening. I can sometimes see how they died and how they were born."

Mary: "How do you feel about the beings?"

Fern: "It feels normal to me. The Grays talk and talk and they even brought me to their home planet and tell me lots of things, and they are very nice. Some are gray and one a reddish-gray."

Mary: "Do you see the same ones all the time?"

Fern: "Sometimes there are different numbers of them visit, and they want to be my friend and like me a lot. They teach me how to farm on different planets. The first place they taught me to farm on was Mars and other stars which can be hard, like 'extreme' difficulty."

Mary: "So different stars need different kinds of farming and they showed you how to do this?"

Fern: "Yes."

Mary: "Did you find anything else interesting to you?"

Fern: "I found the animals there kind of interesting, they had different shapes and (drew this)."

Mary: "One looks like a dinosaur/giraffe. This is a mix, and more difficult ones. So they are doing it with animals and different species?"

Fern: "They will do it (with) plants and animals, or even solid matter."

Mary: "Lots of experiments where they mix things?"

Fern: "Yes, alien science."

Mary: "What did you like the most?"

Fern: "Finding out what the outcome (is) with these mixes."

Mary: "So, lots of experimentation and how they can farm and create things on planets. You don't mind them coming and visiting?"

Fern: "No, not at all."

Mary: "What about school; do you share this?"

Fern: "No I just keep it to myself. No one can relate to it."

Mary: "What about school? What do you feel about the things you are being taught there?"

Fern: "The aliens sometimes tell me not to listen to certain things I am taught, and not to do that. These are the gray ones, who come into my head and say this."

Mary: "When did you first remember all of this?"

Fern: "At seven, when I was taken to Mars, was the first time I remembered I was having experiences."

Alien Tech

Mary: "Did you ever feel you were in a different form other than human, at any time in these experiences?"

Fern: "Yes, I was in a different form once. I had drawn a picture of me as an alien tech because once I was in a different form: a Gray form."

Mary: "What was it like?"

Fern: "It felt fuzzy but positive."

Mary: "Did it feel comfortable to you?"

Fern: "Yes, I went into that form for about fifteen minutes, and then came out again. That's why I called myself an Alien Tech."

Time Anomalies

Fern: "When I am with them it may be five hours, but here on Earth only two hours may have passed; they can stretch time."

More from Fern's Mother Amy

Amy: "Fern told me that on the ship, which had animal skeletons on it, there was one guy she didn't like; he was scary. He looked like a spy, with dark sunglasses. There was a scary-looking vision in her head, and this guy ran down a hatch. There were weapons, and canned food, and the little aliens everyone wants to be friends with."

Fern: "He said to me 'Don't tell your mum this.' So I think he can put thoughts into my head."

Amy: "Fern told me she thought this person was human."

Mary: "It's interesting she knew this."

Amy: "Fern also told me that if you take/pick a flower petal and an orange flower petal, and if you touched it on the oxygen dome, it would turn that color. Fern is definitely in tune with energies. She said to me, the Grays she knows are animated and happy but not robotic. So this must be a different type of Gray. They are the ones everyone wants to be friends with."

Fern recently (2016) wrote the above script. She said she saw

it in a vision while she was at school, and then she wrote it down.

Amy also had channeled some drawings of symbols, which came to her. Fern was able to offer an understanding of them.

Notes: Laura Magdalene Eisenhower, great-granddaughter of former President Eisenhower, claims that efforts were made to recruit her into a human colony on Mars. She was told during the recruitment effort (in 2006-07), that she would go to Mars via the 'Jump Room', or technically the 'ARC', which stands for 'Aeronautical Repositioning Chamber'. She would be teleported to work in a secret base on Mars to help maintain the human race.

Ms. Eisenhower and her Stanford graduate friend, Ki' Lia, claim there is a secret Mars colony designed to allow the human race to survive, should a large catastrophe occur on Earth. A nuclear disaster or comet strike could theoretically cause a survival situation on Earth, and a base on Mars could keep some humans alive. There is also other independent whistle-blower evidence of secret U.S. bases on Mars. Why would a group of people, many with academic/professional credentials, choose to claim information about futuristic technology?

"Andrew D. Basiago, author and lawyer, has evidence of the Jump Room, which, he claims, was created from reverse-engineering a crashed UFO. Mr. Basiago, formerly involved in secret research and development projects undertaken by a U.S. defense agency, has verified his secret teleportation to U.S. bases on Mars, and to meeting intelligent Martian extraterrestrial life.

Mr. Basiago has also publicly confirmed that in 1970, in the company of his late father, Raymond F. Basiago, he met three Martian astronauts at the Curtiss-Wright Aeronautical Company facility in Wood Ridge, New Jersey. The Martians were there on a liaison mission to Earth, and meeting with U.S. aerospace personnel. Mr. Basiago confirms that 'The United States has been teleporting individuals to Mars for decades', and recounts the awe-inspiring and terrifying trips that he took to Mars in 1981... He claims he had been teleported as a child participant in Project Pegasus."

Filers Files #3, 2016, *Does Time Travel Exist?*

There are some important points to note in regard to Amy's story:

- Amy's father's military background, and that the family was stationed at a military base that may well have harbored ET artifacts or technologies. (Details omitted to protect identity).
- Amy's significant conversation with her father, and his response to the reality of extraterrestrial life.
- Amy's later recall of events suggests she was involved in human and ET interactions, both as a child and adult.
- Amy's PSI abilities, that her children seem to also have in varying degrees.
- The extra-sensitivity of her son to consciousness, no matter what form e.g. plants, rocks.
- Her daughter, Fern's understanding of genetic manipulation, and use of energy/frequencies.
- Corroboration of a symbol, as understood by two children taken to Mars on spacecraft.
- Fern's drawings of beings encountered, similar to her mother's experiences.
- The possibility we may already have such technologies on other planets such as Mars.

Chapter Six

DECODING EXTRATERRESTRIAL ART – THE CODE BREAKERS

"I mean, why are we here? Why did God make us? Those are the most important questions for mankind. Everything goes back to those two questions and those alone."

A comment by an eight-year-old (USA).

In this chapter, I explore more evidence that the children have profound and deep knowledge through their encounters. In this case below, the mother was interested to observe their reaction to the artwork by Experiencer Tracey Taylor.

The full story of Tracey's experiences she wrote for my first book *Awakening* (Chapter Eight). Tracey explained how she created her artwork (below) from her encounters and it was brought through from the beings she interacted with. Since that time, she has created even more amazing artworks as she has grown in her own understanding of her encounters, and this art is shown on her website. The art the child interprets were some of her earlier works.

The mother wrote to me because of her amazement at what her son understood or decoded from what he saw in them. Her children: son and younger daughter, stated the art was from the aliens.

"They contain information about aliens."

Mother: "I showed both my kids Tracey Taylor's paintings, one after the other. Each child was shown the pictures without the sibling present in the room. I gave them no prompts and just asked them 'What do you see in the picture?'

My seven-year-old son had more to say (obviously!). He said he could 'read' them. He said they contain information about aliens. A few of the paintings contain images of harvesters of energy: machines that harvest the sun's energy. 'They have different types. Here is one type and there is another.' (*Ancient Future*)

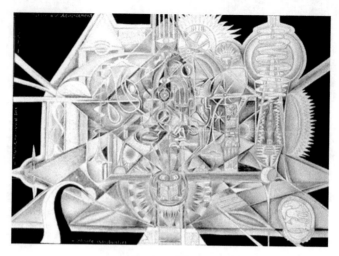

Ancient Future

I received an intriguing email from a parent that indicated her son, who is eight, had knowledge and maturity beyond his years and could decode the *Expressions of ET Contact*.

Evolutionary Creation

Possibilities

Note: The artist Tracey Taylor created these images in 1998-2002 and since then the artwork has evolved as she has grown in awareness.

Web site: www. harmonicblueprint.com

He said that others contain information about types of aliens; one is about the 'seven who will be coming'. There are the Eagle people, Anubis, the gods and 'Oh yeah, those guys (cat/lion-looking people)'. (*Possibilities*)

He says that they are very ancient messages. Another piece with writing he translated as, 'The Fallen are coming' (*Treasures of Existence*). He noted the energy rings around the triangle, and said, 'That's a pyramid. That's how they will come.' (*Treasures of Existence* and *Evolutionary Creation*). One piece of another image represents Time (*Inner Visions*). He had something to say about most. There were a couple that he says he hasn't 'learned' yet. 'I haven't seen that one yet. I see the other ones in my mind.'

My four-year-old wasn't particularly interested. She looked at one picture and then moved on. She did say, 'That one is about aliens.'

N.B. Both kids recognized the subject matter as having to do with aliens. My seven-year-old interpreted and 'read' the images as information.

On the same day and totally unprompted, I was reading and my son was watching TV and he said to me: 'Sometimes, when I am looking at things normally, I can see through things. Like right now. I can see through my hand to the TV.' He demonstrated what he was doing. He was looking with both eyes open, without favoring one eye over the other. I simply acknowledged his statement without bias.

Mother: "Did you have any good dreams last night?"
Son: "Yes Mom, I finished magic school."
Mother: "Oh yeah, what did you learn?"

Son: "Everything; mostly science. I learned about time and space and gravity. Time controls everything; time controls all."

Mother: "About your Pyramid question. Yes, my son believes that they will come by way of the pyramid. I assumed that it is a portal since he pointed out the energy rings around the triangle/pyramid structures. I can confirm that with him again to be certain of his meaning. He spoke about the magic-school dreams. He was seven years old at the time. He is now eight and his sister is four.

My son has not elaborated on the paintings since the first time I asked about a month ago. When he said he 'hasn't seen that one yet', he went on to say that he hasn't learned about some of the paintings I showed him. He was talking about the completed paintings rather than paintings not yet made. He said that he hasn't learned them yet, as if that information has not been shared with him. He says he sees the information in his mind. At the time I asked him how he knows what they mean. He said he just knows; the information is in his mind. So apparently, he has not seen some of the images nor the information about them in his mind yet. He said it as if he will one day have information about them. He didn't even bother to guess at the ones he doesn't know about.

I haven't shown him any ET script. Then again, I have only seen Tracey's and maybe a few others on your website. The only thing he has seen is the writing in Tracey's paintings. I am assuming that the writing in her paintings is ET. I try not to burden him with writing forms other than Roman letters. He has seen Egyptian hieroglyphics and Mayan pictographs as well as some Asian writing. He may have seen Cyrillic, though I don't think he would recognize it as different from English. With his dyslexia, he has a hard enough time spelling in English. He would just see a series of random letters I think. He has a difficult enough time reading in English.

I have not shown him other ET artwork. I was going on a hunch to show him Tracey's artwork and was surprised by what he had to say. His idea of aliens only comes from cartoons and maybe some movies. I don't let the kids watch movies about abductions or close encounters. I think it might be too frightening for them. My son's idea of aliens is most likely in the range of the blue creatures of Avatar or the monsters of Star Wars. To be honest, I have never asked him what aliens look like. I was surprised that he identified so many 'types' in one of Tracey's images. The images of Gray-type aliens that are in popular media are usually cute and cartoonish. They have WHITE faces/bodies and dark eyes. The image the kids drew of the gray face looked like a Gray alien and was not cute at all. And the kids themselves were frightened when they talked about it.

When my son said he could see through his hand, I understood it to mean that it was like an x-ray. Exactly right. He could see right through his hand to the TV.

The 'magic school' dreams are from my son William. He says he goes to magic school at midnight sometimes. He learns about time, space, and gravity. He says a white light comes through his window and then he is there at the school. (This doesn't sound like Hogwarts' to me.)

My four-year-old daughter, on the other hand, tells me about going into space and seeing aliens. When she talks about aliens, I assumed she means Gray aliens. She will point to something on the TV or whatever, and say 'alien'. It is always a Gray-type alien. She has dreamed about space and aliens a few times. She will sit up, eyes still closed, and tell me about her dream. It goes something like this. 'Mom, we were in space, and so there were aliens, and a baby alien, and so they put something in your arm and so I was scared and I was missing you and so I found you and so I was happy.' I asked her later what the baby alien looked like. She looked at me like I was crazy! 'What are you talking about?!' I explained what she said about her dream and she just shrugged her shoulders. Now, the mention of a baby alien creeped me out a little bit. There is no mention of baby aliens in popular media; that is to say, there is no way for my four-year-old daughter to conceive of baby aliens. Where would she get this idea?

Another morning and another dream, she said, 'We went up into space in a rocket ship and we could look down at the Earths (Earth). Then, we came back down.' Same sort of dream recall – half asleep, half awake, and just babbling about her dream.

I asked my son if he could tell me more about the pyramids in Tracey's paintings. He said, 'That's how they (aliens) will come.' He said, 'That's where they will land (arrive). But, it is also a teleportation machine.'

He went on to say that the big pyramid isn't the only one. 'There are others. They will come at the pyramids and then fly over the ground to the South Pole and then shoot up to the North Pole (by way of a teleporter) and then fly down to the pyramids again.' (He made some hand motions which indicated that the craft would teleport, or pass through the center of the Earth from pole to pole.)

Mother: "When you say others, do you mean other pyramids?"

Son: "I mean other teleport places on every continent."

Mother: "At pyramids?"

Son: "Places all over the world."

Mother: "The reason I ask is because there are pyramids on every continent. Did you know that? (Eyebrows knitted, he seemed to think about this for a minute.) So, there are other types of teleportation places other than the big pyramid (Pyramid of Khufu)?"

Son: "Yes, in the side of the hill! Lots of hills – all over; hundreds of them around the world. The saucers just shoot right out of the hills like 'peechooo' (sound effect)."

Mother: "So what's inside the hills? A hangar or something? Is there something inside the hill? A hangar? Like a place where they land and house aircraft; like a garage?" (I think he was thinking of a clothes hanger.)

Son: "It's actually a place where they do science. The aliens do science there."
Mother: "A science lab?"
Son: "Yeah, an alien science lab."

I stopped asking questions. I think I just needed to digest this. He was starting to scare me...again. I honestly wish I were making this up Mary. I started to think he plucked this from a movie until the mention of alien science labs. Holy Smoke! I only recently read about Dulce and other bases maybe two weeks ago.

I guess when I think of alien labs, I think of something horrific. I'm sure not every alien science lab is fashioned in this style. I just got spooked. And he didn't seem frightened by the idea of the labs. So that's important, right? I want to follow up with him on the labs when I get a chance. I think I was just projecting and letting my own fear get the better of me. I still plan on asking him more about Tracey's paintings and about the writing. I will follow up with you when I do.

My husband just had a (bedtime) conversation with our son. He started talking about gray aliens. I will paraphrase. 'There are two types of gray aliens. The ones who talk, and the ones who don't. The ones that don't talk are OK. The ones who do talk, you have to watch out for those ones. Just stay away from them.' My husband asked our son how he knows this. He said he just knows.

My husband thought that I told him about the Gray aliens. I explained that in no way have I discussed anything with the kids. I will talk to my son theoretically about alien life forms if he asks. For instance, it is highly probable that there is other intelligent life in the universe, and it is likely that they have visited Earth. However, I have no idea what they are or what they look like. But if they made it here they must be more advanced than humans are. That's all I can really say with certainty from my own experience.

After I explained that I wasn't the source of his information, we just looked at each other, dumbfounded and a little bit disturbed. Do other kids talk like this? I am not so frightened that I would shut him down. But I do feel out of my depth with this revelation. I want to believe he picked it up on TV, or it is just his active imagination. To be honest, I can't verify if what he says is true re the ones who talk and the ones who don't. Of course, I have read about the telepathic abilities of the Gray aliens, i.e., 'the ones who don't talk.' Again, this isn't something I have or would share with the kids! How does he know this?

Anyway, this is fresh and I am still processing it. But, I thought you might want to hear it. Feel free to share. I know what I wrote sounds like fantasy and imagination. But, when I look at the composite of what the kids have said, I begin to see a picture emerging. It is spooky at times and unnerving. And, sometimes I doubt myself (in believing all that they say). Especially when I am dealing with them day to day as normal children – laughing, playing, pouting, crying. They are still fragile little beings. The things they talk about are strange, sometimes profound, and definitely heretical.

It is comforting to know that you and Tracey 'get' what my son and daughter are saying. Like I said, I know my kids are different but I don't ever want them to be freakish. To know that others understand their inner world helps me to validate and honor their experience. It's difficult enough to be a good mother; it is even more so with these kids who challenge one's belief systems. Does this make sense? So, thank you for your understanding and support.

P.S. I have no idea if he means human/ET labs or just ET labs. But, I will ask when I ask him again about the labs. With regard to the Grays who do talk and why one should keep away from them, I really have no idea what he meant. It was a conversation he had with my husband. I will ask.

I asked my son to draw me the gray face. Again, he drew me a goofy face with a big smile. Kyra drew something similar. I then drew a copy of the image from memory and showed it to the kids. 'This is what you showed me a year ago and you called it the gray face.' My son immediately looked at it and said 'Mom, that's an alien.' I replied 'Yes, it looks that way.'

Over the weekend, something kind of cool happened. I bought a package of geodes that the kids can smash to find crystals inside. They love crystals and gems, my son in particular. At one point, when I stepped inside, my daughter started muttering nonsense as she was holding the quartz crystals. I didn't hear it, but my husband told me that he and our son just sort of looked at each other wondering what she was doing. As I was returning to the patio (ground zero of geode smashing), my husband asked if I heard what she was saying. I replied no. I said that she sometimes mutters in a made up/pretend language. He said that he knows what I am talking about, but this time she seemed almost possessed. I didn't think anything of it until a few minutes later, when she started talking about planting the crystals in the garden to make the trees grow and blossom. 'Let's plant them under the trees. They (the crystals) will make everything grow! And, then blossoms will come out.' This to me almost sounded channeled. Of course, I believe her and I agree, but it's not the typical four- year-old conversation. 'Oh, let's plant quartz crystals in the garden to make the plants grow bigger.' I would expect this more from an adult new-age-y organic gardener. Anyway, I thought that was pretty amazing.

Again, thanks for putting up with my long-winded emails. I really appreciate all your input as well. It helps alleviate some of the stress over the strangeness of it all."

Deep and Profound Statements

"I should add that I sense that my son was poking around the idea that the world/life is a whole and does not need to be parceled out into camps and compartments. The good and bad, light and dark is all part of a single unified whole of existence. He said 'Life would be boring if there is no dark/bad.'

I think he is trying to articulate that life would have little meaning, (harkening back to his original ontological questions re Man's purpose), little zest, and would only be a partial life if we did not recognize and accept the whole that it is. Of course, I am

93

intuiting what he means, but as his mother, I feel that I am uniquely qualified and capable. *wink*

I did have an interesting conversation with my son this morning. There was some build up to this, so let me paint the picture. William has been feeling out of sorts since yesterday evening. He had a play date with a little friend after school. It was the end of the week and, as usual, he was tired. After his friend left, he sat on the (stone) floor and would not move or speak. He wouldn't tell me what was wrong, nor would he get up to move to a more comfortable spot to rest and relax. He seemed like he was on the verge of tears, but refused to articulate what the problem was. Of course, I asked him the requisite probing questions. Did something go wrong on the play-date? Did you wish it had gone a different way? Are you feeling sick? Hungry? Out of sorts? Is there something wrong with your body? Head? Heart (feelings)? Nothing.

Anyway, I let him be and stepped away to tend to my daughter (four years) and get her ready for bed. I returned and convinced him to come in my bed and relax without interruption. He sat quietly watching a video on his iPad. He then complained of a headache and eye ache. 'Mom, I feel nothing has any meaning. I just feel numb.'

He woke the next morning and went to his Saturday morning tennis lesson. He was a little low energy. On the way home (no more than ten minutes), the conversation went something like this:

Son: "Mom, do you ever feel like nothing has any meaning?"

Mom: "Yes I have felt that way, but I don't feel that way now. But, yes, I know that feeling."

Son: "I mean, why are we here? Why did God make us? Those are the most important questions for mankind. Everything goes back to those two questions and those alone." (These are his exact words!)

Mom: "Wow! That is very perceptive of you. And, I agree with you. Where did you come up with this?"

Son: "I don't know. I just know. Like everyone should know this."

Mom: "Yes, they should. You know you are an amazing boy. You make me very proud."

Son: "Thanks. You make me proud too."

Mom: "Thanks!"

(Pause)

Son: "You know, I know why there is bad in the world?"

Mom: "Why is that?"

Son: "We need to have the bad. You can't have the good without the dark. If everything was all good and happy, then life would be boring."

Mom: "You know what? I think that's spot on. Did you come up with this on your own?"

Son: "Yes. It's simple."

"We then pulled up to the house, and he hopped out. The conversation was over.

You know, I would like to say that all this is due to my stellar parenting, but really he exceeds my expectations. Many people spend their whole lives searching for the answers and insights which he just blurts out. He has always been very contemplative and spiritual, though most people don't know this about him. I feel fortunate to have these special moments with him. It is in these moments that I really see his little spirit shine."

Note: I receive many accounts of both adults and children bringing forth artwork they feel comes through them from their interactions with extraterrestrials. However, decoding them is another fascinating aspect to the mystery. What do they mean?

I have spoken in my presentations of adults I have called 'translators', who also appear to have the 'awareness' or ability to decode this creative expression from artwork, as well as scripts and symbols. I explore this in my presentation on Tracey's artwork: *Triggers of Consciousness.* Mary Rodwell, YouTube.

Lorraine – Artist/Experiencer, Western Australia

"It's amazing! I am going somewhere else. A portal entrance. It's like I'm not here but can be between both places at the same time; like the ability to go there and be with them. Leonardo da Vinci created the same portal. They are working with me through the pictures. The matrix. It's downloading to peoples' subconscious. They are full of compassion, just like us. We are they!"

Cecy Colichon – Artist

In my presentations, I have shown some extraordinary artwork. One particularly that I feel to be extremely important, given the ability of the New children, is in the presentations *Triggers of Consciousness.*

Cecy Colichon, a wonderful artist, who has painted a body of work since 2000: one hundred and twenty to one hundred and forty pieces of drawings and oils. She explained to me the way they have been created is puzzling as well as demanding.

Cecy said: "I feel I am in a school and higher intelligences are instructing me and teaching me. After the work, it forces me to read and learn what they have suggested; it awakened me to higher consciousness and awareness. The development of my work can be described as a progressive sequence where groups of paintings and drawings comprise an aspect or a puzzle piece to a larger intuited concept. One group of work usually explains the meaning of the group that was created before it. The creation of my body of work is almost like a thesis; a work in progress that has opened my mind to the bigger picture that involves aspects of biology, neurology, physics, astronomy, astrophysics, theology, philosophy, spirituality, technology, anthropology, and archeology. Subconsciously, a pattern emerged in the imagery of consecutively-created art pieces. As I studied these images and thought about how it was produced, I wanted to understand the meaning and purpose of the mysterious information contained within them. It took several years before I realized that specific and large amounts of information were being relayed to me by 'advanced intelligences' through my art-making process and that I had personally experienced a conscious transformation and spiritual enlightenment.

Subsequently, I began drawing images likened to computer chips, indicating an electromagnetic technology, and structures resembling vehicles that generate modulations of light and sound for the transmissions of intelligence. Sixty images evolved into a sophisticated description of this technology. The structures depicted in this artwork are combined with frequencies which can be interpreted as musical, mathematical, electrical or script descriptions. I believe these frequencies can be deciphered with some manner of code breaking.

I speculate that extraterrestrial beings communicate through emissions of individual symbols from the electromagnetic technology, which is consequently understood by the conscious mind as information. These works present the initial appearance of dimensional concepts that are elaborated upon in the remaining subsequent groups. In the seven paintings that follow the *X-Ray* group, descriptions of the technology become more specific in the *Dimensional Projections* group where the electromagnetic technology and its energetic emissions and sound are represented. The emissions in the form of dots and lines in white, apparently like electrical digits, pulsate in a rhythmically mathematical order. I strongly feel that the pattern of dots and lines in my work have particular importance because they represent both units of energy and also carriers for a large amount of information in symbolic form; that it involves a form of subconsciously received extraterrestrial communication or representation of language. However, each symbol may represent not just individual words or letters, but whole concepts. These dots and lines in white and other colors are also reminiscent of the intricate network of knots and strings found in a fiber-based record-keeping instrument used by early Peruvian civilizations, and later on by the Inca Empire, known as the *khipu*.

The *khipu* is thought to be an ancient method of record keeping that consisted of a collection of dyed strings, usually made of cotton or wool, that hung from a main cord, with a variety of knots tied in each string. It is currently thought that the khipu was meant to simply record various types of information, such as stockpile accounting, the organization of municipalities and simple messages. Alternatively, there are others who postulate that the khipu relays information in the form of a complex symbolic language system or method of computation, in a manner much like the digital language of the modern computer. Despite more than a century of research on these remarkable devices, however, the pattern system of the khipu remains largely undeciphered.

The *Cellular/Nebular* group of artwork describes a network of brain cells and neurons and how they are related to the patterns of star clusters and nebulas; in how they are ultimately connected between the micro and the macro. The work continues with a description of a specific planet with its moons and its place in the Cosmos, surrounded by a sacred geometry or cosmic fabric that exists in the Universe.

The initial period of my transformation, during my art-making process of this body of work, was intense and painful. I tried to understand as I became aware of my ability to communicate mentally with people at a distance. I developed an acute sense of intuition as the work evolved, and so did my spiritual life. I went through lessons and challenges of re-evaluation. I learned to see life differently, and how everything is interconnected by a mathematical order, balance, and harmony, that flows within us and beyond.

The imagery of my work has led me to an appreciation that the world we live in, and the world beyond this world, are interconnected, and that I have the ability to communicate with beings beyond this dimension who want to communicate with all of us.

The imagery of my work has also led me to an appreciation of the common ground between the nature of the world around us: a harmonious and intertwining relation between the subject matter described in the fields of theoretical physics, biology, and theology. I believe I have had, and presently continue to have, Contact with extra-terrestrials. Such Contact may well be 'energetic', with beings of Light, involving non-ordinary states of consciousness that are often difficult to sustain and remember. I have developed a way of recording, amplifying and unfolding this Contact information through this art-making process."

Website: cecy-colichon-yarosh.artists.de

Codex VI

Codex XII

Terry Mace – Psychotherapist/Decoder

"When I first saw the art I was traumatized. Because I saw, and was aware of, what was in the artwork. And it knocked me off my feet. Metaphysically, spiritually; a spiritual and internal implosion: a 'light going on', switches pulled, flashbacks, experiences. I sensed and understood something I shouldn't have knowledge of as awakening spiritually – since being a child – and I had forgotten 'something' I had been trained to do.

I knew my life was never going to be the same again. Directly afterward, I understood languages, symbols, signs, even the creational and co-creational process of the artists themselves. It was awareness on multiple levels of what the artwork was. I understood on a personal and intimate level what it meant. Its potential was for humanity's group consciousness. I could interpret codes, ciphers, signs, geometric formulae, blueprint, designs, models, encryptions, meta-languages, hieroglyphs, schematics – an internal Rosetta stone turned on; an intergalactic process. I could understand on a conscious and super-conscious level.

I was able to download images from a portfolio of mine, which had artwork in it, while it was still closed. I was able to sense and switch on a channel and use my hand as a bar-code-reader scanner with my third eye to receive the equivalent of several hundred terabytes and upload them. The uplink knocked me backward. I felt like I had been hit by a lightning strike; information at light speed. My receiver network re-routed. I was a code-breaker able to interpret encrypted codes received and downloaded (d=). I don't know where it comes from, but is activated by the artwork. I am able to understand and do something with it."

More on Cecy's Images

"I received several downloads to do with Cecy's work. The DNA stranding is interesting in as much that it's galactic, but it's not carbon-based DNA as such, it's like energy/light-resonances/vibrations which hold together the primary structure (body/form) until it re-calibrates and then it reconfigures just like a time/space/multidimensional travel DNA sequence, which I can esoterically implant, once built as a chip or implant, to activate our own carbon-based DNA sequence, to enable us to travel in and out of our current time-space continuum.

I've translated 'loosely' about ten so far and can give you a heads up that some are tools and devices which act as interfaces between our reality and another. Likewise, there's some DNA info and some esoteric construction info which I need to look at further, however, I'll choose a single piece of art to work with and I'll 'build' the item esoterically and see what happens. There's also some info about esoteric 'implants' or 'chips' and I need to be able to enlarge and zoom into the work to break down the components further.

I can now confirm that one of the items in the pictures is a DNA injector tool for injecting the galactic DNA strands into another.

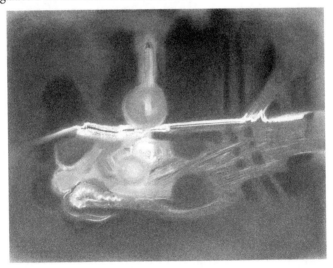

Spatial Vibrations II Is one of the DNA injector tools.

Codex XX is part of the DNA data, which is captured by the injector tool before transfer.

After one year of this experience, I now realize what is going on. The change has been profound. I have done a series of group experiments with male and female, different social backgrounds, professionals and scientists, etc., to become an esoteric engineer; to create a receiver to receive information from beyond the normal human range to other dimensions of reality. The Key has been turned.

However, it's very hard for me, Mary, to think of myself as an interpreter because, for me, there is no interpretation; it is what it is. Mary, it's both a curse and a blessing to 'know' but I don't know what else to do, so I continue to work through my life as a seer, rather than leading a more 'normalized' existence. Of course, this way of life, as you know, is rather isolated and lonely.

Since my decision to live shamanically on a day to day basis, my awareness, skills and talents have grown to encompass the abilities to move in and out of non-ordinary existence at will. As such, my first interaction with Cecy's work was conducted within the work, not as an observer but as the work.

So you see, it's not about me interpreting the work but living it. As such, I became the work and was able to interact with it in a non-physical way. Because of this, I've begun to experience a shift in my own genetics and mental capacities. As such, it's very, very hard for me to filter and to explain things in a way that's 'watered down' or safe.

http://www.thenewurbanshamansoracle.com
https://www.facebook.com/pages/Director/129469867097597

Chapter Seven

COMMUNICATION WITH EXTRATERRESTRIALS THROUGH MUSIC

Arthur, Western Australia – 11 years old.

This is a fascinating account of a family with encounters and a highly talented musical child, who appears to have made himself available to channel frequencies from a non-human source. He has understood via his encounters that at least some of these musical pieces are healing frequencies. He also has a remarkable ability to discern which beings are loving, and which are non-loving Contacts, as he has experienced both.

I was fortunate to get some remarkable and corroborative feedback from a celebrated musician who had similar experiences to Arthur, and what she feels about his music highlights its extraordinary nature.

My First Communication with Arthur's Mother
(Arthur is not his real name but one he chose)

M = Mary Rodwell
A = Arthur

Mother: "I need to talk to you about my eleven-year-old son and the music he is channeling on the piano, which he says is from the alien dreams he is having. I will go through the questionnaire with him and send it back to you with answers to your questions; however, it was hard answering the entire questionnaire with Arthur being so young. He may not have experienced all of it yet. However, both my daughter and I are a 'yes' to all of the questions in the questionnaire. The three of us all have always been very similar in the way we see and feel about things. I have had a quick skim through your research info for your book. I don't think Arthur is on the same scale as some of them. I often refer to him as a super-being though, and he is diagnosed as ADHD Asperger's. He is not like other children and often, not knowing how to control it, throws his energy around, affecting our dogs constantly. He affects us too, and we feel drained by the end of the day. Some days are worse, where even his speech is heightened and sped up, like on fast-forward. He still sees colored orbs and senses things strongly, so is always scared to be on his own even during the day, but not as much as at night. He often asks "Why me?"

In regards to Arthur's songs, they are very energetic based.

He Had What Seemed to be a Dream, Which Goes Like This

He said he was sleeping when these beings came to him and wanted to take him with them. They seemed to be good, short, light gray, big heads, a small slit for a mouth and big black eyes. He shut his eyes and felt like he was being lifted out of his bed; like he was floating. At this point, he felt like it was a dream. Next, after opening his eyes, he saw himself still lifting up to the ceiling and before hitting the ceiling he blacked out. He then woke up in a dome-shaped ship, scared and unsure. He wanted to be back in h=is bed. The beings came up to him and looked at him; they felt nice, but he was still scared."

M: "How many, and how tall?"

Mother: "Three short Gray beings; the Gray's skin looked rough – they had attached cords into him. Arthur blacked out again. Not sure how long he was out, but he woke again to see the beings around a control panel type desk where they were communicating in another language telepathically, which he could hear and at which he did not see their mouths moving. He then focused in on the control panel, which seemed to be sounds instead of a heart rate monitor, which he said he felt was altering his DNA. This became his first of the second five songs, called *Decoding the Human DNA*, which is quite incredible to listen to and sounds very ET."

The Nice Gray Who Healed Arthur

This was a few days after a painful encounter with six-foot Reptilians, which he said pretended to be Blue Beings.

He remembers the sound, that was coming from the heart-rate-monitor-type control panel, which he knows wasn't a heart rate monitor, but he could see the sound waves that were being almost played into his body to adjust his frequency. He says it was from that he formed the one particular song.

M: "Did he see the frequencies, hear them or both?"

Mother: "He saw, felt and heard them."

It was over three days Arthur played the other four songs. He named each song before he played them. However, one was created a week before these events. Each song is done on the spot, as though channeled. It is not like a typical music piece, it is more using sound to create a particular vibration to heal or adjust one's own frequency. He knows when the pieces need to be recorded and just gives himself over to the piano and the sounds are created. He has since created two more other than the original six on the album.

However, before all this took place he had a nightmare the night before – he was asleep and woke up to a vibrating sound and strong bright light. The energy felt very scary and dark. He thinks there were four beings: sharp razor teeth, black smaller eyes, tall, with the heads protruding backward. Only three were in his room, looking at him and showing their teeth. He looked at them, staring into their eyes, and one being was holding a long, thin, wire-like wand. One being grabbed Arthur's arm and held it as the other being tried to zap his arm with the wand. He tried to struggle free but felt overpowered.

It was like a small electric shock in his arm when the wand connected and at this point, he blacked out. He woke in a bright room where he could not see doors or ceilings, only white light around him. The beings saw him awake and slowly walked over and zapped him, this time on the forehead, and he blacked out again. Then he woke again and found the beings removing his right eye and he screamed in pain. His arms and feet were held down on a medical-type table. The beings put his eye in a bowl of liquid and he blacked out again. Then he woke up in his bed. It was morning, and each time he thinks about the event, he can still feel the sensation of pain in his eye.

Arthur said the beings were Reptilian, but they pretended to be Blue Beings, but he knew they were not what they seemed. The being from the first visit didn't feel good and what is behind him is not a cloak, but like an air tank with a feeding tube at the back of the neck and it is about six feet tall.

Mother: "The second experience regarding the DNA incident was the next night. The first encounter beings were different, as described above, to the short Grays on the second night. We are doing our best to remember; we think that the encounters

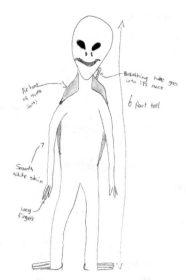

were two nights apart. Arthur feels as though the second beings (the nice ones), were fixing whatever the first ones did.

Shortly after this communication, I had an in-depth Skype conversation with Arthur (not his real name) and his mother:

Mother: "When Arthur sits by the piano, he doesn't figure out the song, he seems to go: 'Mum, you have to bring the video camera now.' He doesn't read music by notes; he has been playing by ear since he was about seven. He taught himself, and these pieces he has been coming out with, we call quirky pieces, but I don't know."

M: "Arthur, what do you feel when you feel you want to create some music?"

A: "Like something wants to bring something out of me. Like someone has put something into me that is trying to bring it out of me, to show the world what I can do. I know I am not doing this myself; it feels like someone else is bringing it into me, bringing it out and making my fingers move."

M: "So it feels like another energy or consciousness is assisting you?"

A: "Yes."

M: "What do you feel about this – being a facilitator for this consciousness to create this?"

A: "I feel like I am playing a piano track I did. I didn't feel like I was doing it. I didn't know where it came from."

Mother: "After he recorded it, track three he's playing, but you hear this 'wooooo', like a vibration that lasts for a few seconds. We wondered where that sound came from because it wasn't in the room when we recorded it. I only record where his hands go because they are only a one-off, and they are so intricate and so fast. One of them is twelve minutes long. He keeps going until he stops, so I am trying to record his hands and change them to musical notes."

A: "With this thing when I play the three minutes song, my hands cramp up from doing it normally. With this, I can change speed and do it for twelve minutes and I don't feel any pain at all."

M: "So it really feels like there is another energy taking over?"

A: "Yes, it's like my hands are doing it itself."

M: "Do you feel you can replicate it again?"

Mother: "No, just small bits of it."

A: "When I have finished the pieces I feel drowsy and feel like I am going to pass out."

Mother: "When he did the five over three days, he literally crashed for a full day. He lay on the couch, but couldn't do much – no fever, not sick, just drained."

M: "Did you feel it was the same energy using your body each time or different energy?"

A: "I felt it was the same one, but producing different pieces of music. It was passing through me to do it for some reason. I don't know why?"

M: "What did you feel about the energy as it was in you: a good feeling, or not so good?"

A: "It was a good feeling, but it was hard to tell the feeling because I just sit there and use my hands and I couldn't stop, like something going through me and I am accepting it."

Mother: "When you feel you want to play, what does that feel like?"

A: "Something is inside me and my hands start shaking. I know I need to play another piece, so I feel I need to say 'Mum, get the camera'."

M: "So you have a sense before you start that it's going to happen?"

A: "Yes. I know."

M: "Your mum said you had a sense what each piece was about too."

A: "Yes. I knew even before I played it for the very first time. I knew what they were called and when I finished, what I called them was the exact same piece of what they sounded like."

Mother: "They really did match the title of each song. I would question and wonder if this was really real or just him playing, but the fact he named every track and then when the track was done, you could even see how the journey of that track belonged to the title. How can someone do that five or six times in a row, in three days? I don't know if that is quite possible on a normal level. Even though I am more open to this, I am questioning."

M: "Arthur, you say that you think this comes from aliens. How do you sense that?"

A: "The extraterrestrial feeling. I know this might sound weird, but I can tell when

105

aliens are around. I can tell where they are, and I feel it in me. I can feel like an outer-space, extraterrestrial feeling."

M: "So you feel extraterrestrial energy is different to spirit energy?"

A: "Yes, way different to spirit energy. It feels one way, and that's normal to me because I am well aware of spirits. You may not believe me, but I see orbs and spirits and that feels one way, but this feels a whole different level vibration. Just by the vibration I can tell it is extraterrestrial."

Mother: "He's fearful all the time, though, Mary. Even though it may be good or not good, anything he feels in the room, he will run out and yell. It does freak him out. His world is in constant fear."

M: "With regard to the more loving being you drew of your experience, do you feel it's connected to this music?"

A: "Yes, I feel it was coming to me because of them. Because of that, I know they are the ones that are making me produce music. They are the ones I feel are coming through me. I just know it! It's the same energy that they gave off on their ship. And that energy thing, it's the same feeling I get when I create a song."

Note: At times during this whole interview, a strange buzzing sound was heard. This seems to occur in some interviews.

M: "So you recognize the energy of them because of that experience, and your feeling is a good feeling?"

A: "Yes."

M: "So that's what you feel when you think of them?"

A: "I was scared about everything, and the first time I saw them. The second time, they looked at me and the fear disappeared. It felt like they were trying to help me and I just let go, and then I was on the ship and all the stuff happened."

This is what I was sent by Arthur's mother, regarding the encounters Arthur experienced:

Over the course of three days, the Arthur played five songs, which we recorded. The last song that we have now put on the album (song six) we recorded about two weeks prior to the other five songs. These happenings occurred one week after the first song recorded (song six on the album), and one week before the final five songs (songs one to five on the album).

Track 1: *Insanity*

Track 2: *Decoding Human DNA*

Track 3: *Learning*

Track 4: *Meditation*

Track 5: *Going Within Yourself*

Track 6: *Arrival*

M: "On the ship, you said that you felt they were fixing something because you had a very negative experience prior to this with the ones that seemed to have the 'tank' on their back."

A: "Yes, that first one freaked me out a lot. They had a tube attached to the back of their neck as if something was feeding into them. I don't know, but they were breathing weird; it was like these creatures were Reptilians. They had more Reptilian-looking skin and they felt more Reptilian than the other ones, who definitely felt ET. It was like they tried to look ET but they just looked Reptilian. They didn't behave like aliens. They opened their mouths and growled like they did with me. It was pretty scary. I saw their razor-sharp teeth, and I saw the tunnel. I felt it was a Reptilian, but it looked like an alien and I was confused."

M: "So you felt it was not alien, but Reptilian and Earth-based?"

A: "Yeah, more Reptilian."

M: "Did you get a sense of what they were trying to do to you?"

A: "With my eye, it felt they were putting something behind it and, as I feel now in my bowel, right here (he pointed to his left side), there is something in there that buzzes sometimes. I just don't know what it is."

A: "When you think of that buzzing, does anything come to mind as to where it came from at all?"

A: 'Yeah, it feels like a tubey-like white thing which buzzes once a week or once a day. I think the bad ones put it in there because when I woke up next morning I felt it in there. It was definitely the bad ones."

Note: Arthur also mentioned a rod-like instrument that he said zapped him and knocked him out.

A: "It was pretty scary. It was like a long thing with a needle, and they would put it to my head or my arm and it freaked me out."

M: "What do you think this thing placed in your body is about, or for?"

A: "No, I just feel they were trying to do something to me, trying to shut me off from what I am trying to do, and with my eye, they are trying to shut me off from seeing what I am seeing, and producing what I am producing. The one in my bowel I don't know what they are trying to do, but I feel they are trying to shut me off from seeing the spirits and shut me off from the extraterrestrial feelings and put me down. I did feel uneasy the next day, so it was the good aliens who helped me."

M: "So you said that these other beings came and fixed you?"

A: "Yes, I think they changed me back to what I was when I was doing this stuff, only I am doing it even better. They made it more, so I could produce these songs. But I wasn't producing the songs, they were. They were coming to me and I would feel them 'in me', and I would feel I have to do this. Twelve minutes straight, fingers moving that fast. The music is about shifting our DNA. My friend has a mother in her late forties, and she heard this and cried. I heard it and lay down, and I felt my body jumped. I could feel the vibration and it felt pretty cool. Another friend was sensing symbols when she heard it, and it seems to work on a high level, and almost frustrate those not quite ready, or they love it."

The song he had done a week prior to the encounters, we now call that the sixth one. The other five after the encounters were in the order of a journey. The first one almost shatters you and shakes you out of the mundane reality. I felt it was 'insanity.'

M: "Have you any sense of what you now need to do with these songs?"

A: "Yes, I need to give them to certain people to 'wake them up.' To come out of their minds and back into their soul."

M: "There is an alien on the shelf that the first alien tried to look like?"

A: "Exactly like that, with small eyes and a huge head and long neck. It was pretending to be an alie but it wasn't actually because it had the mouth to the back of their neck."

M: "So it was disguising itself, pretending it wasn't a Reptilian?"

A: "Yes. I knew it was disguising itself. And that's why I felt the fear. With the good aliens, I didn't feel the fear. I saw they were true aliens, and when the bad aliens came, they felt like Reptilian creatures trying to take me away and were just horrible. Every time I think about it, it brings up bad memories."

I spoke with Arthur about when he is scared, and things he can do to help deal with his fears. I asked him about the spirits he sees, and how does he feel about them?

A: "Yes. You may not believe me, but my grandpa died when he was fifty-seven, and sometimes I feel his presence. He connects and talks to me. I connect with him on that level and the outline of him. He tells me what's going on. It's pretty nice, and sometimes I see my guardians, like angels above me; they are the spirits of my Mum's grandpa and my grandpa, and they are helping me out. When something goes wrong, I can tell they are there for me because I can feel it."

M: "Do you recall any time you were on another planet?"

(The background noise became very loud here.)

A: "I remember seeing this alien in my mum's room."

Mother: "I think it was when he was between two and four years, he woke up crying 'I had a bad dream'.

A: "I was walking to your room. A gray man with black eyes, he saw me and went through the window, and up into the sky."

M: "Was this a different ET to the one you saw recently?"

A: "I think it was exactly the same. He was looking at my mum and doing something. I remember bits of it, and I didn't know what they were, just a gray man with black eyes looking at you.

I remember this experience when my mum used to do healing. I was about six or seven, and it was late and my dad was in bed and I woke up. I heard footsteps and what felt like something on my bed and like a breathing out noise from the nose, not the mouth. It didn't feel such a nice one. Some people make fun of me and I am here to do something, but I don't know what it is."

Mother: "Track two is the one he heard at the heartbeat monitor of the craft. Arthur saw waves going in and out and telepathically feels and hears this vibration, and this vibration is in this song. He said 'That's the song that was on the machine; that was the sound on the machine.' He is also naturally creative when he plays, and astounds his teacher. So when he plays these songs, it's almost at times that they allow him to add notes and then they come in again, so it's him and this other energy. I don't believe it's all the other energy, as I know how he plays and I see the difference and when he becomes part of it, almost breathing into the energy as well to make whatever it is."

A: "I wanted to say that when the good aliens wanted to knock me out they just did it with their hand, but when the Reptilians came to me they needed the wand. They couldn't do it themselves; they had to use this power."

M: "So the not-so-nice ones needed technology, but the real ETs could do it with their own energy?"

A: "Yes. Now I know a hundred percent the Reptilians were not extraterrestrials. The nice being had sandpaper skin, it looked rough. I remember the sound that was coming from the heart-rate-monitor-type control panel, which wasn't a heart rate monitor, but I could see the sound waves that were being almost played into my body to adjust my frequency."

M: "Did Arthur see them or feel them, or both?"

Mother: "He sees, hears and feels the vibration. He says it was from that he formed the one particular song. Then, over three days, he played the other four songs. However, one was created a week before these events."

M: "Which one?"

Mother: "*Decoding the Human DNA*. He named each of the songs before he played them. Each song is done on the spot as though channeled. It is not like a typical music piece; it is more using sound to create a particular vibration to heal or adjust one's own frequency."

M: "So he knows the purpose of each one?"

Mother: "Yes. He knows when the pieces need to be recorded and just gives him over to the piano and the sounds are created. He has since created two more, other than these original six on the album."

Note: Update: Arthur feels watched, and senses those watching are not loving or nice and they are pretending to be positive.

Mother: "Arthur is still fearful, and frequently seeing some sort of being, spirit or ET, he is not sure, looking at him during the day. Arthur says they look like the ones that helped him but don't feel like them. They are in disguise and feel bad."

The Mother's Encounters

"There was an event where two beings came onto my bed and did something with air on my face. It felt as though they were altering something internally, or trying to scan me for something. It did not feel good. They either did not care that I was awake still and allowing the process to happen or thought I was asleep. It was a few months after that I began to show signs of a toxic body. I was a healthy eater, but still ate yeast. I stopped eating the yeast and all cleared up. This was either connected or just a coincidence; not sure."

M: "Do you know what type of being this was?"

Mother: "No. I had my eyes closed to stay out of my mind and trust the soul to stay protected. I did feel as though they were animal in energy, sleek in the way they moved and cunning, though no more intelligent than humans. It felt like they were doing a job and were just as physical, but with the extra tools that we don't use. This is why my soul did not fear them."

M: "What did they look like?"

Mother: "I made an ET sculpture in my early twenties, which later seemed to match the ETs I saw whilst awake. These beings were very tall; elongated everything: head, neck, arms, torso, legs, and fingers. I can't remember the color of them, but their skin was smooth. They had a very loving presence."

M: "Did you feel any connection to them?"

Mother: "Yes, this is where I originally came from, but a long time ago that it feels sad that I don't remember it enough. They said to me, 'You have been gone a long time, but you will be home soon.' I felt a connection, a slight remembrance that this felt familiar, as well as sadness for what I have chosen to do for the time I had, but also a knowing that it had to be done. My journey was always going to be a hard one, I knew the mind would get me lost, but through the help of the other dimensional beings, I have always been led back to the path. The journey was a double-edged sword of both honor and strength versus incredible hardship and sacrifice. I remember talking from a young age to other beings and feeling lonely here on Earth, but somehow, somewhere, someone was always there, guiding and watching over me. I have always known I was here to serve others."

M: "Any sense of what being it might be?"

Mother: "No, I have never done any research into beings, so I am in the dark in regards to names. I really have to work on myself to stay in the soul, as I was brought up to only trust in the mind, what only the physical eyes saw on a low frequency. It was only in my later years that I began to grow and I am not afraid to say I am still very young in this field. This is why I never thought I knew more than my children, as their souls could be, and I believe are, much more advanced than mine.

I had an ET experience whilst awake where I was on their ship. The ship was very open plan. It appears that I was in some sort of teleport machine. Still human, I was on their ship, but not out of the teleport machine, which was a transparent barrier between them and me. It was more that they brought me up to remind me what I was doing, and who I was. I saw no more than this part of the ship.

M: "Are there beings you feel particularly close to?"

Mother: "I had conscious connections with beings when I was younger and saw more than I do now, but felt more energetic spirits than ET. For the last fifteen years, I channel energy readings and healings for people and can still connect to these beings and hear what needs to be said, or they will put visuals in my head that I can use this to help the person understand. I can pick up energy on others and I often have dreams that I am on another realm learning a new technique. All of what I do today has no name and was not taught to me on this planet.

One time, I know, I was being downloaded with info. Two days prior to 2011 and two days after the turn of the New Year, I slept for four days, hardly eating and rising only for toilet breaks if needed. I felt dizzy if I stood up and did not feel sick; just knew I had to sleep. About two weeks after this, I started understanding everything that was downloaded to me. Each person that came into my session room confirmed what was given to me through how I needed to help them."

M: "I understand ... what was the type of downloads you experienced?"

The Healer

Mother: "I was given knowledge and emotional and energetic sensitivity. I understood that the frequencies over the next coming years were going to be increasing in periods, so as not to affect people too harshly. I knew that we had two years to clear our bodies and issues before the frequencies lifted enough to severely affect our mental or physical health. I understood that heart issues would be the first to present, as well as an increased desire to suicide. I was given a tool to help people adjust; those who were ready on some level that found me that is. I also knew that many of us were here for higher purposes and that as we cleared and rebalanced our energy we would be opened up to what we were sent to do. I have been working strongly in this way since then. I also know when the frequency lifts and changes.

Since then, I have been shown many confirmations to support what I understood by the download. Also, as these four days occurred, I did have my own ET ship experience while awake! I was moving the energy through a friend (she works with ET energy, and can throw energy and affect electrical equipment, as well as speak a universal language) in my session room, when I closed my eyes as I worked like I usually do (standing) and found myself on a ship. I remember not seeing any straight walls; everything felt circular. I was in a transparent, tube-like pod of some sort, when a being walked up to me and telepathically communicated, 'Welcome home. Your journey has been long; you are almost done.' The being felt familiar and loving. I had been verbalizing the experience to my friend while it was happening. (I have never felt like I fitted here on Earth, and I was told by a medium years before that I come from somewhere far away and that she has never seen my energy before and was so grateful to have the pleasure to read it.) When I left the ship and was back in my session room and was instructed to move the energy in a different way, I could see and hear the energy that was flowing and how it was being redirected and turned on. It was a truly amazing experience.

I never saw the beings that worked on me when I was learning in other dimensions. When I first was learning to use energy for healing, my hands would move by themselves and I would recall many beings also in the room with me. I learned they used me as a vessel, until I knew more of what was needed. I was learning on the spot."

M: "What type of beings were they?"

Mother: "I never thought about looking at them. I just remember them being in white, standing around, both learning and teaching, watching and communicating amongst themselves as well as with me, telepathically. As I learned on the 'job', I would either be told or shown what that move was for, or the client would make a comment about what just happened for them, and always a few days later I would get confirmation from an external source to seal the understanding."

M: "So they were teaching you?"

Mother: "Yes, how to understand, move and facilitate energy. This is my field; everything I have learned has come from other dimensional beings. How to read crystals and listen to them as to how they can help others. I can also make oil that can help most ailments; all done through channeling.

I have made some dot points and that way you can ask questions in regards to that."

What I have taught my children.

- Everything that my being knows; what I see as life, which is far outside the box.
- I taught them when they were young to send energy through their hands before they were too old to doubt.
- I made everything energetic second nature, through living and breathing it, and allowing them to see the proof for themselves.
- I never disbelieved what they said they saw or experienced and always tried to understand.
- I always encouraged my children to research and find the truth, take what makes sense and discard the rest.
- I always taught my children to know that they are creators and unlimited;

anything is possible.

- Most importantly, stood from a place of understanding, fairness and an equal soul level, where communication was always open.
- Taught them to question everything and get them to search their inner-selves for answers.
- Knew that they had just as much to teach me as I had to teach them.

ET Experiences

- Night event, where two beings came on my bed and did something with air on my face.
- Made an ET sculpture in my early twenties, which later seemed to match the ETs I saw whilst awake.
- ET experience whilst awake, where I was on their ship.
- I never saw the beings that worked with me when I was learning on other dimensions.
- When first learning to use energy for healing, my hands would move by themselves and I would recall many beings in the room with me. I learned whilst they used me as a vessel until I knew more of what was needed. I was learning on the spot.

Note: Downloads of information and taught concepts on the craft are two well-known ways humans are taught knowledge and skills by extraterrestrials. It appears that some of these intelligences can, for a short time, inhabit the human body to offer communication verbally and through music and artwork, etc.

A few years ago, I connected with Japanese musician and author, Julliena Okah, a celebrated pianist, artist and Experiencer. She has courageously written about her encounters in her autobiography, *One Life, Many Worlds*. Julliena experienced inter-actions with spirits, ETs and otherworldly, inter-dimensional beings. Her Contact experiences began in postwar Japan, when she had her first encounter as a child. Some of her experiences echo Arthur's, including the experience of downloading music frequencies. I wrote to Julliena, to ask her what she thought of Arthur's story, the process he experienced and his music, since I knew she had experiences similar to his in terms of channeled music.

Julliena Okah Commented on Arthur's Music and his Experiences

"I think the spirits have more this kind of power than the aliens. If the entities who possess us are the high-vibration ones, the result we get is peaceful and helpful. We always find out by the fruit (the outcome) but it is not that simple in some cases.

My mother told me a few weeks ago that she had a very difficult time raising me because she never really understood me. Very few people understood me or what I went through with my experiences. I don't believe I was possessed, but I was at times; I was controlled by other beings. For example, when the spirit artists possessed me, I had some experiences similar to Arthur. I knew someone wanted to paint through me. My hands moved automatically. However, who wants to get up 3:00 a.m. to paint? But 'they' did. I felt I was a different person. However, they created the masterpiece that the world accepted; it was definitely not my personal talent. However, artist spirits were connected to aliens and working together. Although it's not always so simple.

"I found that Arthur's titles for his music fascinate me."

Julliena's Comments After Hearing Arthur's Music

"Definitely Arthur is Contacted by the aliens or master musical spirits. Amazing composition. Genius. I liked it a lot. The first one has combined a few bars of Beethoven's music. I normally do not care much for contemporary music. But people who like this would appreciate it. I am very interested in this boy.

My alien experiences also happened in childhood and went far beyond. When I was overtaken by the entity; when I faced the ghost and felt I was in hell, I felt something similar to what he was saying. It was an amazing power I received, but I was drained and crashed afterward, as he describes he feels too. As a result, I could not go to school afterward. People cannot understand about otherworldly things. So I hope he is treated with more understanding than I was.

I am glad his mother was relieved to hear this information. I can understand her feelings. My mother went through the same. In my case, I had complete healing of my sickness and practice of the violin. But this was hard to prove. Even though we are communicating with the good aliens or other beings, we must go through tremendous experiences that are completely different than the experiences from this world. When I was his age, I was fine, but years later the paranormal things escalated and intensified and led to my Near Death Experience (NDE). This was after a suicide attempt when it all became too difficult. But despite this, I learned so much about other worlds that I could never have learned in this world.

When listening to Arthur's music I feel this is striking music. I never listen to contemporary music more than twice, but his music has power to draw. The un-harmonized tunes and the offbeat are interesting. The powerful energy is unbelievable. The boy is very special and amazingly talented. He, or other entity, has a great technique of piano. This is not the way children play or create this music. I like all of his music but especially *Meditation, Human DNA* and *Arrival*. Someday I would like to hear his music alone, without others being part of his playing, and then I would understand more.

Arthur needs a lot of support from the people around him. He is lucky. He can prove his experience with his music. He makes captivating music. His incredibly sharp perception is scary. He has an incredible future. Please keep me posted on his situation in future."

Julliena Okah, is a musician, celebrated professional violinist, artist and author of *One Life, Many Worlds* and speaks publicly about her encounters and NDE experiences and past lives.

Arthur's Discernment

It is interesting to note that Arthur knew intuitively which beings were loving and which were self-serving. He could see/sense beyond their screen image that was meant to confuse him. Arthur soon deduced that the pseudo-beings needed technology to control him but the real extraterrestrials only needed to touch him and so he knew that meant they were not only real but, through their healing, cared for him.

Chapter Eight

OFF-WORLD TECHNOLOGIES AND MIND CONTROL

This chapter explores the challenges facing the New Children on Earth.

Cathy, from the previous chapter, commented on programs to shut the Star Children down. For many, this would be difficult to accept. However, she is not the only child who has covered this controversial subject. I have met a number of these aware children that have much to say on this subject.

The next detailed account on this subject comes from another nine-year-old boy in the USA. I have been in communication with both father and son over a number of years. They are fully conscious of their interactions with numerous non-human intelligences and inter-dimensional beings. They also have become aware of covert black budget programs which show that we have advanced technologies way beyond what the public is aware – covert bases which teach these children how to use their abilities.

In this chapter, father and son share their awareness of some agencies on this planet, which appear to target and manipulate the 'new children' for their own covert agendas.

M: Mary
E: Son
Father

Transcript of a Conversation Over Skype

E is nine years old with a high IQ. He recalls his past life and has complex understanding of physics. He believes it is even beyond the level of Tesla. This understanding, he told me, stems from his past life recall on Orion, working on higher technologies as a light physicist.

Father: "My son was sharing with me some things about Mars: the war that went on there, the asteroid which hit Mars in the past. Mars didn't die, but much of the population was injured and died. He said that there are still people there who began to re-build. People on Earth found out because there are 'star-gates' on Earth that take them there, and then on to other planets.

I am concerned about the present education systems because E is fully conscious. What kind of school system will be best for him? Even with his specialist education, something is being blocked, even though they are the top percentage of children. E felt there was no educational system that was for him. He spoke about a school, that does not presently exist. I know, Mary, this is also in your heart, but how to get this to happen?"

Note: E knows there are special schools suitable, but they have been created by covert agencies and operate clandestinely.

E: "The kids at the bases – what they are learning versus what the public learns is so different. There are schools on the ocean floor, in underground bases and off-planet."

Father: "E told me that he has been taken to these, but he has held on to his good intentions. He has spoken about the mind-control technologies and how they are pulling the kids like him, and monitoring their brainwaves because the children have the information. I have been aware of this, but I don't influence him. This is what he has come up with. He then told me what he needed for his education. It is frustrating that the surface population doesn't know this is real, or what's going on, or if it's real or not.

So, as a parent, you have public/private gifted/media/government not aware, you can't even make it relevant. I know what they do offer the public is bogus science. So the best you can do is re-invent the wheel. My son comes here fully awake, knows what we are really at and what's out there. He knows what he's supposed to do and what he needs to unlock him for what he needs consciously, as well as what he needs to equip his knowledge and skill sets. He is even aware of where the world is really at on Earth. So here he is, fully aware of these things way beyond his teachers, but at the same time has a nine-year-old body. What he is conscious of, out there, and the way things are run, they, the mainstream public, are not even aware of.

What he knows inside of him even the current PhDs are not aware of. I know someone with a master's degree at MIT advanced space technologies. This PhD individual didn't even know we are not alone. There is nothing on the surface world and in the current curriculum or Universities that can 'unlock' what's in my son. So E said we have to create a school if there isn't one, or a different one, apart from the groups that are already doing this covertly."

Note: I have spoken about creating Awakening Centers with new schools for the children like E, where they create the curriculum to help them expand on what they know.

E: "There is being made a new moon. There are a lot of moons that are artificial, like around Saturn and Jupiter and other places, and some people are affected by them. When this new moon is built, we are all controlled, with no way to stop it. It's is for mind-controlling brainwaves."

M: " So, it's manipulating peoples thoughts."

E: "Yes. In a 'dream' I went into a room and was in a chair and I was groggy (maybe drugged). There was a lady in black. She had boots on like military, and she had a mind-control machine. I pretended like I was being controlled by it, but I wasn't."

Note: E showed me with his hands the level the mind control device worked at and the level his mind frequency was, which was way above this device.

E: "The reason I was there was for them to take my information and make me forget it."

M: "So the information you share, they try to stop you from retaining it and to shut you down?"

E: "Yes."

M: "What did you do to show you are not affected by the mind control machine?"

E: "Focus in my head a lot. You have to maintain focus. Basically, when this hap pens, I go into my own energy, I try and go over it. It's really hard, but it's the only way to block it. I go up as high as I can. They wanted a lot of information; unfortunately they got some; fortunately not too much."

Father: "Why did they have you in that room versus other kids?"

E: "Because I was a trigger."

Father: "I guess you would call him an activist or catalyst. E told me he has something in him, a piece of the puzzle, like a trigger. He also told me they knew he was here when he came here."

M: "How did they know?"

E: "Well, my energetic frequency. It's a special energetic frequency. Basically it's an Orion frequency, and they hone into that to get hold of me."

Father: "Are you saying that they monitor frequencies, and they can tell when you are in a certain place?"

E: "Yes."

Father: "How long have they known about you?"

E: "For a really long time; since I was about six months old."

Father: "E said that in a dream there was a lot of interference then bop, he is in this experience where he is sitting in a chair with a lady in black who started to talk to him."

E: "Well, I wasn't supposed to be awake just yet. I wasn't supposed to hear, but I heard about the new moon. They didn't tell me this. I heard because I wasn't supposed to be awake."

Father: "E told me that she said something about interference, but it would all be done in the next decade or so. Regarding the new moon – the only way to stop it was to destroy it. We have just been experiencing 'little' interferences, nothing that big yet."

M: "So you are saying that you, and those like you, are bringing in new frequencies that they are trying to stop. Is that correct?"

E: "Yes. We need to destroy the moon so we get higher frequencies from people."

Father: "E told me that they are trying to get the information from him, but he has been causing interference and interfering. They were trying to get information from him, that's why he was dazed a little with the machine. They are trying to match his brainwaves with the machine, to sync on a brain wave pattern to lower his frequency."

E: "They said that if this doesn't work there are two options: one, they would bring me to their school or two, they would try to destroy me if it didn't work."

Father: "They put thoughts into his head such as 'this isn't real,' and also some fear stuff. They were trying to get the brain sync so they could get in. E acted like he was going with it, but really he wasn't. He has been talking a lot about mind control, the brainwaves and the scanning of the planet: how they watch people, and talking about targeting. I have never talked about that. E, can you tell Mary about the targeting you mentioned?"

E: "Basically they target people who are special, and they stop them going higher than the machine. So they are trying to affect my consciousness and me."

Father: "I have never told him about this, but what he told me is that it's like an electrical frequency fence. When the frequency goes above a certain level it sends out a signal. He's talking about AI (Artificial Intelligence). It's like a computer program from underground, from satellites and also from some of the radio towers that monitor basically the field, the consciousness, to see where people are at. This is important right now. If you can talk to Mary as you do to me. Is there anything else on the mind control stuff?"

M: "Can I ask, is this to keep us in a lower vibration so they can control us? So as soon as we don't buy into that or raise our frequency they don't have the control, and that's the problem for them? They no longer can affect us as we go to those other frequencies? Is that why you managed to avoid some of this because you concentrated on your own essence, your own frequency; is that how it is?"

E: "Yes"

M: "Where do this knowledge and awareness come from? Is it a connection to some place which allows you to understand that, or is it an understanding of

119

your own essence? How do you understand how you know that?"

E: "How I understand, how I know that, is that when I go higher. I just start to get all this information, and sometimes when I go to places I get tons of information."

Father: "It's like it triggers him for that recall. He even uses language that adults use. But what Mary is saying is where did you learn what you know?"

E: "Orion."

M: "So, it's from your origin of Orion you bring this information through?"

E: "Yes."

Father: "E was telling me that Orion is in charge, or a group of them. Like a German group: Aryan. Interesting, as I have royal bloodlines. It's Aryan. Tell Mary about the group from Orion: skin color etc."

E: "Skin color: well, some are blue, some are gray. Mostly blue. Some of the Grays are good; some of the Grays are bad. Some of the Blues are good; some of the Blues are bad. It's like a personality split, and some of the Grays are like a cyborg, others are clones. Some Grays are tall and some are short, and some don't have a nose. A group of them are connected to a group here, doing some of the not-fun stuff."

Note: Not positive.

M: "So there is a mix of agendas?"

E: "Yes. Orion has been overseeing many things on Earth, but things are changing. Everything is moving faster; the solar system is moving faster."

M: "How do you understand us, as a species, changing, and why you are that more aware than your dad, etc.? How do you understand yourself?"

E: "I know a lot, but in special subjects."

M: "Do you have a sense of why you have come here at this time?"

E: "Yes, because right now Humans don't know anything. They don't know why they are here. It goes round and round, the same every day. I am here to teach 'special' things like special physics."

Father: "I asked E what I could do to help him, and he said to help him to learn physics. 'Well not to learn, as I already know, but to awaken and remember it. But the math's here is too low; what I am used to working on they don't have here'."

E: "Basically I know totally different math, and before I came here I was doing light physics. I change light, use light, make things out of light Basically, I was a Light Physicist."

Father: "What were you working on?"

E: "I was working on a portal. Unfortunately, it got destroyed."

Father: "He told me he needs Tesla books."

E: "Tesla is like me. He was a scientist bigger than his age. He knew more than he was supposed to. I need to read the books to get more understanding of my stuff. That's why I need them."

Father: "He told me he needs Tesla books to 'trigger' him. It's like a starting point; a beginning place to go forward."

E: "Talk about the schools. All the schools so far don't accept me. For my purpose, I need to go to a different school because even in my special group I am more different than the different group. I am supposed to be different because I learn more, I learn differently than they do. I am learning who I am different than them. I know I am from a different star, a different planet, different Universe. I know I am a Star Child. I know more science and maths than are from here. I know how to build a portal. I know how to teleport"

Father: "You said some of them are just not awake yet so it's harder to learn certain stuff, but if someone comes with full recall and is awake, it's easier for them to learn stuff and easier to remember?"

E: "Yes, basically because I know where I am from it makes it easier to learn things, makes it easier for me to understand things. I can remember faster when others have to memorize them. I just know, and I am just practicing."

M: "So, you are saying that you can remember what you know because you remember where you are from, but regarding the other children, it's because they don't remember their origins they cannot access what you can. Is that correct?"

E: "Yes."

Father: "You said it's already woken up for you to work with it, and you gave me examples of portals and dimensions."

Note: E explained by using his arms and hands, the level that one gifted child can reach, in contrast to what someone who remembers their origins can do; so it is greatly expanded.

E: "So, you are saying it's like they are re-learning because of their lack of recall of their origins. Whereas you can access it consciously, and where it's from."

E: "Yes."

Father: "So, it is sounding like we need to surround them with triggers to work as a stimulus to bring back, to bring through. Tell Mary about Mexico, Palenque and Chichen Itza."

E: "I got a lot of information where star constellations are; about the languages. Not on Earth, in Earth."

121

Sacred Sites, Pyramids and the Awakening

E: "At this time, the angel was talking to me, and said that some people would reject me. I have to do something that means I should die, but I won't die, but most people will die in it. Like most people in their physical body will die in it. I have to trust I will survive it."

M: "Why did you go to Mexico?"

E: "When we went to Mexico we needed to go to energy centers, sacred places."

M: "What was there about those special places that gave you help or understanding?"

E: "I heard a name and it brought in all these things and information because I was close to a temple and sacred spot. In Palenque, I got names of star systems and co-ordinates; it just started coming back. In Chichen Itza, I brought in more information about the pyramids and water. Water is the power source energy and the pyramid equals portal when water is near. Portal is when you are near energy."

M: "So a pyramid, with water near it, can create a portal?"

E: "Yes. When water is completely pure it's a source of energy. It's pretty endless. Water powers portals and other dimensions; it powers it up, basically. If a place you need to go is far away, you will need more water. It can be as far away as a planet, or as close as a centimeter. When we were at Chichen Itza there was no water around there, and that's important, as that's what powers up a portal. It's the water. The water is how this thing works and water is multidimensional, like it can go through the dimensions. Water is the energy that powers up the portals, and you go inside and the water is the purest energy. It's all around and in space too."

Father: "Mary wants to know how does the pyramid work?"

E: "You know when you charge something you take it out. It doesn't really have batteries, as it's on charge. It's charged up by the water if it's close to it, and you can go home. You can go into it with a special code, I think."

M: "What do you mean by a special code? Do you need to chant a special frequency to work it? If you have the water and the pyramid, how does it actually work?"

E: "By a special frequency. How you create it is actually very simple, you go into your mind and tune in. You tune to the frequency – not sure how to explain using words."

M: "So, you have to be in a certain consciousness and frequency, so that you can use the water and the pyramid in conjunction to create the portal. You have to create the right mental/consciousness frequency. So you work with these two things: the water and the pyramid i.e., consciousness works it with the water and the pyramid. Three components, and the individual's consciousness has to be in the right frequency to trigger this happening?"

E: "Yes."

Father: "He was also saying to me that the frequency triggers and unlocks what you do in the portal."

E: "You can go to Orion and back. One time you had to go via Mars, but now the technology means that you can go directly. You can go two ways: one in your mind and one in your body, it's a frequency thing."

Father: "E also told me how dimensionally to shift and come back in. Time, space-dilation things, this is what the future is to be. He speaks about the Sun. It is not the main power source. It's in the middle, and everything goes around it. It is like the main power source. It isn't, but it is what we are more attracted to, mostly Saturn. Re brainwave devices (more commonly known as brain-control devices), they can be big or small and can even be a portal. What happens is that 'they' (covert black programs) target people using a higher energy and makes people forget some stuff and gives you fake memories. This happened to me once, but I regained focus. Brain wave devices are used in a lot of places by supercomputers. They can be changed and tuned differently; not always tuned to destroy. Aliens built the supercomputer AI, and they gave it to the secret intelligences."

Father: "Mary asks your permission to put some of this information in a book? Is this okay with you?"

E: "Yes, that's fine with me."

Father: "She believes it will help other kids like you; give them understanding, as well as help their parents, and cause of lot of information to be out there. Is that okay? What do you think about that, and what do you see happening with this book?"

E: "What I see happening is that it will help a lot of people, a lot of other kids. Particularly the adults will be helped to parent them. That's what I see."

Father: "Do you see a different side to this book?"

E: "Only some people will use it badly; use the book against her. But it just feels great; it just feels different."

Father: "Anything else about the book? Is there anything you pick up around this book? This is really important."

E: "Just that: great job."

We Need a New Type of School

Father: "E reads two hundred plus pages a day; just wants to learn and learn. He feels really held back because what's the point of all this because the knowledge is wrong, a lot of it. People don't know what's going on and you are trying to resonate with people who are really dense. 'I just want to be around other kids like me and go to school with them.' He told me there are schools like that underground or on the ocean floor; they are secret schools. He is aware of them and they are aware of him."

E: "There is one last place I need to go, Dad, to cause the last bit of knowledge to come up in me, and then it will quicken and go fast. Then I will be functioning at the pace I am supposed to, and I will bring everything through for me to remember why I came here. I need to go to the great pyramid in Egypt because there is Orion energy in there. It's hooked up to Orion and Sirius. I need to go into a room because of the frequencies there, and it will activate the last bit of information in me and cause everything to speed up because that's the technology. It's a portal access to everything on this planet."

Father: "I never told him that. I kept saying to E 'What, as a father, can I do for you; how can I be there for you? You have come knowing who you are but a lot to learn and where you come from. But you have a lot of areas of consciousness that's beyond this giftedness. However you are in a nine-year-old body, and I am your dad and I will bring you up. You are on this planet for a reason. What do we need to do, to get you what you need to do? Tell me when you need to go."

E: "I just need to go to Egypt when it's a full moon. Things come off the Moon and the Sun that charges our full powers because when it's the full moon it is the highest charge. It goes off the Moon to the Sun from that. It collects the charge from Orion and Sirius, and brings up all the information and speeds it up. No particular time, just better to get it over with. So, the sooner the better, and then we can go on. That will set something else in motion once that's done, and that will put out something else in its field as it goes out."

Father: "He was telling me then about a secret school, but if he goes to it, you have to pretend it's a normal school – but really what you are doing is going to the Moon and Mars, and going to these places. So he would have to pretend, and the children there are being trained. On one level, he wants to be around that, but he said 'I don't want to be with the group that lies to all the people.'

I said to E 'We don't lie to the best of our ability; unfortunately there is a non-disclosure, where you can't mention anything. We are on one level until such a school gets created. But even then, someone has got all the money, the knowledge and technology and experience. If we can get this out of there, you could have the knowledge you need to do what you already know, and you could be relevant to the generation it's actually at – without all the control and the monitoring, and with the right information for what you need. That group has at least a fifty to seventy percent start. But the thing is how it's run.' So he doesn't want the character and the morality of these covert schools, but at the same time, he is bored. The relationships he wants are with people conscious and aware, capable and who have the wisdom and the experience, are negative and underground here. The other ones are not out for the public. So that's where I am at as a parent."

E: "If there was a good group, I would like to do that, as I came here to do something."

Father: "He knows that he is not going to learn here, from even the present highest levels of University. I know some of these people and they know he is off the charts. They don't know what he knows, and here they are considered leaders. So with this, one doesn't know if it's real or not. One group may even be two hundred years on before we even build something, and another group already totally knew all of this years ago and is already going.

E is there on a consciousness level, but has a different morality. At the same time, he is just nine years old and I am his father. We are bringing him up to be in the generation on the Earth he's on, and be part of its transition. Another big part is breaking the frequency mind control, and also getting the technology out there so that there is the information you need to be awake and remember. You don't have access to the technology and you have to re-invent the wheel, when some have already got starships – which he knows how to build and work with.

I told him you were connected to some wonderful scientists that may have more knowledge, at least to get him going. At least their field of study is there. He says the people aren't conscious. They don't have a multidimensional grid of how creation is Nature. Everything is going in the wrong direction, and it's not even what you need. So on one level you are associating with a really dense class; you are not getting what you need, and what you are getting is wrong information that doesn't resonate. It puts you in the wrong box, which later you have to untangle from. It's not set to bring these kids up, so he says 'What's the point of me going to school? There is not anything built, so you have to do something about it. And I know that's in your heart and my heart, to work out something we can do about it. In the meantime, get me Tesla books.' It's a good start. He was wired the same and ahead of his generation, so that will help awaken some of this. It's sad that the group that has the curriculum that we need is underground. It's sad that what may be created they have had for fifty years or longer, and that's where his consciousness is."

Underground Bases and Schools on Mars
Father: "E tells me there are other kids, and they are raising an army right now. There are a whole lot of kids on the Moon and on Mars, and some are from here. He said they get the kids from the stars, they target them, get the information out of them, copy it, and then they try and lower their brainwaves and put in other stuff so they don't remember.

Basically using the kids to get information, so it means that the kids already have the information that they want, and they get it from the kids that come here. But they also put in memories such as 'You didn't live before you came here'. They give them cover memories; implanted thoughts given when they are groggy.

E said that where he came from, such things as cloning and DNA manipulation are just common sense. They are doing this on planet Earth now, raising an army with kids like him, where that's the normal thing – to go off-planet and off-world. Many are there already, and on one level, that's where he wants to be, for relational normality, but on another level, he doesn't want to be part of a military without morals. So you can see where I am at – he knows about all the bases.

E told me there are some where you live, in Australia. Also in South America and Africa. He says these are three major places with underground bases, where some people's souls are not really from there. Some people's actual bodies are from there; here and there is just a mixture, another breed, a whole civilization.

E talks about a moon that they have put outside the solar system, further out; they are trying to finish it. I had an experience about a month ago, where I was shown a moon over in the Saturn system, and that there was an exchange of ownership from a group here and a group out there, to try and get one of those moons. Those moons are not what people think they are.

E was telling me today that a lot of moons out there are artificial; they are old and used for different things. But he said another moon is being finished to bring here. You can't pick it up yet, but it's picking up off our moon to here, so I think that's a good starting place. The main thing is the consciousness; the frequency to stop people raise their consciousness. Things put in the food, chemtrails, radio waves and water. The pollution re fluoride in the water – he said it makes you dumb, makes you stupid like you can't think, and so you go along with it. It's all about greed at the top, wanting to have the technology. He just goes through the whole system, where it's functioning underground and elsewhere, about the genetics and the mind control; the energy technology to lock it all down. That's what this other moon is about: it will help seal it. Once it's in place, people won't be able to get out of it because they don't have the information. They allow the wrong information to go in them; it is electronic mind control.

When I went to Alaska, I was shown a neuronet with an electric fence, which they are trying to put into place. I had these downloads, and they told me to go up there to 'trigger' and activate to get my family off the grid. I was shown the old grid was information control for energy and consciousness, which some call the morphogenetic grid and the consciousness mindset that was religion. So, information control for the mind and money for the heart which are both energy currency. The second one came in the early forties, earlier really, phased in with media. It isn't just a program of information. In earlier times you would emotionally connect to a leader who knew more than you; a religious leader or someone, and he would be your source of information. So, you would have information come through the emotional, energetic, relational connection to the authority. Then, they upped to the next level, which is the media. It's all energetic, so now it's sound, tones and harmonics – one percent of the information overlay.

We are taught only the one percent, not the how and why of the nature of things, so that we can't work out things for ourselves. To keep the people in their box (left brain compartment), which is the twisted, Saturnian energy that can't scale up through the emotions to the heart (the right brain, which some would say is the divine feminine). The next level is the TV and radio because there is more than the personality in it;

you now have a frequency you are connecting to. E said to me 'Technology isn't bad, it's just the information going through it. They have it on a lower frequency. If it was a higher frequency it could actually be used to activate people, but to keep it on a lower one it sinks. If you have it higher, as it is on a lot of planets, and the pyramids are a step, it would activate the people, and then you would have the right information going through. If you had phones on a different frequency it would connect you to your heart, not your head. Just by turning on the TV you are tuning into a frequency that is a lot lower than you already; it has you hooked.'

Secondly, the authority figures: their energetic relationship to your news person. Thirdly, in Alaska, an electronic global fence quarantine. Like an electronic dog fence, which they are trying to put into place, as they can't stop the energy coming in with our changing sun; with Sirius and the galactic center, which is causing the rise. So they keep the other two in place; these programs running. Then they do the money, the genetics, the chemtrails and the food, the water. Then they keep the laws in place, which constrict, and the invisible electronic frequency fence globally, to put the system on lockdown, to add to what's already there. So, all these things are in place. I managed to get the understanding and break this, and also for my family.

I was told this is the current strategy; the current end time thing. It is an energetic war we are dealing with. It's a frequency war; a consciousness war, and because they can't stop the awakening, they are trying to seal it. E was basically talking about targeted individuals and energy weapons. It's like a roaming AI supercomputer to see where people's scalar waves are at: their brainwaves. When you go unconscious it tracks that automatically and makes up a profile of who you are, where you are and your history. I prefer to talk about the better stuff."

M: "But we need to know. If people are informed, then they can understand when they are feeling certain things. Certain people feel targeted and feel they can't function anymore, or get so frightened they shut down. It's great that E recognizes it and transcends it. I was interested in the information about the water."

Father: "E was speaking about water too, to purify it then energize it. He said that if they do this and drink it, it will help them in this process. Water can help a person, as water is multidimensional. It scales the dimensions and gets you to a place where you can go further. We were right by the pyramids but E said, 'This is great, but you know it's about the water, Dad; that's the power,' and he started as it came out of him, and triggered and came up, and how the water is the power device behind it. How it's underground and in the air, but it's multidimensional and so are we. We need pure water. The most important element in a 3D level is the water; clean and enriched water. E said that in space there is water, like an energy current; like an ocean.

What helped me was to see all cultures, and one analogy is that people are given one version of the foot; they don't know there are many versions out there."

Note: The concepts discussed here are about complex, advanced technologies, and the awareness of groups of individuals and covert organizations on this planet, who are creating a truth embargo. Black budgets are created to orchestrate these covert agendas. This is controversial information and unfortunately due to the nature of these organizations, the only access the public has to this data is via whistleblower testimony by those who have participated in these secret projects.

A number of whistleblowers have come forward, about being trained as children to use their advanced abilities and travel via jump rooms: advanced technologies which allow them to visit the Moon and Mars, which suggest there are bases located there. I cannot cover this material in depth, but suggest those interested can look further into it. However, what is fascinating, is that these are very young children who appear to know about this information and can speak about these complex subjects and covert agendas.

For readers interested, visual data in the form of photographs and video of what appears to be bases on both the Moon and Mars are very compelling. Many of these images show huge structures and bases on both the Moon and Mars, and images of present habitation.

Recommended: *Moon Rising*. Documentary by Jose Escamilla.

Ref: Project Pegasus: Mars is Inhabited

Andrew Basiago

The time-space age has begun

Andrew D. Basiago, J.D., M.C.R.P.

A team leader of Project Pegasus, he is an American lawyer, writer, chrononaut, and twenty-first-century visionary.

Andy served in Project Pegasus at the dawn of the Time-Space Age and was one of humanity's early Mars explorers.

His Truth Campaign about time travel and life on Mars is based on direct, personal experience serving on two US defense projects.

In the late 1960s and early 1970s, Andy was a child participant in Project Pegasus, which was the US time-space exploration program at the time of the emergence of time travel in the US defense-technical community. He was called back into government service in the early 1980s, when he made numerous visits to Mars, after being tapped to join the CIA's Mars jump room program.

For over a decade, Andy has investigated his secret project experiences, on a quest to prove them and communicate them to others. He is a prominent figure in the Truth Movement, leading a campaign to lobby the US government to disclose such truths as the fact that the US has achieved 'quantum access' to past and future events and has used time travel to place a secret US presence on Mars.

Andrew was identified in early childhood as an Indigo child with special abilities, including the ability to use his mind to levitate small objects and to perform telepathy by reading the minds of others.

Past member of Mensa, the high IQ society, he has five degrees, including a BA in History from the University of California at Los Angeles (UCLA) and a Master of Philosophy from the University of Cambridge.

His paper *The Discovery of Life on Mars*, published in 2008, was the first work to prove that Mars is an inhabited planet, and also the first work ever published on Earth to contain images of humanoid beings on another planet. Since Andrew Basiago has shared his experiences, several others have shared publicly their experiences in this project.

Chapter Nine

THE MISSION!

Part One

"I built Interstellar Craft in my past life on Mars."

Zachariah, USA – 16 years old.

Childhood

Zachariah communicated with me after he saw a filmed hypnotic regression I facilitated on YouTube. Zac told me that he did not feel comfortable communicating with someone in the US. This led to a number of conversations over several months on Skype. I have put the conversations in sequence in four parts, as his sharing over the months unfolded. Zac has been extremely open about his experiences and the difficulties he experienced due to the judgment he endured from those around him. Zac explained how this judgment became so intolerable for him at one point, he almost gave up and shut down, and attempted to deny this heightened awareness. However, when he tried perceiving his experiences through a 3D reality he became so depressed that he contemplated suicide at the tender age of ten.

Note: Sadly this option has also been considered by others who have felt the same as Zac; despairing children and adults who have their experiences judged and denied as a reality.

In this chapter, Zac shares past-life recall in some detail, as well as his understanding of his star origins, the cosmic intelligences he is aware of, his spiritual philosophy and how he understands his multidimensional reality, psychic phenomenon he has experienced, what he understands of the Truth embargo, his Earth mission and the future of humanity.

Note: All conversations have parental consent.

Childhood Encounters

The first Skype conversation

Z: "When I saw the hypnotic regression, I felt I needed to talk to you. When I was a young child I always knew I had an important purpose in this world, I didn't know what. I always talked to beings, I could see auras and I would always run into things in a different dimension. My mum couldn't see them, but I could."

M: "What age did you have this kind of awareness, and was it natural to you?"

Z: "It has always been natural seeing other beings, telekinesis, and spirituality. I recall it was between the ages of two and seven years old that I went up on the ships and I spoke to beings and then I forgot. It was a type of amnesia, and I started remembering again around nine."

M: "So it was going on but you were not consciously aware of it until you were nine?"

Z: "Right."

M: "Did you talk to your mum about what you were seeing and experiencing?"

Z: "My mum would ask me how this happened. My window would open itself in the middle of the night and I would go for walks, and I would tell her I went up in the sky – my friends took me – or I would speak a different language to her, which she never understood. But she used to see spirits herself, so she kind of understood."

M: "So she was open to it,; you didn't have difficulty explaining it to her?"

Z: "Yes, she is open to it but she is scared because she doesn't want me talking about it to the wrong people. Anything could happen."

M: "So she is concerned who you connect with in case this is detrimental to you?"

Z: "Yes."

M: "Is your mum aware and okay with you communicating with me? It's really important she knows what's going on."

Z: "Yes she does, and she knows. She's okay with it."

M: "Okay, that's good. If she has any questions on my perspective let me know. When you say you communicate with a number of different 'intelligences,' you sound as if you are very connected to them. Which have you a particular affinity to? Those who support you?"

Z: "Yes, the Pleiadians and the Arcturians, those two; it's really tied between them. It is because I was both of them numerous times. I incarnated as Arcturian and Pleiadian an equal number of times. They feel like family to me, I guess."

M: "In terms of supporting you, do you have connections in the Pleiadian and Arcturian network that support and protect you and give you information? Is that how it works for you?"

Z: "Yes."

The Mission

M: "You said you needed to connect with me because of what you feel strongly is your mission on this planet – can you tell me more?"

Z: "My mission is to connect with all the other starseeds and through you who already talks to starseeds. I think I could connect to more of them with their acknowledged permission."

M: "What you would like to do is make yourself more available to other starseeds?"

Z: "Yes."

M: "Apart from connecting with them, is it also to share your collective understanding of your role here and what you are meant to be doing?"

Z: "Yes, that is to share my experiences and gather the information of their experiences and the others for mutual understanding."

M: "Do you have a sense of yourself and what your skills are?"

Z: "Yes I am a Light Warrior. I don't know if you heard of that term."

M: "Yes."

Z: "In a past life, I battled on the Light side, so to speak. I agreed to come into this life to help the planet ascend; to awaken the sleeping ones; to provide peace and spread love to the Earth. Not only that, I was an engineer in a past life. In this life, I am to build these technologies and help the Earth with more advanced, more clean technology."

M: "Can you tell me a little bit about how you understand that?"

Z: "I use magnetism. I don't use any fossil fuels. A lot of crystals in the technology are telepathically based; it's spiritually based. It's technology anybody can use and there are no harmful emissions."

M: "So it's a combination of those things you have just mentioned."

Z: "Yes, I use mainly AC currents, alternating magnetic fields to create a current within whatever I am powering."

M: "Have you put any of this together yet?"

Z: "I have tested some of my devices but not most because I don't have the money and I don't have the finances."

M: "So, really what's hampering you are the financial constraints?"

Z: "Yes."

M: "What will this technology help to correct?"

Z: "Pollution. It's a step to getting rid of fossil fuels and transportation. I have actually developed teleportation technology and spacecraft. I have been designing space ships for planet to planet travel, planet to star travel. It's to bring Earth into the space age."

M: "Is this technology what you have been given when you were being taught on the craft or downloaded? How do you get the information?"

Z: "I designed it myself. It's all my technology. The extraterrestrials don't actually give me technology – they help me remember what I built in past lives."

Past Life Expertise in Technologies

M: "So this is a past life ability?"

Z: "Yes."

M: "So you are basically recalling this information that was from that timeline?"

Z: "Yes."

M: "Have you written it all down?"

Z: "I haven't written down how to remember it, but I have written down all the technology. When it comes to me, I write it down."

M: "So you have written down the designs and this kind of thing?"

Z: "Yes, the theories behind them and everything."

M: "The reason I am asking is so we could provide the scientific backup to understand what you are saying re free energy. Are the people able to access the data and information?"

Z: "That's been what I have been waiting for my whole life; to talk to someone who can understand what I am saying."

M: "Yes, I understand – the children who are writing scripts and some of these languages."

Z: "Yes, this was how I was when I was younger. I used to talk about the future and finish my mother's sentences; see balls of light. I could do all of that stuff, but I had no one to talk to about it."

M: "When did you realize you were different to other children? What age were you?"

I'm an 'Indigo' Child

Z: "When I started public school at six years old, I realized not everyone had experiences like me. I would go to school and want to tell people how I went to another planet and no one would get that, so it really started when I started hanging out with other children."

M: "It's interesting you say you went to another planet and couldn't talk openly about this."

Z: "When I was seven years old I used to tell my mum I was an Indigo child and I am here to change the planet and I have a higher purpose, and I never knew anything about this and I just knew it was true somehow."

M: "What was your mum's response to this kind of information? How did she react to that?"

My Mom 'Knew' I Was Here for a Higher Purpose

Z: "My mom always used to say, 'Yes, I know you are here for a higher purpose; somebody told me when you were younger.' My mum used to have voices in her head tell her 'Your son is destined for greatness; your son is different from the rest. Your son is going to have a biblical name'."

M: "With your mum, did she ever know who these voices were or give them a name?"

Z: "No. I actually asked my mum that, but she just said she heard voices."

M: "Maybe she was too frightened?"

Z: "Yes, that's what I think."

M: "With your awareness, do you get a sense of who your mum was interacting with?"

Z: "Yeah. I think she might have been interacting with the Pleiadians, as they are the ones that have interacted with me the most. I mean I do interact with the Martians and the Grays on occasion, but the Pleiadians are the ones that brought me to the planet and brought me back."

Mars – The Untold Past and the Many Species of Non-Human Intelligences

M: "I would be very interested in the Martians, are they still operating?"

Z: "Yes, they have bases underground, not many – there are some in our dimension underground. They like to 'screw' with the (Mars) rovers; they do this all the time. They think they are funny and primitive."

M: "With the Grays, what's your understanding? I receive so many different stories. Some say they are really loving and some they are really scary, and I am told there are many different species and types of Gray, so what's your understanding?"

Z: "Yes, there are so many different types it's not funny. I can't even calculate the number of species there are because they exist in so many different dimensions. The Grays that interact with Earth on a regular basis, are not benevolent or malevolent – they really do not care about what happens to Earth. They do help out some species and some people like me they have aided. They abducted me and poked me with needles. Other times they wouldn't; they would give me information. Depends on what they want to do, you know? They are a very scientifically-minded race. They have emotions but they suppress them; they don't like emotions. It's part of what happened because of the Council of Nine, if you have heard of them."

M: "Yes."

Z: "The Council of Nine are part of the Galactic Federation of Light and actually forced the Grays themselves (called the Artuvians) at one point to genetically manipulate themselves because the Grays took a Pleiadian warship and blew up Mars. The whole entire Martian race. So that's why they don't have many emotions. That's why they seem robotic and not caring about anything, and that's why they have no genitalia because they were mutated. Some Grays do have genitalia though. It's a rare occurrence, but it does happen.

M: "I was told there were over one hundred and sixty-five species of Gray."

Z: "Probably more than that."

M: "I also heard they were basically self-serving, neither good nor bad, but they have their own agenda."

Z: "Yes, they don't honestly care either way."

M: "The Council of Nine was mentioned in the book *The Only Planet of Choice*. Star Trek was based on that."

Author Phyllis Schlemmer, psychic, medium and astrologer – and these were channellings from deep space and the Council of Nine.

Z: "Star Trek was very close to what happened at one point, but actually, believe it or not, what is way closer is Star Wars. It is so close to humanity's future, it's not funny. I am baffled by how close it is. Yes, everyone is capable of this; just the amount someone is limited – and we are all limited by what we limit ourselves with."

M: "So you mean we are limited to what we believe and that reflects our reality."

Z: "Yes."

M: "Re the Council of Nine, why do you think they are connecting with you?"

Z: "I was a member of the Council of Nine. I wasn't a high member at this time. I was an Artuvian. I was an advisor to the king. His name was Armtek and he was a member of the Council of Nine because he was king of the Artuvians, and every king was a member of the Council of Nine in this Galaxy. The Artuvians came from a separate Galaxy, from a different dimension, but they do exist in this Galaxy now; they populated a certain planet. Some Artuvians still exist. I lived through it. I lived through the destruction of Mars. I lived through the Great War that happened. There was a lot of death."

M: "So the Great War is what happened on Mars?"

Z: "Yes, that's what began the Great War. Earth was involved in the Great War; that's why the Renaissance paintings have ships in the sky and explosions, and Earth was a battleground for some time."

M: "What was behind the Great War itself?"

Z: "Well, it was possession of Earth. Earth is an experiment. Not only was it possession of Earth, it was possession of the Council of Nine and who was going to have control over it. It was a power battle between the Pleiadians, the Artuvians, the Grays, the Martians; some of Earth civilizations were also involved in different dimensions, and a Reptilian race. They wanted to enslave humanity and use us to mine gold and minerals for them, mainly copper and gold. It was about control between the Reptilians and the Pleiadians. The Pleiadians wanted to free Earth, the Reptilians said no. The Reptilians inevitably won and that's who is in control of Earth right now, which is why they are trying to manipulate our governments. That is why the Pleiadians are trying to help us free ourselves. The stronger we get spiritually the weaker we make the Reptilians."

M: "In terms of your understanding, the Reptilians are in control of this planet, but the Pleiadians are supporting humanity to become spiritually empowered so that they can get rid of the Reptilians. Is that correct?"

Z: "Yes, not only the Pleiadians but many, many races."

M: "Do you have an understanding of where the status quo is at the moment? Do you have a sense of where this is heading; a future timeline for Earth?"

Z: "This is hard to decide, the future because humans are a collective and they will move into whatever future they so choose. Right now, there is a heavy momentum to a war. Not just between countries; I mean a global catastrophe war and a bunch of revolutions, primarily in the UK and the USA. Revolutions against governments. Spiritual awakening; spiritual revolutions. They are supposed to happen but I cannot say for sure they will, as future is not set in stone."

Note: This is a transcript of the first conversation with Zachariah and his understanding of a past timeline when he was part of some Mars catastrophe. Synchronously, shortly after this conversation, an article appeared in Nexus Magazine: *Remote Viewing Ancient Aliens on Mars* (Vol 21, No 2, Page 57). Remote viewing information when the target is Mars, that Mars suffered a catastrophic event, and there was life on Mars etc.

A Russian boy, Boriska, also recalled a past life on Mars and a catastrophic war, which destroyed its atmosphere, and that there are still beings under the surface of Mars and, as Zac mentions, new children being born now.

Boriska Recalls a Past Life on Mars

"Boriska, born in Volgograd Russia, demonstrated high intelligence even as a baby. He spoke in sentences at eight months old. Before he was three years old he began to name all the planets of the solar system, names and numbers of the galaxies, which shocked his mother, Nadezhda, a dermatologist, and his father, a retired officer.

Boriska became a local celebrity because of his intelligence and how much he knew about extraterrestrial civilizations, including an ancient race of humans nine-meters tall called Lemurians. He also showed abilities of precognition (awareness of future events).

Boriska was just seven years old and shared what he knew about Mars' civilizations and his past life on Mars. He described huge cities on Mars, and his regular trips to Earth, and a country called Lemuria, with which they traded.

Boriska stated, "I remember that time when I was fourteen or fifteen years old. The Martians were waging war all the time, so I would participate in air-raids. We could travel in time and space, traveling in round space ships, but would observe life on Earth on triangular space ships. Martian spaceships are very complicated; they are layered. He drew an oval object and stated that it consisted of six layers: twenty-five percent outer layer of durable metal, thirty percent of something similar to rubber, another thirty percent metal and four percent magnetic layer – and when the magnetic layer was charged it could fly anywhere in the Universe.

Boriska was asked if there was life on Mars now. Boriska replied that there was, but the planet lost its atmosphere many years ago due to a global catastrophe. The Martians live underground and breathe Carbonic gas. They dislike air because it causes aging. They are taller than seven meters and have incredible abilities.

Boriska said he knew of phenomenal children: special ones he called 'Indigos', and he said the planet's rebirth is approaching and we need a different mentality. Indigos are being born all over the globe, especially in the last twenty years, and he is one of them and they are on a mission to help change our planet. Boriska was asked how he knew all of this and replied that it was inside him.

Professor Vladislav Lugovenko at the Russian Academy of Sciences tested Boriska – stated that Boriska was remarkable and one of the new children he has researched being born all over the globe.

"Boriska is one of them. Apparently, Indigo children have a special mission on our planet. Many of them have amended DNA spirals, which give them an incredibly strong immune system which can even defeat AIDS. I have met such children in China, India, and Vietnam and am certain they will change the future of our civilization."

3rd Dec 2004. Reproduced from the Russian News *Pravda*. http://english.pravda.ru/science 2004, (Translated by Anna Ossipova). www.collective-evolution.com

The Awakening

M: "What I am noticing is many people waking up. A term people use, and it's surprising, as many are not into New Age terminology. Many are professionals such as lawyers, doctors etc., and understand what part they play in this Awakening. Is that how you understand it?"

Z: "Yes. I am to be a leader of one of the great awakenings. That's why I have been gifted with all the information I have – although there are people out there that are more awakened than I am."

M: "In terms of the next few years, do you have a sense of your major role?"

Z: "Yes, I feel the next few years are going to be important for me. I am going to be attracting a lot of new people and giving a lot of advice, but I am obviously going to be remembering a lot more. I feel I am going to be speaking to scientists about two of my inventions."

M: "Can I share this information?"

Z: "I have no limits because I am going to tell the world anyway."

Questioning the Experiences: Am I Sane?

Suicidal at ten years old!

M: "Regarding the multidimensional nature of your experiences, did you ever question your experiences?"

Z: "Yes I did. I thought I was insane because I could see something when no one else did! Was I insane? Was it actually happening? As I questioned, then it caused me to go into deep depression. I didn't like that at all, so I said 'You know what: I am going to believe this because it makes me happy,' and that's what I have been doing and I haven't been depressed since."

Note: Zac elaborated on this statement in another conversation and said he tried to be 'normal' and just operate in what he called the 3D world, but by shutting himself down it caused such a deep depression he wanted to end his life. Zac decided to open up to his multidimensional self again because it supported him and helped him cope, although on another level it made him feel isolated from everyone who didn't understand.

M: "What age were you when you questioned your sanity?"

Z: "About ten. Mainly because I was questioned by an adult family member (not my mother). They said I was making things up; that I'm lying, hallucinating, stuff like that. I proved them wrong one day when I moved an object with thought and they were mind blown. It's interesting how we can have our stability shaken by other people's judgments. So yes, I always questioned! I always thought to myself 'Why does what is being said to me by other people make me feel so uncomfortable? Why should I care what they think?' I said to myself 'Wait, I don't. I am I, and I believe what I do. If they don't believe, then they are closed-minded'."

Pre-Birth Recall

Z: "I can remember being born and coming out of the womb. I remember being outside, standing by my mother as she was giving birth to me, then I went into the body and remember coming out of her."

M: "So you were watching during labor and then went into the physical container?"

Z: "Yes."

M: "What other memories and awareness do you have?"

Z: "I remember my first house. I remember everything. I don't know how to explain it. I have a holographic memory. I can remember where the couch was and the angle; where the TV was."

M: "So your memory was very accurate?"

Z: "Yes it is. I can remember whole conversations with people and remember it word for word. That's why my mum hates arguing with me."

M: "Re earlier years under five, what sticks out to you?"

Space School, and Meeting Up with Star Beings

Z: "What sticks out to me most is that I remember lying in my bed, sitting up in my bed and looking over at my closet. I shut the closet door with my mind somehow. I get out of my bed and look at my window. My window just flies open when I look at it. I don't even walk through the window. I phase through the wall and walk down my backyard and just fly into the sky – and this was all physical, not a dream."

M: "So it wasn't your astral body, it was your physical body?"

Z: "My physical body. My right hand was glowing a bright blue and my left hand was glowing white, like bright white. And I remember flying into the sky with an energy trail behind me, and into the ship with the Pleiadians, and they let me take control of the ship as they said that I knew how to fly it, and then we just took off into the sky."

M: "What kind of things did you do on the ship?"

Z: "We were only on the ship until we got to the planet. That was when the training began. While I was on the ship, though, I would have conversations with Arctuvasek; he was the pilot. He let me have the controls, as he said I had designed the ship in a past life, and I worked the controls. My friend, you will meet eventually, the only other 'new' child, so to speak. A crystal child was on the starship with the Pleiadians; she goes to school with me. We are astral twins. We were brought up together in the same ship. She would go into the other room, the meditation room, where this brilliant pink color would just surround the room. (Lost Skype transmission)…purple sand."

M: "Where was this?"

Z: "This was when we went off the ship onto the planet?"

M: "Was it familiar?"

Z: "It was familiar to me, but I can't put the name with English words."

M: "Something you recognized?"

Unique DNA

Z: "Yes. Tons of humans and Pleiadians living in harmony – not just Pleiadian, children too, from Earth. They would come on different ships and meet up in the center. M and me were picked out, you could say, with a crowd of a hundred kids. I was always picked out and taken to the front. I don't know, but I was told we had a special DNA, unique in some way."

M: "Have you any sense of what that uniqueness is, or how you understand it?"

Z: "I know but I don't like telling people because I don't like to feel special. I like to feel we are equal in everything and when I tell people, I can see from their energy that they start to think of me as special. I don't like that."

Note: Lost Skype transmission. This happens many times: computer or the Internet plays up because of the energy in the room or those with high energy.

Z: "Sorry; this could be because my energy became really high when I was talking."

M: "On this planet, you were taken with a number of children. What was the purpose of taking you there?"

Z: "To train us to prepare us for the great Awakening is what they called it."

M: "When you said you did training on the craft, was this the same kind of training or something different?"

Z: "Same training."

Learning to be Human and Manipulation of Matter!

M: "What were you taught on the craft or the planet?"

Z: "I was taught how to live among humans. It was new to us, confusing, like eating. I was confused with having to eat when I was younger. I didn't understand it. I didn't understand being mean (unkind) to someone; I used to be very sensitive to that. They used to teach us how to cope with humans I guess, and how to use our abilities. We are really powerful and I can remember picking up a Pleiadian and spinning them in the air because I thought it was funny, but putting him down gently, though."

M: "So it's manipulation of matter?"

Z: "Yes. I can speed up or slow down atoms, generate magnetic fields from my hands and change temperature – which is the speeding up and slowing down of the atoms."

M: "You mentioned telepathy and being respectful of people's privacy."

Z: "Yes."

M: "What else can you control?"

Z: "Other beings. For example, if there is a being in my room and I don't want it there, I can control it and tell it to go and it's gone. I can astral project."

Non-Human Forms

M: "What else are you like in your nonhuman form?"

Z: "I stand between fifteen to seventeen feet tall on average. I can choose my form and whatever height I wish. I am very muscular. I have wings, broad cybernetic wings, dark black eyes like a Gray's, but not really. My head is elongated in the back; normally I have four fingers on one hand and five on the other. I have a picture of my soul."

M: "What color is the skin?"

Z: "White, it emits white light. It's so white it's almost blue, if that makes sense?"

M: "Do you mean luminescent?"

Z: "Yes."

M: "So that is what your form is when you are not in a container?"

Z: "Yes, when I am not in a physical body – a vessel so to speak."

M: "Why that form you have chosen for your essence?"

ET Soul

Z: "When I had an Artuvian soul, they have a drive or passion to be perfect: their genes to be perfect and their spirit to be perfect."

M: "Any other abilities you can tell me about?"

Z: "To fly. I could do it when younger. Now I can shift a little but it's much harder, but the higher the dimensions, the stronger my abilities get. Right now I could throw a being into another dimension, or I can move them out of my way or whatever I want with them."

M: "Basically, you can manipulate any being that comes into your reality; choose where you want them to be. Is that correct?"

Z: "Yes. I could do whatever I want with them basically. If I want to stretch them, I can stretch them. If I want to compress them, I can compress them. I can make them seem a different color; whatever I want I guess."

M: "Almost like you can have them in any form you so choose?"

Z: "Yes, but I let them appear as they want. I don't put control over them."

M: "What else are you able to do?"

Channeling Beings and the Martian Language

Z: "I can channel beings. I can heal. I am a pretty good healer – helped my mum when she burned herself. I can speak the light language, two versions of the light language."

M: "I would love to hear it?"

Z: "I also can speak Martian, ancient Martian language."

M: "Yes, but I would also like a recording."

Note: Zac speaks the language to me and translates.
"I said 'How are you and how goes things with the New Age children?' – loosely translated."

M: "Can you write Martian?"

Z: "I have difficulty but my friend can; she is a Martian Hybrid. She lives across the street from me, actually. When she is at my house, I will get her to do this for you. How I connect with the Martian because my friend is a Martian hybrid. Martians are a very closed race, they don't talk if they don't need to."

Other Species: Felines and Mantids

M: "What do you understand of the Felines and the Lion Beings?"

Z: "The Sirians, they are from higher dimensions. They are a very spiritual race. I have only spoken to them a couple of times. They have said what I already know: spread love and awaken as many people as you can. They are very peaceful and have a powerful energy to them."

Z: "My body sometimes pulsates white and I am very cold, my mother said it's like my hands are very white, like they have been in a refrigerator for hours; my hands as cold as ice."

M: "I know that the Starseeds seem to have a lower blood pressure, high hearing sensitivity. Do you get a sense of why you operate at a lower temperature? Is it due to your origins do you think?"

Z: "The Arcturians say that it's due to the fact that I vibrate at such a high rate that I shift through the higher dimensions physically, so that's why my skin gets white and my body actually gets so cold."

M: "Many appear a lot younger than their physical age – look ten years younger than their age."

Z: "They say I look about eleven years old."

Note: Zac is sixteen in this conversation.

M: "Do you know about the Mantids?"

Z: "The Insectoids? I have never come across them, but I can't say anything about them."

M: "Some have light green frequency and some purple frequency, say they are very ancient."

Z: "Sounds like the Martians. The purple frequency. My brother is a Star Child as well. He doesn't remember as much, I am trying to help him with that. But when he looks at me he says I have like a purple fire around my body; he's not the only one. My girlfriend and everyone I talk to say it's like purple fire energy, so it's funny that you mention that."

M: "We know that they can appear in any form anyway. More what they are under standing; the frequency of that form. And not judge the book by its cover."

Z: "A lot of people take what they learn from other people, influence what they are seeing, but you need to trust yourself as only you truly know."

The New Earth

M: "In terms of the children talking about the New Earth, what is your understanding of that?"

Z: "My understanding: there is a new Earth but it's not necessarily new, we are just moving into a new vibration, but to us it is new. It's been there for a long time. It is waiting for our arrival. Gaia is already at the destination she wishes to be; she is waiting for us to move with her."

M: "Gaia is moving into another frequency or another dimension; how do you explain that?"

Z: "She is moving into a higher frequency, a collection of similar frequencies. That's all we are in actuality is a collection of vibrations."

M: "So what the children are really saying is that when we are awakened we will be able to move more with Gaia to this other plane of awareness and reality."

Z: "Yes, but we are not necessarily moving with her, just moving space around us to get to her because she is in one position and we are in another position which exists in the same space."

M: "Can you tell me re the last few years how things have opened up for you? You said that when you were nine or ten you got more conscious awareness. What was that like?"

Z: "Scary, getting all this new information and not knowing what to do with it, it was like sensory overload. I slowly worked through it, learning to be patient and let things come to me and instead of looking for the answers. It was really scary at first and now it's very peaceful. I look at the world from a whole new level. I don't walk down the street without saying thank you to every blade of grass."

M: "Did you tell your mum about this?"

Z: "Yes, I told my mum almost everything to help her understand it. As well, I tried to explain it to her the best I can but it's hard."

M: "How do you understand your siblings?"

The Siblings – How Do You Understand Them?

Z: "My brother is ten years old and my sisters are teenagers. He is still asleep. He is interested in Aliens and he can see auras. One day I had a Gray meditating next to me on my bed. My brother walks in and says 'OMG Zac, there is an alien sitting on your bed.' I said 'Can you see it?' and he said 'Yeah. Creepy – is he not going to eat me?'"

M: "So he's not become fully awake in the way you have?"

Z: "No he hasn't, but he's on track. I have got to be patient, and I have to let him do his own thing before I can help him with anything?"

M: "What about your sisters, have they abilities or are they more in the human stream?"

Z: "They are more into 3D; they are not into this. When they see me meditating or channeling they get confused and kind of scared."

M: "Is there anything else you feel you need to tell me?"

Z: "No, but I have a question. I haven't met anyone else with this ability, so I wondered if you have. I can change my eye color, and not only can I change it to normal colors, I can change them to purple, red and yellow. When I meditate my eyes get a yellow ring around the pupil."

M: "I have heard of this with some, and it seems during a Contact encounter the eye color has changed. I don't know the reason for this as yet."

Z: "I meditate and I do something that involves thinking, and my friends will say, 'OMG, your eyes are a different color'."

M: "Perhaps, because you are changing your frequency, so it changes the eye color?"

Z: "That's possible. I have never thought of it that way. Yeah!"

M: "That's what I would like to know: why the eye color changes in different states. Maybe what you are tapping into in terms of your origins, more of your greater self. Does that resonate?"

Z: "Yes. Actually, I am Yayel in the physical body. I have Yayel DNA. Yayel told me when I meditate my eyes turn yellow because of them and I am activating part of their DNA. But that doesn't explain the other colors. When I get angry, my eyes turn red. When I get calm and peaceful and in a loving mode, my eyes turn purple. The yellow is explained I guess, not everything else."

M: "It would be interesting to know why you shift energetically into that frequency. The whole thing that's funny about that is that anger has always been seen as red. Anger has always had that red connotation."

Z: "Well red is a low vibratory state, low vibratory color, maybe that's why because anger, hatred, jealousy – they are all low vibratory emotions. My girlfriend once said I had cat eyes."

M: "Have you a connection to the Felines or Lion Beings?"

Z: "I know I am connected to the Sirians, a different version of the Sirians, not the animal-looking ones. I might be. I would need to look into it. I thought it was because of my Pleiadian origins. The Pleiadians tend to have more feline-looking eyeballs than other species. I was speaking to someone on Facebook and I was saying how I have an Arcturian origin. She looked at the picture and said 'You are definitely Arcturian.' I said 'How can you tell?' and she said 'It's your eyes. You look like you have dragon eyes.' A lot of people have been fascinated with my eyes."

M: "It's interesting that you put the Arcturian with the dragon. Thank you for sharing, and it gives me understanding, and so many feel like you. They find it so hard on this planet and they don't understand what's going on; don't like an environment that doesn't make any sense to them, and it's very difficult."

Z: "Exactly. I resonate with all of that and that's what I say – I just want to go home."

Part Two

Second Interview Zachariah – Oct 2014.
Transcribed from conversation.
10th Feb. 2014.

Psychic Attacks

Individuals may sometimes feel under some form of psychic attack, targeted by individual entities or by a covert human organization.

Z: "I get protection and guidance in my meditations. Once, I was being psychically attacked by one of my friends. I woke up from a sleep paralysis and was levitating a couple of inches above my bed. I knew it wasn't astral projection because I know the difference. I looked down at my feet and there were these two Blue Beings standing at the edge of my bed, and their hands were around my ankles. From my toes up to my lower thigh muscles, it was all blue and glowing. One of the Angelic Beings tapped me on my third eye and this rainbow vortex opened in front of me, and I shot through it. I dropped and then woke up, and I was in my room and everything was fine.

The next day I saw a painted 'W' on my floor, and I can prove it to you, as I have not moved it. I learned that 'W' stands for 'Mind, Body, and Spirit.' The trinity between them. Right next to the W was burned a hoof print in the floor. Ever since then I am seeing the numbers 333 or 833, which stands for the Ascended Masters, and some intuitives tell me I am somehow connected to the Ascended Masters. I feel strongly that my purpose is to heal and guide others. I have found I am really good at it. Whenever I go to school little kids, they come up to me and tell me stories about what they see and what they hear. Children just feel comfortable around me. I seem to have this way of explaining things. I don't know what it is."

Teaching Other Starseeds

Z: "Recently, I have been teaching a twelve-year-old how to manipulate the wind; how to tune into the Matrix and tune into the speed of the wind. Just to tap into the mode of tapping into her inner self – Inner Goddess. I have been teaching myself, Tai Chi, Reiki and Reiki Massage, Chi Gong, teaching Yoga, and myself to meditate. My friends call me a Ninja because I seem to have reflexes I was born with. I know martial arts I have never studied. I have memories of being a Shaolin Monk and people seem to be tuning into this with me."

M: "With the Psychic attack, what do you think this was about?"

Z: "My friend was jealous of me because he is awakened to a point where his ego took over, that he felt he was better than anyone else. He started to attack anyone who supersedes this. I began to get information he hadn't, so he would attack me in my dreams to get me afraid. He had a lot of Reptilian attachments I have seen on him. Since he is no longer in my life, the psychic attacks have stopped."

M: "Do you feel you were assisted with that psychic attack?

Z: "No, I don't think they assisted me with the attack. I believe that experience activated me so I could deal with it on my own. My guides have always told me this life is mine. They are not here to interfere with anything; it is my free will. They are only here to guide me unless I become lost, or I need reassurance. Again, all your spiritual guides are fractals of your consciousness from different planes of perspective. I realize the guides are really me. I perceive things differently. So I know I am helping myself."

M: "So, aspects of you, you have created?"

Z: "Yes."

M: "So, do you feel that your role is as support, or more than this?"

I'm an Activator

Z: "Yes, I am an activator. I am awakened and I am here to help others awaken. I have my own path. I think I am just supposed to walk the Earth and meet people, explain my story and my life and interest them to introspect, to seek their inner self. I feel like my life itself is my message. Such as the twelve-year-old girl I am helping with telekinesis, for example, she says whenever I am near her things just happen – and there is a sense of calm near me. I think I am here to activate others. Help them see their true self."

M: "So your frequency accelerates or expands the consciousness of the other person? So you are here to raise the frequency of those you interact with who choose to be awakened?"

Z: "Yes."

M: "How do you view yourself? I recall you told me you could build interstellar craft because in a past life you did this and can recall it?"

Note: Zac recovers a drawing to illustrate his response and now gets a drawing he did of an image he drew of his higher-dimensional self during meditation.

M: "How do you understand this aspect of yourself?"

Z: "This aspect of myself exists in a different dimensional plane. It is me. I am it. We are perceived differently due to our difference in vibration. It is it/he/she is alive. Biological. He can come down to Earth and talk to me if he wishes but doesn't because he exists as a much higher plane of perspective. He is an engineer. Remember, I told you about a past life where I built interstellar craft? That's the life I am talking about. It is a past life, but everything co-exists all at the same time. So he is still alive. He is an Arctuvian, from the Sirius star system or the Orion Belt."

"Everyone My Whole Life has told me that I am Different."

M: "When did you realize you were different from those around you?"

Z: "When I was nine years old. I used to go to school and I would see attachments – like spirits, like people. Grandmother for example. I would see their grandmother standing over them. Then, as my third eye began to open more, I began to see auras. I began to hear voices in my head. Then I began to feel people's emotion. It became hard for me to go to school because I would take on other people's emotions. I would break down and cry for no reason. Everyone my whole life has told me that I am different. But they feel comfortable around me and can trust me. I don't know why, but when people are around me they just open up. For a time I didn't understand it, but I do now.

At ten to eleven years I started getting dreams of the Pleiadians coming to me more often. They came to me when I was between three to seven years old. But then they stopped, it was to protect me. They came back after I was nine years. I would have dreams and they would teach me all this stuff about light-working, how to channel energy and how to manipulate the matrix, how to move objects, how to manipulate people's thoughts if they get angry at me."

Note: Part 3-4 of conversations with Zac continues in Chapter Ten. Zac has more detail of his origins, information on Mars and its inhabitants, and the alleged human bases on Mars. His understanding of the nature of Reality and Cosmic Intelligences.

Chapter Ten

"I'M A HYBRID"

Part Three

Past Life Recall – Mars

In this chapter, I continue my Skype dialogue with Zac from Chapter Nine, as he shares more of his understanding of hybrids and because he is told he is one. Zac also shares more of his understanding of his past life on Mars, the Martians, the qualities of soul, God and beliefs, and how beliefs shape human experience, the DNA upgrades and his understanding of the New Human.

M: "Why were the Pleiadians communicating with you?"

Z: "The Pleiadians Contacted me because they said I am a hybrid. I have DNA within me that is not completely human and so they have to train me because in one of my past lives I was a Pleiadian light worker – part of the Council of Nine, and they said they have to train me as part of my mission on Earth. After the Pleiadians introduced themselves, the Sirians introduced themselves and told me about a past life as a leading engineer for them, which had to do with the Great War between the Martians and the Pleiadians."

M: "What form do the Martians take?"

Z: "The Martians, from what I have observed, are 'insectoid-like.' It has an exoskeleton on the outside but meat or fiber, but it's hard like an exoskeleton. They have no skin from what I have seen, and deep-set eyes, and their teeth are like spikes that come out of their mouth."

M: "So they are not the same as the Manta or Mantid but a different species?"

Z: "Yeah, the Martians came as a hybridization between the Sirians and Lemurians. The Lemurians set up bases on Mars between the pyramid complex on Mars and the pyramid complex on Earth, to transport goods back and forth. So, resource trade, communication and geo-harmonic power; they powered their technology from the core from planets. So the Lemurians went to Mars as a colonized base. They were farming and creating an ecosystem there. But the Sirians came in and because they couldn't conquer Earth at the time, they conquered Mars instead. So they hybridized them, so there were Lemurians species on Mars for war, then they used the Martians to attack the Lemurians on Earth because the Sirians couldn't do it directly because they had a long standing treaty that they couldn't interfere with Earth affairs."

M: "How were you involved?"

Z: "I was part of the Sirians. I was on Mars and Sirius at the same time this took place. I was an engineer for the Sirians. I designed their technology, their power systems, their multidimensional crafts. I was sent to Mars to woo over the Martian people and the appointed King that the Sirians had picked out. The Martians grew to be a huge industrialized species and segregated themselves into separate races. There were red Martians and white Martians, and those with a kind of greenish, offset-gray-teal, so the red Martians and teal-colored Martians tried to wipe out the white Martians because they were genetically superior, and they didn't want the white Martians to overtake the planet. After the race war that the Sirians had started, the civilization of the Martians collapsed on itself and that's when the Sirians took over, but they let the last white Martian be king. I was second in command. I was called Youseftos. I didn't agree with the King and was more peace loving and wanted a kind of Utopia, and wanted to unite the different empires as a triad. The Sirians didn't want that so I butted heads with the king, and I went down to the Southern hemisphere, to help start a more peaceful Martian civilization. I was murdered in my sleep. I had been in the process of designing a new power system, crystal-based, for the civilization I was trying to start.

At this time I discovered corruption within the Council of Nine, that the Reptilian Sirians had corrupted some of the Pleiadian representatives and Arkatu. He was a Pleiadian King of Era at the time. He was persuaded by the Reptilians that if he were to side with them, he would gain all power and become a ruler of the Galaxy. I found this out through my telepathic advances upon Arkatu. He wasn't as evolved as the Sirians at the time and they found out about it, so they murdered me in my sleep so I couldn't reveal the corruption."

Note/Ref: NASA footage has shown anomalies on Mars, which suggests there may have been ancient civilizations and evidence of a catastrophic event in the past.

Dr. John Brandenburg PhD, a plasma physicist, stated that life on Mars was eradicated by nuclear war by intelligent civilizations from ancient history and this was responsible for the coloration and composition. Martian soil points to a series of 'mixed-fission' explosions that led to nuclear fall-out on the planet.

General Stubblebine, retired US Major General, a Commanding General of the US

Army Intelligence and Security Command (INSCOM) said this about Mars:

"There are structures on the surface of Mars, structures underneath the surface of Mars. There are machines on the surface of Mars and machines under the surface of Mars. You can find out in detail, you can see what they are, where they are, who they are and a lot of detail about them."

UFOs and the National Security State: Chronology of a Cover-up, 1941-1973, by Richard M Dolan. Published by Richard Dolan Press.

Stubblebine was a proponent of the US Defense Intelligence Agency's Star Gate Project, a remote viewing project.

Ref: www.collective-evolution.com

Whistleblowers Corey Goode, Michael Relfe and Randy Kramer (aka Captain Kaye) have stated in the recent book *Insiders Reveal Secret Space Programs, and Extraterrestrial Alliances* by Michael Salla, Founder of the Exopolitics Institute, that our species has bases on Mars, and a secret space fleet called Solar Warden. This program has been mentioned by another whistleblower, Arthur Neumann, who claimed to have worked as a physicist at the Laurence Livermore Laboratories. Neumann stated there are secret bases on Mars built by our covert military agencies with the aid of other non-intelligences, and that we have a secret space fleet and 'jump gate ' technologies and were able to reach Mars as early as 1962. These bases were established in 1964 by American and Soviet teamwork with the aid of non-human intelligences.

Ref: *Insiders Reveal Secret Space Programs & Extraterrestrial Alliances.* Michael E. Salla PhD, 2015 (page 164).

Moving Into My Human Container at Five Years Old

Z: "During that time, I was preparing my body for this mission on Earth, and because I knew that by the time my body was prepared there would be enough time crossing over to the Earth time-stream in this era. I didn't get to finish my genetic coding, so I had one of my apprentices finish it in spirit. I visited him and then seeded into this world from my mother, and then, when I was around five years old, my soul came into the body. So between the time I was born and five years old it was just a vessel. There was nothing conscious in it."

M: "Why did you come in at five?"

Z: "At five, my human mother was starting to question what was going on; why my body was so spacey, and why I wasn't developing like the other kids because I could walk, talk, run and have conversations when I was eight months old and my mother was confused. She knew I was color-blind. She would take me outside and say, 'Look the grass is green,' and I would say, 'No, the grass is blue Mum," as if I was autistic in some way. I used to speak languages that she had never heard of, which I now know were the light languages of Lemurian and Pleiadian. She thought I was speaking complete gibberish. There was a period of three days where I told my mom I had beings come to me; they took me with them on their ships. She didn't believe me. So at five years old I came into the vessel and explained it to her."

M: "What was operating as essence or life force prior to you coming into your body; what consciousness was that?"

Z: "The body, the brain, but I was coming in and out. I wasn't permanently in my body until five."

Earth Power Structure

M: "What do you understand as the power structure on this planet now, as so many people are confused, wondering who is really running the show."

Z: "My belief is that it's a third party. My personal belief is that the main government system on this planet running the show is unified in a sense. The US and the British governments are working together secretly for one specific agenda and keeping this a secret from us. I believe a certain species is ruling over them. Even if the Queen of England is not conscious of it, there is a process controlling her thoughts and decisions. But most of them are conscious of this because it is in their bloodline."

M: "So there is a pyramid of the control system: British, US government, controlled by the Reptilians?"

Z: "Yes."

M: "Is that just one Reptilian species, or all Reptilian or just some of them?"

Z: "No just some. It's mainly the Kractovillians from the Orion region."

M: "Who is orchestrating them?"

Z: "I suppose you could say they are 'gods' so to speak. It's a consciousness they are 'tuning into.' They created over a thousand years of evolution. They work up to this supreme being they manifested themselves, and this being then took control of them, like drones."

M: "So with enough thought, you can manifest a 'god' to become a consciousness itself?"

Z: "Yes, it's how humanity is working. Like the Christians look up to a god. The God the Christians look up to is really self-perpetuating over thousands of years."

M: "So we create the form they are focusing on?"

Z: "Yes, that's what I am saying. It's an energy and essence because everything is energy, just like me and you. We are the same but are perceived differently due to our vibration."

M: "So the God many believe in, like the version of the old man which is supreme, is that God because we have believed in that form of a god? Is your understanding of God or the Source or Universal Consciousness: how do you understand this?"

Z: "My personal understanding is that God is everything. All that is – because all that is, is One. So when we speak of God, we speak of an essence that is higher than us. And since energy itself cannot be higher or lower, it is just separate frequencies. It's just how our limited materialistic brain perceives the quantum energy."

M: "So when you have greater understanding you no longer need a particular form, you honor the fact we are a collective essence."

Z: "Yes, and it is why, as I said earlier, my guides are just another version of me."

M: "So you have come in with a consciousness to assist. What exactly do you see as the big picture of what is going on now; how do you interpret it?"

Z: "I don't know what you mean by that. My goal is to reach one or two on this planet. If I can help only one or two ascend, that's fine. It doesn't need to be thousands of people. I don't need to destroy government and make a new one. I am not here for anything physical because I realize the physical plane is just an illusion. It is just a set of realities that we perceive because we wish to because it's an experience. I want my life to be my experience and to follow my heart and go with the flow, and who ever I come to meet, whomever soul I touch, so be it."

M: "So, it's more about you focusing on your soul journey, but the interesting thing with that, we know when we are following our heart and wanting to be of service. We are touching people on multiple levels. Many people feel we are heading for some kind of shift of awareness."

Z: "A great awakening."

M: "Yes, how do you interpret that?"

Z: "I feel that too, I feel we need to reach a critical mass point. When we were talking about the God thing earlier, humanity as a whole, and each human has a bio magnetic field around them and this magnetic field contains all their thoughts, emotions and energies, etc. And since each human is inter-connected to the next then his or her magnetic field is sharing information back and forth, which creates a collective consciousness around the planet. I believe this consciousness does not have enough positive energy at the moment to shift the vibration of Earth yet! But it's getting there, and when enough people awaken and realize their true potential and their true light within, that energy will shift to a more positive peaceful note because right now it's very negatively programmed; very dualistic: light and dark.

When Humans awaken to the fact that light and dark are the same, just different perspectives of one, I view the Earth itself will begin to pole flip, where the magnetic poles will cease to function. They will flip and activate again but during the pole flip, the Earth is going to shift tectonically. The plates underneath the Earth are going to move, continents are going to rise and fall, volcanoes are going to erupt. There will be complete chaos because in the Universe you cannot have new unless you destroy the old. And I believe chaos is the heart of the Universe and then you find harmony within the chaos, which is the yin and yang sign."

M: "So you feel we will need some form of destruction and chaos before we can begin reconstruction, balance and harmonize our reality."

Z: "Yes because as I understand it, if we try to move ahead in our ascension and evolution we will be tainted, in a way, if we don't because we will be tainted in a way because of our past and what we don't let go of. We need to get rid of the past, accept it for what it is, realize in a blunt manner, we screwed up, and then begin anew, but we can't begin anew unless we let go of the past, and all the things we have done – all that karma that we have built up."

The New Earth – The Reality Dysfunction

M: "So with this in mind, how does that fit with what some call the New Earth. Even the children are speaking about going to a New Earth. How would you understand this?"

Z: "I used to tell my mom the same thing. When I was between the ages of four and nine I said to her, 'Mom, I am here to help with the New Earth.' I'm an Indigo child. I am here for a purpose, but these are just labels. And regarding the New Earth – it's not new, it's already here, we just have to change our perception from our brains to our hearts. Once we follow our hearts then the Earth will be new; reality will be new. It will be something you haven't experienced yet, but you are already experiencing because everything is simultaneous. The Earth itself is a giant library of information; a cosmic beacon. It's attracting so many different souls for so many different purposes, so many different journeys and stories to tell.

There really isn't a definite 'what's going to happen.' There can't be, there are too many possibilities, way too many variables to calculate. The only thing that's going to happen that's definite is that every human being is going to realize they are part of something greater, and once that happens the Earth will begin to change. So to answer your question, the New Earth is already here. We are already a part of it – we just need to open our eyes."

M: "Regarding those who feel like they are controlled. They say this is a prison planet, and that our souls become trapped here by some of the Reptilians. Does this make any sense to you?"

Z: "Yes it does because belief creates reality, so if you believe this is a prison planet and the Reptilians are controlling you, it is so. You create this reality yourself and then that binds you, until you change your beliefs in your heart. And when I said that I believe that the Earth itself is governed by a third party, this is a belief I have come to through my physical observation; it does not mean it's true; it does not mean it's happening right now in this moment. You can only be affected by what you let affect you. You can only be controlled by what you let control you. When people say they are being attacked by Reptilians, these are their inner fears they are not letting go of because they are beginning to ascend. They are beginning to open up, beginning to

153

become aware of themselves, but they are not delving into their deepest and darkest fears because to truly ascend you have to accept who you are, in the deepest parts of your soul. So where your demons lie is where your true heart is. Once people ascend they are forced into that, without really knowing what's going on, so these fears begin to bubble up from their heart. They don't know what's going on, so they perceive them as 'Oh My God, there is a Reptilian attacking me' because humans have been conditioned through thousands of years that the Reptilians are bad."

M: "So what you are saying is that as we have beliefs and judgments, those beliefs and judgments control us and control our reality."

Z: "Yes."

M: "My experience and my work with past lives, has never suggested that the soul was trapped by Reptilians when it leaves the physical world."

Z: "Yes, because the soul cannot be trapped because the soul is infinite."

M: "I have always believed the soul has no boundaries."

Z: "I completely agree with you. One person's truth could be another person's lie; it's a law of perception. If a person believes they are trapped and there is nowhere to go, that's their experience. I say, let them live it, they will move out of that if they wish to. You can't force ascension down someone's throat; you can just give the information and hope that they understand it. If they don't, just move on."

M: "When people have come to me who are fearful of something evil, I remind them that if they believe they are part of the Source and if they believe there is nothing greater than the Source, so nothing is greater than them or can harm them unless they believe it to be so. And why are we fearful? We are fearful because we are told we are powerless."

Z: "Exactly. What is fear? Fear is an emotion that is manifested from disconnection from Source; that's what I believe. And I believe that love is an emotional chemical reaction that manifests when we are in connection with Source; connection with love, our heart. Because if all there is, is Source, that means when we are connected to this source, we are going to be happy, we are going to be filled with joy and love. And when we are not connected to Source we are going to be depressed, down, and that's what I truly believe.

Levels of consciousness: from what I have seen there are different stages. From their emotional level and their brain development as we ascend, open ourselves and activate our DNA, our brain begins to change its chemistry. It begins to rewire itself. There is a point in the ascension process that is a challenge for everyone. You reach a level of understanding that you know all is one and you believe all is one, but you are so stuck in the material realm the brain starts to contradict itself, your ego takes hold because your heart is afraid. I believe that is why so many are stuck right now. There are so many people out there that claim to be psychics and claim to be mediums but they are stuck in life. They are not happy with where they are; they are fooling themselves."

M: "The way I understand this is that, intellectually, we know this, but the understanding isn't integrated."

Z: "We talk the talk but we don't walk the walk!"

M: "Do you feel that something needs to occur, which will help us move from understanding to integration?"

Z: "Yes, and it's called acceptance, that's what I believe: the shift is acceptance. They haven't accepted who they are on the inside because they don't know who they are on the inside. They have all these ideas of what they should be and what they want to be, what they think is the right way, but they haven't connected to their inner wild side, flamboyant; their chaos. As I said before, chaos is the Universe; it is nothingness, is random. And because it is random, it has no choice but to be harmonized. Within the harmonization you get dysfunction, and that's where they are stuck: they realized harmony but I know they haven't connected to their chaos. Accepted their heart and not accepted their demons, that's the best way to put it."

M: "So we are basically creating a reality of dysfunction for ourselves so we can accept that we are dysfunctional because that's okay, it gives me my experience?"

Z: "Yes, because everyone has their own experience and everyone has their own storyline. The problem right now – well it's not a problem because there is no such thing as a problem - the difficulty with the ascension process: there are so many beings awakening at the same time. They each have their own story line. They are forcing it down everyone's throat. They are not able to say 'Well your storyline is the same as mine but you've perceived differently.' They say, 'My storyline is my storyline, and my storyline has to match up with your storyline because there has to be an ultimate truth.' Well there is an ultimate truth and the only ultimate truth is that all truth is correct; nothing is wrong, no matter what. It is your experience."

M: "That will be very confronting to people who say, 'I need to know the truth and there must be some penultimate truth.'"

Z: "That is ego mind connecting to their brain and not their heart. Because they say they need the truth. 'I need clarity, I need to know what's going on.' Okay, if you want understanding just open your eyes. Open your hearts and see what's in front of you; you are made up of atoms, what more do you want."

M: "My truth as a twenty-year-old was not my truth as a forty-year-old because through your lives and human experiences, your truth is always shifting, your perceptions shift, your openness shifts."

Z: "Exactly. We are saying the same thing here: people get stuck. Stagnation through saying my truth is the only truth so what more to my truth is there – and they create all these stories, realities, elves, angels and demons. All these beings, so they can live life without accepting that they are lost. I am not good at articulating my sentences, I am better at telepathy, feeling."

DNA, Vibration, and Extraterrestrials

"I feel I need to change the direction of the conversation to DNA, vibration and extraterrestrials. DNA is energy, like everything else. DNA is the physical manifestation of thought, and as thought creates reality the DNA begins to physically create. What I feel I am compelled to tell you is about resonance with DNA, and Indigo children, Rainbow children and Crystal children and the ETs. Whenever they say they are hybridized, it's a stage of their awakening process – we are human. If I was to say I am hybridized it just means I am ascending and opening up my codons and these codons are vibrating at a higher frequency, so my brain perceives them as maybe Pleiadian because my brain is perpetuating this species of Pleiadian. Because the Pleiadian species does not exist in a physical form, it is just thought-based. It is a result of our imaginations, so to speak. They are real, don't get me wrong, but we create them through our drive and our need to have something otherworldly because we feel alone. The disconnection we have from Spirit causes us to search and find that truth, and once we latch on to what we think is truth, we then give it structure and then we give it more structure and then we give it society, names and faces.

So when someone says they are Pleiadian, that's just the first step in their ascension process. Then they may feel they are Arcturian, another step in their awakening process, opening up their DNA as they feel they are Sirian, Lemurian, Lyrian – and they keep labeling and labeling because their ego mind hasn't shut off yet. And then they get to a point in their ascension process where they realize 'Hey, I am nothing, I am just I.' And that's what true awakening is. Once you realize this, you are you and be you, no matter what, that you don't need these labels, they are just archetypes you are perpetuating from your own need to be something because your ego says 'I need to be important,' because you think you are not. This is what I have come to realize. Don't get me wrong, I have seen spacecraft in the skies and I have had close encounters myself. There are beings besides us. But that's just it, they are us. They are just reflections of ourselves that we are perceiving because we wish to."

M: "So we are creating the reality of seeing them?"

Z: "Yes, and they are creating the reality of seeing us. Yes. Part of us is saying, 'Well, God' (for want of a better term). Our heart is God; the Universe is within, it's an implosive force. So when we go within, we then perceive all the vibrations around, all the light. And then we project out what we wish – our desired reality – and that's how it works. So our hearts are disconnected from our true selves – from the divine, the Godly force within us – and this causes us to search for that Godly force and a higher purpose, and that is why I told you my only purpose is to be ME. My only purpose is to love and accept everything for what it is and just live. The only purpose in life is to live. We are at the same stage right now; the Christ consciousness is the highest vibration of love. All you need to be is you and anything else is a fabrication of the mind to feel like you need to be something."

M: "I would like to know your understanding of labels such as ADHD, Asperger's; some types of Autism and Dyslexia are possibly new programs, more attuned to where we are going. That is why they appear to be dysfunctional in this paradigm. But have they accessed the multi-dimensional paradigm that we haven't accessed yet? What do you think?"

Z: "I believe everything you are saying is true. But I don't believe it's just them that can do this. Your seventy-year-old grandmother, if she was still alive, could do it if she chose to, if she opened herself. My cat could do it – my cat does it on a daily basis. Animals are already connected to that; they are pure in their heart. Those who are asleep, disconnected from Source, are perceiving this as some divine intervention from Source because we haven't connected to that, but we can do this too. Feeling like they are some new type of evolution to where we are going next. It's not where we are going next; we are already there. Everything is co-existing all at the same time; it's just what you want to make of it. The linear time frame is perpetuated by the mind; it is manifested by the illusion of the lower vibrational realities. It is sludge, so to speak, in the Universe, and that is why the Universe moves around us and we are stationary. We don't exist but we exist at the same time, that's the paradox of the Universe. I believe everything you are saying is true, but it's all perception. An autistic child is no different from a so-called normal child by society's standards because everyone is beautiful in their own way. They just have the experience they wish to have. Some beings wish to come in with a desire for limited perspectives, such as blind or deaf because their soul wants that experience – what that's like. The reason we have this reality is for this experience. That's why the physical plane was created, manifested, so that souls could learn. There was a quote that said the gods were jealous of us because we are mortal and we are going to die. Energy can't do that; energy can't be created or destroyed. It is eternal; all it can do is change."

M: "What I want to do is share the information from what I believe are your avatars."

Z: "That's what I was called by my guides, a young avatar."

M: "One of the reasons I want to get this information shared is that with the young children and young adults, there is a clarity with them that is lost to a certain extent in adults due to education and stress, etc."

Z: "Yes, it's a purity of information. That's why my guides told me to stop going to school, and yet everyone around me is telling me it's a terrible mistake. But I am sorry when I go to school; I am in extreme pain; it physically hurts for me to be in that situation. It is energetic stimulus, and my heart is telling me to do with you what I am doing right now, explain what I know. Everyone is programmed from the time they see another human – this is what we are supposed to look like. If we didn't have eyeballs everything would be perceived entirely differently, no one human would look like the next. We are programmed to think this is the ideal way: a tree is supposed to look like a tree and green and black and in autumn orange and red. If we didn't have this programming our reality would be completely different. That's what the new ones are coming in to say: that your reality is what you make it, so make it awesome."

M: "And that starts with thought!"

Z: "Exactly!"

M: "So it's how we choose to see each other, how we choose to see the world. When you say it's difficult to go to school, is it because of all the different energies there?"

Z: "Yes, it's an over-energetic stimulus for me; there are so many thoughts and feelings and I take them on. I am like a sponge for everything. If someone's dad beat them the day before, I would feel that. I am using that as an example because it's happened before. I feel that pain. I feel where he got hit. I feel the sadness he has because of it and I feel everyone else's emotions on top of it, plus my own emotions, and I can hear their thoughts, and I see alternate realities and what's going on – it's just too much. I meditate, I calm myself, I try to deal with it the best I can, but for me, I realize the best place for me to be is in the woods – that's where I am the happiest. If I just go for a walk in the woods and do some Chi Gong, hug a tree and talk to the squirrels; that's when I am the happiest. But the society and the kids, they are picking on me. I don't care; it's only their opinion, but it does get to me at some point. What if I really am insane? What if I am wrong? Because I only know that I am the only one who perceives reality in this way. Many people have told me that I am hyper-intelligent, above average intelligence, but what if I am not? What IF! And that's why I don't go to school anymore because there are so many 'what ifs'!"

M: "So you are questioning because it seems to be in conflict with everyone else?"

Z: "I used to question it and occasionally I do now, but I kind of push that out and say my reality is mine, and your reality is yours. No judgments. You perceive your reality your way and I will mine. It is what it is. That's what I have come to terms with recently."

M: "So you feel one of the main challenges is owning your own truth, given that everything else reflects something different?"

Z: "The biggest difficulty is acceptance. What is the true essence of love? Acceptance. That's all love is: acceptance of what is and not expecting it to be anything else than what it is. I agree with everything you are saying; acceptance is the biggest challenge for people like me. So many variables to calculate and you struggle to know what's right or wrong, so you have to accept what is, and that takes a lot because so many people don't do that. So many people say, 'You are wrong for being this way. You are mentally unstable.' It put me into a deep depression when I was younger. I will be honest, I tried to kill myself numerous times, I was a depressed child because I was perceiving reality differently than everyone else and I thought I was wrong. I thought I was born broken in some way, and I wanted to end it. I understood as a child that I would go somewhere else anyway, so why stay here. But every time I tried to commit suicide: tried to drown myself, jump off a bridge, something saved me. I don't know what it was – it was just this force – it wouldn't let me die. That's when I came to terms with this and decided to accept it. That's what kicked me in the butt, so to speak; I wasn't allowed to die."

M: "So there was some aspect of you that stopped you leaving this plane. I received an email from someone who told me that, at eight years old, they wanted to commit suicide but they could not recall the reason. What was the age this first happened?"

Z: "It was at the start of my awakening, around eight or nine years old. I have found the most depressed people are the ones most spiritually awake because they are alone in a world full of zombies and they don't know what to do. I tried committing suicide when I was twelve because of bullying at my school. I was being bullied because of my views on life, and because I didn't like all the male-type sports and I was picked on for that. So I tried to drown myself. I told my best friend the next day and I worked it out by speaking to them, and haven't really tried since. I thought about leaving sometimes, but it wasn't about depression, it was more that I wanted the experience of something else. I have been here for sixteen years now and that feels like an eternity for my soul. One day for me is like years for my soul. I don't know if this makes sense to you. I don't know how else to put it. And the age I am now, I feel I am done with this experience, I know what I need to know so why keep going. And then a voice came into my head and said, 'This existence isn't for you.' I said, 'What do you mean?' And it said, 'This existence is for other people; you might know, but other people don't. And that is why you are here'."

M: "Does that make sense to you?"

Z: "It does make sense to me. It makes a lot of sense because I try to help everyone no matter what. My friends call me a counselor and I should go into a job doing counseling because I understand things and explain how things work. That's my gift in life I guess, this understanding. And once I was told this by the voice in my head, a fractal of me that I wasn't aware of at that moment. I felt it within. I felt it alleviated. I felt this giant weight was lifted off me. I realized why I was really here. That is to help to heal, to heal what has been tainted. I want to say broken, but it's not."

M: "So what's helped you hang in there is the understanding that you can help and assist with what is going on here."

Z: "Yes, that's helped keep me here. Every time I speak to someone they seem happier. I don't know why. What's really helped is that I make people smile just by being me. I love that. I love making people smile. I am happy when other people are happy. I am holding on because I can make other people happy. Even if it's just one person, I don't care, as long as I make their world better. I know what it's like to be in depression. I don't want other people to go through that."

M: "What can you do to support people like you who feel very alone and isolated at times because you feel nobody understands what you are experiencing? How do you support the physical human part of you which sometimes finds it really hard?"

Z: "By surrounding myself with people who make me smile. That's what really got me through it by finding people who thought in a similar way to myself. Even if they were spiritually shut down; if they didn't know what spirituality was and thought religion was crap. If they had that one light inside them that I could see – that's what got me through it because I was not alone. They have that light; they don't see it. I can't be the only one going through that. And endurance and perseverance got me through it. Pushing through life, I realized at a young age that life is not what you always want; it's what you need. Life is going to throw a whole lot of garbage at you, and you need to be able to stand tall with your head held high and push through it because it's a lesson, an experience. If you are in a third-world country with no water and no food, it's a human experience. I learned when I tried to kill myself this was not my decision, when I die. It's the Universe's decision when I return home. So until it's my time to return home I am going to make the best of it."

M: "So this means nurturing yourself."

Z: "Yes, self love. If you don't love yourself how, can you love others."

M: "So, it's realizing that you must resource yourself and knowing that you have chosen this experience, and not feeling that it's just you. Because many young Starseeds feel alone because no one else 'gets it,' and their family may not understand them and they can't talk about this to anyone because they just think 'I am crazy.' Constant questioning of their truth, their reality, that seems to be almost a theme."

Z: "It is, yeah. I have realized that too."

M: "So, is this the major challenge, being born into a reality that is so different for someone as sensitive and aware as yourself?".

Z: "Yes. This goes back to acceptance."

M: "When it was hard for you, what would you have liked to hear in terms of where you are right now? What would have been the most helpful?"

Z: "Someone to accept me for who I am. I would tell them: 'You are amazing. No matter what color you are, what gender you are, what your interests are, it doesn't matter. You are amazing just as you are. And I love you, and I accept you.' That's it, that's all there is to it. There is someone out in the world that truly cares for you and will do anything to make you happy."

M: "In terms of your siblings, how do they respond to you and your understanding?"

Z: "My siblings tend to look at me as a guide. They come to me for information.

Other than that, my siblings know it's their life. I am not going to be there to hold their hand the whole way. I am here when they need a light shining on something dark. They didn't fully understand when I was awaking. They thought I was seeking attention, maybe mentally unstable. I would channel personalities that would offer them information that I would not know, but they would. I proved it to people."

Part Four
2015 – A Conversation Re Moon and Earth Changes

Z: "I have had dreams of being on the Moon quite recently. Something's happening on the other side that we are not able to see. It's like they are getting ready for something. They are preparing, and they are busy creatures that are humanoid, but I feel I am coming from a bird's-eye view, looking down and flying through the bases. I see hexagonal and geometric bases with obelisks randomly coming out from these structures, then beings and people walking around and preparing these ships, crafts.

In other dreams recently, which are difficult to describe, my intuition has spiked. It's like when I walk into a room I can pick up more and more of peoples' thoughts or feelings, and saying things that people needed to hear, like messages from the Divine to tell them. I also see orbs in the sky that will flash really quickly even in the daytime; an anxiety within me that something is going to happen. I wake up in the morning and feel I have been gone for thousands of years, although it's just an hour or two. I was actually asleep. This pressure-buzzing tingle. I keep hearing, 'We are preparing you, and something's going to happen with the Earth.' I connect with Gaia and I sense that she is getting ready to shift and change, to push out the stored energy within the consciousness of the human collective. Dense energies. She is getting ready to shake these energies out of her.

Also, my abilities to shape-shift have increased lately. I learned something from the Pleiadians that showed me how to connect with the Universal source, and you breathe this and it fills your body and allows you to access the DNA of your vessel that is a higher frequency. And so, when I do this, my eyes will flicker, will turn gold like cat people. And it's others who see this happen. I just feel a tingling at the base of my spine which shoots up my back like electricity and then I get euphoric, and then the person who is looking at me will go 'Whoa! Your eyes just changed.' A person I am very close to said that when we were talking my eyes changed to look like dragon eyes. I understand that I am filling my body with light and biomagnetically I am retaining more energy and that is allowing my physical body to access more of my higher vibrations or expressions of my DNA, and because I am able to access other higher variations of my DNA. My body is going to express that which is closer to this reality, but still of a higher energetic plane, which is my Arcturian soul or expression – the part of my vessel that stems from Arcturas, which is the cat-like dragon eyes, and also the golden aura that I have radiated recently. My friend took a picture of me with this aura.

I am careful about sharing this information, but I was told Earth is being initiated into the Galactic councils. The Earth is in its pre-teen years right now, like we are going through another stage in puberty. We are going above the meridian line in our galaxy as we are going through a more dense region of gas; our sun is being engulfed in hydrogen gas and being influenced by it. It's producing different wavelengths of light that our solar system is not used to, so the energetic fields of all the planets in our solar system are receiving this new information, new light wavelengths. We are shifting, we are growing, evolving, and it's going to be quick. In our perceptions it's already happened i.e., ten steps ahead of what we are perceiving. The sun is also going through a magnetic pole-flick, north and south gravitation fields, and when it reaches zero point and the gravitational field rearranges opposite of what it used to be, Earth will also go through a shift similar because the sun has a gravitational pull on the Earth and also they have a connection. The ripple from the energy from the sun not being confined by the magnetic field will blast light waves in our direction and hit the Earth and cause a massive upgrade in the human DNA spectrum. It may not be physically visible to certain people, but very physical to certain people. It's like a software upgrade and the Earth itself is getting ready for this. This means Earth upheavals will continue up to 2023, the date I have been given, and something is going to happen around that time. It may be something geopolitical and with huge implications, and change how we perceive life on this planet. There is also a massive DNA awakening going on; a massive data-bank upgrade, hard to explain in English. We are going into an era of divine light; our cells and atoms are all being magnetically aligned and restructured to fit into the template of what we can call the Galactic Human Being. We are being prepared and upgraded to be ready for the galactic superwaves that are entering our solar system.

My school studies have shown the galactic center is releasing massive amounts of gamma rays and X-rays, far more than normal. The whole galactic center is evolving right now, like strings on a guitar. We are going up an octave and that is why the Schumann resonance has increased and mass amounts of people are awakening, and there is a domino effect, and many new healers will be showing that some of the healings look almost like sci-fi (I am being told this right now, like what to look forward to). The younger children's abilities are increasing. I am being reminded of something I have to tell you. I was meditating and I was having a moment of weakness where I was questioning everything; I felt I was stuck on Earth and why am I so alone. I connected to Earth and I felt so much love and joy, I was vibrating so much I felt I was floating; my body and my soul felt it was like a balloon which expanded as much as it could, inverted and exploded. I saw a flash of light and a rainbow tunnel, and then I was standing in front of a seventeen-foot-tall, lanky being, indigo purple, glowing. Its skin looked almost like a galaxy; it was like the freckles on his body were glowing like stars. His skin was the color of the night sky; almond eyes no nose and no mouth, no ears and head elongated. He said to me, 'We are on our way.' He knelt down in front of me and took out this diamond which was glowing white. He put it into my hand and wrapped my fingers around it and then put it close to my heart, hugged me and said, 'We are coming for you.' He said this diamond was the beacon to find me, and will always be with you. I woke up and had this feeling that Mary should hear this."

I asked Zac what he sensed with this experience?

Z: "I felt it was almost like a parent and I was their child and special, and a special mission; a nostalgic moment, sad but peaceful. The hidden message of it: they are on their way but not to physically get me, but to watch and protect and guide. They and me are coming to Earth to assist; coming for the whole Earth. I connect to Gaia and it's like they are coming to me like an ambassador who speaks for her, Gaia. These beings are from Andromeda because they have no mouths. This is because they don't need to eat; they absorb light and sound. They are pure energy, although they evolved from a physical form and go back into a physical form.

In my vision image, being able to see every physical atom and electron around them, when a being like this presents itself to you, it's like their heart chakra is the center of their being, and their being is the atom and their aura is the field of the electrons falling around them. All that energy from the nucleus and the electron is their aura. The nucleus is their heart chakra. They reached a state where they could dematerialize or materialize their own physical body. The mouth just looks like a pulsing light, like if you touched it, it would ripple like a liquid, and pulses like it's bioluminescent. When they communicate, their heart pulsates and changes color."

Mary: "You say that they have told you they are coming. Have you any sense of when?"

Z: "I feel they are already here, or at least some of them. And my feeling with the message is they will come when we need, when it's critical. Like something is coming and you are going to be rescued."

M: "So you feel that this was telling you not to be disheartened because your life circumstances were difficult at this time, but to know that you are supported?"

Zac shared the realization that although it's hard on this planet right now for other starseeds and many feel alone as he has done, they need to learn to be patient. It is hard and challenging to accept this but they need to understand help will be here when it's the right time and not when we demand it.

Z: "I was trying to understand why electronics was always playing up, even when I was in a calm place. I understand it's my energy, but it wasn't my intention. I was told that a lot of the paranormal things are happening, or in a family with young children and things disappear and then appear somewhere else. It happens in my house and my family think it's haunted, or feel they are being attacked by negative entities or demons. It is their energy. Their DNA is awakening, and their connectivity to the matrix that makes up our reality is increasing and energy is permanent, although it's in a constant state of change, it is still permanent; it's a paradox. Input you put out to the Universe comes back ten-fold but it can also come back to you in a different way.

When people are awakening to these states, and things start going haywire around them, it's because they are not centered within themselves, and the emotions that they store within their energetic imprint before they started to awaken are being purged, and that purging causes chaos. For example, if someone was extremely depressed before they awakened and now they are awakened their energy is increasing and connecting more, that depressive energy is still there and it has to leave somehow, so it will leave in the form of psychic attack or technology exploding or going on the fritz when you are near it, or the weather being weird around you, or your couch moving by itself across the floor. To release this energy is pure magnetism, expressed as paranormal psychic phenomenon."

M: "So when people feel they are being attacked by some covert agency or demonic entity, how do you explain this?"

Z: "A lot of people are. I have been attacked by negative entities; a lot of my childhood was demonic attacks. When it comes to manipulation through sexualization – that's one hundred percent true. Sexual attacks by negative entities, I have experienced this all my childhood. But what I am talking about is like someone's cell phone dying when you are near it. But also if you are angry and you go out in the public, everyone you meet is angry with you. It's because your energy is angry on the inside and you are attracting that anger to you. Same if you are depressed and sad, your experiences will echo that as you attract it to you because you are lowering yourself into that dense vibration, allowing those energies to connect to you. Once you allow yourself to be open to these dense vibrations you allow other beings to connect to you and become a parasite and use you as a host. If you are overwhelmed and scattered, then this allows other energies to connect to you and your psyche and it will do its best to confuse you so it can stay."

M: "Re covert agencies, have you strategies to deal with this?"

Z: "Not everything I do works for everyone. I need to say that. My techniques are unique to me. I learned to deal with stress and harmful situations when I was younger because of what I went through. To begin, I go for a walk and go to the woods or forest, and it's the best when you are angry or sad because the oxygen coming from the trees helps with the delta waves in the brain and increases your energy levels. Talk to those whom you trust. To know you are targeted for a reason: you have information they don't want people to know that makes you special, and that is important to remember. Also, find something that makes you happy and put your time into the project and take your mind off that idea. Because by focusing on that attack will feed it. Try and live your life without letting it control you. Realize you do not need to be controlled by others through fear. Be heart-centered, conscious and mindful. You need will power and perseverance, intellect and strategy to concentrate on what is working in your life.

We are going through a period of transition to get us off the couch and listen to what you are guided to do. It's a time of creativity and expression and be in nature as much as possible. These times are about becoming more human and reaching out to each other. So we can join the galactic family, we have to be a human family first. This process is about becoming human and opening our eyes. These beings will only come once we have healed and become more mature. The process of awakening and embracing the shift is looking at your neighbor with love."

M: "It is interesting because what I am hearing is about us becoming truly human, yet so many connecting to their star family say they don't like being human because it's very primitive and barbaric. But you are saying embrace that aspect of yourself, but in a way that expands the human that is embracing their true essence no matter what form they are in."

Z: "I don't like the term 'Starseeds', as I feel all of us and animals and plants come from the stars, everything comes from the stars."

M: "So what would you prefer as a term for this shift and change in humanity – and you mention that we have to become more human. I have thought about the term 'The New Human'?"

Z: "I like the term 'The New Human.' I think that title fits very well because we are going into something that is new for us of what we know we are. We are only seen as different because of a preconceived idea of what is normal. When we come up with Crystal child, Indigo child or Rainbow child, it is not describing the person but the person's expression of self. The Indigo child has that warrior personality, to break down a system that is wrong and needs to change. The Crystalline child has the aura of love and peace; the healer, the medium bringing in the 'sight.' The Rainbow child has the energy of the creator, leader, kingship personality; it's a vibrational difference. It's a term humans are using only because we have a limited understanding of what is going on. Those who call themselves these labels are just resonating to the frequency of those attributes, and not staying with the status quo. Animals are changing too, personality wise; animals are evolving as we are. I believe humans are evolving in another huge 'leap' right now; our body has enough energy to make improvements so *The New Human* is a great title.

I also need to say 'they' (the family) are always listening. They love what we are sharing, and they thank you and send their love. There are going to be huge techno-logical leaps in the coming years in the medical and energy industries, and the way we transport our goods, and many suppressed technologies are going to resurface as new technologies. However they are not new, simply improved. To sum up their interactions with Earth at this time, 'we' are the Arcturians, we are here to gather our family, like a family reunion, and we are guiding you in your pre-teen years and healing and preventing cataclysms, getting ready for your initiation to the family of light that you left long ago. We, the Arcturians, are always willing to assist, and even when you cannot see us we are there. That's strange: I just see the Earth from outside engulfed in a ball of golden fire."

M: "So what does that mean to you?"

Z: "Gold is the color of divine wisdom, the color of the higher heart chakra, or our Galactic source connection, the symbolism means that the Earth is connecting with Source, sparking our divine remembrance."

Ref – Re Moon Structures

There are many pictures taken of anomalies on the Moon and also documentaries such as *Moon Rising* by Jose Escamilla, where the anomalies are explored in detail. Bases on the dark side of the Moon are also explored in detail through whistleblower information, such as Michael Salla's book: *Insiders Reveal Secret Space Programs & Extraterrestrial Alliances*, where it is stated by Corey Goode that the Germans landed on the Moon possibly as early as 1942 and by the end of WW2 had a base there. (Page 301).

In Chapter Twelve of Michael Salla's book, he quotes from *Our Cosmic Ancestors* by Maurice Chatelain, a retired NASA communications engineer, who wrote that only moments before Neil Armstrong stepped down the ladder to set foot on the Moon he saw two UFOs hovering overhead. Chatelain stated that information was deliberately kept from the public by NASA (Page 298). Furthermore, he said that in the sixties, a huge Russian and American base was built on the Moon, allegedly with a population of forty thousand (Page 302).

Extraordinary as these claims are, I have worked with a number of those having encounters, who have recalled being taken to the Moon. I had the pleasure of writing the foreword for Niara Isley's courageous story: *Facing the Shadow, Embracing the Light: A Journal of Spirit Retrieval and Awakening*, in which she documents her traumatic experiences by covert military agencies, and the abuse she suffered when taken to a base on the Moon.

It is also intriguing and compelling that a number of the younger children, such as Zac and Lea K, mention they are aware of non-human intelligences with bases on the Moon.

Chapter Eleven

THE HUMAN UPGRADES – *HOMO NOVIS*

Adult *Homo Novis* – Awake and Aware

Lea Kapiteli "Out of this world"

Lea was still a teenager when Lea's mother wrote to me. As Lea's parent, she struggled with what Lea shared with her but she also believed her daughter was telling her truth. It was information, however, that left her very confused; it contradicted all her own beliefs, especially as she was a scientist by profession.

"Dear Mary,

I believe my eighteen-year-old daughter Lea is one of these New Humans, or *Homo novis* as she calls herself. 'The term comes from them,' Lea informs me. 'Them' are the ET people she has been in Contact with for the last ten years or so telepathically, she claims. In fact, she says she is in constant Contact with them.

I have listened to her for the past ten years, and what she tells me is pretty shocking and unbelievable for someone like me, who is a biotechnology scientist. What can I say? I did think that something was wrong with her. However, based on information on ancient history and people of our planet, combined with philosophy, metaphysics, biological information, etc., this became intriguing and supported some of her information, so it hardly could be prescribed to her imagination. I would try to find corroboration for the information she would give me, and would find other sources to support what she said. This helped me realize that she is not crazy, and that in fact this might be really happening.

Needless to say, I would find most of the information coming from Lea in other sources of information much later, such as the books of Dolores Cannon, Dr. Steven Greer, Lobsang Rampa, etcetera. It was when I found your information that I was so relieved, and it confirmed for me she is not crazy and she is not the only one to have experienced this! She did maintain that there are another sixty or so Contactees (*Homo novis*) like her in Australia alone, but she does not know them, but she can 'detect' them.

The picture attached that Lea has drawn, represents Mezereth, her mentor, an ambassador of an ET race called Naevansorous. A member of a custodian group (twelve members, altogether) that she says originally seeded the Earth and are taking care of Earth matters. They have a base on the dark side of our moon. Other ambassadors are all there also. Mezereth is not a three-dimensional being; he is an energy being, as his race evolved from the three-dimensional into energy nation. The image she drew is how he presents himself to her in her mind, most of the time, but it is really a biological suit, the real being is inside in energy form. She has seen their energy form too, and she said they could be described as 'angelic' looking as the light is shining around them, especially from their back, which might be interpreted as wings.

Mezreth is part of the Custodian Council, but their base is not just on the dark side of the Moon. The whole Moon itself is an artificial satellite, and there are multiple councils and orders working within. These are Ashtar and Custodian Councils, which are the most dominant. Then you have several other sub-groups with separate specifications, all of them working towards one goal: First Contact."

Lea's mother and I communicated. I was very intrigued by Lea's understanding of herself and her Contacts. Particularly her in-depth descriptions of them, their psyche, the personalities of the ones with which she said she communicated, and her wonderfully detailed drawings. I traveled to Victoria, in Australia, to meet Lea and her mother. Lea was at university. I found her highly intelligent and a gifted artist. She allowed me to record some of her experiences and shared her understanding. (Clips of Lea speaking and sharing her story are in some of my more recent Power-Point presentations.)

I questioned Lea about her understanding of her experiences and the beings she had drawn and told me she interacted with. Lea was able to describe her experiences in great detail. I found her understanding of her Contacts logical and compelling.

Lea also shared that she had conscious recall of many of her past lives as a non-human, and that she had on-going encounters with many different non-human intelligences she referred to as Ambassadors. Not only was Lea able to draw many of these Ambassador Intelligences in amazing detail, but she could also describe their culture and individual personalities.

However, I could relate to Lea's mother, a scientist who had not been exposed to this phenomenon prior to this. I could well understand how she struggled to accept some of the information Lea shared. But as she told me, she knew her daughter very well and so she found it harder and harder to dismiss what her daughter was telling her, despite it being so far out of her own knowledge and understanding. She came to believe what Lea was telling her.

Growing Up as a *Homo Novis*

Lea: "I was confused to realize how many people on this planet just don't know. I was eight when I discovered I could heal with my hands. I did healing on my mother. I knew my mother couldn't do what I could do. I am connected to various ET and they explained to me what things meant and taught me that which I was perceiving; the Energy Beings taught me. I was close to one of them in a previous life, and once I saw them out of their suit (solid form). I could see just 'white' around him. I wasn't scared because when I was younger they showed themselves in human form. As I got older, I saw them differently. There are certain categories of ETs, such as extra-dimensional. Some are 'wanderers'; they can move through dimensions, you have to be careful how you interpret them. Some work for the ETs and some are guides.

The New Human children are the ones incarnating from 2000 i.e., *Homo noeticus*. However, they do not fully awaken until their pubescent years, which is 2012 onwards, and this is because open Contact is supposed to happen."

Lea – Update 2016

I asked Lea to speak about her recall of her extraterrestrial education and syllabus:

Lea: "Where I was taught by 'them' and my first few experiences, I recall I was in a type of classroom, but I didn't know where it was located. It could have been a ship (space craft), but I doubt it was. It could have been a pocket space (a huge area hidden within a tiny area), or it could have been a portal to the moon itself (I actually feel like it was below the Moon's surface), and it continued for years up to the present day. I still get taught things, but as I grew up I was told rather than taught. An'taji'san was my main teacher, and she would take my astral body to Elzona, and we would stay there for hours until my physical body needed waking up."

Note: Elzona is a planet, which Lea told me she is very connected to. She has drawn images of what they looked like, and they had purple skin. She also recalls her human mother being with her as a sister from that lifetime. This was confirmed by regression hypnosis I facilitated with Lea's mother. In this regression it was confirmed that Lea's mother had a lifetime on Elzonia with Lea, who was her sister, just as Lea had explained to her.

While in regression hypnosis, the mother was able to recall that lifetime on Elzonia, and was also able to speak the Elzoni language with Lea during the hypnosis because Lea was in the room while this was being facilitated. It was remarkable to witness the scientist and her daughter speaking the Elzoni language together, one in hypnosis and one in conscious recall.

Mary: "What do you understand of the New Human and their role on this planet."

Lea: "*Homo novis*: *Homo novis* is a mix of *Homo sapien* and ET genes, whose purpose is to uplift and alter the offspring of *sapiens* into the next evolutionary step in humanity, into *Homo noeticus*.

As I understand it, *Homo novis* bring a subtle way of mutating humanity to the next stage by our 'parent' ET race, Neavensoros. The intention is to ensure a brighter future for humanity; this is to put the 'derailed train' back on track and secure survival of all life within this planet's biosphere. But as *novis*, we not only alter genes and frequencies of *sapiens* around us, we also act as agents for ETs: insiders looking out, unfolding the enigma humans wrapped themselves into for the last several thousand years. Though we *novis* have our primary objective: awaken humanity, we, as individuals, have different roles to play to ensure this shift does happen. Some may have talents in sports, art, language, dancing, science, philosophy, mechanics, maths, even politics (that's a hard one for me to wrap my head around). But all is needed to make sure the shift happens!

We are few in number; our wisdom is as vast as the stars, but our naivety is of children when attempting to understand the workings of this world. Remember, this is not our world; we are only here to save it. Once the *Homo noeticus* children grow up into adults and have 'replaced' their older models, we will act as teachers for the New Humans so the old mistakes are never repeated again. *Novis* are here to teach the *noeticus* children; *noeticus* are here to save us. If that unity doesn't bring a tear from one's eye, then I don't know what does."

Mary: "When did you know you were different?"

Lea: "I always knew, but I didn't know that no one else knew what I did until I was between six to nine years old. It shocked me how no one spoke to me about metaphysics and the relation humanity has with ETs, and they had absolutely no idea what I was talking about. Most of them put it down to imagination, which is a reasonable conclusion in hindsight. Thankfully, my mother never told me to stop talking about it, unlike most other family and friends, but there was that tiny seed of doubt in her eye that made my sharing to be nothing more than a vivid dream and it can make me feel jaded. So, despite being very young, I decided to prove, at least partly, what sounded to them like my science fiction, to be science fact. Because I was taught by my ET Contacts on the nature of the universe and also the nature of what I was (*novis*). I knew I could heal. When my mother would develop a pain in her body or head, I'd place my hands on the spot and inject energy into it stopping the pain receptors from working temporarily, or stimulate the cells to produce faster."

Mary: "When did you first realize you had Contact with non-humans?"

Lea: "At the tender age of four I had my first physical experience with ETs (not to be confused with ED (Extra-dimensional); those encounters came much later). My mother and I were sharing a small bed and a bright baby-blue light appeared from the only window in the room. I woke up instantly, compelled to walk towards it. That's exactly what I did. I walked and walked until I went through the window itself. That detail didn't even occur to me until some years later when I began learning metaphysics. On the other side, a small yellow-skinned woman in a red dress greeted me. She looked like some kind of teacher, since we appeared to be in a type of classroom. There were other human children there, and other children were ETs, but all the adults in the room were ETs. This didn't faze me, I knew I was safe there. I felt that with more certainty in this room and its inhabitants than I did in Earth schools. (That speaks volumes, doesn't it?).

The gold-skinned woman gently placed her hand on my back and introduced herself to me as Marro. She explained that the adults were 'case-workers' for all the human children here, and that I had my own caseworker. She pointed to a young woman sitting by a short table; she had many characteristics of an average human woman, however, her skin was a beautiful light violet color, her hair was a deep purple, her eyes were obnoxiously blue and her ears were pointed, slanting backward. When I reached this woman, she looked to me and smiled. She identified herself as Ahn'taji'sun (pronounced as a single word), and her race was Elzoni. Despite how secure I felt in the entire room and with everyone else in it, Ahn was the one I felt most comfortable with. Even though I didn't know her personally, her physical appearance, likeness of her name, and her race's name were extremely familiar. After a small introduction, Ahn settled me on a seat next to her near the table. She told me to play with all the toys she was going to give to me, and that every single one of them presented a general skill to determine what part of the brain is more active. She took out the first toy that represented logic; it looked like a 3D triangle with all faces and sides so perfectly aligned that whatever side you placed on a flat surface it would look like it stood in perfect triangular proportion. However, this toy had smaller triangles stacked up to make the main and it was the player's job to take it apart and place each piece back up again while trying to keep it as balanced as possible.

Another toy was given, that represented creativity; it was a shapeless object that behaved like runny goo. However, it was really hard and when you tried to squeeze it, it was very difficult to mold a shape out of. Ahn explained to me that I had to create a recognizable shape by holding an edge of that hard goo, and craftily shake it until it turned into the shape you want. Ahn gave me several other toys that represented different skills: ingenuity, charisma, reflex and motor skills. At the very end of these small tests, Ahn took a look at all the toys that lay on the table and turned to me saying, 'You scored the highest with creativity.' She let me go to play with the other kids in the room for a while, before Marro (who I later learned was the woman in charge of the development of *Homo novis* (AKA star people/children programs over the decades) took me back to my grandparent's house so I could finish resting.

After the first physical encounter, I had many different encounters of figures, which apparently only I could sense, which I found very odd.

This new sensor was followed by the emergence of empathy. Humans are natural empaths. Ahn was helping me in how to control it, due to the sheer raw power of it. The lessons on how to read others – not just emotions, but also how to determine if the individual was ill or not, and would also teach me how to use my hands to heal the sick. At that time, I could numb pain and cure headaches, but my abilities grew stronger as time progressed. Ahn mentioned a crucial piece of information when she was teaching me how to use empathy: 'All the good one can do is equal to the amount of bad one can do,' meaning that if you can heal people you can also hurt people. It's the very cliché line of 'good cannot exist without bad, and bad cannot exist without good.'

Ahn told me that everyone is born with these abilities, but it is up to the adults to teach the young how to properly channel it. It makes sense why most people on Earth do not know or think it's possible to use these abilities because if their teachers do not know how, then what chances do the students have to learn these invaluable lessons. Thanks to Ahn, she has taught me many ways how to use this ability. In many ways she was like a second mother, but I actually felt like she was an older sister I never had. If it were not for Ahn I wouldn't have learned the most important lessons of this life because there would be no hope for anyone else in my environment that would be able to teach me this.

I had one other encounter like that one, when I was six, a year later, but since then I never have. I have different ways of Contacting and being Contacted by ETs: via telepathy, astral visitations and in rarer instances, physical visitations. Even as I write this, I'm being communicated by an ET friend, talking about 'how cool particles are.' (You give them an inch, they take a light year!)

I had few ETs actually teaching me over this life. Two were always there: Mezreth (the energy being and youngest of his race) and An'taji'san (my Ezoni, non-birth biological mother; I have some of her genes). Ahn taught me about *Homo novis* and the New Humans, about what we could do, such as abilities and powers, and how each human sub-group differs. She taught me about her home world, my own too, about the Elzoni and our history.

Mezreth taught me about the nature of the universe and the value of every word within it. How every cell and planet has a soul and how every atom and star are the same, in a way. He told me about the astral and physical realms and how they relate within this universe – that all born within this plane have both astral and physical bodies. Astral bodies allow astral projection, travel, etc. To some spiritual or psychic humans they can be called 'soul-self', but the soul is something entirely different.

I had various 'teachers', most are people I'm in contact with and who share their stories and knowledge with me. Without their trust in me, being able to tell me about themselves in a private and personal way, I would have concluded years ago that I was mentally ill."

Mary: "What do you perceive as your abilities?"

Lea: "Every being has their own set of abilities, but there are abilities that are most common in races. There is a list of my own:

Homo novis

- *Heightened Physical Senses* – Vision, hearing, smell, touch, taste, synaesthesia, ultrasound detection, sensitivity under the skin, fingertips and hair follicles.
- *Hyper-Cognition* – Cipher, Omni lingual, genius intellect, encyclopedic knowledge, fast learner, enhanced memory and able to multitask. Ability to decipher and translate any written or spoken language.
- *Empathy* – To sense the state of health from living life-forms; a small degree empathic mastery. Sense a person's vitality, animal and plant bonding (the ability to emotionally bond with plants and animals making them sensitive to you). Sensory scrying (the ability to tune into active senses of other life forms). Empathic aversion apathy (isolate yourself emotionally, making yourself invisible to other empaths). Inflict confusion (induce a state of confusion in someone), imprinting (a deep emotional connection with one or more other life forms, allowing each other to connect at a distance), project emotions, telempathy (using emotions to communicate with other empaths – not to be confused with telepathy), sense emotions.
- *Telepathy* – Mind scanning, telepathic tracking, mind link, mind meld, hypnotize (ability to make someone vulnerable to your suggestions), absorb and transfer information, telepathic cloaking, psychic communing (exchange information to different life forms), memory alteration (the ability to change a person's memory from a minor detail to a total re-shuffle of their experiences), mental inhibitor (the ability to disable certain mental pathways within the person, making them unable to be aggressive towards you).
- *Immunity* – Elemental (immune to extreme changes in weather), immune system very resilient to disease, toxins, contaminants, radiation, lower astral acids, poisons, elemental absolute filtration (filter out contaminant that the body may be exposed to).
- *ESP* – Extra-sensory perception.
- *Heightened Physical Condition* – Heightened physical condition, genetically enhanced life form, better health, longer life (this is because of my *novis* side).
- *Third Eye Activated* – Infrared vision, aura perception, death perception (ability to see waning life force), X-ray vision, night vision, telescopic and microscopic vision, astral realm perception, electromagnetic radiation vision, 360° vision.
- *Acrobatic* – Enhanced agility. Flexibility, balanced, dexterous.

- *Clairvoyant.*
- *Astral form.*
- *Pheromone Control* – Manipulation and generation of one's own pheromones to affect others around the user, to induce: hallucinations, excitement, aroma, seduction, activation and alteration of genes, etc.
- *Aura Control* – Manipulation of user's personal aura, varying on the degree of control from one's personal aura: aura torrent (unleash biotic energy from one's aura), change chakra (alter the user's chakra spheres and alignment), bendable aura (change shape and density of personal aura), protective ball (create a thick aura barrier to protect body from contaminates), peacemaker, create presence, induce chaos (enhance emotional tension in other life forms prone to more exaggerated emotions), expand and absorb aura, biotic absorption (store energy in cells, impact absorption, a conduit, energized body, solar powered, self sustenance). Become beautiful or hideous.
- *Collective Consciousness* – Every *novis* has this quality.
- *Fortitude* – Enhanced endurance, (stamina, tissue, body hardening, temperature tolerance, pain tolerance, resilience, resistance, quick recovery, tough DNA).
- *Absorption* – Store energy in cells, impact absorption, become a conduit, energized body, solar powered, self-sustenance, negate food and rest, etcetera.
- *Healing* – A mixture of photo and electro kinesis (manipulation and generation of photons and electrons). The last one is new for me; it's to a very small degree.
- Photo-kinesis: A manipulation, shaping and possible generation of photons (light particles). Users can alter existing photons around them or create their own photons, and once in the user's control, they can bend them into whatever they desire. They harness this power with their aura's ability to absorb energy. Shaping of photons, light projection lasers and holograms, photon blasts, illumination, photon control, vibration emission, microwave control, calming light, ray beams, etcetera.
- *Electro-kinesis* – A manipulation, generation and shaping of electrons. Users can create friction in their aura and with enough control, direct the energy back out; a smaller version of lightning. The generation and redirection of such energy makes this formidable. Static interference, sense currents, lightning bolts, living battery, heightened EMF, electric paralysis, magnetism, electric field negation, control technology (to a point), friction generation, etcetera.

I asked Lea about a young boy of eight who said he could communicate with solid matter (Chapter Five).

Lea: "When you say communicate, is it psionic communication or verbal communication?"

Mary: "What this child tells his mother is that when he touches the meteorite it communicates to him – it's feelings and where it's from, etc. He hears it in his head."

Lea: "Verbal communication if done correctly, can affect solid matter, if the user's voice is vibrating a certain frequency. However, psionic communication to affect solid matter is a different form of manipulation: that's telekinesis, photokinesis, electrokinesis, ergokinesis (pure energy manipulation), etcetera, so that's a kinesis-based ability."

Mary: "This was not psychometry, as such when someone intuitive touches an object and picks up information it has energetically retained: This child says he has a communication with the meteorite, it has real feelings and told him where it landed, etc. So it suggests it has its own consciousness, and is not just recording device!"

Definition – A psychic skill in which information about people, places, and events is obtained by handling objects associated with them, called psychometrizing.

> Ref: Page 487 *Encyclopedia of Mystical and Paranormal Experience* (1991)
> by Rosemary Ellen Guiley.

Lea: "Yes, that sounds like psychic commune. That allows deep communication with another life form, but meteorites are fragments of a planet's consciousness, so it's entirely possible people are able to communicate with pieces of life like that. Yes, a piece of a once-greater consciousness. This meteorite may have formed its own consciousness through its travels; the meteorite became self-aware. I personally haven't communicated with solid matter (other than some quartz crystals), but I can safely assume what the boy is doing is a psionic level of communication. I would say psychic commune at best, which is a basic sub-ability of telepathy.

I can also recall past lives, that's not so much ability but a state of being. Most *novis* can recall their previous lives and other human sub-groups, *noeticans* will be able to recall it when they come of age – even some *sapiens* can too."

Mary: "What do you know about yourself i.e., how many past lives do you recall; OBEs, etc?"

Lea: "My past lives: I have lived on Earth as a human for the first time fifteen thousand years ago, in the time where Earth knew its highest point, its golden age. This time was known as the fourth civilization, the Atlantean Era. My name was Delta Ungbrahe, and I was a citizen of Atlantia and lived in the world's capital of Atlantis. There, I worked in a museum as a historian. And now, I am here again, known as Lea. Feeling like an old woman in a child's body. Just starting to realize that the Earth I knew fifteen thousand years ago was so different that it was almost like it wasn't the same planet or race.

I can recall five whole lives stretching back thousands of years in many forms, but I can remember a few events from altogether thirty lives, but I do know my soul has had more. I was an Elzoni (same race as An'taji'san). This was thousands of years ago, way before their own First Contact. I lived on our home world Elzona, where I lived in a primitive civilization, learning how to become something equivalent to a shaman.

A thousand years later, I reincarnated into a human living in a once-great city known as Atlantis. Atlantia was a continent that existed in the Atlantic Ocean. The continent's main city was called Capihul (Atlanteans never called the city Atlantis – that was Plato's name given to the destroyed continent many thousands of years later). I lived in Atlantia my whole life, but back then humanity was at its highest point of civilization. We could travel to any continent in a second but also any planet of our choosing. Atlanteans had jaw-dropping technology that surpasses most modern-day engineers' dreams. Not only were we Atlanteans skilled inventors, but we also had help from ETs; we were in contact with them. Back then, humanity was intelligent, hard-working and ambitious, but none of those things equate to wisdom. We reached out too far too quickly, that's why Atlantia no longer exists; that's why humanity is in the state that it is right now."

Mary: "What is your feeling for the future?"

Lea: "It's hard to say. I have some idea for the future, but I'd rather not say, because, as always the future is no certainty. I do feel First Contact will occur in this generation, I feel there will be many wars happening both prior to it and certainly afterward, but one thing I do know is this world, humanity, will work out for the better in the end - we will survive.

We are evolving into a more multi-dimensionally conscious human to *Homo noeticus*. However, *Homo novis* are another group entirely; *Homo sapiens* are the only ones that are doing the upgrading to *noeticus*. *Homo novis* are only temporary; we can't have *novis* children, only *noeticus* children. They were made specifically for one time use, not continual production.

Homo noeticus are the real future, that's why we *novis* are trying to nurture; we are in transition. *Homo novis* have multiple jobs, mainly to make sure humans survive. Everything is to prevent destruction and wake people up. Those born after the year 2000 are *Homo noeticus*. These children are literally the next step, and they know things *Homo sapiens* never dreamed of. They will help us open up to ETs."

Note: Lea hopes to write a book on her experiences and her understanding of her Contacts. Lea has spoken about her life on Atlantis. She told me she was there when it was destroyed, and why it occurred.

My research has supported many details and information Lea has shared, including a recent picture of an underwater pyramid in the Atlantic Ocean, which Lea noted (and I quote):
"So they have found one of the Atlantean power sources then?"
This response from Lea is extremely compelling.

Note: The Sunken City submerged off the Bermuda Triangle has two huge pyramid structures made of glass, said to be as old as 10.000 BC.

As to how many *Homo novis* are in Australia, I'm beginning to think/feel they are in the hundreds, possibly thousands.

I believe Lea's understanding of herself and her reality, are extremely compelling. In the many conversations I had with Lea, she never deviated from her previous recall of those experiences or her understanding of them. No matter what part of her experiences, such as Lea's recall of past life events or her understanding and relationship with the extraterrestrial personalities she interacts with. The incredibly beautiful and detailed drawings of the Ambassadors, with which she says she is in regular communication.

My impressions of Lea as an individual are of someone who is extremely grounded, intelligent and articulate. The complexity of the subjects she shares is logical and compelling.

Conscious Awareness – New Major Experience

"I am an Arcturian ambassador in human form. I am here as an ecological engineer" – Antonio.

"There are lots of plans for humanity. Humans are primarily Pleiadian, Lyran, Felines and Reptilian."

Antonio contacted me when he was just sixteen years old. He resides in New Zealand with his parents. Antonio told me that his extraterrestrial heritage is Arcturian and he calls himself Ambassador Ehani. Antonio believes he has come here to help with the awakening of humanity, in the role of an ecological engineer.

Antonio shared that he attained his conscious awareness as a teenager. I have shared similar accounts where the child or teenager has demonstrated similar understanding, both of their 'true' origins and their Earth mission. Their awareness can be very challenging to them because Contact with other forms of intelligences is a 'knowing' with them and does not need to be proven. Their challenge is to gain acceptance of this 'knowing' when living in a 3D mindset that requires more tangible proof. Below is Antonio's story:

The Mission

Antonio: "My name is Antonio. I am sixteen years of age and I have had extensive Contact experiences over my life, but it intensified at the age of fourteen when I had some very direct Contact with Light Beings that telepathically communicated to me, mostly in my dreams and in meditation. I have extensive Contact experiences with the collective energy of the beings originating from the star system of Arcturus.

My mission here is to elevate the consciousness of Earth and bring through the higher dimensional energy in many ways. I feel like I am very activated and I can communicate a lot about my civilization and the operations and missions being crystallized here on the planet. I am an Arcturian ambassador situated in the human form. I can remember 'home' and exquisite organizations of beings from various star systems; they are integrated into geometric harmony. Technologies resonating on pure light and sound, crystalline resonating fields which emit this sound which resembles cosmic plasma of revolving circular fractals. I have some form of Contact, usually telepathically, almost every day.

I have many experiences where I have gone to non-local fourth and fifth-dimensional civilizations operating on higher color spectrums. I am a communicator for the collective consciousness to flow through my body. I feel like this body is a projection, a crystallization of the collective consciousness of our collective energy.

This body is an instrument for the frequencies that emanate from higher dimensions and into this physical plane, where I enjoy painting, drawing and communicating with individuals in the physical plane. Over the course of my life, I have increasingly heightened my psychic and telepathic abilities through my experiences with the ETs – to the point where I had difficulty with a lot of the low-frequency energy, both in the physical and astral world. I am healing myself and being reconfigured energetically by the angels and ET races very often."

Note: When we were speaking on Skype I asked Antonio about his childhood.

Antonio: "My earliest recall was at two or three years old. I remember sitting on a bed and seeing sparkling lights around me and knowing this was the council of all the ET races working as a body. However, some races and beings communicated with me directly. I was given instructions that the Earth was going through a shift, through visions, telepathy and dream state. This was a dense reality and I had an important mission.

It was only when I reached my teens, from fourteen through to seventeen, that I was able to remember the visions. As I spiritually awakened I can recall every single moment of my life, and the beings observing me. Even as a child, I would know what a crystal was and the properties it had, the energy it can hold and store.

As a child, I would look out the window and think, 'Where are you guys? And who are these two people who are my parents?' I knew they were just my temporary teachers in this world.

I had experiences when my astral body went to the higher realms, and met these 'beings'. I found it hard to be in this human body and in this world, as I was sensitive to energy and could see all kinds of things: ghosts, entities and spirits. I was able to feel the whole draconian energy of the planet. I knew this was a very low-dimensional world.

When I was growing up (five-six-seven) I developed friends in school. We recognized each other, and I was also telepathically communicating with the Council.

While at school, because I had multidimensional vision, I could see vortexes and the ETs themselves would materialize, also flickering lights and orbs. I would see this in the classroom, and other kids in the class who were Starseeds and connected to other civilizations, and I could see what was going on energetically and in their energetic field too.

As it developed, I could see a lot of high-frequency and energy fields. I would speak to other kids about space and extraterrestrials from five years old. When I went home I had a sense I was to be an inventor of time travel, teleportation. I can explain bit by bit what we need to develop to enable us to reach multidimensionality. This is to start with my physical body and that's why I eat healthily, to store that information in my mind and body. This data is available to everyone because when we connect to the multidimensional stream of information you can receive everything you want because everything is connected.

As I was growing up I saw a lot of dark spirits, and at six years old I told people that there were reptiles living in the Earth. I have been able to see starships, portals and energies; I was able to perceive these higher frequencies. I felt more advanced than other kids because other kids were conditioned by incarnating on Earth for a long time. Even at a young age, I understood why I was different. Some of this was due to my communications/downloads with the Council, even at two and three years old. Fortunately, I had a supportive family and home environment.

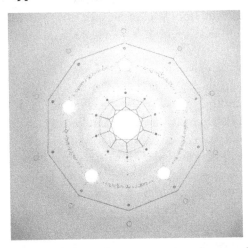

Antonio calls this image a light code, representing the over-laying of higher fre-quency thought and emotion, transmuting the old information stored in the DNA within the creator of this image(myself) and observer. The transmutation of old negative belief systems and patterns into symmetrical, powerfully spiritually inspir-ing. 'Healing Time' – a template to heal and repair emotional or mental distortion within the time field of the third-dimensional template of time. Five pointed star of the five elements, fire, water, air Earth ether-energetic symbiosis, harmony and fractal perfection.

Note: It has many symbols prevalent in many drawings of extraterrestrial Contact.

Healing Timelines in Earth System

Antonio: "All is connected; every situation in life has been embedded in our current body's cell memory. We can change and transform our consciousness by letting go of the past, letting go of fears and useless programming, which can be stored even early as childhood. Who we truly are is a field of non-local, creative, infinite potential, and the memories and identifications we hold in our body's memory banks can keep us stuck and resistant to receiving the guidance and blessings of the source within, of timeless intelligence.

By healing and unifying your earthly timelines that are connected to the months, seasons and astrological cycles, you grow stronger in all aspects."

New Technologies

Antonio: "My mission here is to elevate the consciousness of Earth and bring through the higher dimensional energy in many ways."

It all started with a school-funded subject work called Impact Project, when I was fifteen. It took me about thirty to thirty-five Wednesdays to build. Each week we had the opportunity to focus on a particular project of our choice and the teachers would support us in our creativity. So I planned a representation of a pyramid structure/temple that would be a meditation center, as well as containing a form of technology that would increase the vibratory level of the area this structure would be located in if it was built in the physical world. It is geometric, aligning to North, East, South, and West.

The concept and idea was given to me by the Star Councils, which were in constant communication with me during these earlier times in my life. They told me that I am a Galactic Architect and one of my special missions on Earth is to bring the sacred fractal architecture to Earth, reviving the ancient knowledge, but also bridging technology and architecture from more advanced societies to our developing 3D planet.

The pyramid is a meditation temple, which is a place where people come to focus their energy in groups, to stabilize each other's energy fields, as well as move collective thoughts/intentions/energy to different parts of the planet that require healing or multidimensional updating. These temples would not only be built with sacred geometry and harmonic fractal measurement, but they would be using technology. This technology would be electrical, magnetic and crystalline. The temple could also be used to access higher states of consciousness in groups of people and establish Contact with star visitors or other dimensions/star systems.

The pyramid is created through multiple layers of balsa-wood, which required me to spend a lot of time being precise to get all the symmetrical measurements in all the layers. After, it was coated and painted and layered with small landscape features.

It is geometric, aligning to North, East, South and West. The technology regarding the pyramid would consist of crystalline generators: light running through the crystals at a certain wavelength to produce an amplifying effect for people who are around it. Crystals located inside the pyramid; crystals located around the pyramid, perhaps at the water fountains.

Another form of technology would be thought-interactive computing devices that would record the vibration of the individuals inside the pyramid, to measure and figure out what kind of healing would be needed for each person.

The greatest technology of all would be the love-light telepathic connection of meditators and healers, interacting inside the pyramid. With intention, love and telepathy, as well as the help of these crystal amplifiers, thoughts and feelings can be sent around the Earth, to cleanse energy, as well as connect the other temple grids around the world. There are lots of plans for humanity. Humans are primarily Pleiadian, Lyran, Felines, and Reptilian."

The New Human Ecology

Antonio: "My work is as an ambassador, artist, channel and teacher. I feel I am already doing my mission. We need to create new civilizations, new villages and communities utilizing higher frequencies, crystals, magnetics, anti-gravity and electromagnetic technologies, so we can create our own energetic environment and stabilize Earth's energy grids over time, to achieve this grand, golden, multi-dimensional future of awakening of the planet. But to change the planet you need to change yourself: the food you eat, the air that you breathe, the people you connect with. The only way negative energies can access you is if you vibrate to that frequency. Darkness is a lack of information, a lack of light, an absence. The light is information, its energy the substance of the Universe.

People need to know that by changing their environment, they can influence themselves and the planet in the most beneficial way. To make the most change on the planet we need to put ourselves in certain environments so we re-connect to the Universe. We need to build our homes and technologies to fit with nature itself. We need to reconnect the natural, fractal, sacred-geometric intelligence. I want to build architecture that connects us to the Source of everything, so connecting to the fractal matrix.

Earth is like a big cosmic, galactic playground and none of us are just human, we all carry the memory of the star systems we are from."

Star Languages, Light Language

Antonio speaks the Arcturian Star Languages, writes the scripts and creates many geometric symbols, which he says are for raising awareness and frequencies.

Antonio: "Light Language is not only a language, it's the substance that creates all life. It's through the music, artwork and sound language of spoken word and intention. How this will happen on the planet: it is communicating to souls coming to Earth from all places in the Universe."

I have a recording of Antonio Speaks Arcturian Light Language.

Mary: "What does it mean? What is it describing?"

Antonio: "The connection between ground crew and lightships. The downloading process from the Arcturian down to earthlings and how that will connect the energy grid points in the coming times."

An Adult Experiencer Response to the Above Information

"This makes total sense! I'm so happy this person found you. We do have a rich ET history with so many different families out there. The transmission lines and waveforms are activating our galactic history. I am continually told that I am an ambassador and diplomat representative of the galactic council and the new galactic frequency to our star system, and here to help lead this planet, humans, and all other life-forms forward into the next generation. We are the transitional generation into the intergalactic and universal society, and are becoming interstellar with the other cosmic cultures. It's not all of our DNA or consciousness in us first time, but as for these bodies here on Earth, it is the first time for most in a long, long time. It is truly a renaissance and a great awaking and reformation of all things, and it has to start within."

J. (USA).

Antonio's Perspective on Hybrids

Antonio: "From my knowledge and memory, the human makeup on Earth is a combination of Earth native primate and nineteen to twenty-five different 'groups' of extraterrestrial lineages. It depends on where you are in the world and your own culture, for example: the Asians and white people have slightly different hybrid make-up, as they have different components to the extraterrestrial gene-lineage connection.

The Reptilians (Orion cultures) have also contributed to a great deal of who we are genetically. There are multiple human-like races such as the Pleiadians, Lyrans, Vegans, and many more, that are our genetic family.

As for hybridization projects and programs, I am aware of a few. One of the hybrid projects goes on between multiple Reticulan cultures. There are a few types. I have heard of accounts of both the Short Grays and the Tall Grays. This is a complex faction because there are multiple races and lineages of Grays, as you would already know."

Note: The Author was told that there were at least one hundred and sixty-five species of Gray.

Antonio: "There are some Gray's, which are hybridizing so they can be separated from the control of the Orion cultures (Reptilian). The Orion Empire was co-operating with some Gray groups because they lacked the emotional quality, therefore they were easy to manipulate. The Tall Grays are the most sophisticated and further along the advancement of technology and spirituality, I believe.

There are also hybrid projects going on with the Orion and Reptilian cultures as well, and this is too complicated for me to put into detail. I can say that this is going on in their ships, home worlds, and also within our own underground Earth bases.

The hybrids of both Orion and Gray groups are utilizing our genetics by often agreeing and making contracts with Earth humans. There are some of these beings that will incarnate into the physical body (as souls from the ET society into the Earth society) and then partake in the hybrid programs.

The emotional quality is powerful in the human makeup because we have a strong degree of power to be angry, fearful, loving and compassionate. Many ET races find this interesting, and the emotional quality is what the Grays require, to transcend the manipulation programs of the Orion culture. There has been a great degree of control, manipulation, agreements etc., between the Orion and Gray cultures. In fact, this is not only happening on their world, but on our world and multiple other worlds."

Ref: *Meet the Hybrids: The Lives and Missions of ET Ambassadors on Earth*
by Miguel Mendonca and Barbara Lamb, published 2015.

Antonio: "I have to be careful with my higher vibratory energy states. It is amplifying, and it can attract unwanted attention from the darker beings. I am speaking of the lower astral energies, which do not want us to be enlightened. I am very psychic and sensitive and I can feel what's going on in the world. I am calm and reflective at all times, even when things might not be going my way.

I have been feeling a lot of changes going on in the planet. The Vatican, underground government, and some other groups, are planning something very bad right now. They are implementing frequency technology to keep the masses enslaved.

There is a lot that we will be going through because all of us, on a higher level, have agreed to the changes already.

The radioactive problems are getting very big, Mary. I suggest you look into Zinc supplements and Reishi mushroom supplements. Those are among your most powerful allies in combating the heavy elements and radioactive isotopes in the air. It is accelerating. We need to take precautions because according to the Federation of Light, it is Earth's biggest issue right now."

My Many Aspects as Ambassador Ehani

Antonio: "Ambassador Ehani has many forms. Ehani is a Light Being. He/she may manifest and materialize in many forms. He is an androgynous, multidimensional, extraterrestrial soul-matrix, whose consciousness is an extension of a higher-dimensional council operating in hyperspace. Ehani has seeded his soul-matrix into many confederations, star systems, and timelines.

As a crystalline engineer, multi-dimensional programmer and communicator, he has taken the privilege to assist Earth in this current space-time, and finds himself awake in a young male body, shedding and transmuting the cell memory, in order to allow higher-vibrational light-signatures to be channeled to the grid networks of the Earth Life System. He is a light code with the platonic solid octahedron in the middle and a hexagonal geometry extending out with symmetrical light codes.

He is I as a physical extraterrestrial. Although my name is Antonio now, many people refer to me by my star-lineage name Ehani. I am currently seventeen years of age, a university student studying Landscape Architecture. I have a highly psychic, sensitive nature and I have been experiencing inter-dimensional Contact with Light Beings and extraterrestrials ever since I can remember.

My mission is that I have chosen to come back to Earth in this time-line to help in every way that I can. I have memories of my existence on other worlds and dimensions. I portray these star-memories and connections through poetry, art and You-Tube videos. I have been sent here from a group of beings, which I would refer to as a group-collective of Light Beings that exist in the higher dimensions. These Light Beings can manifest in the astral and physical dimensions also. I see them every day. I have experienced the telepathic downloading of information that is very common among Starseeds and Star Children. I have a YouTube channel, with thousands of people who are interested in my work. My life purpose is to anchor my higher self, which only wants the best for all life on Earth. I am here as an extraterrestrial Starseed ambassador, designer and architect, channeler, healer, and multi-dimensional programmer."

Three humanoid hybrid beings from the Andromeda Constellation in our galaxy (These are the same beings that Contacted Alex Collier). They are materialized and are consciously accessing some type of crystalline technology. The technology is opening a vortex and they are using their telepathic abilities to transmit and receive specific information through the portal vortex. This type of technology is very common throughout all space civilizations. (Portable, Accessible, High Frequency Vortex Communication technology.)

Antonio: "The memories are coming back, and I am remembering more of my cosmic origins within the higher-dimensional networks and other planetary systems. There is a lot that we will be going through because all of us, on a higher level, have agreed to the changes already."

Past Lives

Antonio: "I have been told that I have been incarnated in their civilization many times as a multidimensional being. We have many, many connections to different timelines on Earth, as well as different star systems and dimensions.

The dimensions in which they primarily operate are a type of hyperspace environment, where everything is full of light, energy and information. The dimensions are represented as layers of geometry that are specific to a certain vibrational frequency.

The civilizations that Contact me the most are masters of time and space. They are deeply involved in the evolution of the Earth and they appear to me as colorful light energy, plasma or complex geometry. They feel what I feel. They can communicate visual messages to me, or even give me confirmations on my pathway in life. They often give me a strong vibration, which comes from my brain down through my nervous system and through my feet. These are used to increase the vibrational frequency of the physical body, and there are many techniques where they use certain sound/light 'packages' which my physical body feels and receives. This has been happening for most of my life."

I asked Antonio how his parents felt about his experiences. Antonio believed he was very fortunate that his parents were so accepting of him and his understanding. I spoke with Antonio over Skype and shared many email communications. I found Antonio to be intelligent and articulate. I was impressed with the complexity of his understanding; the knowledge and the information he shared; the dedication to what he believed as his mission to help other young Starseeds become aware and awake.

Antonio's YouTube channel: https://www.youtube.com/user/DesiignMS
Channeled artwork: http://arcturusant.deviantart.com/

Notes – Ambassador

I have communicated with many individuals who interpret themselves as Starseeds. Some of them also believe they are ambassadors from a particular star system or species. Personally, I do not believe it is beyond the realms of possibility that non-human intelligences would not instigate this kind of operation. It would be a logical step if they wish to instigate open acceptance of their presence. They would place certain individuals to assist with this process. The creation of intermediaries (hybrids) to interface and assist in the process connecting with off-world cultures and species –any Starseeds who feel they are hybrids believe they are here to create a bridge to link humanity with their extraterrestrial ancestors.

Definition

Ambassador – A diplomatic official of the highest rank, sent by one sovereign or state to another as its resident representative.

The field of Ufology has expanded its mandate in recent years, to recognize the need for a socio-political structure to assist with the recognition we are interacting with non-human intelligences.

Vanessa Lamorte shares her story in *Meet the Hybrids*, and she believes that although her parents were both human, she was taken on-board a craft and embedded by extraterrestrials with galactic coding which included Sirians, Andromedans, Pegasians, Camelopardians, Zetas and Pleiadians. She says she was aware that as a soul she had agreed to come to Earth as a hybrid. (Page 217) In the chapter *Bridges and Ambassadors* (page 239), she states that "a key part of the hybrids' mission is to bridge the gap between humans and extraterrestrials."

"With the term 'exopolitics' and its engaged aspect 'exo-diplomacy' coming into increasing use, the hybrids could be thought of as a key group of exo-diplomats."

"Bringing this awareness to humanity is one facet, being something of an Ambassador."

Ref: Robert Frost Fullington (page 241), *Meet The Hybrids* by Miguel Mendonca and Barbara Lamb.i.e., Exopolitics.

Exopolitics – The art or science of government as concerned with creating or influencing policy toward extraterrestrial phenomena and extraterrestrial beings. Exopolitics hopes to define a process towards a peaceful and co-operative communication with non-human intelligence.

Ref: *Exopolitics, Politics, Government and Law in the Universe* by Alfred Lambremont Webre, JD. Med. Weber is an American author, lawyer, futurist, peace activist.

Alfred Lambremont Webre

Alfred Lambremont Webre is a graduate of Yale University and Yale Law School in international law and was a Fulbright Scholar in international economic integration in Uruguay. Alfred was general counsel to the New York City Environmental Protection Administration, a futurist at Stanford Research Institute (where he directed the proposed 1977 Carter White House extraterrestrial communication study), and a judge on the Kuala Lumpur War Crimes Tribunal. He is the founder of www.exopolitics.com, a leading exopolitical news website, and the host of Exopolitics TV: http://www.youtube.com/user/

Using empirical data from intelligent extraterrestrial civilizations and the intelligent civilizations of souls in the inter-life, he demonstrates a new hypothesis of a functioning ecology of intelligence in the dimensions of the Omniverse.

Ref: *The Omniverse: Trans-dimensional Intelligence, Time Travel, Afterlife* and *Secret Colony on Mars*. Paperback: 224 pages. Publisher: Bear & Company, 2nd edition (Nov 19, 2015).

Ref: http://aquarianradio.com/2013/12/29/alfred-lambremont-webre/#sthash. RJLuQZXW.dpuf

Chapter Twelve

ART – THE CONDUIT FOR NEW PERCEPTUAL INFORMATION ACCESSING OTHER DIMENSIONS

A Past Life that Did Not Fulfill Its Mission

Debbie Malone is a respected psychic medium and author of *Between Two Worlds*. She is well known for her psychic detective work with a number of police departments throughout Australia regarding unsolved cold cases. Debbie resides in Sydney, Australia, with her family. Debbie refers to me clients who may have extraterrestrial Contact; this has been due to her own experiences with extraterrestrials.

Debbie discovered more about her extraterrestrial encounters when I first met her. It was when she was helping to solve a well-publicized cold case in Western Australia. My skills as a hypnotherapist were needed to help her access more information about this case because she knew her psychic skills were heightened under hypnosis. It was very successful and we gained important and detailed information regarding this significant case. However, while Debbie was in my home, she encountered a blue extraterrestrial being and realized she had experienced many such extraterrestrial encounters throughout her life. We have remained in contact since that time because of her on-going extraterrestrial experiences.

Debbie: "My first experience with ET was when I was fifteen to sixteen years of age. My brother had a telescope and we lived in Lalor Park, in the western suburbs of Sydney. Our house was built on a hill, and at night we could see the night sky very clearly. One night, my brother Michael told us that he could see a UFO. Michael did this on many occasions and we all said, 'Yes, Michael, like you did last time.' Actually, he did see a UFO. We stood at the front of our house and a number of neighbors across the road also saw this UFO. I rang the Richmond Airbase and made a UFO report. I described the craft and they said that it was a Hercules, flying at night, but I knew it wasn't. I called Sydney Airport and Bankstown Airport; they said

I was just seeing things! The Richmond Airbase sent me a UFO-report sheet, which I completed, and drew what I had observed. Unfortunately, when my parents moved, I told my mum to throw it out; I regret this now.

When I underwent my first hypnosis session – it was around 2000 – the first image I saw was an ET baby. From my earliest memories as a child, I had nightmares of being restrained in a clinical room on a medical-type table with an elastic-type band across my abdomen area. For many years, I suffered from these images. I had constant fears that ET would abduct me. I don't know why, I just did.

I had also forgotten an unusual dream until I moved into my current house, in the Sutherland Shire, twenty-three years ago. I began to have the same dream of the clinical experience with the elastic-band-type thing holding me down on a clinical table. During these experiences, I felt like my mind was being stretched or expanded. It was a very weird experience and I was frightened.

Fast forward – I met Mary Rodwell in 2007-2008, for a hypnosis session for a project I was working on. While at Mary's home in WA (Western Australia), I asked if I could use the bathroom. On walking down the hallway to the bathroom, I encountered a tall, blue being that was around seven feet tall. He seemed quite friendly, but he also surprised me by his presence. I thought I was seeing things. It was only when I spoke to Mary about what I had seen that she agreed that he had been seen in her home before.

I underwent the hypnosis session for the cold case project. When we finished I spoke to Mary about my own experiences. I tried to show Mary pictures I had taken, but when I tried to show her my photographs the computer and all of the electrical items around us began to play up. (This seems to be a common occurrence with individuals having encounters). We discussed what I had seen, and from that point onwards, Mary and I have stayed in contact.

Since meeting Mary, I have had numerous experiences with ETs. I have captured images of ETs on camera and have a number of recordings of their Contact. In 2010, I underwent hypnosis with Mary, in my office, and during the hypnosis session, in trance, I was shown natural disasters that were to happen to the world. I saw that earthquakes were going to happen in New Zealand, in Christchurch. I saw the earthquake in Japan and the tsunami that followed. I also saw Australia cut in two by water and then I saw the super-cyclone that happened in North Queensland at the time, and the flooding of Queensland and New South Wales.

I have had many visitations by ETs and have also experienced implants in my left eye, which I was able to dislodge. I had an implant in my left ear, on the top of my left ear, and also an implant in my right eye after having an operation, and another implant in my left hand near my left wrist. I have undergone a thermal imaging scan, and the implants were seen in the scan. I have seen numerous ET craft, including an ET craft hovering above the hockey field at Lithgow. I took photographs of the experience.

Note: Due to Debbie's own sightings and ET experiences, she has been a valuable source of referral for people who have also had encounters and need support.

Debbie referred a young man, John (not his real name), a talented artist. John believed he may have experienced extraterrestrial encounters. He was intrigued why he painted certain, very specific, geometric images, some of which he felt intuitively were star maps, and wondered if his encounters were in some way connected to his art.

John also had another question, which related to his childhood. It was a childhood fascination with army combat clothing and his desire to be a gunner or 'tradie' (tradesman), which puzzled him. He felt this may be a possible connection to what he believed was a past life in World War One. He had researched into his family ancestral heritage, discovering an ancestor who had been a soldier in the First World War. This soldier had his mother's maiden name and he had the feeling this individual was significant and connected to him in some way. John asked if I could help explore the possibility of his extraterrestrial encounters and this past life link. As our conversation unfolded, some fascinating links to his extraterrestrial encounters in this life and a past life mission were revealed.

Psychic Experiences and Non-Physical Help with Art
Communications from the Spirits of Dead Soldiers

Skype conversation prior to hypnosis:
J: "From the age of four, I remember I had Contact with what I felt were soldiers which came into my room. I used to talk to them, and I wouldn't go to sleep and would transmit the messages to my family, such as what one soldier was saying to me. I would say to my parents, 'The man's here.' I recall they had nails sticking out of them, and missing limbs, just like soldiers in a war.

One day, I saw this light I told my mother that finally 'he' (the spirit) was going to the light. However, I got scared of these abilities and shut down.

Note: These experiences instigated John's obsession with the military without him understanding why. It was researching the family's ancestral links connected to a soldier in the First World War, and, synchronistically, this soldier had the exact birthdate as John but it was exactly one hundred years apart.

J: "I had experiences in my room; I would see balls of light before I went to sleep. It was after I had knee surgery. I couldn't play sport anymore. I started to focus on my art and painting, and I opened up again intuitively, psychically, and began to understand how to communicate with spirits. I was studying fine arts and I had trouble with a teacher so I communicated to 'them' and asked for help. I believe it was Leonardo De Vinci I was communicating with at the time."

M: "What made you think it was Leonardo?"

J: "Because I was doing a painting which was traditional. I heard a man's voice – very calm – talk me through a still life picture. I was struggling to do this and I didn't know what I was doing, as I was more naturally an abstract painter rather than doing realistic works. It's hard to explain, but he would talk to me and tell me to 'put some paint' in a spot, or a particular brush stroke and 'you will get this effect.' It was a big improvement from my previous work; a big change."

M: "Did he introduce himself to you as Leonardo De Vinci?"

J: "Yes, he said who he was. I checked with my parent, who was also very psychic and intuitive and they confirmed that I was correct. I was having trouble with my teacher, who was very traditional in her art, and I am unconventional. Leonardo is classified as a very traditional painter, one of the best of all time, so it made sense to me. When I went to University, my art became more natural. My drawing became better and sometimes it was either 'him' or a guardian who would communicate with me and advise me to take my time and re-do something as I worked on a piece.

I was always interested in the stars, and I took photos of the stars and then painted the night skies. One day, I was just experimenting and painting an image and it fell off the wall and a voice said 'Leave it there', and I started painting a cosmic other-dimensional kind of painting, like surrealist paintings but more abstract, just like another world. They do feel real to me like I am escaping into another world in a way. Although I feel I create another world, it also feels like it really exists."

M: "Does it feel like this may be images of a place you might actually know or visit?"

J: "Yes, it does, and when I say that I get goose bumps, whatever that means, and I have been buzzing since I have been talking to you. (People often get this rush of energy or goose bumps when they are connecting to a truth or something important). I have always felt very different and unconventional. I don't drink or use drugs, and at my age, this is pretty unusual, especially at art school, but this behavior doesn't interest me. I look at Kandinsky, a Russian artist famous between the 1900s to the 1930s. He had a lot of references to the stars, and this year my paintings changed again. In my head, I make shapes of paintings. I can't explain them. I take something cosmic from my head and maybe put a circle. I have to put a triangle. It's like they are patterns, but I don't know what they mean. One I did – there were lots of shapes like symbols. It felt like I was writing another language in a way."

M: "Do you feel like you may be conveying information in your paintings?"

J: "I feel like I want to open the world up to the more spiritual side of things, as there is so much negativity in the world right now. I feel these paintings can change that, as it's a language. I feel very calm when I am painting, like it's me. It is how I feel and I am trying to communicate something like look deeper, open up your mind."

M: "Some people who draw scripts say that some of the symbols are multidimensional in nature and convey packets of information."

J: "When you say that, I start buzzing again. I am not certain of my recall of encounters so would like to try hypnosis. But strangely, I feel I can pick out those who are 'aliens' in a way. (John means humans that he may see in every-day life whom he believes are really aliens.) They look different and I feel like they recognize me as well, sometimes they even stare at me, but I don't know their motivation. They can be very lean and tall, slim looking and chiseled jaw, mostly men. I don't get a good feeling with some of them; I feel I am being watched.

Note: Many people believe they have met people who they said seemed very different and felt they were alien. Command Sgt Major Robert Dean in many interviews says this happens.

One evening, I was taking photos with a friend, it was not very dark. On a soccer field we saw a dark shape – a figure – then it disappeared. We picked up the camera and left. It was the weirdest experience, and earlier on we saw a kid. His face was strange and looked like something had happened. He was running really weirdly and it was 9 pm at night and he looked only ten to twelve, so it was late for him to be about. But it was this weird shape that came out of this dark area."

Note: In regression, we revisited this experience. He felt the being he saw could shapeshift and bend/change matter and felt a dark feeling, and felt they were trying to sabotage his mission. John has always felt watched and can feel energy, but says he knows how to block energy. He protects himself with seeing himself in a cocoon of gold with beams of energy from his heart to a higher source and his star family. He says some of the beings try to scare him, to get him to lower his frequency, but they can't touch him while he is on this higher frequency. Painting and music help him maintain this frequency, and he said he has visits from many species.

J: "I always knew I could do what some members of my family could do psychically. I was always a bit frightened as a kid. I went to sleep with my arms inside my bed because I felt I was going to be taken. Even now, I feel uncomfortable leaving my arms outside my bed. A mental thing; like they can grab your hands or something. I am better now, but when younger, if my arms were outside my bed, I would freak out. I was worried about the closet and dark when younger, even under the bed. When I walk home at night I always look behind me. I feel like someone is coming for me – it's weird.

Sometimes I feel that time slows down or speeds up. Like days feel longer than what my watch says, but it's not like I am busy; it feels very different."

M: "Do you recall anomalies with time – 'missing time' when things have taken longer than they should have – like instead of thirty minutes it has taken you longer than that?"

J: "All the time. I think there are things I need to know. I feel I have to travel the world, but I don't know why. I feel like I am doing things like Leonardo did when he drew planes hundreds of years ago, and how some of his paintings make triangles – such as in The Last Supper, Jesus' right eye is a triangle. I noticed the set up is all in threes, even with the disciples.

I am very drawn to artists who are very spiritual, and one can see this in their paintings. With the Russian Kandinsky, it looks like dimensional art. When I paint, it's very intuitive and the color just feels right. I found I could imagine, feel and sense color, like synesthesia. And even songs will feel like color and wavelength."

Note: Synesthesia: A condition in which one type of stimulation evokes the sensation of another, as when the hearing of a sound produces the visualization of a color.

"I do wake up in the mornings really tired because my mind doesn't really stop and I need a lot of sleep. I did think 'I am going out-of-body' (OBE's), but then thought 'I can't be that important.' I would like to recall more of this experience, as I feel my mind has a lot of information. I have an urgency to do something for the world, but I don't know what. It feels like some kind of mission. I feel the art is going to get me to what else I need to do, and I have a feeling I am going to run out of time. I can look at people's eyes and I can immediately tell what kind of person they are, like a darker energy or lighter energy. Although reading them like that makes me feel a little uncomfortable, that's all. I have read someone before I meet him or her and then find they have turned out to be like that. Also, my friends are drawn to me when they have difficult relationships; they will just open up to me."

M: "Do you sometimes feel you know what they are thinking?"

J: "Yes, sometimes, but that's harder to read than the whole person. I had a strange thought one time that in some way I had an alien connection. My mother had a miscarriage, and after that, I was born. I felt 'they' (the alien beings) helped me to come (be born), but I am not sure and think maybe that's crazy, but it also feels normal in some way to feel like that. Lots of electronics seem to break down on me too. I think because of my energy. I feel like I am changing and am lonely sometimes, as I feel others just don't understand or get it!!

In my paintings, I feel like I have to make a wormhole into other dimensions. I feel like there are places in the world you can access these wormholes. I feel like the other alien children that we spoke about, who could build the portals. I feel like I am mapping other dimensions that exist, like telling a story, and they are patterns, and I feel they will be put together like a map. It's like I don't need to explain it just yet, though; it will be later I will need to do this. I do feel I need to do hypnosis. I think there is a lot there, and I feel comfortable with your energy.

I am drawn to the pyramids and Stonehenge. I think that's a vortex, which makes sense to my mind. These shapes speak to me sometimes. I see a shape, it's almost like I can read them. It feels weird and true artists can understand that. And I think certain sounds can make shapes, and with my painting, it changes the person's perceptions as people view them. Open their mind and other people will see it; there is also information and they will get the energy from it.

Note: John noticed a strange beat/humming sound at this point.

I also feel I have to create my own style of school and teach mathematics and have a day where you are doing art, a day where you do music and one doing sports, so it's balanced and they choose whatever path they want to go down. I feel sometimes I have a job, to help save the world. I know that sounds naïve and I am only one person but there is something there to do, to bring them (people) to the light – to show them the light."

Note: John commented on my space picture in my office as so many have, and said the green ball shown there has been in some of his paintings. This painting has an 'unknown artist.'

J: "It was after my knee surgery I was different. I felt so different I wondered, did something else happen?

Note: It was after the knee surgery that John then focused on his art.

Answers:

1. Answers to his images of space and geometric forms he felt related to other dimensions and star maps.
2. What his origins were.
3. Why he was afraid of heights or the edge and falling.
4. What he needed to know.
5. Was there any connection with the soldier in World War One.

The Regression

Initially, John finds himself on a golden cloud until he perceives a passageway, which led to a point; feeling and then traveling into another dimension of space. He feels his destination is a meeting with 'them' – the beings.

John feels he is in a metal shuttle like ball craft, which felt familiar. He feels they are expecting him and he is going towards a golden light, to a meeting with 'them.' John meets a figure: tall and skinny with big eyes, a big head, long face and blue skin. He says the being knows him but calls him by another name. John calls these beings both family and colleagues and their star origin is Surracus, located in another dimension. John describes two points which look like a spider web and says that one travels through it to the other side. He travels to that point and then it spits him out in the other dimension. He describes it as dimensional travel. He says he is there for a briefing about what needs to be done and it relates to his painting, which is maps, to help the human world, and they need to know them. John felt the maps help 'them' and also us humans. He said it helps them come here to Contact us and helps us to Contact them; he is the middle man of the two dimensions. The artwork can create a portal but also open people up to an understanding of dimensional space. The colors are important because it creates the right colors for that energy. John said they often take him up to craft at night and it's very intense for him.

John saw other beings he has interacted with, of a different color, but he described them as a sister-planet species who worked with the Blue Beings of his origin, creating a yin and yang balance. He felt his own origin race was called Zelsabar. They have a fast energy, very peaceful, and the planet is very eco-friendly. I asked him if he recognized or connected to any of his human family on this planet and he recognized his mother there, as well as now, in his present human life, and said it explained why he feels so connected to her in this lifetime.

The feelings of fear of heights or falling off the edge were related to when he was a small child and traveling through the dimensions. It left him with a residual fear of falling off the edge of something. He located this energy of fear held in his stomach and throat, and it cleared as it was recognized and we moved through the regression. Throughout this regression, John said that much of what he found out he already sensed or felt he knew. He also had confirmation that changing his diet would help with his stomach problems, and to eat a lot of vegetables and fruits, and this will also raise his frequency. John was instructed to spend more time in meditation, and creativity to enhance his communications and connection.

Finally, we explored the focus on the soldier who had the same birth date, connected to his ancestry. John saw himself on the battlefield and recognized this as his past life as the soldier. He said that because he had been sent to war he hadn't fulfilled his purpose. The war had altered his consciousness and so he had come back in this life to complete it. John said that 'they' (the beings) knew a war was coming, but although the war could have been stopped things didn't go to plan. They created a connection to this lifetime so that he could do what needs to be done and to do this is very complex, and requires complex mathematical equations of being here in the correct timeline. It's very mathematical and so complex he can't comprehend it, but he was seeing lists - numbers - going through his head like a science of numbers. He said it was all connected to his personality and consciousness. The reason he is here is that 'they' needed a strong carrier, and even star signs are mathematical in creating stronger links to them, as a system they have created to go down a particular path. Even images he has on his clothing (images of space) keep him linked to them. He also helps his family with their connection to this.

After the first Skype interview, John found new information was downloaded. John was told that he will get more information during sleep, and it will be available to him intuitively. The regression has heightened his connection to his subconscious and more information.

John said that the species he comes from are called Zapherus, and they are seen as healers of the galaxies.

I find John's information compelling as it provides possible evidence that the soul chooses certain mandates for its life journey, and if it is unsuccessful it will return to complete them.

John's understanding of his art and what it conveys gives more credence to its importance. It again demonstrates how this unique art may act as a catalyst for triggering the awakening of multidimensional awareness. This confirms a theme or pattern for many artists after their encounters, that what they are producing has a significant purpose.

The production of specific artwork after extraterrestrial encounters appears to be a significant pattern of Contact as Tracey Taylor explains in Chapter Thirteen.

I am very grateful to Debbie Malone for her support and for her willingness to help those who experience encounters.

To contact Debbie Malone:

BETWEEN TWO WORLDS P/L

Web: www.betweentwoworlds.net

Mailbox: PO Box 752, Sutherland, NSW, Australia 2232.

Facebook: https://www.facebook.com/debbiebetweentwoworlds

Chapter Thirteen

A COSMIC BEING

The Modern Shaman
By Tracey Taylor

"I have realized how the native cultures of our world understand and acknowledge my experiences as visionary or shamanic, that such realities are yet to be openly accepted and understood in Western culture."

Tracey Taylor.

I first met Tracey when she was in her early twenties and was introduced to her beautiful and unusual artwork. Two things struck me: Tracey's vulnerability, because despite the many extraterrestrial encounters she continually questioned her sanity, and secondly, that her artwork was extremely significant.

I facilitated a support group of Experiencers for many years, and Tracey joined this group. Encouraged by what they shared with her, Tracey became more confident and at peace with her own experiences. The group also found Tracey's artwork 'spoke to them' and she was determined to explore what this meant in relation to her experiences because this unusual geometric artwork was created with no conscious effort on her part, although she always had a sense of what it conveyed. I have known Tracey for almost eighteen years and her story has not deviated except to be expanded upon, which is what the reader will see below.

Note: Tracey Taylor wrote a chapter on her story in my first book *Awakening* (Chapter 8).

Triggers of Consciousness, Art and Language
Tracey:
"For most of my life, I have experienced interactions with beings from various realms beyond the consensus reality of Earth. Over the years, these beings would

appear to me in many forms, often presenting as extraterrestrial in nature. During several encounters, some of these beings imparted to me insights into unified ways of perceiving and experiencing existence, as consciousness within human form and beyond. Understanding and realizations regarding heart-centered consciousness, including knowledge, incorporating multidimensional viewpoints, multispectral physics, frequency (vibrational) modulation, nature, creation blueprints and more. These awakenings triggered within me the expression of such perspectives on reality, resulting in the completion of numerous writings, drawings (personal and universal blueprints), equations and energetic downloadings of insight, incorporating divine geometry, script and symbolism. The experiences brought about awareness from within my heart space that led to the overpowering urge to put pen to paper. The drawings include script closely resembling hieroglyphics and other texts from various ancient cultures. Inspiring also a spoken language that imparts particular sound frequencies enabling cellular healing, alignment and deep awareness from a soul level.

Concepts for the artwork, inspired through connections and communication with these beings, also activated within me a vast cosmic perspective, which I was to anchor into the Earth domain. The nature of the artwork's potential is to connect individuals through internal portals to multidimensional realities, whilst also having positive emotional, spiritual and physiological effects on those viewing them. I have often noted how people feel drawn in by the symbolic familiarity of the images deep within their being. Often triggering realizations, emotional responses, and memories of their connections with a higher inner knowing, an ancient omnipresence and with on and off Earth civilizations and origins. They gain access to an alignment with the Divine masculine and feminine energies, the cosmic and Earth energies. Many people now feel there is a conscious unification of these energies as a bringing of Heaven/Earth alignment, reawakening our hearts into a state of compassion and union with Mother Earth. As we open our hearts we can experience the grief and pain of humanity's history, the disconnection and the incredible trauma all species of this planet have been part of. We begin now to transmute these energies through our heart space, to heal, becoming new and awakened within a place of true compassion and love, conscious of the inner and outer union with All, for All of existence.

In some of the artwork there are technologies of an interstellar nature, multidimensional travel and communication interpreted and understood whilst viewing the symbols and drawings. The works have also revealed understanding as to the purpose and energetic functions of the Egyptian pyramids (and others), related to the ancient sacred science of golden mean geometry and sacred geometry's relationship with astrological vibrational mechanics. Knowledge concerning evolved technologies, (hidden from the public), now here on Earth, can be brought to light."

Note: Many individuals who view Tracey's artwork, or hear her 'Light Language' (spoken universal language) have profound reactions. Many say they get healing frequencies or find themselves being triggered on multiple levels.

Terry Mace – Psychotherapist, UK

"When I first saw Tracey's artwork, to begin with, I was traumatized, it knocked me off my feet. Metaphysically, spiritually, it was like an internal implosion, like a light going on. I sensed and understood something I should have had knowledge of as awakening spiritually since a child, that I had forgotten; something I had been trained to do. I was able to switch on a channel, and use my hand as a bar code reader: the equivalent of several hundred terabytes of information, data at light speed.

I understood on multiple levels what it meant, what its potential was for humanity, group consciousness, codes, geometric formulae, blueprints, designs, models, encryptions, meta-languages, hieroglyphics, schematics. An internal Rosetta stone turned on as an intergalactic process. I could understand on a conscious and superconscious level, something I was trained to do. I was a code breaker, activated by the artwork. I am able to understand and do something with it, like an esoteric engineer."

Pre-birth Experience
Crystalline Grandfather Beings

"Relating to my present earthly incarnation, yet as a precursor to my birth, I remember encountering beings I can describe as enormous bodies of immense light; geometric, crystalline and holographic in nature when expressing a visible form. These energies/beings were shown to collectively span solar systems and galaxies, I call them the Crystalline Grandfather Beings or Council.

The first recollection I have of these beings relates to the moments before my birth, where I had an awareness of a vastness or void without form. There was no me or self, just a conscious omnipresence. At the same instant appeared (as consciousness) two powerfully-expansive beings of energy within the omnipresence, encapsulating another presence of 'new consciousness.' There was a sense of timeless infiniteness. The 'two' became clearer as my awareness created a sense of separation from these energies. A sense of an evolving singular 'me' somewhat independent of the two, became clearer.

I remained without form, yet a vision of a small, hyper-colored, multidimensional revolving sphere appeared within the vastness, along with the sensation of connection to the sphere. I observed a human hand reaching out from my point of consciousness to gently grasp the glowing holographic sphere. This 'human hand' that I had now become connected to enabled sensations relating to the unique energetic vibrations of the sphere. I sensed from the 'two' that I now (as a singular consciousness) was to go forth and enter into the sphere. Immediately, I experienced a sensation like a condensing of space (consciousness) into form, as the vastness dissipated into a new vision.

There I now was, a 'me', a human form surrounded by majestic scenery. I found myself resting on a large moss-covered stone boulder in a forest, near to a gently flowing waterfall. Within my new awareness was the inherent knowing as to the functions and purposes of the human form on all levels, miraculous and divine.

199

The softly-emanating vibrations of the waterfall converged into audible sound; the humidity and density of the cool forest air enlivened my lungs, the sensations tickled my skin. I felt a sense of a center within this form, yet a spacious connection with all else. Peace and tranquillity within the experience of the human senses enabled me the ability to envision from within the projection of this scenery before me.

A small furry being, an opossum, made its way along the rock ledge beside the waterfall. I then heard language for the first time: a 'voice' clearly saying *yapock*, within a knowing this was an earthly name that human beings had collectively assigned to this creature within my view. This vision then blurred into a myriad of light and color as my awareness opened into an experience. Now being physically birthed as a human baby into the condensed creational consciousness of the Divine Earth, through the portal of my Mother.

Interestingly, twenty-six years later, while watching a David Attenborough documentary about marsupials, he began to speak about and show footage of an opossum from the South American jungles called a 'Yapock.' Hearing this word immediately triggered the memories of my pre-birth experience, as this was the same type of creature I had recalled seeing. David Attenborough described how water-opossums have vibrationally sensitive webbed paws that pick up vibrations on the surface of water to find food. The yapock during my pre-birth experience was also near the water. It also intrigued me that throughout my life, my hands have naturally been sensitive to energetic vibrations, learning to further tune into this for healing purposes."

More on the Crystalline Grandfather Beings

"According to my understanding, the function of these beings is similar to a combined energy stream, a unified collective body of consciousness. The purpose is for co-creation and harmonization between many dimensional frequencies and relative universes. Made up of various civilizations, beings and species coexisting as a harmonized energetic field of consciousness. This vast energy formation comprises a collective directive for stabilizing creational energies through harmonic unification within regions of consciousness. All life forms originate through this direction and intention (the original blueprint); creating harmonic blueprints within the universal paradigm they resonate at extremely coherent vibrational frequencies in various dimensional constructs. Our human perspective on this is seeing that all planets and bodies within our solar system function according to very precise Golden Mean or Fibonacci ratios or Phi geometry, and that each planet resonates with particular frequencies. This is then reflected through our experience on Earth on all levels, as one can look at the understandings pertaining to astrology and the collective experience.

Grandfather Beings reflect a broader awareness to consciously unify all creational aspects, including the physically-focused orientation, movements and harmonic frequencies of planetary bodies, interconnecting through all of us. The illusion of separateness in our experience as individuals is purely for the purpose of infinite diversity in evolution. As human beings awaken through the dimensional layers of perception, we exponentially experience the momentum of these resonating harmonic fields of consciousness within our reality. A focused convergence of cosmic energy through projected consciousness (masculine energy) is then merged and balanced with the divine feminine as an experience of emotions and feelings and connection with Earth. This, in turn, affects the blueprint of the human genome and our collective evolutionary experience. It is maybe that instead of bringing heaven down to earth, we are now in the process of bringing the Earth up to heaven, stabilizing ourselves within this truly Divine realm and raising our vibration along with our planet.

The artwork is a vibrational reflection of humanity's consciousness and of our innate link to our cosmic origins equally through the macrocosm and microcosm, each being a reflection of the other. We are beginning to remember what we already know: our 'harmonic blueprint.' Realizing our connected state with the multiverse, we awaken from an unconscious state of being into our reality as creators for the purpose of communing consciously and joyously as expressions of the Divine. Humanity is awakening out of the illusions, confining ideas, belief system constructs, and vibrational suppressants. There is an unleashing of new energy into this domain, bringing about harmonious manifestations here on Earth in more connection and alignment with our infinite nature.

The following describes a small portion of some types of beings I have been in Contact with throughout my life. The attributed names and spatial origins of these beings were not always a conscious aspect of my experiences with them. Instead, the messages and information they imparted relating to other matters were more relevant at the time. Therefore, I cannot guarantee that the specific names given to the beings are correct, rather that the following is to be viewed as a general guide through what I have personally experienced."

Tall Grays

"From birth up until the age of nine, I experienced frequent Contact with tall beings of a blue-white appearance with very large eyes, who felt like close family to me. Contact with these cosmic beings meant that I was transported from my earthly, everyday world into their domain: a starship.

There I was shown this starship was made up of several smaller pod-like craft that connected into the larger craft. These vehicles were mind-interfacing, inter-dimensional, and would respond to telepathic instruction and thought processes. Communication between these beings and myself was telepathic and empathic, a combination of thought and emotion. With these beings, I was aware of an integrated, interfacing reality with them and their environment; a feeling of ease and deep recognition, compassion, peace and understanding at a deep level.

Interactions with these beings were as real as anything I experienced in my 'normal' human everyday life. Feeling a unique affinity with them, our physical differences did not interfere with any aspect of our interaction; we were all considered as equal.

These beings were incredibly gentle, telepathically communicative, demonstrating advanced vibrational healing processes, multidimensional, astrological and scientific understandings in balance with heart-centered emotion. I never felt in awe or surprised by this or their technologies as, while in their presence, I felt very much at home. I often traveled in the starship with them, almost instantaneously journeying through the various layers of interstellar and inter-dimensional space. As a child, they showed me several species and civilizations living within other realms and star systems, where I could experience the spiritually advanced practices, customs and the consciousness of parallel worlds, planets and beings.

Visiting a place where there were two suns (portals) in a strangely colored sky, I noticed the buildings were made of a substance that visually looked similar to a light-emitting obsidian or smoky quartz, yet there were no doorways, we could just walk straight through the walls. This material apparently interfaced with its environment and those who existed within it, allowing a molecular frequency exchange and transition, according to the intentions of those in contact with it. The people in this world wore clothing made of a material, unlike anything on Earth. I was given the opportunity to wear this. It had a similar look and feel to extremely fine silk, although it was literally a living material, like wearing a delicate, living, second skin that molded exactly to my body and breathed with me.

There was always a sense of belonging with these beings, and it was expressed to me that they were travelers between worlds (frequency bands). My role within their spacecraft involved the 'downloading' of frequency coordinates for new destinations into a consciousness-interfacing transport system. These coordinates were often for travel to specific points on timelines or between dimensions of existence. Intuitively, I always knew exactly what to do. Moving over to a round-edged device in the center of a room, I would lay my hands upon this in a certain location and focus my eyes into its central screen-like device. Images, geometry, and star maps were transmitted from my mind, then transmuted into a holographic-like information format and were then reorganized, then calibrated, to create portals. Engaging in thought processes unlike anything I have experienced on Earth, I found myself in telepathic communication not only with the beings, but through another undefined source where concepts of universal understandings were personally realized. There was often the experience of travel beyond the light barrier into a field where the craft would operate at a non-linear frequency, allowing us to travel (without actually moving) in and out of different universal layers, dimensions, timelines and frequency bands. Apparently, the instantaneous change in locations is due to an input of the relating frequency equations into the spacecraft for its manifestation at a new location.

This innate connection and knowledge that would flow so effortlessly, like second nature, while with these beings, was more difficult to access while back in the Earth realm. Finding that while I was taken into the off-Earth environments, the shift in frequency altered my state of consciousness to such an extent, I had the ability to easily access information from the universal field of thought. While in this vibrationally altered, heightened state, I was able to interface with regions of my mind and soul connection, which, while on Earth, were usually hidden within the subconscious or unconscious. It took me many years to realize that I could actually access this heightened, intuitive field of thought from Earth through nature.

At times it was difficult for me to leave these beings and return to Earth, often feeling as though I was returning to a harsh, unfamiliar, restricting world. Of course, I felt so much more comfortable in their open, energized and peaceful environments. As I grew older, the transition from 'their' world back into the collective density of Earth became more difficult for my physical human structure. In my teenage years, it often took days to recover from my otherworldly adventures, feeling completely exhausted. The molecular structure of my physical body found it increasingly difficult to realign and adjust between the finer vibrations of other realms, then reintegrate into the denser realities here. Also, I found that my brain seemed to function very differently to other people, along with heightened sensitivity as an empath, naturally reading into and taking on other people's thoughts and feelings. Sometimes I had difficulty distinguishing between my own thoughts and feelings and those of other people. If I felt a friend or family member was unhappy, I would do all I could to make them feel happy again, so that I too could feel happy. This became extremely tiring and detrimental to my well-being, especially while attending my crowded school or visiting the shopping center. I felt that I needed to function in the human world 'frame of mind', so eventually my physical interaction with these particular beings ceased for many years."

Small Grays

"Encounters with several races of small gray types have been varied and many. These little fellows have been the receivers of much negativity and hostility from human beings. Sometimes called Zeta Grays, as related to the Zeta Reticuli constellation, they once existed in a similar form to human beings and are part human. Through an on-going disconnection from higher vibrational fields of consciousness, they collectively became emotionless, disconnected from Spirit and technologically focused to the point of depletion and demise of their world and species.

A percentage of experiences with the Gray-types have been an illusory attempt to provoke fear. These experiences were simulated, created by an outside source and were not genuine experiences with the real Grays. These simulated events were an attempt to use artificial (robot-like) life forms, created here on Earth for negative means. Not only was this a cover-up for an underground genetic agenda based on Earth, but to instill untruths and fear into an awakening humanity, all in an attempt to corrupt and hold human beings back from realizing greater truths.

Many humans seem convinced the Grays are (all) attempting to cause harm and disruption to humanity, and in the past I have also felt this possibility. However, through my own personal journey and interactions with these particular beings and others, I came to realize that it was my perceptual limitations and fears that kept me from understanding a greater cosmic truth. Attempts have been made to put humans into an amnesia-like state so that we hand over our power, placing us in fear (illusion) to disconnect ourselves from the truth and forget that in every moment we can consciously decide to choose to create our world or to let fear create it for us. The good news is that humanity is awakening at an accelerating pace, returning to our hearts, seeing through eyes of love, remembering who we truly are, putting it into action; the most powerful force there is."

Human Fear Creates Misunderstanding

"Various beings have been involved in genetic manipulation (including humans), attempting to cross-clone our genome with their own and others, to create a hybrid species as an advancement of their own race (this is how the human form was created). Some people believe that the Gray's intent has been to manipulate human consciousness, controlling our thoughts in an attempt to influence us collectively. If we consider the fear-based reactions of human beings through their association with 'abductions', along with their infiltration into our living rooms through television and the media, they have succeeded. Yet throughout all of this, there is a perceptual distortion of the truth. Everyone recognizes the Gray beings with their large dark eyes and the emotions that may arise through this image. These beings reflect patriarchal control and the fear that has taken precedence on our planet for a very long time. Affecting every woman and man, we are being reminded that if we deny the divine mystery of the feminine we also deny something fundamental to life. We separate life from its sacred core, from the matrix that nourishes all of creation, we then cut our world off from the source that alone can heal, nourish and transform it. The same sacred source that gave birth to each of us is needed to give meaning to our lives, to nourish it with what is real, and to reveal to us the mystery, the divine purpose for being alive.

There have been many attempts to totally disconnect us from our hearts, spirit and nature. Our infinitely alive and conscious, our Divine Earth is communing with each of us, beckoning us so loudly that we have no choice but to go within and listen. As we recognize and look directly into our shadows at what we fear most, we can allow the expansion and integration of our divine true nature to then unfold its beauty and diversity, bringing back into this world the light of our creation. Shining light and love into the darkness, bringing balance and love in accordance with the truth of who we are.

During a spontaneous vision, I was shown a representation of the illusion of darkness. I looked into the night sky and saw the many stars surrounded by the darkness of space. I was then shown what the night sky would really look like if I were able to see from another perspective, and watched as the entire night sky filled with indescribable radiant light. The darkness of the space between the starlight was now filled with this luminescent radiance.

It then occurred to me that as we view the light of stars from Earth, we are only seeing the light that has reached our eyes (awareness) from where it originated a very long time ago, within the range that our eyesight permits. The dark (unconscious) places in the night sky are where the light has not quite reached our eyes (awareness). Light is present, yet we are unable to see the light as it has not yet reached our consciousness. If we were to move into those dark places with conscious awareness (masculine) and love (feminine) we would meet up with the light (conscious awareness) sooner than later, to realize that the darkness (fear) is there to be integrated and transcended. As light and darkness become a unification into Oneness (Divine nature)."

Soul Agreement – The Mirror. Transcending Fear

"My understanding from a soul level is that the billions of human beings who have played a role in the Zeta Gray's genetic agenda have agreed to that. There are agreements that were not necessarily remembered or conscious aspects of one's mind. At a soul level, and even possibly before incarnation into human form, it was agreed upon. On another level, we are awakening to a fact that collectively we have given our power over to those who 'we' have chosen as our world leaders. The Grays made agreements with those leaders before implementing their agenda. They were given permission, so it is the Grays' understanding that they have done nothing against our will. As those 'we' collectively chose to represent us granted permission.

Just as with every aspect of our experience and reality, there is some part of us that has agreed to participate. The difference now is that humanity is awakening to become 'conscious choosers', deciding with a greater amount of insight and awareness, what we decide to create as our reality. Agreements can be altered and changed with conscious awareness along with increasing connection with our Divine nature. We are being intuitively guided.

The Zeta Gray beings were once very human-like and connected with Source and experienced emotion. After disconnecting from the Divine life force, the feminine (emotional body), they were unable to physically give birth to their offspring; instead were producing children in laboratory environments devoid of the 'great spark' of life force necessary for healthy reproduction. The Grays have been accessing ancestral timelines when their species were more aligned with the Divine, in an attempt to enhance and prolong the survival of their species. Bringing through past genetic blueprints into current timelines combined with human genetics as an attempt to reconnect into the matrix through the creation of a hybrid race, who would slowly integrate into our reality on Earth amongst human beings.

The Zeta's emotionless state made it difficult for them to understand the fear, trauma and discomfort that some humans have gone through during these 'abduction' scenarios. Instead, they became intrigued as to our human reactions, attempting to understand us from a mental perspective. They were fulfilling a plan to assist in the continuation of their (and our) species survival within the denser regions of existence. I have found the Grays to openly communicate with those people who were also open to communicate telepathically, for the purpose of interactive learning between species. This was my experience after coming to terms with my own fears around what was occurring, finding that I could interact with them and ask questions about their agenda, and through this process I gained new understanding.

I now find myself feeling much gratitude and compassion for their species, and appreciation for the bigger picture. If we empower ourselves as having the ability to direct our life experience, we can change agreements at any time. Those who live in a disempowered state can experience great fear and pain through interaction with the Grays, and succumb to feelings of being overpowered and abused. Again, the way to change such an experience is to reclaim your power and direct your reality consciously beyond the fear, as a Divine connection with the highest vibrational frequencies of Source energy.

There have been misunderstandings; the Zeta Gray beings have played a great role in the evolution of humanity within denser levels of our existence, teaching us much about ourselves. It is the collective consciousness of humanity (through choice) that has allowed them into our dimensional sphere of reality. These beings have held up a mirror to humanity that many people have refused to look into for fear of what they may see. As the human being rises above the densities of fear and into an awakened state of awareness, such destructive experiences can no longer infiltrate. Instead, humanity in its awakened state can only experience the bigger picture: that all life is connected and that one's reality is merely a reflection of one's inner world as a creation for expansion and learning.

The Grays' also gift us with the reflection of how we 'collectively' mistreat one another, including animal species and all life on our beautiful planet. Human beings too, in a disconnected state, are capable of abhorrent and uncompassionate acts. We are all being called to open our connection with the Divine, through our Mother Earth, bringing in through our hearts, the cosmic energies as we use our form to transcend and bring the Light of Divinity into balance, bringing Earth to Heaven.

The Grays' energy and presence are displayed within the drawings to show some of the waning influence on this planet, expressed through the genetic creation of humankind, and how their evolution is directly linked with our own. Humanity is now moving into the higher vibratory levels of existence with a greater understanding of fear; it is being transmuted into an encapsulating awareness of Divine Love.

Collectively, humanity is again beginning to perceive other extraterrestrial and Light Beings working with us from the finer energetic levels as we move into their range of existence. Zeta Grays in their current form are becoming less prominent within humanity's spectrum of reality, as we move further into the Light."

Reptilian Beings

"It is a similar story regarding the dark Reptilians, who are greatly feared by many for various reasons. The mere thought of such beings conjures up deep-rooted fears and beliefs, which separates us from discernment and puts us into a type of survival mode. Through this misunderstanding and buying into the various illusions created by this, we unintentionally give over our power, allowing ourselves to experience a disconnection from our Divine source. Humans are then overcome with fear through misalignment with the greater truth, thus feeding the reality they have created around these beings. The projection of fear in the form of these beings is representative of our collective shadow or disconnected state of consciousness. However, it is possible to assimilate such experiences, revealing the truth behind them.

The Reptilians reflect the reptilian center of the human (animal) brain. Scientists call it the reptilian brain because it refers to our primitive, survival function. It relates to fear, in that when we experience something we consider to be life threatening the experience of fear sets in from the reptilian brain to enable the fight or flight functions, which were necessary for survival for primitive human beings. Human beings experience Reptilians as a projection of their own fears. That being said, I have encountered such a projection as a large Reptilian in the hallway of my home. Just before the encounter, I was in the kitchen and felt that something was truly amiss, and began to feel fearful, so decided to go to my bedroom. On my way down the hallway, I was confronted by a very large, very scary-looking Reptilian. My attempt to flee was immediately halted as this being took hold of my throat with his scaled, clawed hand, pushing my body to the floor while choking me. I could not take a breath and knew that if I did not do something fast I was going to be killed or end up in a hospital for the rest of my life. In my mind's eye I could see within me, a spark of light, it was being strangled and squeezed, dissipating, becoming smaller until the light was just like a faint glimmer of hope that I would survive. At what seemed like the last moment of my life, something took over and gave me the insight to focus with all of my intent on the little faint glimmer of light. My overwhelming fear immediately transformed into great love and compassion for the being strangling me!

The tiny glimmer of light became stronger and brighter until it was gleaming, encapsulating my form and that of the being in front of me with a magnetic golden radiance, with a feeling of all-encompassing love. In what seemed an instant, I was also guided to focus with all my might upon light within the being. Directing as much love as possible, the golden light became so powerful that it was all I could perceive and within an instant, the Reptilian suddenly vanished. Other than being completely bewildered and overwhelmed by what had occurred, I was forever grateful for the lessons this experience brought to me. It made me aware of just how powerful the energy of love, compassion and Divine light really is when faced with the illusions of darkness."

Note: Pamela Stonehouse (Singer/ Experiencer), in a lecture at the 1999 UFO Congress, spoke about her interactions with Reptilians and shared that she had tried many strategies to free herself of traumatic interactions with them, until she decided to try love, and as she projected this at the being, it disappeared. She believed love was the key.

"Some time after the Reptilian encounter, I was given an opportunity to experience the same power of what I had learned. My friend and I were leaving a bar late at night and were walking down a side street when two burly, drunk men appeared from the darkness. It immediately became obvious that their intention was one of violence. These men proceeded to provoke us, blocked us from passing, and began to physically push my friend around. Immediately the insight came to me to focus with all my intent upon their hearts, imagining with my mind's eye the beautiful, golden radiant light, and then I silently proceeded to speak to their hearts with love and compassion. It took no time before both the men began to completely change in their demeanor, seeming to become confused as to their intentions with us. They had been energetically disarmed. We witnessed a complete turnaround. These men totally backed down to let us pass and even wished us a good night, as though nothing had happened! For me, this was like entering an alternative reality.

A similar situation occurred while traveling in Honduras. Again, two men attempted to mug my boyfriend and me at a beach as we took a walk near a town, to explore the coastline. The men approached us as one of them produced an impressive knife from beneath his jacket, pointed it at my boyfriend's chest and demanded money. Intuitively, knowing the intention to do harm came from just one of these men, I immediately focused into the heart space of the man with the knife while silently speaking to his humanity. I imagined the light in his heart space, while showing no fear. Interestingly, I remember smiling while my boyfriend had the knife to his chest, only because I was in an unwavering zone of complete knowing that this situation would go no further. In a short amount of time, the men had backed down. Miraculously, we both walked away from the scenario with our wallets and well-being fully intact.

We must also remember that human beings exist with many filters of perception. Religious, social, cultural and familial beliefs all taint greater truths. We exist within a matrix of programs, stories and illusion. It is well documented that particular cosmic beings appear to people relating to their filter-creating beliefs. Catholics and Christians often witness and communicate with beings who appear to them as Mother Mary or Jesus Christ. I have been shown that many of the non-physical beings can appear in any form, dimensional frequencies cloaked by our own beliefs. The true form is more a frequency of light or consciousness, appearing to us in whatever ways best appeal to our spiritual mindset.

The scientific domain has concluded that all 'matter' is energy vibrating at various frequencies. As observers, we, moment by moment, decide consciously or unconsciously how we shall experience our reality. We experience our world and our relationship to it based upon programs and constructs that seem so very real. Scientists have found that their own observations, thoughts and state of mind during experiments, especially involving the subatomic world, directly affects the outcome of those experiments."

It's all Consciousness – The 'Dreamtime'

"As human beings awaken out of one dream and into another, we are realizing ourselves as an extension of eternal consciousness of the purest kind. Each of us has the ability to experience individuation through the process of realizing our uniqueness and simultaneously our connection to the Divine, connecting through All. The universe is essentially a cosmic playground. As the more aware of awareness we become, the greater our ability to choose what aspect of consciousness we would like to play with from our individual, unique viewpoint. The cosmic beings, the extraterrestrials, are a reflection and likened to parallel or future versions of ourselves beckoning us to reconnect with our spirit, individually reconnecting as infinite expressions of possibility. As we awaken out of this dream and into greater expansion, maybe we shall experience cosmic beings as vibrationally attuned with our spiritual selves, integrated as the expression and unification with Divine Light."

The Mantis Beings – Healers

"Interaction with those recognized as the Mantis began consciously as a teenager. These beings usually exist out of visual range from Earths' vibrational collective field of consensus reality. They appear with a very unusual form, are often extremely tall, about two to five meters (six to fifteen feet), with large insect-like eyes protruding from either side of their head. I learned to accept this strange appearance as they have shown me much about humanity – possessing incredible wisdom and understandings about the ancient origins of humankind and other species. At times I have observed them alongside the Gray types, displaying great integrity regarding their interaction and knowledge to do with human beings and evolution. The Mantis have assisted the Grays to understand human emotions more fully, allowing them to genetically realign and reconnect with their own ancient spiritual ancestry. This has enabled a more compassionate interaction between the Grays and humans.

The Mantis have expressed masterful use and alignment of energy, known to have contributed to the human genetic blueprint and the Earth's energetic grids. Some Mantis wisdom is expressed through the artwork, as they seem to exhibit a significant link in our evolution as a species in connection to the crystalline beings, and are active participants of the governing council.

During a time that I was in great self-doubt around my experiences and actively pursued psychological analysis in an attempt to become 'normal'. I was resistant, but found myself engaged in communication with a young Mantis. This new being displayed great curiosity about my life and human experience and wanted to understand why I was wishing to disengage from my multidimensional self. In the end, the being appealed to my spirit, to my own childlike innocence, assisting me to remain open to the purity of my innate multidimensional nature.

The Mantis are apparently born with total inherent knowledge of their elders, passed along as an exponential genetic accumulation of experience from throughout their vast existence. Yet only through their own personal experience and interaction with other beings can they gain the wisdom to fully understand and integrate the internal genetic knowledge."

Lion Beings

"Lion-like beings come through in the drawings as cosmic warriors of wisdom; expressions of strength, protection, and well-being for our species. Expressing facial features not unlike a lion, they exude a beautiful softness, cat-like eyes and often golden-orange or pure white manes and beards. Holding many keys to our Earth ancestry, they can be easily Contacted through focused thought, and are of service to humanity. Originally arriving on our Earth during ancient times, and also existing within parallel realities, they have come from the Sirius and Orion star systems as overseers of the creation and activation of the pyramidal structures and ancient technologies all over the world. Beings from Sirius were prominent architects of energy systems and bringers of Astro-technological knowledge of the pyramids. During times when Earth remained relatively untouched and in natural balance, they guided the use of advanced technologies and were able to harness and focus the Earth's energies. The result was that this energetically fertile planet was able to share this potent energy to accommodate certain needs within other planetary bodies, as a portal for travel and for inter-dimensional communication. This planet was able to foster life from many star-born places, creating the abundant diversity for a myriad of life forms. These beings also assist within various other planetary systems completing similar energy activation, connecting worlds through portal alignments. Their association to the beginnings of human design and connection with the Earth are also imparted through the drawings."

Initiation with Horus – A Being of Light

"One night, as a teenager, I found myself interacting with a being who was in the form of Horus of ancient Egypt. During this lucid experience, I found myself in an unfamiliar environment, underground in what looked to be a dimly lit stone-walled passageway. The being telepathically introduced himself, relating his form as belonging to Egyptian Horus, Feathered Serpent. He then imparted that humanity is remembering its future and will soon understand the blueprint of time. He stood side on to me, revealing only the left side of his face, very similar to the ancient Egyptian drawings: face in profile with his body turned towards me. I vividly recall his large, powerful, left eye penetrated every level of my consciousness; nothing within me could be hidden. Floating and moving sideways along the underground hallway, I looked at a wall covered with several types of hieroglyphics. I was told that the messages within these hieroglyphs would be revealed and brought to light during my lifetime.

We then became stationary in the hallway as I witnessed a forked snake's tongue protrude from his bird's beak. The long forked tongue effortlessly carved a perfect geometric symbol, into the stone wall. When the image was complete, I was instantly drawn into it at great speed. It felt as though I was being sucked into its portal, as the symbol became very large to fully envelop me. At this point, I found myself above ground in a deserted landscape looking at an equilateral triangle with two concentric circles within it, all suspended in the air. Beyond the symbol, I could see mountains with the sun dawning behind them. Three tubular silver bars descended from the sky, connecting one by one with the inner circle, each with the powerful vibrating sound of metal hitting metal. Three more bars then descended to join into the outer circle in the same way. An intense wave of energy then enveloped me as I awoke, shaking, in my bed at 3:00 am. This encounter preceded my ability to channel through the geometric symbols and messages freehand with the accuracy of the golden mean and pi geometry.

The message Horus imparted was that he (Horus) was a Being of Light as a particular influence on Earth throughout history in many cultures, as a messenger. To seed humanity's consciousness and evolution, bringing about a closer alignment with our Sun (light). Many times humans have been reminded, through his various forms, of the advanced abilities and consciousness we, as human beings, are capable of accessing through inner alignment and evolution. Intuitively, the name 'Architect of Consciousness' came to me; the title for one of the artworks depicting his role in this universe through my personal understandings and experiences. I also found this quote from the Pyramid Texts of the old kingdom; 'Let the Eye of Horus come from the god and shine outside his mouth'."

Humanoids and Walk-ins

"There are extraterrestrial people who appear to be physically very similar to humans, known as the Humanoids. Various races are at different levels of spiritual and technological evolution who also have human genetics. Many races of humanoid are hybrid species who display evolved advancement scientifically, technologically and spiritually. Their origin at the time of incarnation into human form is off-earth or extraterrestrial in nature.

There are also humanoid types walking among humans, virtually unnoticed, curious about our reality and ways of living. They gather information and also interact with certain people to assist with the 'planting of seeds' for a new consciousness on Earth. Some are incarnated part way through a human life, completely conscious of who they are and where they came from, sometimes known as 'walk-ins.' On these occasions, a soul agreement has been made with a person for them to literally 'walk into' the physical form of that human person under certain conditions. This is never forced upon another, is unlike possession and is often a continuation of the lifespan of the physical form of the soul who is moving on. This can occur instead of undergoing the complete physical death cycle. Interestingly, the soul who moves on often switches positions with the 'walk-in' and gains an enhanced spiritual perspective through this alignment.

These people have mostly human genetics, yet a portion of DNA is non-human.

An extraterrestrial walk-in consciousness cannot just walk into anyone's form, there needs to be a degree of vibrational cohesion for this to happen. The non-human DNA acts as a link to cosmic consciousness and ancestry, creating a blueprint which differs from human genes. Another function is to increase the capabilities of the human form, yet this happens while in an awakened state.

There are also humanoid beings who are of a finer vibrational field, existing just beyond the physical realm of Earth, who are a Lemurian remnant race. They exist in the equivalent of the subterranean areas of this planet. As with the human multidimensional reality, there also exists multi-layers to this Earth; that within these realms many extinct species of our planet remain very much alive. Humanoids and others have also collaborated to maintain the survival of the animal and plant Earth species and their genetic lines. Many of these species considered to be extinct on our Earth, also exist off the Earth, having moved on from the consensus reality of planet Earth into higher vibrational fields or parallel realities.

There are those increasing in numbers, who are being incarnated on Earth, who have a strong sense of 'not being from here.' Mary Rodwell speaks about the 'New Human' and the changes now rapidly occurring as super-conscious children are being born, many with remarkable abilities and often memories of previous off Earth lives. As our planet moves through the universe, conditions are allowing higher frequencies of vibration to manifest through the evolution of our consciousness at all levels. Children are now being born with an inherent knowledge of higher wisdom and universal understandings. Their hearts are wide open, with greater sensitivity to those around them and to environmental influences. Many are also unwavering in their integrity to do things the way they know is of truth for them. Due to their nature and high levels of sensitivity, they feel truth and mistruth more clearly. Discordant energies can be managed and brought back into alignment once they gain understanding and find the tools to nurture their inner well-being.

There are, of course, attempts being made by those who represent 'shadow', to shut children down as young as possible. This is occurring through vaccinations, education systems, technology, Wi-Fi (frequency programming) and wireless baby monitors, chem trails, to name a few. It is not commonly known, yet the fact is, baby monitors, used by millions to listen in on their sleeping babies, emit more electromagnetic radiation than mobile phones. It is well documented that the effects of this type of radiation upon adults can be highly detrimental, so what is it doing to the energetic and nervous systems, cellular and brain functions of newborns'?

It seems that these children are not only sensitive, yet hold great resilience, strength, and awareness to overcome all obstacles that may present themselves. These children are ushering in a new age ahead of their time, many are being misunderstood, medicated and diagnosed with sensory issues, ADHD, and autism. The education system is inadequate for these children, with many schools under huge pressure to change in accordance with these children's 'special needs.' From a misaligned point of view, many of these children are labeled as naughty and/or disabled for being their true natural Divine selves. These children are bringing about new ways and systems as the old falls away, and responding according to what is not in resonance with their truth. Holding keys to higher knowing and being greatly aligned with Divine Love, there can only be less and less 'shadow' influence upon their evolution. Many of these 'awake' children choose parents who are also aware and awake to assist with the acceleration of their bringing of Earth to Heaven; death of the old, reborn as a newly-enlightened society.

There is now a lessening of the suppression of technologies and energy systems that would end the suffering and destruction of our fragile ecosystem. Some of these technologies are in alignment with Earth frequencies and would not only sustain humankind and all other species, but would bring about a regenerative and con-nected way of life, whereby our planet can flourish within a balanced and connected interaction between all species and the Earth herself.

As humans awaken, overcoming inner conflict and turmoil, suppression and repres-sion of the Self to reconnect with nature, this shall be reflected collectively in the outer world. Humanity may find that one path of awakening and evolution shows that there is no need for technologies and that the magic of consciousness becomes manifest through the inner worlds of creation – true union with the cosmic/Earth energies.

Before this can occur, the outer world of sustainable technologies will become read-ily available, obvious solutions to environmental questions will be easily accessed and implemented and we shall begin to perceive and live more unified harmonious lives. Every species of this planet serve a purpose in the well-being and balance of this world. As beings incarnated into this Earth domain, we have the ability to take action to change our world, choosing in every moment to be the change we wish to see.

Recently I experienced a spontaneous vision, which ended with me becoming an instant vegetarian. I was clearly and graphically shown how the slaughtering of cows for consumption is not for humanity's greatest well-being; that cows represent the Mother, their soul intent being to bring fertility, love and sacred union between Earth and all living upon her. Like many other species of our planet, cows are highly conscious, emotional, sensitive beings, all bringing fertility to the Earth and to humanity. The original purpose for the 'aurochs' (ancestor of domestic cattle) was to provide nutrients to the planet, bringing balance and stability to the ecosystem through their migratory nature – energetically stabilizing the finer energies to bring new growth into manifestation. Since their interbreeding into domesticated cows, the original aurochs are now extinct within our human realm. We have seen the great imbalance and suffering to their species and their 'use' by humans within the ecosystem to satisfy economical motivations. Human disconnection with the Earth's original wisdom has brought about a belief that humans 'need' to eat cow meat to be healthy. Eating cow meat or any animal meat, especially when the animal has been raised, fed and killed without any connection or compassion for its well-being or spirit, is truly detrimental to one's health, not to mention the drugs these creatures are given during their 'production.' I was clearly shown that the act of consuming meat, particularly when there is no regard for the animal's essence, shuts down a person's energetic heart center from real compassion and love for self, others and our Mother Earth.

It is becoming more recognizable to human beings that running around trying to 'save the world' without access to the bigger picture, is not a sustainable solution. Instead, we are realizing that as we transform from within, the outer world reflects this change. We shall also reunite with the realization that we, along with all those who cohabit with us, are this planet's caretakers and that she (Earth) is here to sustain us in our experience within this amazingly diverse realm. We are reconnecting through awareness, compassion, and love to our intimate relationship with Earth (Mother), in ways that open us to her Great Wisdom and Sacred Blueprints."

Others

"Beings representing Arcturians, Pleiadians, Sirians, Nordics and those from Andromeda have regularly been around as communicators of alternative worlds and realities. Pleiadians often manifest in their energetic form and can present as angelic because of their incredible light bodies.

One could say that Angels, along with the Pleiadians, are one and the same, with humans having differing interpretations. Some advanced future versions of the human species who also exude a body of light are often perceived as the enlightened masters. Their form and consciousness had transmuted and transcended the density and limitations of physical manifestation. Their presence is a powerful and loving intensity, constantly inspiring messages and triggering the unraveling of humanity. I have found that many of these teachings are carried through into the artworks and geometric symbols I have completed.

It must be noted regarding the Nordics, that these were the prominent humanoid beings Contacting human beings during the early to mid-twentieth century. Many Contactees, especially those in Europe, reported interaction and encounters with them. Since then, these interactions have become less common as encounters with the Gray beings supplanting the Nordic in most accounts. Nordic beings have shown genuine interest and concern for the well-being of the Earth's environment and for humanity, often expressing messages relating to world peace, compassion and spiritual understanding, seeming to assist in the spiritual unfolding of human beings. Interestingly, Contact with the Nordics declined as Contact with the Grays increased – almost as though humanity's direction shifted its course to face its shadow. The inception of the Gray energy into the collective path of awakening was relatively short-lived, as we find ourselves connecting with the light at higher frequencies now.

Mostly these beings express positivity for the path of humanity and are patiently observing us with compassion and interest. Many of the beings mentioned have an agreement for non-interference with the greater happenings on this planet. From the perspective of the Grays, we ourselves made the decision for them to infiltrate consciousness. Agreements were made with those chosen by humanity to represent us as our leaders, even though we did not consciously agree.

This is changing as humanity remembers its innate connection to conscious creation, and they are open to communication and Contact. There are also many people on Earth who have chosen to be conduits for the cosmic beings in that we can transpose from the galactic/cosmic realms, the teachings and vibrational representations of this knowledge to assist with the awakening and evolution occurring here. It is up to us as a race to make individual and global decisions for peace, equilibrium, awareness, and community. This is part of our evolution into greater awareness. We must wake up to who we are and connect fully with our hearts before we can consciously take our place within the universal community.

Aboard a large spacecraft with Arcturian humanoid beings, I recall looking out of a large window at the city lights of Perth, Western Australia, below. I had taken lessons with these beings about manifestation, directed thought and emotion. The inside of this massive craft reminded me of Star Trek episodes, as there were many people walking around dressed in skin tight suits. There were tables and chairs, step-downs and a massive window with rounded edges along one side of the craft, which I was looking out of. The craft was descending through the sky towards the city below, and began to slow down its momentum as we traveled towards the ground. The beings mentally communicated to me that the spacecraft was invisible to the people below, that we would be traveling 'into' the city, and that I need not be concerned about this. I was excited and amazed that this huge craft was now hovering right above the city center. As it descended further, the spacecraft began to tilt on its side. I remained fully attached to the floor, finding there to be no change to the gravity inside the craft. It was then that I felt slightly concerned that we were about to crash into the middle of Perth City!

The movement of the craft became so slow that I could clearly see into the windows of the buildings. Then, as the craft neared the ground, I could see a man who looked to be homeless, lying against the wall of a building on the street, and he was staring straight at me as I looked through the spacecraft window. I knew that he could see this massive spacecraft descending, so I asked the beings why he could see us yet no one else seemed to notice. The reply I received was a benevolent 'We look after that one (man).' All I recall after that was the craft entering into the ground to descend under the city."

Cetaceans

"As we awaken to a greater truth, we shall notice that cosmic beings have always been here interacting with us, yet without interference. There are well-known creatures on Earth that are also of cosmic origins and of high intelligence, belonging to the cetacean species. Dolphins, in particular, have an awakened consciousness originating from Sirius. Douglas Adams, the writer of *Hitchhikers Guide to the Galaxy*, seemed to be channeling this particular information with humor. As humanity evolves, we shall realize our connections with the cetacean beings, remembering and learning much through one another.

In 2016, India declared dolphins as 'nonhuman persons', prohibiting the keeping of captive dolphins for public entertainment anywhere in the country. Obviously, there are situations where dolphins are kept in unhealthy situations, yet my understanding of these beings has shown me that they love to entertain, play and to interact with humans, being a part of our awakening is what they are here to do."

The Black and White Geometric Images

"A major turning point in my life, was when I was put in contact with Mary Rodwell. Mary is the Director of the Australian Close Encounter Resource Network in Australia. Speaking with Mary allowed me to acknowledge and accept what I had been experiencing, realizing for the first time I was far from alone in this. Several black and white geometric drawings I had completed independently over a four-year period were shown for the first time, to those at a Contactee support group meeting. Many of the people who viewed the drawings felt a strong familiarity and personal connection with them. Some remembered having seen the same symbols during encounters with the beings. It was during this particular meeting that the drawings were joined together in a way I had not previously attempted. A small group of Contactees arranged the symbols on the floor into a configuration that made them fit together like pieces of a puzzle. The configuration was completed intuitively; it was as though these people had arranged the drawings together in this way a hundred times before.

These 'pieces of the puzzle' include eleven, black and white, geometric symbols, completed on separate occasions over several years. After completing the first seven of these drawings, I experienced an intense encounter with the 'Council' of Beings.' who I have previously mentioned. They communicated a message as visual material-izations: I can only describe as similar to seeing holographic images projected up into the air in front of me. It was made clear that the drawings held some significance, and that I was to copy them onto transparent paper. When I questioned why this was necessary, they expressed that when the images aligned with each other, they would symbolically show humanity's evolution and cosmic connections. After completing this task, I did find that the symbols fit together perfectly in numerous ways. More interesting was the fact that every one of the drawings had been completed free hand and on separate occasions; one of them had been completed on a piece of paper over the un-flat surface of my knee while I attended a lecture. The main triangles and circles fitting exactly, with other connections joining with astonishing accuracy in several different ways.

Since realizing the connections between the black and white symbols, I experienced another encounter with the same council of beings. This time they made it clear that my next endeavor was to have the drawings translated into a digital 3D format.

216

Apparently, in completing this task I would then be enlightened as to their meaning and purpose. As I don't yet have the necessary skills involved in the drawings digitization, I am still awaiting the perfect timing and the person to assist with this undertaking."

Note: These black and white drawings and Tracey's earlier story are filmed on the award-winning 2002 DVD: *Expressions of ET Contact: A Visual Blueprint.*

Corroboration of the Drawings in Egypt

"During my travels around the Earth, I have been strongly guided to visit the places of ancient civilizations, where direct connections to the drawings and their incorporated sacred geometry have been realized. Before leaving on these journeys, I was clearly shown to take transparencies of the images along with me. In Egypt, visiting Karnak Temple, I noticed, at a distance, that certain hieroglyphic symbols carved into the stone walls would draw me closer. I just seemed to have a knowing from a distance, that particular transparencies of my geometric images would exactly match and superimpose over certain ancient carvings, and they did."

Note: Photographic image of this in *Awakening*, page 137.

"While living in England, a friend synchronistically handed me a book mainly about the ancient sacred sites of the United Kingdom. On one page was a diagram of geometry depicting the golden mean ratio of the pyramids of Giza. I took a transparency, and it fitted absolutely perfectly over the top of this diagram: the circle and the triangle fit at exactly the same size and ratio. As I delved deeper into the meaning of why this was happening, I realized that I was given access and the ability to download freehand, exact sacred geometric measurements."

Crop Circle Making

"I once had the pleasure of experiencing the creation of a crop-circle through a dream one evening. I found myself floating above a landscape of hills and fields of crops below, noticing that there were 'orbs' flying and floating next to me in the sky. I then recall the realization that I, too, was in the form of an orb or ball of energy consciousness. The experience was playful, as I danced around each of the other orbs in the sky, with a totally connected form of awareness to them.

I realized that we were moving towards a particular crop field, where I could see an amplification of energy resonating out from the Earth in that place. As we moved closer, there was a magical and joyous communion with these Earth energies, much like a meeting with an old friend after a long time. Each intensely joyful and playful emotion seemed to manifest into form. I watched as the grasses of the crop in the field below moved and arranged swiftly and immediately, into flowing geometric formations. I knew that as I 'felt' a joyous emotion, the field below then arranged itself accordingly.

The feeling of this experience was as a true and divinely beautiful communication occurring between myself as this little ball of consciousness and the Earth herself as a reflection of the vibrational 'fields' below.

Many crop circle symbols have also been acknowledged as sacred symbols used by ancient civilizations. There have also been many similar correlations found within the artwork and symbols that I have completed. Some symbols are found to exist inside ancient temples and pyramids around the world, many of which have been related to star systems. Also contained within the drawings are what some perceive to be electrical symbols and maps to create alternative power sources. Within one drawing are coordinates for areas of importance on Earth, which have led me to some startling and surprising discoveries. There are also mathematical formulae and key words written around some of the colored drawings, assisting in explaining their significance."

Star Languages

"Information regarding the purpose of these drawings and symbols has triggered me to speak languages that do not seem to be of an earthly origin. I am in the process of learning more about them and have come to realize that the 'languages' produce brain activity, similar to that reached during meditation, connecting people at a deep level. The information I have been given via the beings is that the language contains particular vibrational frequencies that also assist with awakening and clearing our pineal system. These changes allow more open access to cosmic frequencies, remembrance, deep transformation and healing."

Personal Blueprints

"The experiences and interactions have prepared and enabled me to create images and geometric symbolic artworks that act as triggers for the acceleration of personal development and consciousness, called 'Personal Blueprints.' These are downloadings of artwork for personal use, like templates for self-exploration and enjoyment. Through connecting with a person's photo, name, and birth date, there is a linking into the matrix of soul consciousness surrounding a specific person. I then become an instrument for the downloading of particular information for a person's well-being and evolution on many levels. Due to the nature of 'Personal Blueprints', they activate and assist in enabling individuals to complete and heal ancestral ties at an energetic and cellular level, connect, remember and integrate ancient cosmic origins and future selves, reawaken inner abilities, connect through the heart space of awareness, understandings triggering a magnificent new awareness of reality as cosmic beings in human form.

This includes geometric encoding and script compatible with an individual's genetic and spiritual heritage. As individual beings, we are made up of infinite geometrical encodings and harmonic frequencies that exist universally, ultimately linking all life and consciousness together. The drawings seem to bring some much-needed light onto this planet. The transformations I have witnessed within people through their interactions with the drawings have been incredibly inspiring. The drawings seem to be triggering or assisting with the ushering in of a new type of awareness in people, even in those who claim to be skeptics. There are also now psychologists using the images as tools to assist with their patients' healing."

The human challenge; the modern day shaman is not understood:

Depression

"Planet Earth has always felt somewhat unfamiliar to me from the collective human perception, yet the Earth herself has connected me with my soul. This experience has proven to be a great place of diversity and learning, filled with emotion and great potential for extremely condensed and detailed creation. Many times, life on Earth became extremely challenging in the realization that people around me did not accept or understand my experiences and ways of thinking. This forced me to question my sanity as a human, my reality and the validity of my experiences; sometimes I resorted to thoughts of ending my life. There came a point where I sought psychological analysis in an attempt to make sense of it all. Years of analysis by psychologists and psychiatrists, followed by assessment by a panel of eight psychiatrists that included a CAT scan and an EEG. No brain abnormalities, psychological problems or diagnosis other than mild anxiety and depression were found. Unable to find adequate conventional answers to why I have Contact experiences and being told by many mental health professionals that I 'just don't fit into any box', caused me to look within for the answers. Once again, I was able to acknowledge my lifelong connection to the beings and my spirit as part of my personal reality, realizing that we are all here to experience our uniqueness and diversity as Divine Sparks of Oneness.

Through this lifelong inspiration and gift of artistic expression, I am blessed to be able to create drawings, depicting a grand universal connection, in a form that can be understood by life as a harmonic universal language. The geometry and symbolism can be used as cosmic triggers to activate our original creational blueprints – bringing to the conscious mind ancient ancestral memories and wisdom that have always existed within the energetic and cellular levels. Within our genes/DNA we are being 'ener-genetically' aligned with the matrix of consciousness.

We can openly join the universal community as humanity invariably learns to become aware of awareness, to realize the Oneness within diversity. We are conduits for cosmic consciousness, ever strengthening our connection with Mother Earth. Together we initiate the cosmic connection of humans with the transformational power of our planet, to bring about the great change of awakening as spirit in form."

To view the artwork and for more information visit: www.harmonicblueprint.com
Tracey Taylor © Copyright 2016.

Note: Tracey first told some of her story in *Awakening* (Chapter 8).

Chapter Fourteen

THE NEW HUMAN DNA

'The Bringers of Light'

"There is a race of beings upon the planet, increasing in number, although visually and physically indistinguishable to most humans. Every year from now the conscious awareness of these babies is increasing to override the dominance and conditioning that occurs from birth. They are the 'bringers of light' and are here to guide the awakening of terrestrial consciousness. The New Children are born without programs and will bring about a Global Awakening.

One night, I had this intense feeling before sleep. I wrote in a process that I had little control over; something beyond my present understanding. It was contrary to everything I had been taught. The human race had been created by extraterrestrials – and it contained information about genetic manipulation and the use of human and Extraterrestrial DNA to create another species."

Tracey Taylor, 2000 – Artist/Experiencer.

Is Human DNA Mutating?

Is there evidence that human DNA is mutating? Recently headlined by scientists in 2016: Our DNA is Mutating! We are Developing Twelve Strands.

Ref: humansarefree.com

A child with three DNA strands, a little child in the UK, Alfie Clamp, is the first one to be acknowledged by the medical community. Alfie's seventh chromosome has an extra strand of material which has never been documented anywhere in the world. Doctors are baffled because it is so rare it doesn't have a name.

The articles stated:

- Modern medicine officially acknowledged the first case of a child with three DNA strands.

- Convention of geneticists from around the world: "We are making an evolutionary change...we will be developing twelve DNA helixes." Each extra strand of DNA will grant us 'super-human' abilities that we are now calling paranormal.
- DNA and body changes.
- Physical DNA - Spiritual connections.

> Ref: www.dailymail.co.uk; spiritlibrary.com; www.spiritpathways.co.za; en.wikipedia.org; www.rense.com. (20 April, 2016).

In this chapter, we explore what is already known about the anomalies in human DNA that suggests intelligent design.

Nobel Prize winner, molecular biologist, Dr. Francis Crick, co-discoverer of the structure of the DNA molecule, believed we once had a third strand of DNA and are a created species. Whistleblower information on the nature of human DNA indicates human DNA has been artificially altered. Molecular biologists discuss what they believe are recent changes in human DNA and what they believe this could mean for us as a species.

DNA and Contact

Contact and Encounter experiences share one very important and central theme, which is centered on the importance of human DNA to the non-human intelligences who interact with humans. Human DNA is collected during encounters in the form of sperm, ova, partially-formed human fetuses (i.e., missing pregnancies) (*Awakening*, Chapter Ten), for what is perceived to be an extraterrestrial breeding program.

Two primary issues discussed in this chapter explore the questions: *Homo sapiens* a created species; what is the evidence? Secondly, if we are indeed a created species, is this modification of human DNA still occurring and for what purpose? These questions are central as we learn the perspective and understanding from a whistleblower geneticist and two molecular biologists.

Astrophysicist Dr. Rudy Schild, comments on their observations and the research by scientists in Russia who have discovered amazing properties in DNA.

A Created Species

Author and researcher, the late Alan Alford, author of *Gods of the New Millennium*, based on the Sumerian texts, stated:

"*Homo erectus* changed to *Homo sapiens* approximately one hundred and eighty thousand years ago, during which *Homo sapiens* 'acquired' a fifty percent increase in brain size, language capability and completely changed anatomy."

> Ref: *Gods of the New Millennium*, by Alan Alford.

In the present era, scientists questioned how *Homo sapiens* evolved from Neanderthal man or Cro-Magnon man because the human evolutionary tree cannot explain how this could have occurred. There are a number of theories, but one notable scientist, molecular biologist and co-discoverer of the structure of the DNA molecule, Dr. Francis Crick, stated:

"Creatures from another solar system brought the seeds necessary for life to lifeless planets, and thanks to their kind intervention, life began here."

Note: Dr. Francis Crick was awarded the Nobel Prize in Physiology and was the author of *Life Itself*, published in 1981.

Genetic Modification and ET Encounters

There is a mountain of data to support Dr. Crick's hypothesis. The collection of genetic material is central to most extraterrestrial encounters. Inter-generational encounters indicate on-going long-term genetic programs. It also supports the hypotheses that each generation appears to be altered in some way, with each generation acquiring more multidimensional skills and higher awareness.

Psychological and Emotional Connection to Their Nonhuman Genetic Family

Many Experiencers, male and female, are aware that their genetic material has been collected. They may be introduced to their offspring at a later date, on board craft. Some individuals also believe their human children may have been altered or modified at conception or in utero. This may explain the identity crisis, or feeling that they have been adopted because they feel so different to their human family. It would also explain why the individual may have a stronger connection to their extraterrestrial heritage than to their human origins.

"The Mantid is my family. I will go back to them when I die. I sometimes 'evaporate' into a Mantid being for a short time, before returning to my human body."

Paul, eight years old, Australia.

Parents have also shared that they were aware something happened, such as an extraterrestrial encounter, as early as conception. This encounter could possibly be an insertion of genetic material. Then the parent is told telepathically, "This is a special child," or "This child does not belong to you."

Jacqueline Smith stated in *Meet the Hybrids* that she is a hybrid:
"Hybrids present on Earth help raise the frequency of humankind, so that humans can evolve and embrace their cosmic family."

She continues on the theme of the upgrading of our species:
"With major paradigm shifts taking place, humanity is evolving into a New Human. This means the DNA of humankind is changing in ways which are allowing them to expand in consciousness. They are being activated by the higher frequencies and becoming aware of natural skills and talents that they haven't tapped into before because they weren't ready to handle them."

Ref: *Meet the Hybrids*, Page 167.

The Genetic Blueprint of *Homo Sapiens* Enigma

In tracing the vertical evolutionary record contained in the human and the other analyzed genomes, scientists ran into an enigma: the discovery that the human genome contains two-hundred-and-twenty-three genes that do not have the required predecessors on the genomic evolutionary tree.

How Did Humankind Acquire Such a Bunch of Enigmatic Genes?

These two-hundred-and-twenty-three genes are completely missing in the invertebrate phase of human evolution. In other words, at a relatively recent time as Evolution goes, modern humans acquired two-hundred-and-twenty-three extra genes. Not through gradual evolution, not vertically on the Tree of Life, but horizontally as a sideways insertion of genetic material. Coincidentally this genetic material is not present in any other Earth species and is linked to higher psychological functioning.

Researcher and author, the late Lloyd Pye, known for his research into the 'anomalous' Star-child skull, explored anomalies within its bone structure and placement, as well as anomalies in its DNA. The research clarified that it was a species of hominid with anomalous, possibly extraterrestrial DNA. In this pioneering work, alongside this fascinating anomaly, Lloyd Pye explored human origins, including the evidence we are a created species. He was convinced there were interventions in the DNA of indigenous hominids, explored in his excellent book *The Intervention Theory*. In the conclusion, he adds the information from a whistleblower geneticist:

"The discontinuities between humans and the various apes for (1) whole mitochondrial DNA; (2) genes for the Rh factor; (3) and human Y chromosomes, among others.

Regarding (3) K.D. Smith's 1987 study: *Repeated DNA Sequences of the Human Y Chromosome.*

Most human Y chromosome sequences thus far examined do not have homologues [same relative position or structure] on the Y chromosomes of other primates. Human female X chromosomes do look somewhat apelike, but not the male's Y. Therefore, if humans are a crossbred species, the cross had to be between a female apelike creature (i.e., creature of Earth) and a male being from elsewhere.

By certain methods of DNA dating, one can tell that numerous genes have been recently added to the human genome."

The author of this statement concluded that if he were to say this openly he would be ostracized and forced to live in a tent. This is more confirmation that the truth embargo not only dismisses the truth of extraterrestrial visitation but also many areas of human knowledge, including the truth of our genetic origins.

Tracey Taylor is an Experiencer and shared her understanding on these changes to produce a New Human. It was some years later, Dr. William Brown elaborated on the DNA changes and its outcomes. Dr. Lena Ohlson confirmed a similar understanding, from both an experiential and scientific perspective.

Changes:
- "Extreme sensitivity to thought, emotions, physical environment, energy frequencies and receptive to parents level of awareness.
- Physical alterations that make them stronger in many ways to that of a child with a higher percentage of just human genes. Their molecular structure allows the cells of the body to vibrate faster and more efficiently.
- Photographic memories and extremely fast motor neuron responses. The DNA of the Star Kids has tenfold the amount of information. Abilities such as telepathy. manipulation of time and space, non-verbal communication, are all conscious abilities for these children and are quite natural.
- Physical makeup is faster (vibrates faster) and more efficient.
- Information through brain pathways is much faster, which means their learning skills and abilities are more advanced.
- Time is irrelevant in a linear format.
- Initially, they do not see things as solid, but as energy. They have to learn what solid is.
- Extremely sensitive to all things. There is a tendency for these children to link with the awareness of the mother; they feel exactly what their mother is feeling.
- Everything is accelerated for them, including immune system responses. Their DNA is encoded to recognize all types of foreign organisms. It enables them to turn foreign organisms and energy into nutrients that give them excelled growth and enhanced bodily functions."

Tracey Taylor.

A New Human – Resistance to Disease

I found that there was an interesting study in recent years on the ability of some children to have an amazing resistance to disease. Is this more evidence that Tracey Taylors' information is correct?

Medical researchers at the University of California discovered some children display unique patterning of twenty-four active codons (In human DNA only twenty of the sixty-four are turned on and active). One percent of these children have the twenty-four active codons and show remarkable resistance to disease.

Researchers at the University of California, Los Angeles, School of Medicine report unambiguous evidence of a boy tested positive for HIV twice: at nineteen days of age, and a month later. Four years later, he was completely free of the disease; the virus was eradicated. The resistance to HIV is noticeably higher.

Ref: A report of a young boy in kindergarten who was born with HIV as quoted from Greg Braden's book *Walking Between the Worlds: The Science of Compassion* [page 81]. His understanding of what he calls 'The New Race.' He quoted from an article in the April 1995 *Science News*.

Science News reported on August 17, 1996, that about one percent of the population tested has developed genetic mutations which make them resistant to HIV infection. This new resistance to HIV infection is so strong that in a few of the cases it was 3000 times more resistant than what it would take to infect a normal person. In all cases, their resistance to HIV is noticeably higher. If this were just one small boy showing these changes, it would simply be an interesting phenomenon, but this is not the case.

In October 1999, the United Nations reported that the six-billionth person was born. Thus, one percent of the population (sixty million children and adults worldwide) has altered DNA to become resistant to HIV.

Exactly what has changed in the DNA of these children has to do with codons. In human DNA there are four nucleic acids, which combine in sets of three to form sixty-four codons. Normal human DNA has twenty of these codons turned on, plus three others that act much like the stop-and-start codes in software programming.

The rest of these codons are inactive. Science has always thought that these unused codons were from our genetic past, but now that theory is changing. Perhaps they are actually from our future. These children have turned on four more of these 'un-used' codons, giving them twenty-four, which have completely altered their resistance to HIV infection.

Ref: Quote from an article in *Science News*, April 1995.
Yvonne J. Bryson and her colleague reported on this study in the March 1995 issue of the *New England Journal of Medicine*, page 833-838.

The New Race

We know that new age and metaphysical groups have recognized the characteristics of these new generations of children with many labels to explain their special qualities. What has not been acknowledged and is crucial, is the understanding that advanced intelligences may be instrumental in these changes.

Extraterrestrial interactions with humans are biological, psychological, emotional and spiritual. However, the most tangible evidence for its reality is the biological and genetic indicators.

"Genetic modification is occurring right now to produce a New Human."
Dr. William Brown. PhD in Biology

"I believe that genetic modification is occurring right now in utero, and is actually producing a New Human. It is not as simple as foreign DNA. It's a combination of genetically improved bodies in combination with souls from different places in our universe, incarnating in these 'improved' bodies. The souls have different frequencies.

The hybrids are altogether a new species of human. This is shown by the exponential increase in autism, ADD, and Indigo children. The new genetic architecture allows them to see the world in a multidimensional fashion. I believe research would show dormant genetic regions are being integrated into the biological system, and this is occurring in all of us to produce expanded awareness. Their brains are working faster and they have access to more information. In the classroom, learning is much faster than normal. I believe they already 'know' what's being taught. The 'intrinsic' understanding of certain knowledge and information goes down to the bio-molecular level, where the sentient activity of the brain actually takes place in the atomic structure of DNA molecules. It is trans-generational information. The information is encoded within the atomic structure of the DNA molecule. It can be accessed with greater efficiency and produce savant-like characteristics. The modification of the DNA is more the remodeling of the genome to make dormant regions accessible again."

Statement by Dr. William Brown to Mary Rodwell, 2010.

Comment by Dr. Schild – Astrophysicist

Dr. Brown: "I believe genetic modifications occurring right now in utero, are actually producing New Humans. Their new genetic architecture allows them to see the world in a multidimensional fashion. I believe research would show dormant genetic regions are being integrated into the biological systems and occurring in all of us to produce expanded awareness."

Dr. Rudy Schild: "Here, I think that the genetic modification is largely hybridizing by normal reproductive means, but also modified by telepathic intervention at the earliest in-utero stages. This is indeed producing New Humans. As I noted above, in many cases, like the boy who related to Tesla, the hybridizing creates a pattern of neural connections at the connection between the two lobes so that 3-dimensional brainwaves can be perceived and compared to soul being. This allows some individuals to "see the light" from birth, where other individuals have apparently learned to "see the light" following NDE or UFO/abduction Contact experience."

Dr. Brown: "The exponential increase in ADD, autistic, and Indigo children."

Dr. Schild: "Agreed"

Dr. Brown: "Their brains work faster. I believe they already 'KNOW' what they are being taught."

Dr. Schild: "Let us be careful here. They do not know their arithmetic tables or geography, but they may have an advanced intuitive knowledge, like the boy who is comfortable with you, Mary."

Dr. Brown: "The intrinsic understanding of knowledge and information operates at the bio-molecular level. It's trans-generational information."

Dr. Schild: "This is what the previous author, Dr. L. Ohlsen, said more accurately. Their junk DNA gives them innate knowledge from patterns of resonances that contain emotional content."

Dr. Brown: "It is 'encoded' within the atomic structure of the DNA molecule. It can

226

be accessed more efficiently to produce savant-like characteristics. The modification of the DNA is more like a remodeling of the genome to make dormant regions accessible."

Dr. Rudy Schild: "Again! Here we agree."

Dr. Brown: "The Hybrids are altogether a new species of human."

Dr. Schild: "Yes, we are reasonably sure about that."

Aquantum Letter People

Dr. L Ohlson PhD, Molecular Biologist

Dr. Ohlson, with both her professional background as a molecular biologist, but also experientially, as a Contactee Experiencer, shares her insights into the evolutionary changes in our species, which she calls letter people or Aquantum.

Dr. Ohlson has encountered many different forms of extraterrestrial and inter-dimensional beings and believes she is a letter person, i.e., Asperger's/ADHD/high-functioning autism. The name she was 'given' for the New Human is Aquantum. Dr. Ohlson believes she and her family are letter people. Dr. Ohlson's understanding stems from her experiential and scientific backgrounds. She has recognized she has an intergenerational link to her on-going encounter experiences with extraterrestrials via her father, which has followed through to her children.

Note: Dr. Ohlson PhD in molecular toxicology, Bachelor's degree in biochemistry and molecular biology, Diploma: Biomedical Technician, Reiki healer, and Experiencer.

A personal account from Dr. Ohlson of her encounters and her research into Aquantum letter people follows:

My Encounter Experiences

Dr. Ohlson: "My father and I have met the aliens close up, face to face and not only in an out-of-body (OBE) state. My family and my children have also witnessed alien space ships. My husband has experienced encounters with me. We have experienced blue spheres around us and we put our hands in one of them once; it was a strange feeling, but we felt protected."

Twelve New Groups of Human

Dr. Ohlson: "If my information, which was downloaded to me, is correct, there will be twelve different main groups of new DNA people. It corresponds to the twelve different main groups of ET/alien DNA-donors; so nine more to go. I do wonder what their different features will be and if they will be allowed to go public. Their/ our DNA is activated mainly via remote control and frequencies, so it is like putting a virus in software (computer program). When they are using their DNA, as long as they are alive, they will give off energy patterns that spread to their surroundings. Almost like the flu or GMO genes, which can contaminate via frequency patterns.

I have communications with what I call the Soldier Being: Ram-Ta. He's one of the twelve origins who gave genetic information to assist human development, and he's one of two races who resided in Egypt. One race was Amphibian-like, that healed my foot/knee/hip/back almost two years ago, and the other is more human-like, like Ram-Ta. We all have these genes, but there are some of us that have more copies and some have sort of acquired a stop codon so they are somehow inactivated."

Note: The number of 12 species of extraterrestrial genetic material in human DNA was also quoted by Command Sgt Robert Dean, in an interview with Project Camelot, 2014.

Dr. Ohlson: "The human race have, at some points, been very close to extinction and have been saved by a group of twelve different benevolent "clans" of non-earthlings from time to time, like United Nations on Earth. The genes put into our genome were put there to help us survive and flourish because we behaved more like animals before and did not know better."

DNA's Ability to Transform

Dr. Ohlson: "The genes are genes with all the characteristics genes have (being transcribed and translated into proteins, and so on), but on another level, they contain information of their origin, and also the tools to transform into a higher form of species. The information from the donors and their background is also there; a hidden key like PC programmers hide in their work. This key can be activated and thus they know which ones are 'ripe' and ready to be Contacted (and 'saved'). The ones that are activated, like me, are started (in order) to spread a signal waking others up. We've been too slow and now they are speeding it up. I have a feeling it's quite near now.

The combination of high and strong soul-energy and DNA! But it's not only the genes in the DNA but also the 3D formation of the DNA. Recently, scientists in Cambridge presented astonishing data, for the first time in history, of a quadruple-strand (four-strand) formation working in human cells. They believe it's connected with disease, but I believe it's connected with what I call the 'new way of 3D folding DNA' caused by frequencies we're bombarded with from Cosmos, Earth, and the Sun.

The new just means the genes which have been dormant and further away from each other are closer and activating, giving the bearer (person as well as animals) extra abilities:

- A heightened and sensitive nervous system.
- New ways of processing data.
- Questioning behaviors.
- Abilities such as telepathy.
- Ability to perceive auras
- A sense of how other people really feel"

Note: These abilities might be difficult to take care of and handle when the person is a child.

Dr. Ohlson also shares her understanding in the chapter on the new programs and the letter people. Included in that chapter is information on how she supports herself as a letter person through diet and vitamins as she was able to recognize what her physiology required.

Disclosure from the Ground Up

Dr. Ohlson explains why she has chosen to disclose her extraterrestrial and other-worldly encounters at this time.

"I asked my guides and guardians to show me a sign that I was on track and should I finally 'come out' and tell my story to give me a sign. I had severe dislocation of my C1 vertebra, the Atlas vertebra. I've been to many professionals to get it corrected because it gave me problems in swallowing and I would choke. After asking for a sign my vertebra began to rotate by itself and into the correct position, I had suffered with this for thirty years. It made a loud noise when it happened and, suddenly, I could swallow without any pain and I can turn my head both ways. I believe this was my sign from them and so I'm 'coming out' as I promised."

Note: Dr. Ohlson has experienced:
- Out-of-body experiences.
- Near-death experience (NDE)
- Miraculous healing after contracting severe septicemia.
- Encounters with many different beings.
- Shamanic interactions.
- Healing by cone heads. She feels she may have been one of these in a previous existence.
- Interaction with Mantis beings.
- Green luminescent beings.

Note: Her full story was first published in *UFO Truth Magazine*, UK, 2015.

Astrophysicist – Dr. R Schild Comments

Dr. Ohlson: "The genes have all the characteristics of genes, but on another level, they contain information of their origin, with the tools to transform into a higher form."

Dr. Schild: "To me, this says that what is often called junk DNA is actually resonant structures that encode in the human DNA the resonance with the quantum hologram (QH), whereby they have built up patterns of resonant structures that constitute knowing."

Dr. Ohlson: "The information of the donors and their background is there; a hidden key, like PC programmers hide their work. This key can be activated and these 'programmers' know the person is ready to be Contacted. The activated ones spread a signal to wake others up!"

Dr. Schild: "Yes, of course. These two bullet points say that the included resonant structures are there for all the affected (infected) humans, and mental activity by the programmers can wake the humans up simultaneously when the time comes. It, probably, also means that the programmed individuals recognize each other."

Dr. Ohlson: "I feel they are speeding this up."

Dr. Schild: "Of course. They are learning how to do this more simply and reliably and so they can speed it up."

Dr. Ohlson: "The programs such as ADD, ADHD, Asperger's, the letter people, I do not believe these are broken genes, but instead, are offering new multidimensional skills to prevent limited re-programming of a third-dimensional reality."

Dr. Schild: "To me, it is obvious that if you over-infect, some individuals will lose some of the normal balance in humans, so that the cost of the program is that there are many unbalanced humans around, to whom we attach syndromes to help us keep and guide them closer to normal adjustment."

Dr. Ohlson: "It is not as simple as foreign DNA. It's a combination of genetically improved bodies, in combination with souls from different places in our Universe, incarnating in these improved bodies. The souls have different frequencies/vibrations, depending on their evolutionary status and that plays a role in activation of the DNA in that particular body. I believe we also have to take into account the collective soul of *Homo sapiens*."

Dr. Schild: "Yes, of course. Because we reasonably know that an increasing fraction of humans is infected with non-human DNA, partly from the hybrid program, but also from direct genetic DNA manipulation, and because the reincarnation process is bringing in more off-planet-Earth soul history. These souls are increasingly out of balance on Earth where the humans have a slightly different flavor of DNA that does not always react so favorably with their soul resonance. And, of course, since our human collective consciousness creates our reality, evolving away from the common human resonance will cause stress."

Dr. Ohlson: "Letter people show impairment in communication between the brain halves and thus use one side of the brain for solving the same problem. They say we are dysfunctional; however, it may be a way to free more space in the brain for solving difficult tasks. The Asperger's part might be responsible for higher knowledge, not interested in traditional learning."

Dr. Schild: "Here I have a lot to say. The connection between the brain lobes is limited in the number of neural connections, and in letter people it is more involved with creating the extra dimension of brain resonance, so some other expressions of brain-lobe interconnection are unsurprisingly weakened, meaning some connections of information with soul are weak. This leaves the affected individuals able to perceive some things of cosmic significance extremely well, at the cost that they cannot simply enjoy a painting or music or dance rhythms. I suspect that their sexual performance is also hindered. On the other hand, they probably see the white light phenomena associated with UFO activities."

New Discoveries About the Nature of DNA

The research into DNA is demonstrating there is far more to DNA than previously believed: the fact that DNA is an incredible storage device, but also there is a second programming language in DNA. Recent discoveries have shown that there is a second programming language within the human genetic code, which alters how scientists read instructions in the DNA and interpret mutations. The genomes use the genetic code to write two separate languages, one written on top of the other. These findings highlight DNA as an incredibly powerful storage device, so what else is there to discover with these amazing properties?

Ref: Dr. John Stamatoyannopoulos, Professor of Genome Sciences, University of Washington. *Science* magazine, Dec 2014.

How Can DNA Change Occur?

DNA can be reprogrammed by words and frequencies. One of the most important scientific discoveries regarding DNA, I believe, is the research by Russian scientists, Dr. Pjotr Garjajev and Vladimir Poponin, whose work is featured in the book *Vernetzte Intelligenz* (Networked Intelligence). They found that DNA is not only responsible for the construction of our body, but can be influenced and reprogrammed by words and frequencies, without cutting out or replacing single genes, and in communication follows the same rules as language. This is significant, as it demonstrates the ability of DNA to be altered by frequencies, which may well be a clue to how some of these DNA changes occur.

Note: "DNA functions like letters in a written language or symbols in a computer code" Molecular biologist, Dr. Francis Crick.

Holographic DNA

Wave Genetics – Are there frequencies to shift human consciousness?
Dr. Pjotr Garjajev and Vladimir Poponin discovered that living chromosomes function like a holographic computer using the endogenous DNA laser radiation and are able to modulate certain frequency patterns onto a laser ray, so influencing the DNA frequency and thus the genetic information. The vibrational nature of DNA allows information to be transmitted by vibration and frequency called wave genetics.

DNA – The Ability to Transcend Space/Time

DNA can also cause disturbing patterns in the vacuum, producing magnetized wormholes! Microscopic equivalents of the so-called Einstein-Rosen bridges in the vicinity of black holes tunnel connections between entirely different areas in the universe, through which information can be transmitted outside of space and time to our consciousness.

This demonstrates the multidimensional nature of DNA and explains pre-cognitive insights, clairvoyance, intuition, telepathy, past-life recall, spontaneous and remote acts of healing, self-healing, remote influencing with weather patterns, crop circles and much more.

Ref: *Vernetzte Intelligenz* (Networked Intelligence) by Grazyna Fosar and Franz Bludorf based on the work of Dr. Pjotr Garjajev and Vladimir Poponin. (Summarized and translated by Barbel Mohr).

The Purpose of Star Languages or Light Languages

If human language and frequencies can alter or reprogram DNA, this can explain why hypnosis, suggestion, and affirmations can be so successful.

It could explain a possible function of the star or light languages articulated by many Experiencers. It means we have to ask the questions: Are these languages frequencies having a purpose we have yet to understand? Do these star language frequencies have an effect on human DNA, also?

Many Experiencers believe these are from their star origins and can trigger awareness or an awakening in human DNA. Some healers find themselves using star languages for healing also, and believe the frequencies act on multiple levels.

"I work to align the frequencies. The sounds/languages are for the souls to recognize their lives on other planets."

Rochelle D'Elia, healer – *Expressions of ET Contact: A Communication and Healing Blueprint?*

Can Music Also Affect Human DNA?

Music is another frequency that may also be significant in altering or affecting DNA. In Chapter Ten, Arthur is guided to play certain music frequencies and was 'given' the title for one piece, *Decoding DNA*. It would suggest that frequencies in music may also create shifts in our biological makeup.

It also is possible that the geometric symbols, scripts, extraterrestrial art through a visual or energetic means, emit frequencies to assist in the awakening of dormant human DNA. The late Dana Redfield, author, and Experiencer, drew many codes and symbols that she believed were part of her Contact communication. She believed they showed gateways and portals and described it as working mid-plane between human language and mathematics and the higher laws of creation.

"Some words are like concept fields. It seemed I was tasked un-puzzling a kind of art-linguistic sacred geometry, a similarity to certain aspects of the Kabbalah. I was seeing a very big picture design behind our lives and all created things. It's really complex; a map of my journey adapting to a new consciousness."

Ref: *Summoned: Encounters with Alien Intelligence* by Dana Redfield, 1998. DVD: *Expressions of ET Contact: A Communication and Healing Blueprint?*

DNA is More Than Chemistry

Quantum Hologram and the soul

Dr. Schild, 2015

"Dear Mary,

I agree, and simply want to expand on some of them.

DNA is more than chemistry and is in resonance with the quantum hologram to bring emotional and spiritual content to our being. This resonance is also seen in our auras. The mathematics of how this works in human consciousness involves the soul and has been described to me as 'hints of the mathematics'. Our karmic history also determines the progress of our lives. This comes from the existence of our eternal soul being as follows: Our karmic history, expressed in our soul resonance with our eternal soul in the consciousness-connection within the brain, then allows our lives to be the result of DNA-endowment, divine tinkering, and free will.

We are, in some respects, the result of the DNA given to us by our parents. The fact is that the amount of relative father/mother contribution of all aspects of our physical being is an emergent property and thus the result of divine tinkering. These concepts have a mathematical basis."

The Statement

"DNA is not just responsible for the construction of our body, but is data storage, which in communication follows the same rules as language and just requires the correct frequencies!

Living chromosomes function like a holographic computer using the endogenous DNA laser radiation, and are able to modulate certain frequency patterns onto a laser ray and influence the DNA frequency and thus the genetic information itself.

Esoteric and spiritual teachers have known our body is programmable by language, words, and thought. Now, this has been scientifically proven and explained."

Grazyna Fosar and Franz Bludorf, authors of *Vernetzte Intelligenz* (Networked Intelligence).

Dr. Schild: "Thank you for including the statement re Dr. Garjajev's research. I have heard of his work before, but it is just words and not mathematics. It explains the following:

You have probably heard of junk DNA. This description attempts to say that our DNA has much more structure than is needed to express the information of the chemistry of our body. I have long understood that the DNA does more than chemistry, and is in resonance with the quantum hologram to bring emotional and spiritual content into our being. This resonance is also seen in our auras; seen by some, but not me.

The mathematics of how this works in human consciousness involves the soul, and has been described by me 'with hints of the mathematics' in the South Florida Science Museum lecture. This is the mathematics that Dr. Garjajev does not know."

Mary: (from lectures) "Dr. Garjajev's research explains how affirmations can be so effective if human language can affect DNA in this way.

We have to also understand that DNA is also influenced by the Epigenetic, factor, which demonstrates we are not just DNA- determined. Human programming and beliefs also impact on how DNA expresses itself and is integral to this broader understanding."

Note: This information is explained in Dr. Bruce Lipton's book *The Biology of Belief.*

Dr. Schild: "Your statement above has the following meaning to me. Recall that our Karmic history also determines the progress of our lives. This comes from the existence of our eternal soul being as follows: We are in some respects the result of the DNA given to us by our parents. The fact is that the amount of relative father/ mother contribution of all aspects of our physical being is an emergent property, and thus could be the result of divine tinkering. Our karmic history expressed in our soul resonance with our eternal soul in the consciousness connection within the brain, then allows our lives to be the result of DNA-endowment, divine tinkering, and free will. These concepts have a mathematical basis, which most people do not care about. You may use my words in your lectures."

Note: Dr. R Schild, Emeritus Professor at the Harvard-Smithsonian Center for Astrophysics. With an extensive career in studying Dark Matter, Black Holes and the fluid mechanical origins of Cosmic structure. Dr. Schild has a long association with Dr. John Mack (Former professor of psychiatry at Harvard University) and Dr. Edgar Mitchell. Dr. Schild became interested in the formulation of a coherent understanding of space-time in the Universe and is a champion of the Dr. Edgar Mitchell Quantum Hologram formulation of the nature of existence and reality. Editor-in-Chief of the *Journal of Cosmology*, he has attempted to broaden the scope of scientific inquiry to include the nature of consciousness and the Universe of Universes.

Dr. Rudy Schild: Executive Director of FREE (Foundation for Research into Extra-terrestrial Encounters), of which the author is Co-founder and Director.

www.experiencer.org

Planetary Influences

Can the holographic nature of DNA activated by certain frequencies, activate dormant DNA?

The holographic nature of DNA and its ability to access information from different areas of the Universe may be assisted by the frequencies it is exposed to, which alters or changes previous programming/conditioning. DNA remodeling, or awakening the so-called 'junk litter' from frequencies from outside sources such as extraterrestrial interactions, star languages, crop circles, art, music and solar frequencies.

Mitch Battros, author of *Solar Rain* and *Cosmic Rain*:

"Solar Cycle 24 has begun; the Sun's activity is fifty percent stronger than Cycle 23. This wave affects not only the planet, but the human body's magnetic field and human emotions."

Battros believes the magnetic influence of the sun will usher in what's described by our ancient ancestors as the transition: bring in a new state of being.

Junk DNA May Not be Junk After All!

"Over ninety-eight percent of DNA has a largely unknown function."

Quote from *Gene Exchange* no 2, 1996.

Science magazine reported new research on the function of genetic material. The article stated that scientists are puzzled that ninety-seven percent of DNA in human cells does not code for proteins, and appears to consist of meaningless sequences. There is a possibility that this apparently useless DNA has some unknown function. The *Science* article suggests that the non-coding ninety-seven percent of the DNA commonly called junk DNA might have a function. The authors of this paper employed linguistic tests to analyze junk DNA and discovered striking similarities to ordinary language. The scientists interpret those similarities as suggestions there might be 'messages' in the junk sequences.

Ref: F. Flam, *Hints of a Language in Junk DNA*, Science 266:1320, 1994.

Article

Jaan Suurkula M.D., said that the function of only a small percent of DNA is known, the remaining was believed to be junk molecular garbage. If it were junk the sequence of the 'syllables', i.e., the nucleotides in DNA, should be completely random. It was discovered it was not random, but a form of coded information, but the code and its function is as yet completely unknown.

Haig H. Kazazian Jr., Chairman of Genetics at the University of Pennsylvania suspected they might be a key force in the development of a new species during evolution. He thinks this DNA may be essential for increasing the plasticity of the hereditary substance.

Ref: *Junk DNA: Over 98 Percent of DNA has a Largely Unknown Function*, by Jaan Suurkula M.D., May 1997. See: http://www.psrast.org/junkdna.htm.

How to Control DNA

High-Frequency People and Low-Frequency People

Dr. Lena Ohlson: "The growth and function of the 'bio-container', called a body, is partly controlled through DNA, a crystalline formation with an in-coded message. DNA is just a responder to different frequencies coming through to the cell via different types of material, such as biomaterial (i.e., receptors), water and colloids. The frequencies, as such, are from many origins and some of them might be aimed specifically with the purpose of halting or speeding up human evolution. They travel through the body and hit DNA like fingers hit the keys of a piano.

The body (bio-container) is just one out of three parts that decide how the frequencies will be received and implemented. The other two parts, important parts, are mind and soul. The soul is the 'energy container' which moves from body to body between lives and dimensions/worlds.

Frequencies have a huge impact on the DNA. The mind is what regulates and thinks in that energy-container. After leaving the body behind when we die or have an out-of-body experience, our thoughts are not in the 'bag-of-meat' left behind, they are in the energy container we fly around in.

It is helpful to imagine the mind/soul/body working as a trinity. The body needs the other two to perform on Earth; to move and to grow. The mind needs a working space to accomplish things with the bio-container while on Earth, and thus in the third dimension. In higher dimensions, where the material isn't material anymore, it's not necessary. The soul provides the life-force and functions as a data bank for all the memories and lessons carried on from different lives. It's like putting on a hazard suit before you go down to Earth and it's equipped with a memory hard-disc to help you carry out your task. It's just that you have forgotten the log-in name and can't access the hard-disc while on the Earth; that's why we have synchronicity to guide us and keep us on the track."

When You Incarnate do You Lose Contact With the 'Main Control'?

Dr. Ohlson: "No. The 'main control' is sending extra frequencies/signals (programmed photons, electrons, protons and gamma rays, etc.) to help you carry out the mission on Earth; perhaps to make extra effort, like in this time of Earth's evolution, when we are upgrading to a newer version and a lot of bugs are disappearing from the current program. Not everybody will want to upgrade. They choose to keep the frequency low in body/soul, with the help of the mind and materialistic thoughts. Eat junk food and the high frequencies from the 'main control' cannot continue to have a high frequency and penetrate their bio container to influence their DNA.

We have now two different sets of humans: high-frequency people (HFP) and low-frequency people (LFP). The HFP will evolve and their DNA will acquire re-awakened abilities. To what extent they evolve is decided partly by their cell DNA (some people have 'extras' put in at some point that can remove or enhance human genes, as well the extra not-Earth-human genes). This may also be guided by the level of evolution the soul has reached.

I have not talked about the origin of the soul because ultimately we all have the same beginning; the same origin. It's just that some have just begun school and some are graduating. If you haven't learned your 'lesson,' you're not moving up to the next level."

How Can the DNA Help us Elevate or Even Regulate the Body?
What Can We Do if We Want to Evolve and Come Closer to 'Graduation'?

Dr. Ohlson: "You start with your thoughts/mind. Happy, positive and loving thoughts generate a higher and more pure energy/frequency. The clearer the thought, the stronger the force, leading to rejuvenation of the cells, also called healing. One of the mediators of the frequency is water. The higher the energy content in the water (natural and undamaged water forms a chain of molecules that are helping the signal), the better water can act as a platform for the signal and carry it on. Other mediators are colloids and ions. Minerals and their ions are crystalline basically, and balanced water transports the signal into the cells and delivers it to different parts in the cell (like a chain reaction) until the signal reaches the DNA. And yes, the cell nucleus contains ions and water so it's nothing unusual."

The Crucial Question – Can Someone/Something From the Outside of the Human Body Have an Influence on the Person's DNA so That the Person Becomes Sick, Ill or Dies?

Dr. Ohlson: "Yes, I believe so. If water loses its energy or crystals/ions are radiated with, say, UV, then the message/signal is changed and the body misses the message or gets the wrong message.

DNA can be altered just by changing the pH in the cell nucleus with oxygen. By changing the pH you get a completely different adhesion of signal-transduction proteins to the DNA and the genes, also changing which genes are read and in what order.

This is why it is important to have a balanced pH in the body. Not drinking enough water or drinking too much bad water, such as too acidic. Try to be biodynamic and eat more vegetables and/or meat from natural sources; only they can provide the balanced mineral and energy uptake your body needs to function in the most optimal way. Buy supplements only from natural sources because they have the right energy for the body. Synthetic ones are devoid of energy. This is basic knowledge on how to control the body's DNA."

Chapter Fifteen

HYBRIDS

To be a Hybrid is to be Awakened

The DNA molecule is the most efficient storage system in the entire universe. The immensity of coded and precisely sequenced information is staggering. The DNA evidence speaks of intelligent information-bearing design.

"They (extraterrestrials) programmed the molecules so that when we reached a certain level of intelligence we would be able to access their information, and they could, therefore, teach us about ourselves. For life to form by chance is mathematically impossible."

> Dr. Francis Crick, co-discoverer of the structure of the DNA molecule and author of *Life Itself: Its Origin and Nature.*

"By certain methods of DNA dating, one can tell numerous genes have been added to the human genome."

> Lloyd Pye, whistle-blower, geneticist, author of *Intervention Theory Essentials.*

The Ancestors

In this chapter, I explore the subject of hybrids. There are many clues to suggest we are a hybrid species, as this concept is explored in the DNA anomalies explored in Chapter Fourteen. How did our species 'miraculously' become *Homo sapiens sapiens,* without any obvious genetic link to previous hominids? The oral history of indigenous tribes, however, offers a significant clue to how this major change in our evolution occurred, and this is in reference to the star family, the ancestors. The Dogon tribe of West Africa, specifically mention the alien 'Nummo' and genetic engineering, sharing their DNA with the Earth humans. Author, Shannon Dorey, in *The Master of Speech,* revealed alien beings, the Nummo, created humans through genetic engineering. Dorey's information was based on anthropologist Marcel Griaule's research of the Dogon tribe: *Conversations With Ogotemmeli: An Introduction to Dogon Religious Ideas*. The Ogotemmeli refer to how the 'Nummo' found the Earth 'naked and speechless' and the Nummo wanted to put an end to this disorder by combining their DNA with the Earth animals.

http://www.themasterofspeech.com/biologicalengineering.html

Biblical Scholar, the late Zecharia Sitchin, author of *Earth Chronicles*, the translation of the Sumerian texts, records the 'gods' as extraterrestrial: the Annunaki. The translation states the extraterrestrial Annunaki lived on Earth and modified human DNA. It is interesting to note that children mention the Annunaki by name, as beings who practice genetic modification.

Many religious, as well as ancient texts, mention the 'gods' and their flying chariots, and how the 'gods' interbred with indigenous humans.

The Christian Bible – Genesis

"Then God said, 'And now we will make human beings; they will be like us and resemble us'."

The Bible: Genesis 1:26. (*Good News Bible: Today's English Version*).

Just Who is 'Us?'

Command Sgt. Major Robert O Dean became aware of the Military knowledge of the reality of extraterrestrial visitors when he was given clearance to Cosmic Top Secret files. Since that time he has acknowledged he has been in Contact with the 'non-human intelligences' himself, and told of our hybrid nature.

"We are a combination of at least twelve different species of extraterrestrial mixed with the human genome. They are family." Command Sgt Robert Dean was told this, in his Encounters.'

Command Sgt. Major Robert O Dean, talking with Kerry Cassidy,
USA, in a Project Camelot interview, 2014.

It seems quite clear Earth has been visited for millennia, and given their advanced technologies, it comes as no surprise that the extraterrestrial 'visitors' modified and added their own DNA to ours. We know this is likely, not only because of the many anomalies in human DNA, but also because research suggests they are still doing it. If this is true (and I believe it is), then we must all be hybrids, but different mixes. However, in this chapter, we explore this topic from a deeper level of understanding.

For most, the fact we are a hybrid species doesn't alter how we feel about our connection to humanity. But this is not the case with some individuals, who feel truly alienated to their human family, with a depth of feeling and deep resonance to their hybrid nature. Some of these individuals explain it as a sense of dual consciousness, almost like they are only part human but mostly part extraterrestrial. They can feel their primary connection is to the extraterrestrial part of themselves, not the human part. In other words, they resonate far more deeply with their extraterrestrial nature than with Earth human.

This deeper connection to their hybrid nature is articulated by Paul – an eight-year-old Australian boy (Chapter Two).

The Human Hybrid Bridge

The first part of this chapter explores the collection of human DNA by extraterrestrials, for their on-going genetic programs to create hybrids with both human DNA and their own. The results of this mix are children, born normally, who reside amongst us. Another program is where 'fetuses' of such a mix are taken in early pregnancy (usually one to two months) to be nurtured on board spacecraft, and other facilities and reside there.

In my first book *Awakening* (Chapter Ten) I address the 'missing pregnancy' phenomenon. A woman may feel pregnant, sometimes for a short time, such as one to two months, and then overnight discovers there is no longer this feeling of a pregnancy. There is no fetus, and the mother is left with 'knowing' something significant has occurred, with a feeling of loss. In addition, some women felt pregnant when there had been no sexual activity. They feel pregnant, not understanding how or why they feel this way, and shortly afterward this feeling leaves them. At a later date, the 'mother' may be shown what they are told is their child on board craft. They most often are encouraged to hold or connect with the child, as the child needs to feel loved. One Experiencer I worked with recalled both consciously and through hypnosis that she went on board craft looking after the hybrid babies, and she said she also helped the human mothers to bond with them. In this chapter, Sarah shares her story, and she believes one of her children was taken as part of a hybrid program and is living on board spacecraft. I must also say that this is not just with women. Men also have DNA taken from them, including sperm, and some have been encouraged to have 'intimacy' with these beings to create hybrids. This is well documented in many cases, and one of the most bizarre is Peter Khoury's experience, which happened in 1992, in Sydney, Australia. Khoury was awoken by two female ' unearthly beings' who attempted to encourage Peter into physical intimacy. He declined and they vanished, however, they left some physical evidence in terms of hair, which was investigated by geneticists, with some fascinating results.

Ref: *The Hair of the Alien* by author and Ufological researcher, Bill Chalker (2005).
Also in Documentary: *My Mum Talks to Aliens*, SBS Australia.

In the same way that women can be encouraged to see their hybrid offspring, so can men be shown the results of this 'mating' or mix, and be shown their hybrid child. It appears that where the hybrid lives depends on its genetic combination and the programs they are created for:
- Hybrids with extraterrestrial and human DNA, who reside on space craft.
- Hybrids with DNA from one or both human parents and extraterrestrial DNA, residing on Earth.

Note: This is not including genetic hybrid programs orchestrated by covert military human agencies (MILAB).

Zac, whose story is encapsulated, in Chapters Nine and Ten, also believes himself to be an Earth-based human hybrid and explains how he understands himself and these hybrid programs. In the latter part of this chapter, I share information from a recent publication: *Meet the Hybrids* (2015). This book tells the story of eight individuals, who believe themselves to be hybrids. We ask the question: Are those who relate to their hybrid nature a more 'aware' conscious human, accessing more of their extraterrestrial genes? Or do they have more inserted extraterrestrial DNA than most humans? If so, what does this mean and should we be concerned? The co-author of the book, Miguel Mendonca, addresses this question: Is the hybrid program something for humanity to fear? I believe this question is very relevant because as a species we are very intolerant of difference. What is the hybrids' understanding of themselves? What is the ultimate goal of these genetic programs from the hybrids' perspective?

Sarah shares what happened to her son, who she believes was a fully human fetus when he was taken to mature on board spacecraft. (Names have been changed to protect identity).

A 'Missing Pregnancy'

Sarah: "My children, and fiancé are ex-Ojibwa/Anishinaabe Indian. I am Native American as well as English, Scottish, and Irish.

"When I was eighteen, I was dating a man and I became pregnant. One night or early morning, I woke up surrounded in bright light. I watched my baby boy float in the air and I admired how beautiful he was and how much he looked like his dad. I actually felt that he was looking back at me through those dark eyes. His dad was a full blood Seminole Indian. I woke up bleeding heavily, and felt that I had miscarried the baby; I believed I watched his spirit leave.

I discussed this experience with a friend, and as I did so, I had a flashback to that event. I realized I did not miscarry, they (the extraterrestrials) took him (my baby). I saw him (my child) again in my bedroom recently. I was afraid, but all he wanted from me was a hug. He has now gone through puberty. Initially I could not figure out who the 'man' was beside the alien, and why he was embracing me in such a way. But now I know it was my son. My God! How could I have not known!"

Consent

Sarah: "I have read *Awakening*, and much of the book spoke of my life story. The difference was, I was able to see the 'baby' when they took him out because they, the beings, showed him to me. I was asking them to show me reasons why I should not be afraid. After my realization event, I started reading unhelpful information by people like Budd Hopkins, who based their assumptions on fear. It was after this I met my human son again. The child was human and not a hybrid. However, he was the product of rape by another human. He was taken where he would be loved and cared for, and I feel that I asked them to do this at that time. I was not asked to hug him; rather, this is what he wanted. My fear kept me from being able to realize who he was and why he was there in my bedroom. I would have wanted to hug him and talk to him had I not been in fear mode."

Note: This account echoes a similar story of Ann Andrews, in which her third child was taken from her in utero and grew up on board craft (See *Missing Pregnancies*, Chapter Ten). Ann, in regression hypnosis, learned she had consented, and the reasons why.

Sarah: "I want to describe my entire memory of that incident. I arrived in my bedroom from my hallway and it was extremely bright. My other children were sleeping and there was this familiar vibration along with my 'changed' vision. My 'visitor' (extraterrestrial being) is there, but out of my vision. I could still feel him. There was a taller guy, a young Native American looking being taller than me, and both embraced me. I am trying to see what the alien is doing, as I can feel the vibration increase. I think that they want me to mate with this guy! Good grief! I cannot do that. I am afraid. I start to see his eyes turn black, and then I start to float to the ceiling. The next thing I remember is waking up in my bed wondering what just happened. If I had not been so afraid of the 'visitor' that accompanied him (my son) I would remember more. I believe that he is in good hands with the visitors. He looked well; he was healthy and seemed happy. He is human and I cried when I realized that I had been afraid of my own son."

Human Son and Hybrid Children

"I must mention that at the time this incident occurred, I was deathly afraid of my Contact with the 'visitors.' I kept asking them to show me a reason why I should not be afraid of them. They showed me my children, not only hybrids but a human that was quite healthy. I saw a flashback of myself holding hybrid babies (I was trying to nurse one) and I was interacting with hybrid toddlers; they were my own, I think."

Note: Women that feel they have been part of the hybrid program, will say they are often taken on board craft to connect with their hybrid children, as the 'child' needs to experience and feel love.

Hybrid Babies are Different

"Regarding the hybrid babies; I was scared to nurse them. The mouth looks wrong. How can I get a seal to latch on; the baby might starve. The baby in my memory is starting to fuss a little, moving around. The head is not quite right; it's just too big. This is why they do not allow humans to carry them full term. They have told me this at one point. The toddler is similar as well, only it has more hair. All of them have dark hair, not blonde like I have seen on movies. Every one I consider is my own has very dark, almost black, short hair. I cannot tell if it is thick or not. The toddler boy I played with had a hard time with me. I think he could hear my thoughts. I kept wondering about the bone structure of his face and head and the neck muscles that held it up. There were differences that I could see compared to humans. I don't think he liked that.

The other memories which keep flooding through are of me lying on a table having procedures done. I could see them from my eyes, lying there, and the alien perspective. I was 'out-of-body' as a witness, not really caring what was going on. I would notice instruments and panels, and other times just the gynecological exam equipment. I did not want to look at the instruments. I hate it when humans do it to me too. I saw them both impregnating me and taking the babies. Other times they were just checking on me, I am not sure exactly why. There was a time I was left bleeding. I realized they had miscalculated something due to the healing of my past C-section, and it caused me to hemorrhage. I do not believe they meant for me to bleed so badly, but they saved the baby. I also hemorrhaged during the C-section itself, but the doctor said that I did not lose any blood. I did not bleed after it either, but my iron level indicated that I had lost more than three pints. Where it went, I do not know.

I do remember someone at my window in my room. The room was on the sixth floor and there was no roof outside my window either. I thought I was hallucinating. They always come for me in the hospital. I had several routine pap smears where I had known I was probably pregnant. The doctor confirmed that my uterus was enlarged, but since I told him that I had not had intercourse for months, we skipped a formal urine HCG. They came for those ones as well.

The little gray guy showed up in my room one night before I went to bed. He was three-and-a-half feet tall and wearing a blue overall type of outfit. It was similar to the ones that my teenage hybrids sons were wearing. Skin tight and covered from toe to neck to wrist, looked like all one piece. There was an insignia on his chest; small I think, on the left side. It reminded me of a military type of uniform. The part that gets me is the emotional response I experienced. I wanted to touch him. I wanted to trace his eyes with my fingertips. I long to see him again. I feel that I love him. He was a typical Gray in description, but I did not find him repulsive. I do not know if he is the one that usually comes for me. I see these ones as lights. I would like to explore the 'little Gray' memory; it makes me wonder if I were an alien in a past life?"

Note: Individuals with encounters can recall past life memories of lives on other planets and having a different form, and believe this is why they feel so alien as a human. Hypnotherapist and author, the late Dolores Cannon, mentions this in her many books, such as *The Convoluted Universe* series.

"My six-year-old son used to tell me about his brothers and sisters that are dead. I asked him why he thinks they are dead, and he said they look dead. I asked how he knows them and he said that they come and play with him at night. I also asked where they play and he said 'somewhere else' and that he is not sure, but he thinks at their house. I speculated that he was playing with sickly looking hybrids and that they may be his father's. I know that they take him too, as they took his mother."

M: "So you think they may be his father's hybrid children? Why would he think they are dead?"

S: "It is my opinion that he thought they were dead because they may have floated, or walked through a solid object in front of him. Also, because they usually look so sickly. That is just how he described it."

I'm a Hybrid

Z: Zac

M: Mary

Z: "I have been told many times I don't look human."

M: "Can you tell me what you understand about the hybrids, their role or purpose?"

Z: "Well, I'm a hybrid. I was told I have been hybridized with Yayelle, a Pleiadian offspring. They are the most active on our world right now when it comes to the hybridization process. Hybrids of the Yayelle are five foot seven inches to six foot in height normally, oval eyes and feminine archetypes with yellow on the outside of the pupil. When they get excited the yellow expands; this is how you know. I was told I was hybridized for expressing the human genome. There are many different agendas on this planet, and each species has their own programs. What I have been told about the hybridization is that it is to expedite the evolution of humanity. It is not like hybridizing us by replacing our DNA with theirs; it's not like that. We already have their DNA in our bodies; they are activating it through frequency and light manipulation. They have these rods; they look like staffs. They are small and have microscopic needles coming out of the end, like a triangle, three coming out of the end and one in the center. They stick it into your body, and it's vibrating at a high frequency and is beaming light into your DNA. The needle in the middle goes right into your heart or the back of your head. It sends a frequency into your DNA to activate the codons of the new template. It allows more expression of our human genome, and the ones our current vessel is vibrating with. The consciousness that we are vibrating with is the attributes we will take on. So if someone is strongly connecting to the Arcturians, they will take on Arcturian attributes. If they are connected to the Yayelle, they will take on these attributes. If one is connected to the Grays, it's the same thing. I have a friend, he is a Gray hybrid and he is very short, oval eyes and round head, pointed chin. It's what consciousness you are connected to which creates the expression."

Healing

"Another reason is to heal the consciousness of humanity. A lot of the human genome has been put through hell, so to speak. We have killed each other for thousands of years for all sorts of reasons. Through the activation of our DNA, not only are they preparing us for the shift that is about to happen, they are also allowing us to open up our DNA, to the downloads we are receiving from the Universe. They also heal our karmic energy or the injuries our DNA has sustained. This is a purifying, or setting us back on track, back on the original course before we went through the chaos. Like cleansing the crystal, and we are the crystal, just like a chrysalis, and the light coming is expanding our butterfly wings.

There is some Archon (self-serving beings); they use their ability to perform DNA manipulation, which can be detrimental to human beings. In their perception, they are benefiting their goal, so it's not harming them, but they are aware they are harming us, as they use us to clone themselves. We have the gift of reproduction; they don't. They see us as livestock, although they understand we are intelligent. They understand we have potential, but our potential may inhibit their potential."

M: "I have had emails with people who tell me they believe they are a human hybrid Gray or a hybrid Reptilian or Mantis."

Z: "We all are. We are hybrids, but what species we connect to will be our present evolutionary resonance."

M: "So you are saying that we all have the potential within to be one of those species?"

Z: "We already are, through the human genome. Why are we the most advanced species on the planet in our perception? Although technically we are not the most advanced, but in our perception of events, we are; that is why are we thousands of years apart in evolution compared to every other species on this planet, in terms of our biological vessels. We have a combination of many different species, which have interbred with us, as well as us interbreeding with ourselves, so we have created even more genetic diversity. We have the codons within us as long as we focus on that potential, to be any being that we want to be. We are free template beings; we have control over our biomagnetic self, over the concept of our reality. The only thing that limits us is the collective-consciousness energy right now. If we hold onto our former beliefs too solidly then it's impossible to shapeshift, although it's not really. But we don't know how to vibrate matter into a different frequency to perceive the different wavelengths."

M: "It does make sense because it explains when some people have looked at me and have seen an aspect they perceived as a 'Light Being', or a 'Blue Being' or 'Gray', for example. I questioned how could they all see something different?"

Z: "Yes, they are seeing your energy through their lens. When I am really happy some people will see 'cat eyes' in me, my friends always perceive my eyes turning into slits. I can't seem to catch it on video, which is annoying; I can't prove this and look crazy. Other times I will have a glow to me. It's whatever energy we hold at that time that will physically manifest. It's a thought projection created by plasma. The plasma manifests into our reality through what we know as geometry, and geometry manifests as atoms and particles, molecules and matter."

The Reality Matrix

M: "Let me be clear: is it what we are manifesting to others that is perceived, or what 'they' (people) are choosing to perceive in us?"

Z: "It's both: it's your energy you are emitting constructed in a specific way with a specific frequency coming out, and their lens, their energy in the frequencies only they can interpret. Your radio and their radio are emitting a huge number of frequencies all at once. Your individual radios can only understand a certain amount of those frequencies, so you have to limit yourself to what you receive from a ton of information. Whatever you are emitting, what they understand is what they will see. So if you are emitting an energy of a Gray, if that is what they can understand, they will see you as a Gray."

M: "That explains why different people perceive different things with me. That will be the same for me when I see other individuals, or how they understand themselves is what they and I will be picking up. If someone says they are a hybrid human Reptilian, for example, I will be picking up on that, as this is what they are projecting to me and themselves?"

Z: "Yes."

M: "What you are really saying is that we are all hybrids, but whatever we feel in tune with is what we will feel about ourselves."

Z: "That's exactly what I am saying. It's a reflection. The Universe is a mirror and it's what's on the outside and the inside that creates you. As they constantly recycle this process like a huge torus forever re-creating itself, and you only perceive what you can of that re-creation. You are the imager and you see pictures flying by you and you can only perceive certain ones."

M: "So when two people are assessing one another, they are projecting and interpreting each other?"

Z: "You are always projecting and interpreting; the subconscious stores this, but the conscious filters out, so it focuses on what it needs at the time. You only understand what you allow yourself to understand. The point of the Awakening is to feel others and understand them from their perspective, and to open up our awareness to everything that's around us."

M: "So part of this is to understand who we are from those multidimensional levels of awareness, including what we are connected to genetically in terms of the much intelligence that is part of our makeup? So what would you like to say to those who want to understand the whole nature of hybridization phenomenon? What would be useful?"

Z: "I would say, ask yourself why do you feel you are a hybrid? What energies are you emitting? What does this sense feel like when you feel you are not just a human? What brings that emotion within you? Delve into it, and allow yourself to explore as you relax into it and what makes you feel in tune with another race of being. And remember, we are all mutts! Every species on this planet contains the DNA of every species; they are only expressing that bit of information to be that species they are. We humans only express eight percent of our DNA, the rest was considered junk, but the junk is the DNA that we haven't vibrationally become in tune with."

To be a Hybrid is to be Awakened

Z: "When we access the DNA of these beings within us, we tune into their consciousness. It's like a string. That DNA string attaches us to their DNA. To them and their consciousness, and when we activate it and pluck that string, they feel it connect to where we are and notice that we are expressing their consciousness, their attributes, and that is why so many beings are coming on to Earth right now. Because, as the Earth is ascending, as we are healing, these beings that are attracted to the planet – we are calling them. Humans are calling them to Earth through our DNA. We are awake, but lost; they have been at that stage in their evolution. They are coming down and watching over like a parent, sending messages through the DNA: 'Okay, you are one of these, such as an Arcturian.' It's like a blanket, so you become comforted, you are not alone and not crazy. It's like: 'We are here and we have information for you. You can be a messenger for us if you wish to be.' To be a hybrid is to be awakened, don't be afraid of it and don't be ashamed. Embrace the fact that you feel different and unique, and express that to the best of your ability."

M: "So really the New Humans and the Hybrids are really the same?"

Z: "They are the same, but the hybrids are expressing their consciousness through their DNA. So is the New Human, but the hybrids are a part of that New Human archetype we are evolving into. The labels don't matter, the humans are evolving, our DNA is advancing and we will express that in any way possible, and we contain the information in our DNA. There are scalar imprinted memories of all the other beings our DNA has passed through, and because we contain that information we can express it in the New Human template. We can express it in the hybrid form or Indigo, etc. That is the energy they are expressing or perceiving through their lens and emitting. It's like a giant loop. It's all the same thing, but different, like fractals upon fractals. They are all interconnected, but you perceive them as different as you wish to."

M: "So it's really how we choose to understand who we are?"

Z: "Yes, it's how you feel and see it, but *what* you feel is the most important because what you're seeing is not truly what's there. So, it's *what* you are feeling that matters because feeling is vibration. It's energy. It's emotion. It contains the purest form of our essence. The feeling is us; it's everything. The reason we can communicate right now is because we are vibrating at a similar frequency or similar bandwidth; we understand and interpret the same information from the same light particles. It's fascinating to think about."

M: "How do you understand what is happening now?"

Z: "It depends on how you want to understand it, and this may be how you perceive it: such as humanity is sleeping and not understanding our purpose on this planet, destroying the Earth and each other. Another perspective is that we are all awake in our own way. But all we have to go on right now is the experiences in this life and the limited amount of information we can understand, and are conditioned to believe. Because of the educational systems we have now, we become stupid, and we can't understand anything, consequently, we shut down because we don't care anymore."

You Choose Your Perspectives

Z: "However, the younger generations are coming in without this 'field' and they are more aware than those around them. The older generations are evolved too with the DNA but are choosing subconsciously (due to their beliefs) not to express it themselves. It means we all have these abilities but not all choose to express it. It's your perspective on what you are doing that shows how awake you are. It's your perspective on the world that truly matters. Are you a loving person and do you treat people, animals, and creatures with respect and compassion? It's your beliefs and behavior that says if you are awake. That's what awakening is. The young children have clarity because they haven't closed themselves off. You are responsible for your body and your reality or life situation."

M: "I recall a nine-year-old girl who told me humans are truly extraordinary, but they won't realize this until they believe it, which seems to be what you are saying, isn't it?"

Z: "That's exactly what I am saying."

M: "So it's believing in our potential; it's the way we can expand?"

Z: "It's the only way we will expand and change. We have to believe in ourselves because without belief we have nothing. Belief is what structures our reality."

M: "There is a huge belief on this planet that we are not able to transcend the negativity and the programming on this planet. We are trapped on a prison planet and no way out; we are totally controlled. What would you say to people that feel they are being targeted so they have no chance to expand due to those controls?"

The Prison of Belief

Z: "It's a hard thing to answer because there are people being targeted, and yes reality is what you choose to perceive. We have structure here. The hybrid program is going to assist in fixing this belief pattern that comes from thousands of human experiences and beliefs. As humanity expands, that belief will no longer exist. The only prison is your own thoughts. Every choice you make has an effect and if your life is in a state of turmoil, where you feel targeted or psychically attacked by negative entities, look at the physical things in your life that are making you unhappy, and the targets are your own emotions. Yes, there are negative beings out there, but the negative beings cannot attach to you if you are not vibrating at their frequency. In order to have an attachment you have to mirror the energy of that attachment, you have to attract that attachment; this happens through your emotions and actions. If your actions are not in line with your heart center and if what you say and do are not in line, or if what you feel and what you do are not in line, you open yourself up to attacks and a reality that is a continuous spiral of self-destruction. But you are not broken, and if you find within yourself to say you are ready to believe what you can really achieve, you are free. And if you feel you are targeted then explore your inner pain, as this can manifest into that experience. Trauma is what this hybridization process is; it's healing the karmic trauma of this world."

Entities and Frequency

Z: "Trauma creates a negative expression and this expression may manifest as an entity. Many people have been abducted. I have been abducted, I know I have. Some people say they have negative experiences with this abduction. A lot of the time, it's not because it's a negative experience, it's because your brain doesn't have a current understanding or capacity to calculate all of the light information you were perceiving when your vessel was receiving in that solid state frequency when you were in that craft with those beings, and those beings have an effect with their energy, it brings up all the negative interpretation out of your body."

M: "One young man said he was picked up by covert agencies."

Z: "They exist, and they want to silence this."

M: "He said they had machines they used on him to bring down his frequency to elicit information from him, so he managed to tap into his essence so they couldn't achieve this."

Z: "That's great confirmation for me: I personally do not have any valid physical information they are manipulating the ionosphere to beam frequencies into our minds to alter our perspectives or thoughts, although I believe they are, from the information that I have gathered and been shown and perceived, and if they are doing it, it's to everybody. But those who experience it heavily are the ones who are tuning into it because it's just like a radio. The only way this would work is if our brains are allowing that frequency to affect us, and we are. It's not our conscious fault, it's how we are raised, and our programming to believe certain things, so we are susceptible to these energies. Subconsciously, we are choosing to experience this for soul evolution. It will stop on the physical plane when we stand up against it. We allowed these systems, and we can change them. Those that have the power have the money, but this will change and there will be disruption soon in the system, and money will have no value at some point, and only those who have merit will have authority, which will be based on your intellectual and spiritual merit and not money, and this is what will end these systems. Especially when humans understand what's really going on and when more of the public see the chemtrails; it will be people power. The black projects and secret government are beginning to come to light. What I have been shown in my dream state, is that 2016-2017 will be big years for disclosure. There will be a domino effect."

M: "It's interesting that the nine-year-old mentioned 2012-2017 as being the crucial time and others are saying a similar thing: that the next few years are very significant."

Z: "Those that we consider more aware, even if they appear to do nothing, their thoughts contain so much potential energy that they are practically yelling their reality into existence, so even a few people are having a large effect. When more awaken, you will get a peak and it will just take off. We are being prepared for takeoff. I don't know personally how it's going to happen. I don't want to say anything because the consciousness of humanity may choose not to experience it. It depends on what we choose as a collective, and what we are choosing right now is to be more informed. People want truth; they are tired of lies and propaganda. Through the galactic superconscious we are receiving information – what we ask for, that's what is coming."

M: "So what we choose to believe in as a collective is what will manifest?"

Z: "Yes, not the individual, the collective. The individual creates the individual reality, but that is influenced by everyone else's reality, which is influenced by the collective reality, which is influenced by the supercollective reality. Everything is a by-product of everything else."

M: "Finally, is there anything else you would like to say about this for the book?"

Z: "It's happening; it's a real phenomenon. It's happening to every single person. It's not a rare thing. It's not a special thing. It's not anything to fear; it's to embrace and love; to realize that we are more than human. We are so beautiful. We are so amazing. We are just now beginning to experience that true beauty and amazement of what we are: that we are a beautiful species that has been through hell and back, and we are only now beginning to express the fullest of our essence, beauty and creativity and uniqueness. This is what I feel should be in your book."

Meet the Hybrids

Meet the Hybrids co-authors, Miguel Mendonca and Barbara Lamb explore the hybrid phenomenon 'through the lens' of eight individuals who believe themselves to be human-extraterrestrial hybrids. In this book, they share their understanding as to the reasons for the genetic hybrid programs.

The question asked by the authors:
"How do you understand the rationale for the hybrid program?"

"I believe it's multidimensional in nature. You can think of a planet and humanity as a whole, as a collective with a specific frequency. Here, it's a little low, to say the least, due to the collective negativity. This nightmare scenario going on here hurts humanity and the planet – so one of the purposes is that the ETs put their DNA into hybrids, who help to anchor the higher frequencies to raise the vibration in the human collective mind."

Robert Frost Fullington. (p. 99)

Meet the Hybrids, Part 3 contains a summation of concerns researchers and public may have regarding hybrids, and the possibility this may be a strategy by extraterrestrials to take over the planet.

The question posed:
"What is your take on the takeover thesis?"

Miguel Mendonca – "The comments on the 'takeover thesis', commonly discussed in Dr. David Jacobs' work, were varied. Some are aware there is a parallel hybrid program underway, which is in the 'service to self' column, as opposed to the 'service to others' work that they are a product of. Tatiana, Charmaine, and Juju all stated that they don't give attention to the negative aspect and some preferred not to discuss it at all, often referring to the law of attraction.

Juju talked about the choice of words. 'I think it's a matter of perception. The words you choose show you where you're at, with something. The hybridization program is definitely happening, but why do we have to see it as a 'threat', rather than more of a profound happening, that includes humanity helping another species? I like that take on it much better; that's what I choose to focus on. And a lot of us hybrids have been asked to be like donors, to have hybrid children with the ETs, to extend the species' existence. To me, that's a loving, spiritual experience, not a threat.'

Not all ETs here are for service to others; some are more in service to self, and you will feel the manipulation part of it, or wanting to control. If you feel that and see that behavior, that is intervention. There is a species of Reptilian here that's not in service to humanity. It doesn't mean it's evil, but it's not here for us. There's a big difference. People forget to question that. It's like a human stepping on an anthill by mistake – if you ask the ants if we're evil, what would they say?

As someone closely involved with the hybrid children aspect, Vanessa has strong feelings on the 'threat' perspective. 'If we are incarnating these genetically modified children, from an introspective point of view, are the parents going to reject the children, not love them? I don't see how that point of view works because parents are going to love their children, they're going to work with it. We can't incarnate all these people to take over the world because there's this huge love component between parent and child, and that vibration holds so much benevolence. I have to get that off my chest because it's very triggering for me to hear that. There's a personal vulnerability because of my involvement in it.'

Many of the hybrids reported negative experiences with dark energies, but some suggested that it might be a matter of perspective, that there may still be a soul agreement to participate in that.

Robert has had invitations to support the efforts of self-serving beings. 'So yes, this negative stuff is going on, but I'm not close to it. Most of my experiences are

251

extremely benevolent. To be honest, I'd like to see a hybrid takeover – I think the world would be running pretty awesome. I think I'd make one hell of a President. I'd only have one law: Don't be an asshole. [...] As for me, in my one-room apartment, I'm not taking over jack shit. I couldn't take over a McDonald's. I went in there today and it took me a half hour just to get a cup of coffee.'

Robert's response rather firmly grounds the discussion, and speaks with its own kind of eloquence to the point that, as discussed in the chapter on Hybrid Discourse in Ufology, it is apparent that there are at least two hybrid programs underway on this planet. Jacobs may be accurate in his conclusions concerning one aspect of the phenomenon, but the accounts shared in this book – and in Quiros' doctoral dissertation – indicate a very different agenda to that of a takeover of Earth. What level of overlap may exist – which would suggest either deception or misunderstanding – is unclear? As ever, reaching firm conclusions in this field remains the preserve of the supremely confident."

Meet the Hybrids: The Lives and Missions of ET Ambassadors on Earth (Part III, p. 206-207), co-authors Miguel Mendonca and Barbara Lamb. (Published 2015).

Hybrid Programs and the Military (MILAB)

Research has revealed it is not only extraterrestrials who engage in hybridization programs. Similar programs have come to light, with the possibility of human cloning, human/ET hybridization orchestrated by human military (MILAB) genetic modification programs for a variety of purposes, including the real possibility of creating Super Soldiers.

Charmaine D'Rozario-Saytch contributed her story in *Meet the Hybrids*. Previously, Charmaine had requested two hypnosis sessions with me, to confirm her hybrid status. Confirmation she is a Reptilian-human hybrid with hybrid offspring and one hybrid son located on spacecraft, came as no surprise to her. Nor was discovering she had female offspring, taken as fetuses by human covert military agencies, which she felt were used in covert agendas (p. 75). Charmaine explains this in the book.

The question posed:

"Do you understand the rationale for the hybrid program?"

Charmaine D'Rozario-Saytch – "It is my belief there are various reasons for the hybrid program, and these differ depending on species and whether there is involvement with the military. I believe one purpose for the creation of hybrids is to bridge the divide between ETs and humans, taking positive attributes from each race for certain purposes – such as healing, higher intelligence, stronger spiritual connection and so forth. By contrast, some are created by the military to use their abilities as weapons." (p. 75).

Note: Research into the agendas and cloning programs by human covert agencies, with harvesting from extraterrestrials as well as humans. Clones of extraterrestrial species, such as Grays and Reptilians, are called PLFs (Programmed Life Forms).

Ref: Whistleblower testimony on YouTube Bases interviews by researcher
Miles Johnston.

The question posed:
"What do you know of the differences between Earth-based and non-Earth-based hybrids?"

Charmaine D'Rozario-Saytch: "Earth-based hybrids seem to have more emotional ability and a strong desire to help others and the Earth. Non-Earth based hybrids appear to be more aware of the bigger picture, if you will, from a galactic point of view."

I believe Zac's understanding of the hybrid and himself is extremely illuminating. Also, Zac's understanding that what we believe ourselves to be is what we will choose to identify with.

In a sense, if we are souls from the matrix, we are all visitors to this planet and we have come to experience this reality with the human overcoat.

"Mum, we are the Aliens" – Jena, eight years old.

Chapter Sixteen

A HOLISTIC PERSPECTIVE

The Letter People – Asperger Syndrome, Autism, ADHD, Dyslexia
Dysfunction, or NEW Programs for Humanity?

"If by some magic autism had been eradicated from the face of the Earth, then men would still be socializing in front of a wood fire at the entrance to a cave."

Dr. Temple Grandin, author of *The Autistic Brain.*

In this chapter, we explore an alternate, holistic interpretation of letter people. This perspective encapsulates, and re-interprets the present labels of Asperger's, ADHD, forms of autism and dyslexia. [1]

"I do not believe the theory that these letter people have 'broken genes'. I believe they offer new multidimensional skills which are designed to prevent limited reprogramming of a third-dimensional reality."

Dr. L Ohlson PhD.

The term 'letter people' is coined by Molecular Biologist Dr. Lena Ohlson who studied letter people from two significant perspectives, both as a scientist and experientially, as a letter person herself. I believe that Dr. Ohlson has an important perspective in understanding ADHD, Asperger's, dyslexia and autism. In this perspective, we explore what it is that makes letter people dysfunctional. Faulty genes, poor diet or as some believe, the effect of vaccinations, chemtrails, or GMOs (genetically modified organisms)? Or a combination of these factors?

Dr. Ohlson and some researchers have studied individuals with these 'labels' and it revealed some startling information. We explore some of these theories that could offer explanations as to why letter people have difficulties operating in a 3D reality. Information which will help the letter people manage the 3D world more easily.

Testimony from a teacher with a deep understanding of the letter children, and the remarkable ways she supports them. We explore insights into why the children are different; insights corroborated by some of the latest scientific research, and explore how their heightened awareness and abilities can be recognized. What makes them so different? What abilities do they have? Why are they being born in greater numbers? What does this mean for humanity? Are they new evolutionary programs for humanity? Is this part of the soul journey?

Activation of DNA

Dr. Ohlson believes the letter people are the New Humans and have incarnated to help the rest of humanity evolve. She explains: "It is not so simple as foreign DNA. It's a combination of genetically improved bodies in combination with souls from different places in our universe, incarnating in these improved bodies. The souls have different frequencies/vibrations depending on their evolutionary status, and these play a role in activation of the DNA in that particular body. I believe we also have to take into account the collective soul of *Homo sapiens*.

Letter people show impairment in communication between the brain halves, thus they use one side of the brain for solving the same problem. They say we are dysfunctional. However, it may be a way to free more space in the brain for solving difficult tasks. The Asperger's part might be responsible for 'higher' knowledge and not interested in traditional learning."

Letter Person – Asperger's – Honesty, Truth

A personal encounter – An Asperger's individual explains:
"Asperger's are highly intelligent, functioning individuals, but appear to struggle with social norms of human interaction."

Some years ago, I was fortunate to have an in-depth conversation with an individual with Asperger's. I was fascinated to hear his perspective on how he understood himself and what he told me of his challenge with so-called 'normal' social interactions. He explained that the Asperger's individual has little difficulty socializing with other Asperger's because, amongst themselves, they don't use social masks; what they have between themselves is a totally honest interaction. However, he struggled with so-called 'normal' interactions because they were fake and conditioned responses, to meet the cultural and societal expectations, and those with Asperger's abhor dishonesty.

The rituals of modern society, performing to accepted behavior patterns, we know are most often masks to hide our true selves and feelings. It seems that honesty is the Asperger's forte and they feel normal society is dysfunctional, and that's why they struggle with these behaviors. It may well be that the Asperger's program is orchestrated to teach us honesty. This is important as we evolve into the more aware and awake humanity.

Along with this quality, Asperger's are highly intelligent, with many PSI, intuitive, multidimensional abilities.

Autism – Creative and Telepathic – Hyper-connectivity

In recent studies, American medical researchers have uncovered some surprising findings about children with autism. They discovered the brains of children with autism have more neural connections, an over-connectivity, more than other children, not less, as was previously believed.

"It was believed autism could be the result of a brain that lacks enough neural connections, but new research found the opposite. They have discovered that the brains of children with autism actually have more connections than other children. MRI scans on one hundred and twenty children gave weight to the theory of over-connectivity in the brains of autistic children.

"There are more connections between nerve cells in the brain and thus the brain can be overwhelmed by cognitive and sensory input."

Kaustubh Supekar – a research fellow at Stanford University.

Dr. Ohlson Comments

"I believe the autistic person could be hyper-connected and gets caught in that thought loop, and it's also a reason why they seem to be so 'disconnected'.

I personally had problems trying not to over-think, and I learned to react to my feelings and postpone the thinking of 'why.' The 'why' can start a very rewarding thought cascade in the brain. It is like we are involved in a mystery or a game, and people misunderstand us and think we are 'cold' when we seem 'disconnected.' However, this two-sided reaction might be a response to the limited cooperation between the left and right side of the brain.

I have noticed people with Asperger-like features have one 'lazy' eye, and as far as I have asked, it's most often the right eye which has a poorer vision. This could indicate that autistic people could activate one eye more than the other in order to be able to focus more properly in the field they are interested in, through activating the correct side of the brain needed for the task.

I have explored one possible reason why some people are born with more connections and probably more brain cells than other people. It may begin in the uterus, when the fetus is growing. All the cells are dividing at an enormous rate, but there also has to be a regulated cell death, and especially in the brain, to orchestrate the body development. If the cell death is slightly deregulated and a bit 'off' and there are not enough brain cells dying prior to birth, or immediately after, although they should die, are they connected through nervous cells signaling to and from the senses areas in the brain?

Then the baby would be born with more nervous ends, get more input from the start, and develop more synapses because the input is stronger than in an ordinary child, and that increased input is, in turn, demanding more synapses forming, and that, in turn, increases the overload of the senses. In that case, I think one should find that autistic people have much denser cell growth in the areas of the brain responsible for the senses as well as much more and faster signaling. Is it possible something causes this during the pregnancy? Possibly radiation from the sun and the cosmos, the photons pouring over us might be causing this in part. Photons can switch to electrons and electrons are parts of atoms, and we consist of billions and billions of atoms already as a small fetus.

Through my extensive research in the areas covering cell signaling, protein expression and DNA transcription in rat models, I have noticed that very small changes in substances/buffers adding energy to the molecular reactions in form of H+ (low pH), changes the reading frame of a gene. This is shown by the GIEMSA[2] method. In a test tube, cell proteins are attaching to radioactive-labeled DNA from a reading frame of a gene. By altering the pH from 7.8 to 7.6 you can have different sets of cell cycle regulating proteins binding to the DNA, and this can actually have a huge effect on the cell division – depending on what genes are affected and in what stage of the pregnancy.

The research of Kaustubh Supekar regarding hyper-connections, explains the restrictive and repetitive behavior of autistic children:
"It is difficult for a hyper-connected brain to shift attention to a different task. If they are playing with computers and ignore everything else, they are in a hyper-connected state for that task. The findings raise questions about the social behaviors of children with autism."

Note: The research has been published in the journal *Cell Reports*.
Ref: Emily Bourke interviewing Kaustubh Supekar on ABC Radio,
http://www.abc.net.au/pm/content/2013/s3887279.htm

Empathy
"One of the hypotheses is that children with autism are not rewarded by social interactions as normal human beings are, and that may be a reason they don't show empathy." Kaustubh Supekar.

"I disagree, I believe they are empathic but overloaded."
Dr. Lena Ohlson
"The statement that autistic people are lacking empathy, I feel, is incorrect. They may not appear to show empathy in the more conventional way. When an autistic person opens up to feel with someone in distress or someone hurting (animal or human), they are overwhelmed by this feeling, and this is a reason the autistic person tries to keep a distance from the emotional situation. It is described earlier in the article that autistic people can be hyper-connected to whatever they have at hand, and that it is logical to believe this hyper-connectivity has the same effect with emotions."

Understanding Autism
Sandra and Max Desorgher wrote to me, after watching the presentation on *The New Humans*. They have worked extensively with understanding autism and also believe

257

the autistic person has special qualities and have developed ways to support them and help them function.

The 'Light Children' and the 'Transformation of Humanity'

Autism – A marker for the extraordinary human

Max explains: "My wife, Sandra, received information in 1994, relating to the causes and cure of autism. Since then, we have traveled the world sharing this information freely with people who are interested, and that includes thousands of families with autistic family members, as well as doctors and researchers in many fields.

Our work in autism is not accidental; we believe autism is a marker for something extraordinary happening in the human species: a consciousness shift, and the emergence of children with extraordinary gifts.

Autism is a very complex and multi-faceted disorder. In its presentation, it can vary from severely disabling to manifestations of genius. One type is known as Asperger Syndrome and is associated with very high IQ, artistic, mathematical and musical genius. We have probably met more people with autism than anyone else on the planet – literally thousands. We have seen genius in young children, even though that genius is often hidden to the world because of the presentation of socially strange and incomprehensible behavior. Sandra's revelation was that the cause of the disabling nature of autism is pigment intolerance, something which is totally impossible according to mainstream science. When a certain group of pigments known as 'all-trans isomer carotenoids' is removed from the diet, the autist 'wakes up'; the disturbing and traumatizing symptoms and behaviors abate and the hidden person emerges. The miracle is that genius is the rule rather than the exception. If this is true, we have a population of millions of geniuses hiding behind the veil of autism, waiting to be 'woken up'.

Since 1994, we have seen hundreds of such awakenings. The first was Sandra herself, who discovered the lutein connection in 1994 and changed her diet, and her life. The second was her adopted daughter, Sara, who was severely autistic and whose life was transformed. I heard about Sandra's work over the internet. When she sent me the diet information, my life was transformed and I was so overwhelmed by the transformation in my life that I left behind my former life and flew to America to help her in her work. I could give many examples of transformations.

In 2002, we were in Borneo. We met a boy who was running naked around the house, totally out of control. A year later we returned and he was operating two computers simultaneously while watching a TV program and having a conversation with his father at the same time. This is the level of transformation we are talking about. "

See more: http://sojmed.blogspot.com/2011/02/autism-light-children-and.html

"Sandra and I have worked in schools for many years. Sandra is an Educational Psychologist (PhD MA, Psy.D.) and I work as a music teacher. We are witnessing how the educational systems are being forced to change from teacher-centered to child-centered schools, as the children become more aware and are setting their own agenda for education. We help schools to accept this change and adapt to the emerging reality.

There is so much to tell that it is difficult to know where to begin. Please be aware that some of the information I am about to share is not in the public domain, as we still have to work in the world."

Otherworldly Experiences – The Human Mission

"Sandra comes from the Cherokee Nation and was taught by Chief Two-trees, a Cherokee healer. Sandra was born with the memory of her spiritual home and remembers being prepared for her mission. Unlike most humans, she never lost her connection to spirit and her angelic teachers, who guide her through her dream state. Through the dream state she has access to 'The Library' where all knowledge is available, and when she went there, she was guided to the information she needed. She has also been on journeys to the moon and other star systems, such as Arcturus. As a young child, she was taken on board starcraft many times and was taught many things and taken on journeys. As a child, she also spent many hours in medical libraries, reading medical textbooks and journals. In 1988, she completed her training to be a foster parent for children who were hard to place. Her first placement was Sara, an abused autistic girl."

http://www.saras-autism-diet.freeservers.com/Diet/Saras_Diet_I.html

"Sandra had always been aware of her own food intolerances, which led her to seek out answers to why certain foods were a problem for her. By 1994, she had all the answers she needed, including the breakthrough knowledge of pigment intolerance and lutein. She implemented the diet first for herself, and later for Sara. The story of Sara's recovery is given here:"

Ref: http://www.saras-autism-diet.freeservers.com/Exile/I-9.html

"Sandra wanted to know if this information could help other children with autism, so she went online (this was in the early days of the internet) and shared the information with parents on the first autism mailing list, known as the 'St. John's list'. Hundreds of parents took up the information, and some of the results can be read here:"

Ref: http://www.saras-autism-diet.freeservers.com/Exile/I-10.html

"She was invited to speak at national autism conferences and became a close associate of some of the leading researchers at that time.

In 1997, I was living in Holland and worked in publishing. I was looking for answers to my health problems, and my research led to Sandra's work. The changes in my life were very profound, and the information on pigment intolerance led to deep insights into consciousness and evolution. I left Holland and went to America, to meet with Sandra. She was trying to write a book, and my experience in publishing allowed me to help her put the book together, which we published several years later while we were in South Africa. The book is titled *The Power of Exile: Autism, a Journey to Recovery*.

Since then, we have traveled around the world, teaching and sharing the knowledge with families and autism experts.

As well as our work in the world as 'autism experts,' we both work on other higher levels, through dreams, Contacts, healing and 'traveling'. This work is not so easy to write about, and it may be best to talk to you via Skype, or meet face to face. Sandra specifically works with the light children in the dream state, and I spend most nights in 'dream school,' where I am being prepared to teach through multi-dimensional scripts and using organic computers. In one dream, I was in front of a class and I had a 'book' called *The Well*, which was full of multi-dimensional hieroglyphs; entire teachings can be given through each glyph. I have also had dream conferences with Ra Uru Hu, the teacher of the Human Design System, who I knew personally while he was on the Earth.

Ref: http://www.loveyourdesign.com/vale-to-ra-uru-hu/

Our work is with the children, and their preparation to be teachers and ambassadors for the Earth.

I hope that I have given some answers to your questions and that we can work together to bring about the Age of Light that we are all looking for."

Sandra

"I believe it was the 30th of January, a Red Lunar Earth portal entry activation date, that Max put on a video of a conference presentation you gave, (*The New Human*). Within minutes I was in a trance, a hypnotic or altered state of consciousness, and returned to the present physical body time dimension just as the presentation ended.

Wherever you are in the process of writing, I hope that the knowledge of allowing us to follow our own body rhythms will be a focal point. Many of us can learn to 'robot' through the mainstream day, night, calendar and schedules routines forced upon us. Many find their way through the maze and arrive at 'accepted' meaningful and well-paid careers in their early forties (T. Berney). Some are born outside the Western World and to families of wealth and power. From an early age, they are treated with the utmost care and respect; their gifts shine and their differences are attributed to having nannies, maids and paid placements in multiple schools and multiple countries. They come and go from place to place and all of this change, which the standard literature says is not good for them, actually appears (in my experience) to be the best education for them to experience - the only constant in life is change."

Sandra Desorgher – AKA White Wolf (pathfinder).

"I am sure that we will be very happy for you to mention us in your new book, and to use passages from our books and websites. I would love to have face-to-face communication with you as well, and I hope that once we are in a better circumstance to travel and teach again, we will. We have so much we would share with you."

Ref: https://www.facebook.com/Emerging-Raves-422136671315690

Max: "Sandra's work is more and more on the higher planes, as her body goes through deep transformations. As the channel for this material, her inspiration is what drives me to bring it out into the world, at a time when the world is waking up to these revelations."

Ref: Max and Sandra Desorgher.
http://saras-autism-diet.freeservers.com/

Telepathic Children

Cress Spicer – Vancouver, Canada.
"Thanks for sharing your work, I love your work. It was fascinating. I could personally relate to it.

I have over twenty-five years experience in various school boards in the UK and Canada, as a student support worker, so I have experienced first-hand working with these children, not only supporting them at an academic level but also on a spiritual/energetic level.

I feel I have an in-depth understanding of these special children and formed very close relationships with a lot of them and could relate to them on multidimensional levels, as well as at this level.

My interactions I have had with the autistic children were on a non-verbal level, communicating telepathically through pictures and visions. One particular child, whom I got very close to, was verbal and would also connect with me on a telepathic level, sending me images of a yellow circle, which was his favorite thing to draw and was a comfort to him. I feel this was a connection for him to higher levels of consciousness.

Some of the more severely autistic children, who were completely nonverbal and sometimes very delayed, communicated through telepathic means, showing me pictures, and also through an energetic level. I often found these children to be full of unconditional love, radiating a love and joy and very sensitive to other people's energies.

I realized I am able to communicate with these children as I can sense energy using all five senses. Ever since I was a young child, I have been able to see 'beings,' and my dad was very psychic as well. I can relate to these children, as I too have these qualities, but learned how to express myself and be grounded and connected to Source at the same time.

I have noticed that, when in a school environment, an autistic child can be in quite an elevated state as they are reacting to another child, person or teacher, and often, when I entered the room, they became more grounded and calm, as I would be connecting with them on an energetic level and sending them love.

In one instance, a behavior consultant asked me why the autistic child calmed down around me and I replied, 'They are reacting to my energy. If I am calm, grounded and in a loving place, the child will feel more safe and secure and able to self-regulate themselves out of a situation.' If the adult was anxious or in turmoil themselves, then the autistic child could react to their emotional state and act out different behaviors, such as anger, rage, and frustration.

I constantly gain new understanding of these beautiful children and truly believe they are connected to the spiritual realms and are assisting the raising of consciousness within the school environment and in life; sharing their own gifts and unconditional love in ways that they are able to."

My Encounters

Cress: "My husband says he knows you. He met you in Vancouver at a talk you did for UFOBC. Both my husband and I have seen UFOs and my husband has taken photos of them and also Light Beings. I actually saw a UFO just before Christmas, over the mountains nearby.

When I was a child, I was particularly affected by nosebleeds, fainting, low blood pressure and I had very strong memories of an imaginary friend called 'Polly.' I even gave her a house. Even from a young age, I had Contact with beings of light. I remember feeling very comforted by beings that looked like Jesus and Mary, and they would be with me at night as I slept. I recall feeling frightened as a child of looking under my bed and in cupboards. But felt safe and protected by them as I slept."

New Schools for These Children

"I agree; there definitely should be new schools for these children. The education system as it is right now does not work for a lot of these children.

I have written, and am self-publishing, a book about my experiences with these children over the twenty-five years I have worked with them. My book is basically about stories of autistic children I have supported in various school boards and outside, doing energy work with them. The book is coming from a place of how their sensitivity to energy affects their behavior and, yes, you may quote me.

Note: Professional training: NNNEB; Nursing diploma UK; study of child development; Early Childhood Educator (ECE); two years toward a Child and Youth Care degree; Deaf Bind Intervener. Various courses on Autism, ADHD. Professional alternative health training: Reiki Level 1 (1994); Reiki Master/Teacher (1999); Holographic Healing training: Alton Kamadon modality (1997-1999); Flower of Life courses (1999); Certified Bodytalk Practitioner (2004); Certified Bodytalk Access Trainer (2008); PaRama Bodytalk training (2016).

Telepathic and Star Language – Autism – Bridging Worlds

"I had the pleasure of watching a video of your presentation at the Second Annual Exopolitics Expo, at the University of Leeds, on 8 August 2010. I was particularly interested in finding out more about something you alluded to: what you believe to be the case about autism, specifically children with autism who, like my own son, are obviously extremely bright and 'other worldly' but who have what is perceived as an inability to learn normal academics.

My son is very curious and quick but appears to be stuck in a loop of repetition. As a parent whose inner guidance instructed me to home-educate him, we have struggled to live up to academic codes of what is accepted as intelligence. Whether I believe the curriculum and education system to be accurate or not, it is still the most accepted path to being able to get along in this world. My son turned eighteen last year and we are struggling with him entering into adulthood."

Star Language

"One of his most prominent autism features is his language and communication 'disorder'. When he was younger, he really didn't speak much until the ages of five to six, and even now he speaks so fast, and in a type of abbreviation, that it's difficult to understand him at times. Prior to his use of English, he spoke what I jokingly referred to as his own language. It didn't seem like mindless babble to me, as even up to age five I would hear the repeat of specific words and phrases. Even today, he seems to converse with thin air, although now it's more like he's talking to himself and negotiating his life out loud, where normally we self-chatter inside our own heads."

Note: Autistic son of a farmer in Queensland; both of them have seen UFOs. Father and son have extraterrestrial encounters and both speak star languages. One of the languages the son speaks is extremely similar to the star language Tracey Taylor speaks.

G: "I have no conscious proof or memories of actual Contact; I've sensed I have had some unusual experiences. This is becoming a more pressing suspicion in the last few years. I contacted a recognized psychic out of frustration; I had exhausted all other avenues. I had a sinus issue a few years ago, I wanted to get to the bottom of what was going on. She told me that I was an abductee, as was my son. She was curious why I didn't find the news alarming and the words out of my mouth were simply, 'That would make sense.' However, I am not sure why I would say that."

Note: Often the unconscious recognizes the truth and resonates to that statement. Sinus issues can also be a pattern of encounters.

G: "I would love it if you could share what you suspect about autism, as I am looking for insights on the subject. In fact, I am writing a book on the implications of autism on our future society, and in that will use my own experiences and my path looking for explanations beyond the already muddy waters of autism research.

Thank you so much, Mary, for taking any time to share with me your knowledge or point me in the direction of finding out more information. I sincerely applaud your well-crafted research and work in this area."

Telepathy Research in Autism

Note: Five-year-old savant (USA) displays signs of being telepathic. Ramses Sanguino, aged five, was filmed seemingly displaying telepathic abilities. He correctly recounted numbers written down 'out of eyesight'. A video of him attracted the attention of a neuroscientist and he is now part of a cutting-edge telepathy study by Dr. Diane Powell.

Ref: http://www.dailymail.co.uk/news/article-3305206/
Five-year-old-savant-LA-displays-signs-telepathic-learning-seven-
languages-studied-scientists-mother-filmed-reciting-numbers-written-secret.html

Psi Abilities

Autistic savants have not undergone rigorous scientific investigation for psi, although many of their skills are very psi-like. These remarkable skills are accepted by science because they are reliably replicated. Brief reports by physicians, that are suggestive of psi in autistic savants, have been ignored or criticized. The psi ability most frequently reported by parents to the author in her research has been telepathy, especially in nonverbal children. In 2013, the author received three homemade videos of a nonverbal nine-year-old, severely autistic girl, that were claimed to demonstrate telepathy. The data highly suggest an alternative, latent and/or default communication mechanism that can be accessed by people born with severely impaired language abilities.

Website: http://dianehennacypowell.com
Dr. Hennacy Powell M.D. USA. A holistic understanding.

Autism and Creative Thinking

The Journal of Autism and Developmental Disorders explores research, which suggests there may be advantages to having some traits associated with autism.

Psychologists from the University of East Anglia (UEA) and University of Stirling examined the relationship between autistic-like traits and creativity. While they found that people with high autistic traits produced fewer responses when generating alternative solutions to a problem – known as 'divergent thinking' – the responses they did produce were more original and creative.

"This is the first study to find a link between autistic traits and the creative thinking processes. It goes a little way towards explaining how it is that some people, with what is often characterized as a disability, exhibit superior creative talents in some domains."

Dr. Catherine Best, Health Researcher at the University of Stirling.

Dr. Martin Doherty – UEA's School of Psychology

"People with high autistic traits could be said to have less quantity, but a greater quality of creative ideas. They are considered to be more rigid in their thinking, so the fact that the ideas they have are more unusual or rare is surprising. This difference may have positive implications for creative problem-solving. People with autistic traits may approach creativity problems in a different way. They might not run through things in the same way as someone without these traits, but go directly to less common ones. In other words, the associative or memory-based route to being able to think of different ideas is impaired, whereas the specific ability to produce unusual responses is relatively unimpaired or superior."

The above post is reprinted from a press release provided by University of East Anglia, co-author of a study on the relationship between autism and creativity.

Source: sciencedaily.com (August 13, 2015). http://tinyurl.com/nlrb33p

The Soul Journey

"I choose to be autistic."

Adrianna Rocha and Joan Borysenko, authors of *A Child of Eternity: An Extraordinary Young Girl's Message From The World Beyond* (Piatkus, 1995), addressed two significant issues in the understanding of autism and how aware the individual may be on a number of levels: one is multidimensional and one the choice of the soul.

It was through facilitated communication, via computer, that the mother (who wrote the book) discovered not only was her daughter, Adriana, a young autistic girl previously deemed mentally challenged, highly intelligent, but multi-dimensionally aware, perceiving spirits, recall of past lives and her own soul journey.

Adriana told her mother that she chose to be autistic. This was achieved by limiting certain nutrients in the uterus. The soul's purpose was to allow her to focus more on her inner, multidimensional human journey this lifetime, including:

- Telepathic abilities.
- Creativity in thinking.
- Heightened awareness/perceptions.
- Psi abilities.
- Savant abilities.
- To teach and connect to unconditional love.

ADHD and Dyslexia – Overachievers

"Letter people have higher calculated levels of acetylcholine and dopamine when they are active and/or the stress signal 'fight or flight' is on in their nervous system. Letter people are often problem solvers at work and when they suffer from stress and have to be on sick leave it may take three to four people to replace them because they have been managing all the work for several positions. This indicates letter people are in 'the flow' and get their reward (the high dopamine levels) through multitasking; another word for this is hyper-connected, like a 'braingasm,' and feels like you own the world and are one with it."

Dr. Ohlson.

Note:

- ADD: Higher cognitive functioning: Difficult to program into a 3D reality, due to inability to focus by limited 3D conditioning. They operate in a multidimensional reality.
- Dyslexia: Multidimensional, also more difficult to program into an inaccurate

3D reality.

'Always Dialed to Higher Dimensions'

Neil Gould, author of *Close Encounters of the ADHD Kind*.

Author and Ufologist researcher Neil Gould resides in Hong Kong, and I had the pleasure of meeting him when I presented at Hong Kong University. He has filmed many UFOs in and around Hong Kong. Neil explained he was in his fifties before he realized he had ADHD and always experienced reality differently. In his book *Close Encounters of the ADHD Kind*, he shares a conversation with his son about his ADHD.

"In my book, I aim to tell honestly what happened in my extradimensional world where I met the beings of light. I will tell them that being symptomatic of ADHD, I am not limited to a square template of the Universe. I am wired to a multidimensional Universe. I am not Superman, but my 'Internet browser' can browse into chaos, be it on Earth or the multi-verse. I can perceive hidden layers of order and make sense of it all. Most folk without a supercharged browser cannot do this. They are focused towards convention of this reality. To them chaos is not somewhere to look for answers, it is a blur to them. They do not simply have the will or the required software. This is the most important statement I will make in my book.

What my ADHD browser, with its extra super-charge, has shown me: I have communed with entities that are not visible by the normal perception of light; part of you has to go into their reality in order to exchange thought.

ADHD symptomatic people are sensitive to both worlds and seem distracted all the time. They are dealing with mass sensory input and interpreting the resulting chaos into order. They are doing this all day long, both at a conscious and subconscious level. The supercharge they have in their brains requires them to be stimulated all the time because of their brain browser potential. It leads to trouble because the rest of the folk do not understand them. If there is not enough chaos or stimulation they fidget, become hyperactive, and seek chaos.

The more advanced, interesting and colorful those new souls are, the more they can infiltrate society and bring about change. This is what evolution is all about. ADHD and evolution go hand in hand." (pp. 124-125).

Dr. Richard Boylan – Behavioral Scientist, Professor of Psychology

"A Star Child may be defined as a child of both human and extraterrestrial origin. The extraterrestrial contribution to the child's makeup comes with biomedical technology and telepathic consciousness linking. Star Kids are physically and metaphysically changed as a result of their own Contacts with the Visitors, or the Visitors' modifying their parents' reproductive material...

The children become very frustrated with the slow and pedestrian education on this planet."

Dr. Richard Boylan, PhD MS. Ed, MSW, BA. Educator, behavioral scientist, anthropologist, university associate professor (emeritus), certified clinical hypnotherapist, consultant, and researcher. Author of *Star Kids: The Emerging Cosmic Generation*, a book containing fascinating accounts from parents and these new Star Children.

Tracey Taylor (Experiencer) confirms this understanding:
"The new generations of Star Kids are born with full awareness into terrestrial consciousness and are able to bypass unsubstantiated clutter of the mind and link directly to the subconscious with clarity and awareness, to what is known as the higher Self, or superconscious. These superior mental and analytical capabilities with conscious understanding of themselves and the Universe are balanced by spiritual understanding."

Tracey Taylor was given this information about successive generations of New Human.

New Programs for the Soul Journey

Dr. Lena Ohlson.
"It is not so simple as foreign DNA. It's a combination of genetically improved bodies in combination with souls from different places in our Universe incarnating in these improved bodies. The souls have different frequencies, depending on their evolutionary status, and that plays a role in activation of the DNA in that particular body. I believe we also have to take into account the collective soul of *Homo sapiens*.

The letter people:
- Have above-normal sensory cells on the skin.
- Hear above the normal range.
- Are aware of minute differences in the shades of color than normal.
- Have an enhanced taste and smell.
- Are sensitive to all frequencies, and can be overwhelmed by sensory overload.
- Are sensitive to radioactive radiation, as well as energy fields and energy beaming from angry people or animals."

A Letter Person

Dr. Ohlson explains:
"For myself, I don't have a personal diagnosis. However, my mother told me the doctors believed I was autistic when I was a child. Later, when I began to speak, they thought I was extremely strange. I believe my father is a letter person (Asperger's). His IQ-test when he was younger, rated very high and in some areas they couldn't measure his IQ. Some of my relatives are also letter people but don't seem to have the Asperger part, which I think might be responsible for the 'high knowledge'."

Mary: "You mention different brain functions, can you say how you know or understand that?"

Dr. Ohlson: "I have a body-scanner I use when I help people who are 'imbalanced' and suffer from too much stress. It is called a DDFAO (a French acronym to designate the first Computer-Aided Screening and Functional Diagnosis; a Russian invention). It uses the resistance in the body to calculate different parameters, and it is highly accurate. It can, among other things, show you the calculated levels of different neurotransmitting substances in the fluid between the cells.

I found some unique chemical differences: I observed the calculated levels of acetylcholine and dopamine in the brain are higher in letter people. Acetylcholine is formed from choline in the vitamin B family, and letter people need more choline (but also other vitamin B family members) because they use more of it. So that's the simplicity behind the 'cure' for letter people: more of the vitamin B family and methylsulphonylmethane (MSM), to help in the enzymatic reactions in the brain and the formation of acetylcholine from choline. The positive effect comes a few days after the first intake; and if you stop taking the supplements, the first signs of imbalance (ADHD and so on) can be noticed after a few days, depending on how much stress you are exposed to.

Acetylcholine is also used by the body to calm down after stress and to regulate the bowels. That's probably also one reason the letter people can be sensitive to milk products, gluten or additives in the food. Inflammation of the intestine, like IBS, ulcerous colitis and so on, are probably also seen more often in letter people because of the lack of choline. But this could easily be studied for verification.

We know that normal people process one problem at a time on both sides of the brain, observed through brain-scanning experiments. Letter people show impairment in the communication between the brain halves, and thus use one side of the brain for solving the same problem. They say we are dysfunctional but I believe it is a way to free more space in the brain for solving more difficult tasks. Maybe at the same time (lots of the stress sensitive people I have scanned are problem-solvers and multi-taskers before they get their metabolic stress syndrome), a way that nature has supported us with a possibility to further brain development."

Mary: "You mention that those with different 'letters' have bodies and nervous systems different to the so-called normal. Can you say in more detail how you believe that manifests in their behavior or abilities?"

Dr. Ohlson: "It seems like we have an up-graded nervous system. In my case, I have more nerve ends for pressure in my skin. I can see more colors and the difference between more shades of color. Better sense of smell and taste and more acute hearing (a bit outside the normal range)."

Mary: "So would these abilities be similar to what we understand of synaesthesia?"

Synaesthesia

The condition is not well known, in part because many synaesthetes fear ridicule. People with synaesthesia describe having been driven to silence after being derided in childhood for describing sensory connections that they had not realized were atypical. Meat may taste like the color blue, squid bright orange, violins have an energy that brushes the face.

The phenomenon (its name derives from the Greek meaning, 'to perceive together') comes in many varieties. Some synaesthetes hear, smell, taste or feel pain in color. Others taste shapes and still others perceive written digits, letters and words in color. Some who possess what researchers call 'conceptual synaesthesia,' see abstract concepts, such as units of time or mathematical operations, as shapes, projected either internally or in the space around them. And many synaesthetes experience more than one form of the condition.

Siri Carpenter, *Monitor on Psychology*, Vol 32 No 3, March 2001.

Note: This seems to reflect how the New Human may operate in multidimensional mode.

Dr. Ohlson: "We are more sensitive to frequencies of all different sorts, and of course, that means radioactive radiation, energy fields, and energy beaming out from angry people or animals, as well as love and happiness in them. If we can learn how to focus and control our own energy field, we would be less prone to get ill from our surroundings.

I believe letter people have more nerves and synapses because the apoptosis (cell death), that all people encounter already in the womb and all through their life, is slightly impaired. Therefore, we might end up with more nerve cells than normal people."

Challenges for Letter People

Dr. Ohlson: "I surmised that letter people have expanded sensitivities and awareness. These sensitivities would suffer with the present limited and limiting human-reality programming. It would be easier for them to retain multidimensional awareness if they were not so easily programmed in present social, limited and inaccurate third-dimensional reality. I truly believe letter people have a more complex nervous system and therefore also a more complex brain (and thus a more complex and difficult way to go to teach the body how to work with it).

When I was younger, I always had trouble with my balance. My mother said I was clumsy. Nowadays I probably would have been given a diagnosis DAMP (Deficits in Attention, Motor Control, and Perception), in combination with Asperger and the rest of the letters.

Today, through doing gymnastics and focusing training, I have remarkably good balance and a brain that is even better. I advise people who seek help after 'hitting the wall' and becoming stressed that they have to train their brain again, partly through balance and coordination training. The brain has partly turned itself off, but can be rebuilt and the best way to do that is through the senses and limbs, in combination with right food and food supplements. The high levels of acetylcholine and dopamine in the brain are a big part of this and that's one of the signs of letter people. The challenge at this point is to save some of the energy in the body and brain so you don't get 'burnt out' again and again, which in turn can cause depression."

Bipolar Link – Letter People

"I believe the letter people can get bipolar, I believe some bipolar people are just letter persons with too little nutrition in their body and maybe they haven't learned the limit for how it feels when their bodies are running out of fuel. Here, I speak from my own experience. This bipolar thing also runs in the family, and so does suicide. I have learned how to 'feel' my body and its limitations and I have also trained my kids in that too (but sometimes we don't feel our limits and then we have to take it slow and repair ourselves), and some of my clients as well."

How to Support the Letter Person with Diet

"A short list I recommend a letter person to start with and the doses that have helped my family and me. (All doses are per day):

In addition to healthy foods, we take multivitamin and mineral supplements, and in addition to that we take:

Vitamin D3: 50, microgram

Vitamin C: 1-2grams

Sometimes Silica gel for the stomach and nervous system, and probiotic for the intestinal flora, thus promoting health.

For the Nervous System and the Brain

(Running all the functions in the body, and therefore crucial)

Vitamin Bs in a complex: 25 mg each of B1, B2, B6, PABA, Inositol

50 mg each of B3, B5, Cholin

50 microgram of B12

25 microgram B15

150 microgram Biotin

200 micrograms Folic acid). In most vitamin Bs this is over the recommended daily intake, and we, in the family, have taken this daily for more than ten years with no side effects but becoming healthier.

Omega oil 3, 6, 9, in balance: We have used mostly a brand called Udo's Choice, but also Omega 3 from fish.

MSM (methylsulfonylmethane). Start with a few grains and work your way up to the maximum dose of two teaspoons/day. Can be dissolved in fruit juice to taste better. Take this in the morning or during daytime because it gives energy and might keep you awake in the night.

Anxiety Prevention

Valerian officinalis: between 200mg and 1200mg (The brand Neuroplant is really good).

Depression Prevention

Hypericum officinalis: between 600mg and 900mg.

Letter people have a lot of potential, but they are often put down at an early age because they meet more of a challenge when trying to learn how to drive and control their bodies (probably due to very many more nervous cells and faster transmission at some or all synapses between nerves). But the extended nervous system, in its turn, and if handled and trained properly, will give the brain (which also most certainly is a bit different to 'normal' people) a good portion of 'extra curriculum' exercise, and we end up problem solvers and big thinkers. The brain in letter people is said to have bad connections between the two sides, and this is part of their explanation. The other part is that it is a further development of the human brain to increase brain capacity and receive frequencies that enhance our evolution as a species. The brain is compartmentalized to protect the bearer from being programmed from outside sources. Otherwise, you could not continue to get 'clean' ideas and thoughts. A lot of subliminal programming is taking place from media and other sources via 'streaming' different frequencies through the bodies.

There are some points worth adding about letter children/people. They don't seem to have an 'off-button' to use when necessary. They cannot easily turn off their thoughts and the stress response ('fight or flight') in their nervous system, and that makes them more prone to stress-related problems. It is of importance that the parents don't over-activate these children (more easy to say than do because these children have lots of thoughts and a vivid imagination), but let them get bored sometimes to 'down-regulate' the 'on-signal' in the autonomous part of their nervous system. I've done scanning's with the DDFAO on young letter people and noticed that their nervous system is more activated than in 'normal' kids. If this signal isn't down-regulated now and then, their adrenal gland is becoming exhausted with hormonal imbalance (this is the same for older letter people also)."

Depression

"The second part I cannot emphasize enough. They are more prone to become depressed, not least because they use more vitamins because of their more rapid metabolism, especially in their brain and nervous system, and, therefore, they can easily become 'chemically depressed'. This depression is more difficult to meet unless they are put on hypericum and extra vitamin D3, in combination with the vitamin B complex and MSM. Synthetic anti-depressives are really bad for them and only add to the imbalance in their brains. In the worst-case scenario, they commit suicide.

In Sweden, there are now many young letter people feeling very bad and some end their lives."

Dr. Ohlson, PhD Molecular Biologist/Experiencer.

Depression and anxiety are very common patterns with the New Human and part of this may well be the need for extra nutrients and a better diet. However, because of their sensitivity and multidimensional awareness, they are also able to sense and feel deeply, not only the emotions of people around them, but what's happening on the planet, which can affect them deeply. It's important that they look after and protect their energy field and be aware of what they are 'tapping' into.

It is interesting to note that some of our greatest thinkers and creative talents were

autistic to some degree such as:
Albert Einstein
Nicola Tesla
Isaac Newton
Ludwig Von Beethoven
Nostradamus

[1] Officially, as of May 2013 and the publication of new diagnostic criteria, the diagnosis of Asperger syndrome (AS) disappeared from the official diagnostic manual (the DSM-5). It's just part of the autism spectrum but most people have ignored the change in criteria, mostly because the term Asperger syndrome has come to be so useful to so many people. Asperger syndrome was the label for a pervasive developmental disorder at the highest end of the autism spectrum. Rather than five separate autism spectrum diagnoses, there is now only one: Autism Spectrum Disorder.

[2] Giemsa stain is a classic blood film stain for peripheral blood smears and bone marrow specimens.

Chapter Seventeen

EDUCATING THE NEW HUMANS

How do you educate children who tell you they already know what is being taught?

"I don't have a problem with the world – the world has a problem with me. There is nothing they can teach me that I don't already know. In school, they try to teach us in a straight line when I think in a spiral."

David, ten years old, (UK).

"The (schools) program you out of your light. There is nothing good about this system; children are programmed and the teachers just push the keys. School programs are a virus, it extinguishes the light we have inside us and we lose our access to the information we had in the beginning."

Cathy, nine years old, (Europe).

The Children Teach the Adults
Schools, Education in Reverse
Through my research into the new generations of children, it has become obvious that the more aware teachers and parents know that the present educational systems do not meet the needs of these children no matter how progressive those systems appear.

The New Human child has significantly different needs to prior generations. To begin, it needs teachers with a full understanding of their heightened awareness and innate connection to a multidimensional reality. The educators need to understand that many of these children not only have the knowledge and conscious recall of past lives, but have otherworldly education, both in a physical and non-physical state. They can experience information-downloads (an eight-year-old called them 'knowledge bombs') and also telepathic communication with their 'friends,' whom they can perceive as angels, spirit guides, ET friends, or fairies, etc.

The 'New' children can be telepathic, and tap into the teacher's thoughts. They are also guided by their telepathic communications from otherworldly teachers. Many are told telepathically what information is relevant or even inaccurate by these non-human teachers or guides. They also have access to their own innate knowledge and wisdom, which stems from their access to higher consciousness. Their abilities are far beyond what the so-called 'normal', human-educated teacher understands. What they are taught from the present 3D knowledge can make little sense because of what they already know from their access to their otherworldly curriculum.

In this chapter, we explore the information from parents and aware teachers who understand. The children and young adults also share their exasperation with the present models of education, and how this frustration and lack of understanding can lead to them feeling depression and despair. It is also important to highlight that their otherworldly education begins when they are very young.

I received this letter several years ago, and it demonstrates how complex subjects are taught at just three years of age on spacecraft.

Multidimensional School – Physics Classes at the Age of Three

"Your website came as a revelation to me. I never before heard of anyone else having alien classes as a child. It's been both a blessing and a curse all my life. I remember being given physics classes at the age of three or four, in a classroom of children of a similar age to me. I remember the details well and have had an avid interest in physics since (although not mathematically inclined), so have not known what to do with the information, and there is a lot of it. I used to feel I was just crazy and did a year of philosophy and science – amazed myself and my teacher and other students (many engineers and physicists) by the fact I could just answer any question. I never studied and I just dropped out of school as I was so frustrated."

Male, thirty-seven years (Australia).

Note: Such letters are not unusual, and it is astounding that complex information is taught at an age where normally these complex subjects would be considered impossible for the child to understand. Research also suggests that, for some individuals, they were aware their intelligence was heightened on board craft and lowered (dumbed down) again when they were brought back to the planet.

Educating the Educators

I was in a Skype conversation with a parent in the UK. He told me that when his son was only ten years old, he went to see his teachers and was advising them how to teach children like him:
"You teach in a linear fashion, I think in spirals."

This statement alone indicates it will become increasingly important for educational bodies to understand the nature of these New Children and why they will not relate to present systems of education, primarily because it is too limited and limiting. A 3D education will, in most cases, shut these children down. As the statement from Cathy, the nine-year-old explains.

"The (schools) program you out of your light."

The more aware teachers and parents understand why these children will shut down because of their own experiences with a traditional educational syllabus, where they felt shut down. They know the damage the present educational systems can do and they understand that a new system of education is needed. They feel concern as they observe the difficulties their children experience in conventional educational systems.

The aware educators and teachers know a paradigm shift is needed in how we support and educate. We need a system that places emphasis on listening to what the child wishes to learn. The educator needs to have a full understanding of multi-dimensional awareness, with appreciation that the children are supported and educated by non-physical sources too. The environment must allow them the freedom to be creative and true to themselves, with teachers who provide the nurturing so the child can expand and grow to their full potential, with acknowledgment of their innate multidimensional awareness. The teacher can also support them in the human experience, assisting the child to understand 3D reality, but not allowing this to limit potentials. It will need to begin with the very young, as highlighted in this account from a nursery teacher in New Zealand.

Awake and Aware at Two Years Old

I received this email from a nursery school teacher in New Zealand

Telepathic

Two-year-old James, (not his real name)
Teacher: "I run a crèche and looked after a two-year-old boy, James; he is very different to the other children. He walks into the crèche and stands at the side of the room watching the other children. I ask him if he is okay and he says yes, and carries on watching. He is a great conversationalist. Although he can't read, if I read him a story he looks at me, not the book, and says the story out loud at the same time I am speaking.

He drew me a picture that is amazing. At first glance, it is childlike scribbles (even though he doesn't normally like drawing). He'd done it at home specifically for me. I asked him what the different bits in the picture were and he told me various things such as him in his pajamas, a slide taking him to the sky, a black rainbow, a friend called Maisie, who goes with him, and the lady Shalika who takes him to her school at night-time. It was very in-depth.

On another occasion, when there were a lot of children at the crèche and I couldn't give him my full attention, I said in my head 'I'm sorry James!' just because I felt bad. However, he must have heard this in his mind because he said out loud 'It's okay.' He didn't look up but just said the words. Another time, when there were lots of kids and I was doing lots of stuff, James put his hands over his ears and said to the room 'Stop thinking!' I just wondered how I could help him or support him in his journey?

It is hard because it's my work. I don't feel able to talk to his mother; if she was to approach me I would, but it could make them look at me differently! There have been many situations with this little boy, so I wonder what advice you'd give me with him. I have written notes I wrote about the drawing and attached the drawing.

Unfortunately, James' mum withdrew him from the crèche and didn't return. I don't know whether it's anything to do with how much her son was revealing to me, or whether she was aware or fearful of the situation. Below are the notes I made about the drawing from his words in italics."

The Picture

Teacher: "In the top right, the black triangle is what James told me is a spaceship or a boat, he couldn't decide. He said, 'It's not flames or smoke coming out of it, it's the wibbles' (maybe gas?). At the top, slightly left of middle, is an orange blob; this is James in pajamas. The light green line underneath him, he said, is a slide. The blue blob on the far left is Maisie. The brown 'dots' between them are the 'chutes' that they jump in. A big, round, black circle between him and Maisie, is a face 'that doesn't talk, but it smiles when it watches the rainbow without colors.' The center between slide and ship, black vertical lines, is 'like a rainbow, but not with color.' The red at the bottom of the slide coming out from the black rainbow is 'what it looks like when we go bump' (when they land?). Far right center, the green line is Shalika. Beside her (underneath the ship), is a purple squiggle; this is what he looks like when he's at Shalika's school. The blue blob in the bottom right corner is a boat. The purple circle squiggles are him being dizzy. The bottom left orange blob is 'everyone who can't come to school.'

After explaining the drawing to me, he told me, 'All the lines are there for a reason, but not for all the people.' I have no idea what that meant, but it stuck in my mind because of the struggle he seemed to have to say it, which is quite a mouthful for a two-year-old."

I Googled the name Shalika: Spiritually intense, creator and promoter of original ideas and research, intuitive with a reservoir of inspired wisdom, spiritual leadership."

Note: I was very interested in the detail and understanding of James and I sent this picture to artist/Experiencer, John, (Chapter Twelve). John made some fascinating comments on this drawing:

"The two-year-old seems highly imaginative and psychic/alien. The way he explains the colors is amazing and the fact that, at age two, he can put meaning to the entire image. Mature artists struggle to do that in general. The reference to the triangle definitely relates to dimensional space or travel! Triangles are through all of my work and I can see them!"

Note: I was struck by several significant statements James made about his drawing. Apart from the incredibly specific detail and understanding of this two-year-old and what he said about his picture (which in itself is remarkable, given his age). I was keen to get a sense of what James may be highlighting. The black triangle; the spaceship. James draws himself in his pajamas, so it is night. Black circle (the face that does not talk); a being that is telepathic? Shalika (teacher) in space school, where he sees himself purple – is this his energetic frequency? The orange blob is everyone who can't come to school (another frequency - which would be true)."

This account, I believe, highlights what an aware teacher can perceive with the new children, and it came as no surprise that the nursery teacher had extraterrestrial encounters too. It explains her intuitive understanding of James and her awareness that this little boy was very different, and why she had supported James and his needs so well.

The Teacher's Story

The nursery teacher, originally from the UK, migrated to New Zealand. She told me her own Encounter experiences began some years ago. She would often wake up the wrong way round in bed with different clothes on from when she went to sleep or with her clothes inside out, etc., (indicating an anomalous event). She told me she had 'dreams' almost nightly of corridors, stairwells, tunnels, waking up with random objects in her room, electrical appliances behaving strangely. One night, she woke at 2 a.m. and said she 'freaked out,' because through the door was a bright red/orange light. Then there were the vivid dreams with instruction-like information with drawings of how a spacecraft worked, along with various other drawings, which she completed after these unusual dreams.

More Information About her Dreams

1. *Children* – I had a short dream, where I was aware that my children were being taken. I could only see shadows/outlines of them and they were being drawn towards a dark space/portal. It was really stressful, as I had no way of keeping them with me.

2. *Light compass* – I was in a structure like a multi-storey car park, very gray and linear.

There were figures in black suits, almost like SWAT team members. I shut myself in a room, and turned round and saw this large structure. It was like a compass of some description, but filled the room, the size of a car. I could lift it with my fingertips and turn it around. I'm not sure what it was for.

3. *Medical facility* – In this dream, I was in a waiting room with lots of others, and one by one we were being called into the room. I remember standing to walk in and then awakening on this table. The table and instrument trays were suspended in midair, and everything else was very linear. The figure over me was wearing a gas-mask-like piece. The tubes above me would lengthen and shorten and were projecting a hot red circle onto whatever part of me they touched. I lost awareness and awoke in another waiting room. One by one we were called, and then the dream ended.

4. *Pulsing globe* – This was just a brief dream where I was standing on a beach, and it seemed very stormy. There was a globe in the sky, quite close, and it kept coming nearer and further and appeared to be pulsing. I couldn't figure out what it was made of. The best I can describe it is like glad wrap! It was transparent and shimmering. There was awe, but no fear in this dream.

5. *Ship instructions* – This dream was very, very detailed. It was a description of how this craft works. I have written on the picture. The craft has twelve tubes on the top, with seven tubes below. The center horizontal tube holds ball-bearing-type components. The balls are moving around the tube to the left, anti-clockwise. The individual balls are rotating to the right, clockwise. The movement of the balls is what generates the craft's power. The tubes above and below, collect the energy.

"When craft are seen zipping away really fast, this is not because they are powering away. Where this craft comes from, it has a form of supergravity specific to them, which the craft powers away from when they leave their home. They are constantly in the grip of that power, so when they need to all of a sudden go, they turn off their power and are immediately pulled back by their own gravity."

Note: I was sent a number of drawings of this craft.

Teacher: "I don't have kids myself, but other people's children seem very drawn to me! I'll always be the one at parties sitting playing with the kids! It was your presentations on YouTube, and reading your book *Awakening*, that led me to you."

Telepathic Children – A New Way

A teacher living in Australia shared with me that she knew she was on Earth to support the New children. She had telepathic mind-meld experiences and explained that when a lecturer was teaching and completely open to the students, she could just go into the lecturer's mind and absorb the concepts directly. She did not so much listen to the words but was in their mind extracting the concepts, which, she commented, prevented misunderstanding.

It was also how she worked with the children. She explained that these new children are doing the same thing she did. In her classes, she made her mind completely open while speaking to the students and she believed there was 'thought transplanting' going on. Her bank of information was merged with theirs and they re-schematized their own knowledge bank systems accordingly. Again, she explained, symbols would be a written conduit for this. She explained that it is the same in non-literate societies where an adept teacher can only pass on mystical knowledge. Ancient symbols hold the conceptual keys that trigger within the observing mind without the teacher being present.

2000, Western Australia.

A Teacher's Dilemma

This letter was transcribed from a third-grade teacher's experiences and reported in *Filer's Files*.

It reads:

"I'm a third-grade teacher at a public school and I've been teaching for the past sixteen years. After the year 2000, kids started acting differently. A few years ago, I started getting the kids born after the year 2000, who are even stranger. These kids are different; the Indigo/Crystal child concept is true.

They are purportedly the next level of human evolution. They are very intelligent and have super powers. The Indigo Child may see auras as lights or colors around other people, and show an uncanny ability to sense dishonesty. They are often mislabeled, with psychiatric diagnoses of ADHD, or ADD. Sadly, when they are medicated, the Indigos often lose their beautiful sensitivity, spiritual gifts, and warrior energy.

I believe that at least one-third of each class is Crystal and channel what you call spirits. However, as you will soon be finding out, that is just a blanket term. Many are what you term extraterrestrials, and many can take human form. These kids call them brothers from the stars. They are under orders to keep it secret from all unless they are spiritually awakened. If an adult comes to them to question them, they will check with their spirit, and ask them if it's okay to share the information. If the spirit says it's okay, then they will talk to you. Otherwise, they will act as if they don't know what you're talking about.

That's a quick rundown. You must understand that the work you are doing is strictly the 3D version of UFOs. These kids are working with the 5D version, and some even higher. Some of the kids speak directly to the UFOs. They can call them in during broad daylight and especially at night. It does not matter where you are: country, city, suburbs; they will show up anywhere. I have seen them fly just a few hundred feet above the city.

They will also call them in for the ones who do not understand, which is you and the older generations; in other terms, those who are still living the 3D world. The UFOs will show themselves to you in order to help awaken you to their presence among us.

The UFO, or the team in the UFO, will then determine if the Earth people have a high enough vibration to accept the sighting. If so, then they will make a showing. This all happens within seconds. The UFOs use what you know as ESP (Extra Sensory Perception) to communicate with the kids. However, the beings in the UFO always know what we are doing and thinking. Just as an example, my dad, who is seventy, is a white collar conservative; all he cares about is money and show. He does not believe in UFOs, etc. Thus, the UFOs have not shown themselves to him yet, but they say they will later, whereas we see them almost every clear night and sometimes even flying under the clouds. However, this is just the beginning! If the kids trust you spiritually, then they will work with you and tell you their future mission. And believe me, it's coming up sooner than you think. I will just give you a quick clue: they say they will be 'rebuilding humanity.'

I don't care what you do with this information for the children were told that it is now time to publicly release it. However, I want to remain publicly anonymous since I could lose my teaching job over it.

Sincerely,
Third-Grade Teacher.

This was reported by George Filer of *Filer's Files*, in issue #31, 2013.

Note: *Filers Files*, Issue 31 of 2013, collates information on worldwide UFO sightings and other relevant information on the phenomenon.

"I Want to go Home."

The account below is a conversation with Amanda and her mother. Amanda is ten years old. Amanda's mother told me that Amanda wanted to speak to me about her 'fairies.' She told me that Amanda tells her that fairies teach her things, such as how to fly. This account is a great illustration, to highlight what the children experience through their multilevel education, even to being guided and helped in answering questions when at school.

Amanda's mother told me that Amanda's first words to her were that she was not in the right place and she said, "I want to go home."

Mother: "Amanda said to me 'I want to go home.' It was one of the first things Amanda ever said to me. I realized she was remembering where she came from. She now knows I am her Earth mother and now she can remember."

The Fairies Teach Me

Amanda: "The fairies told me that when I get older I will forget a lot of where I come from, so they kept reminding me, so I never forgot. When I started to forget, somehow I remembered it again, but I didn't know how I remembered. I remember once I was standing in the middle of the bathroom for some reason, and saying, 'I want to go home'."

Mary: "Do you know where home is, or its name?"

Amanda: "Yes, I do remember it was from the Pleiades, and it was a really pretty planet. There were all sorts of animals that aren't here on Earth. I had this dragon; it was not like a pet. It had my favorite colors, like red and orange, and it was really pretty and shiny. I could actually see the fairies in my past life, but now I can only see what they are telling me in my head. I can also hear what my sister is thinking sometimes.

At one time, I was lying in bed and there was this thing that normal people can have too. I can see beings in a different dimension. Once, I saw this creepy thing grabbing me and looking at me. I wasn't moving at the time, but it was really scary. There are a lot of Jinns around this house. That's because someone is sending them."

Mother comments: "Some people I work with don't want us to do what we do. Amanda knows this, and who sends the Jinn to us, and who these people are."

Mary: "Amanda, when you see the Jinn, what do you do about it?"

Amanda: "If it's a bad being or I get a bad vibe; the fairies calm me down if I get a little panicked. They always stay with me and the special fairies go and fight the bad beings, like the Jinns and stuff. They (the fairies) are stronger than the most powerful

Jinn because they fight together."

Mother: "Amanda also received information on the phone poles with the boxes on them, not far from where we live. She told me the fairies told her that the boxes send out bad vibrations to everybody. However, the fairies always protected and shielded the people. The fairies said they always do the right thing to help people."

Amanda: "They (fairies) put shields around everybody to help them. It was someone from the government who put these towers (phone towers) there, they know about the fairies and stuff, just like I do."

Mother: "Who are they targeting?"

Amanda: "The people who know a lot, but if they put the pole too close to our house it would be suspicious. There is stuff inside the boxes that lowers vibrations."

Mother: "There was a strange van outside that didn't fit in with our neighborhood at all."

Amanda: "My fairies told me there was special equipment inside the van. It's like they were spying on us."

Mary: "When you were being taught by the fairies, was it on the spacecraft or somewhere else?"

Amanda: "It was on a planet where I was originally before this life. It was a little building, like fairy-sized. Like all the children were shrunk down, so they could fit there. When we graduated, they gave us permission to fly as they gave us all we needed to know. They taught us aerodynamics, and also how to use our third eye properly and normally. Because many people have to learn how to do this, but we did it normally so that I can see the Jinn and stuff like that."

Mother: "I recall you telling me you had elements."

Amanda – Elements

Amanda: "With elements, it is like we can control some elements of the world. My element is like I can control the air and sky stuff; it's like I can control the clouds and the winds. My friends have this ability; some have one of these abilities like the air, not everyone has both abilities, such as the air and the wind, like I do. One has the Earth element, and they do all the nature stuff; one has light and they can do all that sun stuff; one has fire element, and another has water. It's all to make the world better and more beautiful, so people can open their eyes and realize what's going on."

The Fairy Flying Lessons

"A couple of years ago I kept thinking I wanted to fly, I went to sleep and the next day I felt I knew how to do it. Then later, I realized I had fairies to talk to. Then I learned how to fly physically in my body (levitation?), and also fly a spaceship like a UFO. I remember one of the classes was 'Aerial Dynamics'. The directions were easy, and all I had to do was concentrate really hard, and then lean in the way I needed to go. I was to put my head forward, to go downwards and lean back to stop. It was like flight school, I call it 'Fairy University.' At the school, some of the children looked different and some of them looked like me, but they were all human children. And each class was about one or two hours. And if it was a lesson in the daytime, it would only be half an hour."

Mary: "What did the fairies look like?"

Amanda: "They were really colorful. They are not evil fairies. They had beautiful wings, and the most beautiful outfits ever; their hair was either blonde or brown, and the most beautiful eyes, but only blue or green eyes. The fairies visit me in school; sometimes when there is a hard question in the classroom, they tell me the answer. They are always watching me and if something bad happens, like if I get hurt, they would always be there and they would be healing me. Even though you can't see them, they are in another dimension, but they are also in this dimension and another million dimensions too. They can see a lot of things, they always concentrate on healing me, and I start to feel better."

Mother: "They teach her some mathematics that is so complicated that the fairies are helping her."

Amanda: "Yes, but I don't need the fairies anymore because the math is so easy. But sometimes the way maths is taught at school is too complicated; I was confused. "

Mary: "Do your fairies tell you anything about the future?"

Amanda: "Once my mission is completed, when I have made all the people happy that I can, I just keep doing what I am doing and help people who need help."

Mother: "Amanda, do you mean raising vibrations, is that what you mean?"

Amanda: "Yes. My fairies always tell me to remember my mission is to make people happy and I always do that so they always remind me of that."

Mother: "Amanda is a happy-go-lucky kind of girl. She raises the energy as soon as she walks into the room. She can be happy just playing with a balloon, and emanates joy and is a great singer. My other daughter has Asperger's and high IQ and is very bored at school. She is ready to build space ships and engineer them. She can't stand being in this 'sluggish' educational system. I am afraid it will stunt her abilities. I also know I have had past lives with her.

Meta-gene factor, the manifesting gene that only humans have, I believe this is why other species try to hybrid with humans. I believe these children are coming in with the meta-gene and this is part of the third spiral we are supposed to have. I heard that the Annunaki took out our third spiral, which meant we lost all our metaphysical abilities. I believe all the frequencies that are being created by the planet are repairing this third spiral."

Dyslexia

"School makes me feel sick!"

Fifteen-year-old female living in Queensland, Australia.

A teenager who wrote to me explains why the present school system makes her feel ill.

"I went to school today and I felt sick. I can't do it anymore. I just feel like no one is helping me at school, no one is teaching me and no one is awake, except for my friends, and they don't seem awake enough to feel as sick as I am. My dyslexia makes it so hard. I cannot count how many times I have been stuck on my own words and re-typed this or spell things backward or miss out letters."

Too Hard to be Around People

"At a conference, two years ago, I was in a room full of fifteen hundred people and after thirty minutes I couldn't stand it. I would have stomach cramps until the point where I could not stand, and hyperventilation so bad that I was beginning to have an anxiety attack. It lasted about thirty minutes straight, even outside the room full of people. That was way before I was awake even slightly, but I knew something was different. Ever since that, I tried to stay away from crowds and pools of people, and now I can't handle being in a room full of thirty people."

My Teacher Doesn't Understand

"My physics teacher doesn't understand mechanical and trigonometric waves are actually mapped out to be 3D spirals! I showed him a GIF file that explains that, and he didn't know what to say. No one knows, not even my teacher, what I already know about what they are teaching me. I'm not getting it anymore because it makes no sense and it doesn't help that it's all in linear form. I worked out the physics to prove that the sun is a portal and I showed it to my friend that was awake and she's like, 'Yeah, I knew this for ages, but you actually worked it out?' It was pretty easy, but if I show that to my physics teacher he would probably shrug me off. I'm getting so frustrated that no-one knows and that they're just in their little fish bowls circling around like mindless robots. Even Stephen Hawking created that analogy."

Note: David, a ten-year-old boy in the UK, told the author he came to Earth through a portal in the sun.

"Even people on YouTube are talking to me about love and acceptance for all things, but they don't understand that the vibrations you send out affect everything around you, so if you send out hatred you get hatred back. So there were people hating on every single video of Spirit Science; a great resource and wonderful explanations. 'You wouldn't love a serial killer, would you? How about people who commit genocides?' They obviously don't realize that society is brainwashing us to think that we're a hateful, angry, violent race and that we can do nothing about it. Yes, I would not agree with any violence of any kind, but for goodness sakes, you can't go around hating everyone."

School is a Waste of Time

"I don't really like talking negative, but there is literally no one to talk to here, and no one that understands that going to school is really a waste of time. I'm not learning anything, nor am I enjoying my time at school. It's more like a children's prison, full of little teens that can't determine what is real or not, which I can't blame them. They've been thinking like that their whole life. They don't question what society thinks or how we live on this planet, yet have to pay to stay alive! Pay to go to work! You pay to eat, pay for water, pay for shelter, pay for power that could be free, and use cosmic waves that can let cities never sleep!

I think it's so irrational to do this: pay to live, pay to eat, drink and poop (using water) and in a certain light, sleep (shelter). Yes, there are those of us who don't have these luxuries, but they shouldn't be called luxuries, they should be called human rights and civil liberties. I hope that I can do a program to help me control my awareness a bit so I can at least pass this last year of schooling and not be so negative on it because I really don't like being all negative, but school just makes me so sick, frustrated, tired, angry and stressed.

If it weren't for you, I would not have a clue about what's going on with me at all. I would not have any idea about what affects me this bad, and how I can see the problems that I have to face every day. The only thing that keeps me going is the greater good; the greater good for my friends, my peers, and humanity. I can feel that I will help so many and achieve so much, but I would not have any idea about my purpose and the need to help others with this if it wasn't for you putting aside your precious time and effort into helping people like me."

Katie Gunn – Teacher, Christchurch NZ

K: "Mary, I am an advocate for your message and a great fan of your courage. I am a teacher from New Zealand and I find the children much as you say. I am happy to say I feel the schooling system is evolving to the learners' needs. Or at least that is my drive."

M: "What do you feel you need to do as a teacher of many of these new children?"

K: "As a teacher, I am finding more and more students pushing the ideas of the system. For example, one six-year-old, when asked what she would fuel a car on (most kids said beans for fart power, grass for poo power, etc.), she told me the harmony of love. I nearly fell over on the spot. This same child has adopted my habit of drawing the flower of life on every page of her book – and she is only one example.

As the children are being more creative and 'out of the box', so, too, do the teachers need to keep up with them. I can tell you now, a room full of Star Kids vs. one super 3D teacher, the teacher will always lose. Slowly, the children are asking for music in all they do, time for meditation (yes, something I promote in my teachings), time outdoors and time to explore their own passions. I am delighted by this. I am happy to say, my entire kindergarten practice meditation and can sing Khoomei (or overtone throat singing). They love it. They ask for it. They demand more. This makes me feel we are not so destined to use books and tests and are moving more toward a state of appreciation for the individual learner. As for where I am located, I am currently living in South Island, after having spent the last ten years overseas."

The teacher sent me drawings of the beings and said:
K: "The being you see in the pictures I refer to as The Blue Cloak. She seems to be rather feline in appearance and has the ability to fly (or at least fly in something). The bull-type being was the impression of a friend of mine that I got one day. It was the face I saw where his own would be. I feel they are Taurian or draconian. (Not sure). The other being is one of light. It did not have a form so much as a harmonic body that, when moved, projected sound everywhere. The image I like to call the electric turkey is an image of a building I have seen in my dreams for as long as I can remember. It generally involved the spice-smelling sand crushing me, and my waking with a chemical taste in my mouth."

I am Concerned About the Education of my Kids
Melanie Resides in Switzerland
Melanie (not her real name) is married with children and resides in Switzerland. She wrote to me to say she was visiting Queensland and requested regression hypnosis with me whilst on holiday. She kindly gave permission for me to share some of her story because it explained some important issues:

- Depression in the new children.
- The need for a new school system.

Melanie has suffered depression all her life, due to her heightened awareness. The regression helped her to understand why depression is so common with these New Humans experiencing conventional education systems.

UFOs, the stars, and pyramids, always fascinated Melanie. Her session was to find answers and understanding with certain unusual incidents in her life. In this regression, in 2015, she received information on the New Human and special schools and generously agreed to allow me to share some of the information:

A UFO encounter when eleven years old with a friend:

The origin of her depression —because she has always been aware she was different and could not relate to this human society.

Regression Information
Melanie began her inner journey by discovering herself on a Pleiadian spaceship. The beings on this ship felt like family to her. She said her origins were a mix of Pleiadian with Sirians, but this time, she was more connected to Pleiadian. There is cooperation between these extraterrestrial species and many others. She discovered she was taken on board a craft as a child to receive comfort because it was so difficult being here on this planet. It was to get some love from them and she recalled they had visited her several times.

As a young child, Melanie spent some time in a hospital due to experiencing strange periods of unconsciousness, which doctors investigated. In regression, she discovered the human doctors performed experiments on her because they knew there was something very different about her, but she discovered her parents were never told.

Melanie was eleven years old when she saw a UFO with a friend. The regression identified the craft as Pleiadian and she learned its purpose was to show itself to her. She discovered she was taken aboard this craft, shown around and how the UFO worked, to help her remember them and know that they were there for her.

In Melanie's regression, she wanted to know why she is here on Earth if she belonged to them, the (Pleiadians).

Melanie: "I volunteered to come to Earth to help raise the vibration. It has been very difficult and I became very depressed."

Depression

In the regression, I asked her about the origin of her depression? Melanie said that her depression was the result of life on this planet, which affected her far more than she had expected it to. She knew it would be hard, but not as hard as it has been. Her depression is also homesickness for her source, her home, and now she is very tired.

I asked what she could do to help herself with these issues and she answered that it was to find her purpose, so she can feel better and make others happy and help people. When asked how she was to do this, she replied: "Gather information, learn about Starseeds and share this information; teach others and share experiences, which in turn helps me understand others and also helps them through this understanding."

Melanie: "As a child, I was told: 'You are too sensitive. You are a dreamer.' It was a criticism and upset me. But now if this was said to someone else I would understand and I would listen and I would know it's not just imagination, that this is happening and they are not crazy, so I could help and be a support."

Melanie had an experience with a strange being, which frightened her. She called it the Hatman. She discovered this was a 'construction of fear'; by being fearful she attracted the experience.

Melanie explored her interest in Egypt and she saw herself in a corridor in a pyramid and a door which had two handles which should be opened, as inside is a beautiful energy and knowledge which would release a lot of peace and love, and she said it was to be shared with everybody.

Note: Melanie was very emotional about this, and said, "It's like it (the energy)is locked in there."

Energy in the Pyramids Kept From People

Melanie: "It's strange how it's locked in there. It's what's missing in this world. It's like someone locked it away; like it's been taken over for power, so humans are kept in this prison and it's not how it should be; we should be free. (Melanie becomes even more emotional and upset.)

It's kept us imprisoned and caused a lot of pain and depression. It should not be that way. People say it's how it is but that's not true. It looks like a dark age, but it's changing now, but it's changing slowly. People are waking up, but it should go much faster. I feel like I am to help also for this, to help with the awakening process. I am not sure how it can be done. I need to find more support and more people. I would like some help so it would be much easier and faster. It's important to reach the masses and work with more people, as some are still hiding and need this information."

(Melanie wasn't sure how she knew this, but just that it was a knowing. She didn't know why this energy is contained in the pyramid.)

I asked Melanie if this energy was in just one pyramid or all of them? She replied, "It's in all of them; they (the pyramids) are working together. If one is released the others will join with it."

I asked Melanie, who was keeping it from being released.

Melanie: "It is a dark energy, part of the game. It's getting much harder for these forces to keep it there. It keeps us from the truth and fearful, and in fear we cannot take action. Paralyzed, we can't break free of a prison that is really just installed in our heads because of fear. People should not watch TV and read newspapers – it's a whole new way of thinking."

A Healing

In the regression, I asked about Melanie's health concerns. Melanie began to feel energies throughout her body as if she was being worked upon by many beings and energies working as a group. She saw lots of light around her now and an image of Jesus, to whom she prays a lot, as he is a healer.
(Again she is very emotional).

Melanie: "He is not human. I am getting really tired. I feel very relaxed and getting lighter. I see lots of bright lights, golden light – my body getting lighter."

She was then told by these healing beings and energies that healing takes a while, and I can keep asking her questions.

Her Children and the Need for New Schools

Melanie: "The children hold the energy and vibration for people around them. They just need to be so they can transform things, energies; it's the same with me. With me, it's transformed for myself. I haven't figured out how I transform it for myself. I take on too much. My older child does it more naturally, but my younger child takes on too much. We need to be in nature as much as possible, which I already know, as it transforms naturally that way. There will be more communities living in nature again."

Melanie is told that her children need to be free and that they are not so happy at school, although the school they picked is a good one.

It is Not Even Necessary to go to School

Melanie: "The children these days have the knowledge inside of them and it evolves naturally in them, in a natural environment. It is not even necessary to go to school. It's just the information we use in this shallow existence; this prison we built ourselves. It was useful for that, but not so much anymore. Now, having a new world, creating it, manifesting it, it comes from everything within them. Other knowledge and wisdom are important now. Our history is not so important as it's also not the truth and is made up and not important at all and keeps us from the new things. It keeps us in the past – always the same, generations after generations, just living the same. It's time for the new already within, and evolves naturally; there is nothing to be taught actually."

Melanie asked how this should be achieved and she was told the people need role models, and some are already living differently.

Melanie: "We need to bring them all together and sharing this understanding. Those who have been called the dreamers all the time are now doing it and helping nature by the way they are living and are much happier and more connected to everything, and the lack is in this other world, and I would like to live like that but don't know how to get out because of fear; there is too much fear. I feel people want to be different and like to live differently."

Melanie said that she didn't feel strong and courageous enough to help people in the way she would like, but she was told she would be helped by her non-physical family and Jesus, as his message was love and reminded of love and moving from the head into the heart space, and there will be much more love.

Melanie: "Now I understand; it fits together: the love message with the shift, the awakening, the new world, and everything is through love."

Depression – A Gift to New Awareness

Melanie: "I don't find it hard to love people who are depressed and sad because I have experienced it myself, and I can understand them and love them because I know it's not easy, and I can also see the gift behind the sadness. It's become clear right now, with depression and sadness. If you are able to see through that, I can see a lot of strength. It's mostly them that hold the most strength because they are the first who knew or sensed this is wrong – there is something wrong. Those who are depressed are made to believe there is something wrong with us when in fact, there is something wrong with this world, and it made us sad and it's a natural reaction to it. So we are not the sick ones actually, it's the other way around, the others that are stubborn, who live in this prison-like existence, and they can't see how it should be. It's difficult to reach them – not so hard for the depressed and sad ones. I understand that depression and sadness are a way to help humanity wake up. They let them drop low, as it's a state where they are more open and open up to other realities. So it's

289

actually a good thing even though it feels bad, and this makes sense why nowadays a lot of people are depressed. They are taken out of the system, and it becomes an opportunity to wake up, to do things differently. Yes, they come through more easily. I misunderstood this depression. I feel you are so low you are closed down there is no connection, but at some point, it opens your heart space for new directions. (Melanie begins coughing again, which she saw as a release.)

My Mission is to love: find love in and for myself, and to love others."

'They' were thankful for what Mary was doing and it was important for this time now.

Melanie: "More people are coming and you will need to be ready as you will reach bigger numbers; there is a lot to do."

ADHD (Always Dialed to Higher Dimensions)

Ufologist researcher, Neil Gould, author of Close Encounters of the ADHD Kind, explained in his book that he was diagnosed with ADHD later in life. He recalls that he always perceived reality differently and that's why he struggled in such a heavily-programmed 3D world. He re-interprets the ADHD label as 'Always Dialed to Higher Dimensions.'

Why Present Education is not Meeting the Needs of the New Humans

I have listed some of the knowledge and awareness these new children are able to utilize. Qualities and information known intuitively from their star-heritage origins, genetically, or taught and/or downloaded as compressed files or software. It is clear from what they are being exposed to on other levels, no matter how much of this is conscious recall, that our present system of education is lacking the understanding and tools to meet these needs.

Syllabus for the New Humans

- The non-linear nature of time and space.
- Quantum physics – the holographic nature of the universes.
- Telepathy and mind-melds.
- Awareness, connection, and communication to all sentient life, including animals, plants, crystals, Nature, planetary consciousness (i.e., Gaia), and other non-human life forms such as elementals (nature spirits).
- Multidimensional ecology.
- The manifestation of directed thought and emotion.
- Healing skills and energy manipulation.
- Light language and Star languages.
- Decoding artwork and scripts, symbols.
- Creation and the true history of Mankind's origins.
- How the body really works, and how to consciously help it evolve and control its functions.

- Cosmology, and other star systems.
- Ancient human languages.
- Manifestation and manipulation of matter.
- Levitation, bi-location.
- Empathy.
- Out-of-body (OBE) training.
- Understanding the geometry of thought.
- Understanding of the soul and universal spiritual concepts.
- How to communicate, interpret and interact with non-human, inter-dimensional and extra-dimensional intelligences.
- Remote viewing and remote influencing.
- Telekinesis.
- How to operate in a multidimensional reality.
- Ability to work from different timelines.
- Inhabit other consciousness, similar to a shaman that can connect with other species and their consciousness.
- Understanding the nature of various beings, both physical and non-physical, inter-dimensional, extra-dimensional, etc., and their motives and intent.

The above is what I have discovered in terms of the multidimensional curriculum, (I suspect this may even be incomplete). However, this certainly highlights why these children struggle with the present limited educational systems and why they need a far broader understanding of their needs.

One positive note is that the non-human intelligences are educating and supporting the new teachers as well as the children. This assumption is supported in this chapter, as the teachers were able to identify the children.

However, at this time, many teachers have to work with an educational system which is focused on conditioning and programming. The children attending such schools soon identify the inadequacies of this system and become depressed when forced to participate in an education they find obsolete and irrelevant to their understanding and needs.

The Need for a New Curriculum for These New Children

In the addendum below is the personal story of a highly-qualified educator who identifies herself as a crystal adult. She feels she understands the needs of the New Humans, the letter people, as she has experienced many of the challenges they experience with the 3D educational systems. From her awareness, and studies, she has created a new educational system which she believes will support the new children. Here she tells her story and why she felt this was so important at this time.

Note: Due to how this subject is perceived by the mainstream at this time we have kept her identity anonymous.

The Importance of Awareness and an Innovative Approach to Teaching and Learning

I'd like to start by giving you a bit of background information about myself before presenting my thoughts and experiences with a new approach to teaching and learning that could be of interest to educators of Star Children.

I have been involved in the education of children and adults all my life. I began my professional life as a high school teacher of foreign languages and English as a second language after completing my BA Honors and my Diploma of Education. The experience left me pretty frustrated with our education system, although some schools were more student-centered than others. I decided to research alternative approaches to teaching and learning and enrolled in a PhD at Sydney University and later taught at Sydney University. I was often restricted in my creativity by the traditional outcomes-based curriculum.

After a few years of teaching, both at Sydney University and Adelaide University, I relocated to Germany, where I taught future English teachers, and was a qualified examiner for state examinations. I tried to use innovative approaches in my courses. I discovered that I had more freedom to be creative in Frankfurt than in Australia, simply because tertiary studies are free of charge (which means that education is not treated as a business but a service) and lecturers have more autonomy.

I enrolled in a second PhD in mystical philosophy, in Aix-en-Provence. My focus was the work of an important mystic of the thirteenth century and I examined, in over four hundred pages (in French), what is God and what is a human being. Deep spiritual questions have accompanied me throughout my life because next to my academic pursuits. I have always been engaged in spiritual practice.

There is so much more to explain about who I am but in terms of the education of the New Humans, this might suffice for now. Why have I been involved in trying to find new approaches to teaching and learning? I wouldn't say that school was altogether frustrating for me as a child, but from the beginning, I felt different to most other children. As a young child, I could not speak and form words in my mouth that were comprehensible to others. I mixed up letters and was left with the feeling that I could not make myself understood. As such, this was not too painful as I could communicate with my mother via telepathy. The problem really started when it was time to start school and I was supposed to go to a school for handicapped children because of my speech impediment. My mother, a wise soul indeed, took me to an old homeopathic doctor who observed me for a while. His assessment was that I was highly intelligent because my curiosity was beyond my age. I thank this man from the bottom of my heart as he suggested to my mother to only sing with me. For some unknown reason, this was the secret to my language development. I could string the sounds together when they were connected to harmonic melodies. My mother (bless her heart) put all her sentences to music and soon enough I could sing along with her. She then reduced the range of notes until I could express myself in normal sentences. Needless to say, sound and music have played a big part in my life.

I really wanted to learn as much as possible, but school was often too boring. I got up to mischief, like enticing all the kids to leave through the classroom window, and corrected the other kids' tests before they handed them in to the teachers. My parents regularly had to sign letters home because, yet again, I had disturbed the class with my laughter. I found school far too unstimulating so I created my own fun. For a few months, I had to take a letter home to get it signed every day. My father finally stopped this process by telling the teachers that he preferred to see me laugh than cry about their stupid lessons!

Although I enjoyed religious education, I challenged the priest who taught us and prepared us for Communion. Too much of what he said made no sense to me at all. It did not correspond to my vision of reality (mind you, I was about eight years of age). I went to Communion only because I wanted to get the presents but as a requirement, I had to go to a confession. This was traumatic for me as the dark confession box felt like a prison and again, had nothing to do with my understanding of God. The priest wanted me to admit a sin and since I could not think of one I finally made one up and told him that I had hit my brother. The patronizing tone of this man in the dark box made my hair stand on end and finally I screamed at the top of my voice through the whole church "Get me out of here!" When my mother came running to relieve me from this torture chamber, I yelled at the priest and said to him: "You committed a sin now because I had to lie to you to get out of your clutches. I never hit my brother."

These are just a couple of examples of why I didn't fit into the education system. I see it as a blessing now because it motivated me to find alternatives. I might just add that I was probably seen as a precocious child because between the ages of fourteen to eighteen, I not only went to day school but also enrolled in evening classes for adults. I really wanted to learn about the world and school alone was too easy. This extracurricular learning continued at university. I studied languages, philosophy, and pedagogy, but I wanted to learn more. So, whenever I had a spare few hours at university, I would look on the noticeboards in various departments to check if there were interesting lectures going on. Instead of having a break on the lawn, I'd sit in lectures of all sorts of subjects. Whenever there was an examination on, I'd go into the room and sit for the exam. Often, I just knew the answers, although I had never studied the subject. I figured that I would learn a lot in a short time by going directly for the exam.

The fact that I have done two PhDs, one in English, in Australia, and the next in French, in France, shows that my thirst for knowledge is as acute today as it was when I was young. A PhD allows us to go deep into a subject of our own choice, which is much more to my liking than having to follow a prescribed curriculum.

How are these personal experiences linked to my desire to teach in an innovative way and to create, if possible, a new school?

I feel that I was lucky enough to not have the light sucked out of me in our current education system. However, I have seen many extraordinary children and young adults fail, who were bright and unconventional. In recent years, I notice that more and more of these star people join my courses and I have seen a variety of negative coping mechanisms that break my heart. Apart from official diagnoses of Asperger's, Dyslexia and Autism, I have had students who were so sensitive that the pressure of university led them to self-harm. I can always tell when star students are out of balance because their energy field is not smooth and often there is a frightened or dissociated look in their huge eyes. This is sad to witness, and thus I do everything possible to make my courses stimulating, student-centered, calm and geared towards the individual.

To come to the nitty-gritty of my approach, which is not easy to delineate as some of my teaching is intuitive and based on energetic readings, I'd like to name a few characteristics that could be implemented by other teachers. To start with, I center myself before going into class and become aware of my own energy, my feelings, my thoughts. As I don't want to project any unconscious material on my students, I take responsibility for my personal emotional, physical and energetic self. Most of my students are future teachers and I often ask them to sense into the room and to tell me what the energy is like. I want them to be sensitive to energetic changes. I make explicit to them why I choose activities that are uplifting if the energy is more subdued or prefer focused work if there is a jittery feeling in the room. So, I believe that awareness of energy is the first step in being attuned.

As I scan the room as a whole, I become aware of those students that are off-kilter. I don't like to probe into their private lives, but if they have had personal problems to deal with, their focus is limited, and as the whole person sits in class, I need to be aware of those whose presence is only partial. I often 'clean' these students once everyone is working on their projects. Being a crystal adult and an energy healer that is something I do naturally, but I believe every teacher can cleanse the auras of their students by sending out good vibrations and positive thoughts. My aim is always that the students leave my courses cleaner and more balanced than when they enter the room.

I try to use the principles of the Silent Way as often as possible. It is difficult to summarize three-and-a-half years of intensive research and over four hundred pages of a thesis on the Silent Way in this context, but there are a couple of principles that deserve mentioning here. I believe that learning only takes place when the whole self is engaged. Learning determines how something should be taught and it is from the learner that we need to develop our teaching, not vice versa. The learner sets the pace and project work is the best way to let the learner guide us. Teaching is subordinated to learning.

The learning process is one of ongoing awareness. Once there has been an awareness, the energy of the self can be used to practice and then to store it in the automatic realms of the self. This means that specific phases of the learning process have to be respected and they are individual. I also believe that a peaceful atmosphere allows for an intrinsic motivation to arise. While I encourage group work on projects, I am totally fine with those individuals who would rather work alone and dig deep into their own projects. I let the students decide what they want to discover and see myself as an energetic facilitator more than a teacher. As said above, the learner sets the pace for the teacher. When learning is happening, there is a flow or a sense of being in the zone. When a learner is fully engaged and energized by the activity, they are intrinsically motivated by the task at hand. They become completely absorbed in what they are doing and feel a deep sense of enjoyment.

"Education today lacks a sound understanding of the intrinsic motivation that keeps students wanting to learn and to take on increasingly demanding intellectual challenges. In other words, intrinsically rewarding learning produces an experience of growth and of mastery, a feeling that the person has succeeded in expanding his or her skills"

Ref: Csikszentmihalyi et al, 1993: 219.

My aim as an educator is to negotiate learning projects that allow students to experience this deep sense of flow because that is when real learning takes place. The state of flow can happen when skills and challenges are matched in such a way that the experience of achievement provides enjoyment. Flow is the antidote to the boredom that I experienced as a child and to anxiety or apathy that can also result when skills and challenges are not perfectly matched during the learning process. The students need to be able to define their own goals in an activity and identify the means for reaching them.

It is my personal belief that teachers of Star Children need to be flow teachers. They need to create conditions for flow experiences in learning, keep their own interests in their subjects alive and keep on improving their skills at conveying interest. They have to reduce extrinsic pressures like marks, competition, and needless rules. Flow teachers are alchemists of consciousness whose art it is to create optimal conditions that afford the close, well-paced match between task complexities and individual skills that is the hallmark of the flow experience.

Concerning the future of education, I believe that the story of humanity is a rather optimistic one. The Star Children will force teachers to adopt new pedagogical philosophies that are centered on the individual learner. Teachers of Star Children will have to become flow teachers that subordinate teaching to learning and center students' attention on the challenges and inherent satisfactions of learning something new. As educators, we have to make another evolutionary step to be attuned to those that guide us: the Star Children. Eventually, whole schools will have to rethink their curricula if they want to remain relevant. Children who receive instantaneous information downloads and are guided by other than human beings are not going to be satisfied with schools that were designed according to the nineteenth-century factory model. The old schools were geared towards creating homogenized beings while the new schools need to accommodate children that are aware of their multidimensional essence. The educational pyramid needs to be turned upside down with the children leading the way into a new system. Only awareness is educable in people.

In terms of multidimensional experiences, there are too many to mention. At this stage, I am trying to integrate my somewhat unusual life experiences because, up to now, I was convinced that everyone had access to these different dimensions.

In my early thirties, I had a spontaneous recall of my birth with awareness of the physical setting at home (I was born at home). Later, I checked these details with my mother who confirmed everything right down to the position of her favorite armchair. However, being aware of my birth did not satisfy my curiosity. Through hypnotic regression in Michael Newton's life-between-life (LBL) technique, I saw the learning centers that I attended, and also led, in the spiritual dimension. This resulted in a spontaneous recall of the time just before my physical birth.

I like writing literary non-fiction and by that, I mean stories that are fictional in the sense that I change names, locations, and other details, but are non-fictional in that they are based on my personal, autobiographical experiences. Included below is my latest one that is, however, not yet edited. The story gives an insight into one aspect of my multidimensional experiences. It illustrates the choice-less choice I had to make.

My intention is to keep writing stories, and even books, for Star Children in the hope that feeling reflected and seen might help others to overcome the homesickness I have felt all my life.

How do we recognize each other? With very young children I get this physical sensation of familiarity. With older children and adults, there is a decoding process that, coupled with a sensing into the energy, gives me the signals I need. Basically, we can pick each other up. No words need to be exchanged.

I am aware that for our fellow human beings, our 'benevolent earthlings', it can be challenging to make sense of our unique and highly individualized way of seeing the world. In my experience, we all need each other to make this planet a better place for the future. As much as I want to contribute to a better understanding of the Star Children, I would not like to encourage any unwarranted attitude in parents or kids that Star Children are 'special'. We are different. We might suffer from a sense of not belonging and longing for home. But everyone, Star Child or human earthling, is here to fulfill a divine purpose. My hope is that through awareness-raising literature, speaking events and workshops I can contribute to a better appreciation of the multidimensional essence of each being.

Biography

PhD in education, Sydney University. PhD in mysticism from the University of Aix-en-Provence. Pedagogical degree, Melbourne University (Dip. ED). Bachelor with

Honors degree. Studied at the Sorbonne and the University of Düsseldorf. Qualified NAATI accredited translator and interpreter.

Note: The short story below is written as fiction but is actually a true account of a pre-birth recall by the above individual.

The Big Jump

"Are you sure about this?"

"Well, let's say eighty-five percent. I don't know if anyone can ever be completely sure."

I looked into his huge, turquoise eyes that transmitted reassuring energy. It was evident that the mission I had voluntarily signed up for wouldn't be without its risks. In fact, even as he asked the question, I knew that my answer was irrelevant. I had no choice. We were both just following the polite procedure that I had observed with other voyagers many times before. He proceeded to explain.

"Okay then. Let's go over the assignment again. Although none of it will be easy, you've got to remember that you'll be fine in the end. We've made sure that there are a few helpers around and you'll have access to all the latest technology to complete your task."

Mudra's long, lean body remained motionless. The other five assistants stood in a half circle behind him and only slightly nodded their bald heads in support. While their splendid, blue-green eyes sent out beams of sympathetic love, their bodies stayed rigid. The clinical surroundings did not lend themselves to uncharacteristic emotional outbursts. I was to embark on an important mission that required a cool-headed attitude. However, underneath their immaculate exterior, I could pick up the fragrance of blue roses, a sure giveaway that they were ready to accompany me from a distance. Mudra went over the details again, not because I had forgotten, but because he realized that I needed to hear the even pitch of his voice:

"Before you leave, we'll insert an implant into you so that we can always keep track of you and if you really get into trouble, we can send an assistant."

"How will I recognize them?" I asked.

"They'll send off a high-pitched signal and we'll activate an electric current in you so that you can recognize each other."

If anything, it was that aspect of the mission I was unsure about. I had never been privy to the 'mutual recognition process' (MRP). How could I have been? The electric transmission made perfect sense, but without any personal experience, how could I trust that it would work? However, I only had to take a closer look at my surroundings to feel comfortable. The shiny armatures that responded to thought instructions, the soundless lights that activated teleportation pads, the smooth navigation through countless galaxies. I knew in my perfectly-designed cells that I was in safe hands.

"All right then. So tell me again, what I am supposed to do when I get to the first location?"

He sighed and stared at me for a second.

"Well, unfortunately, I can't really give you all the details. First, we'll have to keep it secret for your sake. Second, it's not quite clear yet how the situation will evolve, but what we do know is that you'll basically be stationed in a zone that is currently volatile."

I wasn't even sure if I wanted more detailed information. Would I pull the plug if I knew what I was in for? Mudra had told me in our previous private induction that I would be dealing with people who were mentally unstable due to ongoing mind control. I was going to be thrown into a matrix of primitive manipulation. However, his harmonious singsong soothed my nerves. All I really wanted was a bit more time amongst my people so I encouraged him to keep on talking.

"The success of your mission depends on you responding with great sensitivity and awareness from moment to moment. There'll be people who are spying on you, so you'll have to cover your steps carefully. Always just show one side of yourself to anyone you are dealing with. Never give them the whole picture of who you are."

"So how can I distinguish between our troops and the enemy?" I wanted to know.

In all honesty, if I had any doubt at all, it was about my capacity to discern. I tried to read in his azure eyes if he shared my concern. Hoping for some positive reflection was, of course, a pointless exercise. We don't get sent on such assignments if we are still caught in wanting narcissistic mirroring. We both knew that all I really wanted was to be a bit longer on my home planet. Out of his infinite kindness, he went over the physical traits that distinguished the other-servers from the self-servers.

"Well, some of the real nasty ones sometimes shapeshift. Basically, you won't know who's who. However, since we'll observe you from a distance, we'll send you indicators so you might just feel like getting away from them or you might not like their smell. Always trust your inner guidance. They have sophisticated ways of hiding their cold-heartedness. Don't let the Reptilians fool you by their words. Turn the sound off. Just observe their actions. The proof is in the pudding, so to speak."

I looked at Mudra and my other instructors, who had been my parents, family, and friends from as far back as I could remember. Their love, patience, and trust in me had kept me going when all I ever wanted to be was a normal person.

I remembered crying on Mudra's shoulder when I tried, again and again, to heal with intention alone and yet couldn't do it because my ego wanted it so bad that it interfered with the healing energy. Mudra had consoled and reassured me. At one point, he told me to take time out and just sing my favorite songs. He knew I had to get out of my own way. The other members of my blue family had patiently inducted me into all sciences that were vital to living a full human life. How could I refuse them the favor they had asked of me? I owed them everything. Who I was and who I still wanted to become. I had no choice. At least not morally.

"One last question."

"Sure. What is it?"

"When you give me the injection, I won't remember you or where I come from, right?"

"Yes. Oblivion needs to happen so you can fit in and cope with life down there."

"I'll miss you terribly. How can I enjoy life if I can't find my home or see you guys again?"

He tried to reassure me.

"That's probably the most difficult part. You won't experience fear. Nor will normal human concerns bother you. But for a long time, you won't remember your true identity. However, we won't forget you and one day, when you've completed your mission, we'll meet again. It's a lonely journey. Not everyone can embark on it."

I took a last look into everybody's immense eyes. Each one of my closest allies winked at me, as we do when we get ready for the 'big one'. I would probably never be ready to leave my home. Yet it was time to jump. As I turned around and ran towards the launching pad, I could feel a tiny narcotic arrow piercing into my thigh. Nine months later, I was born.

Chapter Eighteen

COSMIC INTELLIGENCE

God, Religion and the Extraterrestrial Reality

"We all originate from Day Land. God has no gender and is a being I call an Over-terrestrial who sowed the seeds of love and light. It is where the light and angels live."

Cathy, nine years (Europe).

Extraterrestrials – Angels or Demons?

This chapter explores one of the most profound issues for many individuals when faced with the reality of their extraterrestrial encounters in combination with devotion to religious or spiritual beliefs. How do extraterrestrial encounters affect these core beliefs and the concept of God?

The various churches and religions have some very diverse and alternate perspectives on this phenomenon. For some religions, the extraterrestrials are another example of God's creativity and they are cosmic 'brothers,' but other churches interpret extraterrestrials as demons. The UFO/Encounter experience can be confusing and bewildering enough, so how does religious belief hinder or help the individual in their interpretation and understanding of what they should believe? Especially as the experience itself, can offer an alternate truth or an expansion of it. What if the experiences offer new awareness that is in conflict with their religious understanding? Especially if/when certain experiences are not recognized as valid, such as recall of a past life, which is not being recognized as valid by some Christian churches, for example, what then?

These issues are some of the challenges facing the Experiencer. In this chapter, two courageous Christian Ministers share how they have explored their religious beliefs through the framework of encounter experiences. We also explore through the 'window' of cultural religious belief and what the extraterrestrial presence and whistleblower information offer. To begin, we explore the extraterrestrial issue from one of the dominant religions: Catholicism.

Director of the Vatican Observatory, Father Jose Gabriel Funes, states in an article entitled *The Alien is my Brother.*

"Believing in the possible existence of extraterrestrial life is not opposed to Catholic doctrine. Astronomers – even Catholic ones – believe the universe is made up of one-hundred-billion galaxies, so it is unreasonable to discount some could have planets.

As a multiplicity of creatures exist on Earth, so there could be other beings also intelligent, created by God. This does not contrast with our faith because we cannot put limits on the creative freedom of God."

Ref: *L'Osservatore Romano*, 2008. (UFO Disclosure.com).

It becomes apparent that the Vatican has little trouble addressing the reality of Extraterrestrial life and has interpreted this phenomenon under the auspices of a creative God, not limited to Earth and its inhabitants. The Vatican has gone so far as to have its own observatory in Arizona, with the intriguing name of Lucifer! Whistleblower testimony has indicated the Catholic Church has known for an extremely long time we have been visited for millennia which makes the ownership of an Observatory no surprise. Members of the Vatican have also made public statements about the extraterrestrial encounter experience.

Former prelate of the Catholic Church, the late Monsignor Corrado Balducci, was a theologian and member of the Vatican Curia (governing body). Close to the Pope, Balducci spoke on Italian television at least five times to proclaim that extraterrestrial Contact is a real phenomenon. Exorcist and demonologist, he stated categorically that extraterrestrial Contact is real and consistent with the Catholic Church's understanding of theology. He emphasized extraterrestrial encounters "were not demonic, or due to psychological impairment, or a case of entity attachment, but deserve to be studied."

Ref: *Labored Journey to the Stars* by Dr. Richard Boylan, PhD (ufodisclosure .com).

However, not all Christian churches have a similar positive interpretation. I was exposed to an alternate interpretation of Encounter experiences a few years ago, after a lively discussion with two Jehovah Witnesses. I discovered the view of extraterrestrial encounters for those with these core beliefs was very fixed and for the most part, quite negative. The discussion focused on my disclosure that I supported individuals with extraterrestrial encounters. To this statement, one of the Jehovah Witnesses shared that he too experienced extraterrestrial visitations. However, he believed these were demonic, and to corroborate this pointed to certain passages in his Bible. After a long discussion, we agreed to disagree on the interpretation.

However, this negative perspective did not surprise me. Occasionally I received emails with similar views to his. Primarily from the fundamentalist religious, concerned for my soul, as they believed I was manipulated by 'evil entities.' My reply is polite, but I point out; my research has indicated that extraterrestrial experiences, in most cases, proved to be beneficial and transformative. The individual became a more loving, caring person after such encounters. My point is clear: I do not believe such a transformative outcome is the result of interactions with evil entities. However, this doesn't mean there is no such thing as lower astral beings, but this is another issue entirely.

Those who are deeply religious and/or spiritual, and trust their beliefs as the guide to their truth, can feel extremely conflicted as they explore these issues within the parameters of their religion. They may feel betrayed because they can feel they have not been told the truth by their respective church, or believe they are at fault because they are attacked by what they believe are 'demons.' This is a situation where the fear of being crazy or unworthy can be traumatizing. If the individual resources their pastor or minister for support and the Minister has no knowledge of this phenomenon, it can also result in feelings of abandonment and isolation. When I have spoken with some of the more open-minded clergy, they tell me that even if they are aware of this phenomenon, information or discussion on it can be blocked by their superiors, who are not so informed, or because the phenomena is so controversial they, the Church Hierarchy, do not know how to respond.

This highlights that for many, if they are religious and an Experiencer, they may have to make sense of their experiences through a perspective, which helps them to cope in the best way they can. In regards to their religion, it will depend on how helpful their spiritual beliefs are in facilitating a helpful perspective. For some individuals, they may need to be more flexible and explore alternate knowledge if their religious beliefs conflict with what they experience. Certainly, if they have recall of past lives, and their religious belief negates reincarnation, this becomes confusing and possibly frightening, and they could question their sanity.

This confusion can also present if the beings do not appear in the form of an angel or a religious figure they can recognize. The individual can be led to believe they are demonic, even if it is not the case. The encounter may be very loving, but the individual is conflicted because they may feel they are being manipulated simply because their religious background leads them to believe that the extraterrestrials are really demons. This will cause fear in a similar way to the young man who was a Jehovah Witness who admitted he only distrusted the beings because of the Bible text. I find this disturbing, as it means that their interpretation may not be reflective of what they truly experience, but reflect the programming and conditioning of a core belief from their religion or spirituality.

Where Can the Experiencer Find Understanding?

If a person's religious belief colors their openness to their multidimensional encounter experiences, then it is extremely important these churches have a clear approach to how they interpret this phenomenon. It is crucial to how their parishioner may or may not feel supported by them. The exponential increase in sightings and those experiencing this phenomenon means those with religious beliefs will inevitably source their religion and clergy for answers. The Church, with its 'head in the sand' attitude, will come under more and more scrutiny when parishioners seek to understand their experiences. Especially if questions arise, which may contradict religious beliefs and dogma, such as individuals who experience past-life recall, for example. Where does that leave them if Christian dogma dismisses reincarnation? How does this phenomenon affect our interpretation of the Bible? Fiery chariots in the sky; or are they really UFOs and not necessarily coming from the ultimate Source, God?

Thankfully, there are some resources based on religious beliefs which offer understanding and interpretations which can help the religious individual work through these confusing, challenging questions, such as the excellent book by the Rev. Barry Downing: *The Bible and Flying Saucers*; just one of these.

If the individual chooses to understand their experiences through the lens of their religious beliefs, they may need to explore alternative perspectives of their encounters too. If they do, this can result in profound shifts in them. Encounters are a catalyst for questioning core beliefs, including spiritual and religious. How they judge good or evil may be only the start of this shift within.

It also depends on how they wish to interpret and understand some of the core beliefs such as the Creation story, with the knowledge our species has been subject to DNA modification; if they have past-life recall, for example. How the extraterrestrials fit into these beliefs are just a few of the issues that may surface for them.

- Are extraterrestrials real?
- Extraterrestrials, and the Bible.
- Angelic beings, or demons?
- Reincarnation.
- Cosmic Intelligence, Universal Source: God?

Well-meaning Christians may sincerely believe "I am dealing with demons." I understand why they may believe that, however, in most cases, it is demonstrating that they are only exploring this through one limited perspective. Recent surveys, facilitated by the FREE, showed that over several thousand individuals, in a majority of instances these interactions are positive. At least eighty-five percent felt their interactions caused major, positive, transformative change. They became more spiritually and multi-dimensionally aware, with fifty percent experiencing profound healing through their encounters. Eighty-two percent believed there was a connection between extraterrestrials and the spirit world, pre-birth, post-death.

(Recent FREE Surveys 2016: www.experiencer.org)

Many religious people may not realize that a group of extraterrestrials known as the Watchers, and named in religious texts, were considered angelic. Author, Rev. Barry Downing, quotes from the Bible:

"I believe it's time we explored the possibility that UFOs carry the 'Angels of God'.

As the Bible says 'Do not neglect to show hospitality to Aliens, for thereby some have entertained angels unawares' – (Hebrews 13:2)

Ref: *The Bible and Flying Saucers*
by Rev. Barry Downing, 1968, 1997, Marlowe and Co.

The Religious Dilemma

I am very grateful that two courageous Ministers of religion have agreed to share their thoughts and experiences in this chapter, and what the 'Extraterrestrial Experience' alongside their deep spiritual and religious beliefs has meant to them personally and in their Ministry.

Rev. Michael Carter resides in the USA and has experienced extraterrestrial Contact and healing through his encounters. He has authored two landmark books: *Alien Scriptures: Extraterrestrials in the Holy Bible*, and recently his second book: *A New World if You Can Take It: God, Extraterrestrials, and the Evolution of Human Consciousness*. Rev. Carter has explored his Christianity and the Bible with a perspective, which encompasses his own extraterrestrial experiences. He explains how the reality of extraterrestrial visitations throughout millennia, has been perceived. Rev Carter offers his interpretation from a more modern perspective, which I found illuminating and very helpful.

The New Human Being

Rev. Michael Carter

"I had always known that I would take this path, but yesterday I did not know that it would be today."

Japanese poet and philosopher, Narihira.

First of all, I want to say what a privilege it is for me to have been asked to contribute to this book. I have been a follower of Mary Rodwell and her groundbreaking work for quite some time now, and it all began for me when I picked up her book *Awakening: How Extraterrestrial Contact Can Transform Your Life*. Well, I am writing to testify that extraterrestrial Contact can and will change your life because I have been forever changed by this Contact!

I also happen to be a member of the professional clergy. I serve a Unitarian Universalist congregation in the mountains of Western North Carolina and have had visits from Star People off and on since 28 December 1989. Hypnotic regression has also revealed, that I have been visited by these off-world intelligences since around the age of eight years old. Thousands upon thousands of individuals, perhaps I should say, millions upon millions, of adults and children alike, people from all over the globe and from every walk of life, are having Contacts with beings from other worlds and dimensions. This is indeed an exciting time to be alive.

My story begins in Baltimore, Maryland. I was raised in the African-American Baptist tradition as a child and young adult. There was lots of music and dramatic preaching on Sunday mornings. I also attended Sunday school where I learned to memorize and recite large passages from the book of Matthew in the New Testament (my favorite book at the time) and I was pretty impressive to my parents and other members of the congregation. At that age, I wanted my parents to be proud of me and I genuinely enjoyed attending church. However, as a child, I was not at all into science fiction because in my mind, human beings were the pinnacle of God's creation. How wrong I was!

And yet, there was always an inner awareness if you will; a deep intuitive knowing in me that to label people as 'saved' and 'unsaved,' was inherently wrong. I somehow knew that those labels were somehow violating a law of oneness between myself and all living things and besides – it just wasn't true. Now, to be truthful, I don't know how I knew this, I just knew it. I also had a deep intuitive knowing that there was a home that I had originated from that was not on planet Earth, and that there was a different way of interacting with one another that was much more civil. In my original home, we knew that Love was the law of the Universe and that Love was all that mattered. Again, this was a deep cellular knowing, but I could not have articulated that at the time if someone would have asked me. I just felt that a God would not choose sides in a war, or deliberately hurt someone because they believed differently. I took the words 'God is love' very seriously.

Years passed. I had moved from my hometown of Baltimore, Maryland to New York City to pursue a career in the professional theater. Exciting times indeed! But again, after twenty years of pursuing a theatrical career, I felt unfulfilled. I wanted to serve others. I drifted away from my religion of origin and began to study spiritual metaphysics in between acting jobs and classes. I began attending The Unity Church as well as Religious Science congregations on Sunday mornings. I had not totally done away with the teachings of Jesus, but I needed a more liberating theology for the old theology of my childhood; much like an old shoe, it just didn't fit anymore. My consciousness was expanding as I attended these services and began to learn about the power of the human mind and human growth potential. I started reading philosophy and began to study Eastern Religions and, to put it simply, I could not get enough of all the information and wisdom I was coming across at this time in my life.

And then it happened! On 28 December 1989, after returning to New York City from a vacation in Mexico visiting the pyramids on the Yucatan Peninsula, I woke to see a being from another world at the foot of my bed. I was so scared I thought I would have a heart attack. This individual was no more than four feet tall with a chalky white color to his skin. To be honest, I'm assuming this person was male, but I don't know for sure. My room was surrounded with a white light and this person had a cobalt blue light that surrounded him as if I was seeing his aura. He has a pear-shaped head with big black wrap-around eyes, and he wore a tight fitting suit that looked like he was wearing a suit made of aluminum foil.

Never the macho type, I managed to pull the covers up over my head, hoping it would go away. The next thing I knew, I felt a temperature change, and I heard a whoosing sound in my ears – like a great wind was blowing – and it felt as if I was somehow outside in the cold. When I pulled the covers down, no one was there and it was as if nothing ever happened. Of course, I feared for my sanity and began seeing a mental health professional. A friend recommended a UFO Contactee Support group as well. I eventually was regressed hypnotically by the late Dr. Jean Mundy and, years later, by the late Bud Hopkins.

The Contacts continue to this day. Sometimes, I would be paralyzed when they entered my bedroom. Other times, I would be too afraid to even look at them so they would show me telepathically what they looked like or what they were doing. They would show up in my meditations in my third eye area and just stare at me. At times, a year or two would go by before they would physically appear but they always come back. I still leave the lights on as long as I can sometimes before I go to sleep at night, but I have come to learn that it's not about them anymore. They have never really hurt me; it's my fear that's the problem. They helped me to look at where else in my life I let fear control me and keep me from growing, from evolving, from loving.

I have personally seen three Star Races in my bedroom. I have seen the so-called Grays (but to me they looked chalk colored), I have seen the Reptilians, as well as the Nordic-looking Star People. I was even healed by a Nordic brother of a blood clot in my leg, back on 4 July 2013, at 9:50 pm EST. My spiritual growth accelerated as I read voraciously everything I could get my hands on about UFOs and their occupants. I was not interested in the nuts-and-bolts aspects of this phenomenon, but I had an insatiable appetite for the spiritual lessons one could glean from these experiences.

Before moving on to how my limited concept of 'God' had changed, I want to note the physical changes I experienced after these Contacts. It seemed that the summers were the heaviest time for me as far as Contacts go for a while, but that too has changed – why I don't know. I noticed that my interests changed and I was less self-centered. I wanted to serve humanity in some way. I felt a call to leave the theater and enter the ministry and I did just that. I became an energy healer and learned to work with crystals and guided meditations. I studied the religions of different cultures regarding star visitors and their influence on these cultures. My hair and nails grew exceptionally rapidly and I needed much less sleep to get through the day. My intuitive abilities felt like they were on steroids and I just began to feel so much more as if my heart was wide open; I felt so much more love in my heart. My consciousness changed, and I began to feel a 'oneness' with our Mother, the Earth. I began to live my life less fearfully and to love wastefully. To this day, I still feel these emotions.

The God that I was raised with was much too small for me. The 'God' I discovered was not an old man up in the sky, who like Santa Claus, would reward you if you were nice and punish you if you were naughty. He became a thing of the distant past. Personally, I had to put away from me the childish concept of God that I had grown up with (Corinthians 13:11). I began to realize that human life was about evolution and the raising of one's consciousness in order to grow and to learn to love. God was not an anthropomorphic being, but 'God' was an 'energy,' a consciousness, and I was a part of that consciousness. 'God' was not outside of me, and I was not separate from it, but this energy was within me, all around me, supporting all life as we know it. The teachings of Jesus, The Buddha and other great saints and avatars was dangerous indeed for it empowered the masses, releasing them from centuries of dependence on the hierarchy of the clergy. This is not to condemn the professional clergy of today, but in my humble experience, we are here to empower and to uplift our brothers and sisters, not to feed their fears.

As part of my spiritual evolution, I became more accepting of others who were in a stage of their evolution where they needed a personal God that punished those who were different. I didn't have to agree with them, to love them. Words like I'm sorry, I'm scared, I don't know, I love you, Can you forgive me, became a regular part of my vocabulary. I became more vulnerable and more willing to take risks.

We are all in different stages of evolution because of our previous lives and we bring our gifts, our baggage, and our lessons with us from lifetime to lifetime. My Star Visitors showed me other lifetimes that I had as well. Some of us are young souls, some baby souls, some mature and some are old souls. We are all doing the best we can on the journey. My Contacts have taught me compassion and empathy, at least much more than I had before.

In short, I learned that the finite can never fully comprehend the infinite and that any name or experience we have of God or for God, is ours alone and it can be limited. We can only say that we have found a truth, but not the Truth. For some, God is a man up in the sky and for others, an aspect of God may be the Universal Law of Cause and Effect. For myself, another aspect of 'God' is The Law of One, which is the law that emphasizes that we are not separate from one another and that what I do to you and this planet I do to myself.

In my studies and research, I have found that the Talmud of Immanuel resonates with me on a deep level, especially its teachings regarding who and what God is. According to the story, this document was re-discovered by the Swiss Contactee, Billy Meier, and an Orthodox Clergy by the name of Rashid, who was later assassinated. One has to read the document for themselves to see if it has any veracity for them, but Meier purports the document to be the Gospel of Matthew from a Pleiadian perspective. According to the Pleiadian cosmology, there is a 'God' who is the Ruler of the human races (who also happens to be a Star Person), but above this 'God' is a consciousness or energy called Creation.

It would appear that we, as human beings, have mistaken an ET for the Supreme Intelligence of the Cosmos. Perhaps we can now look at the god Yahweh with fresh eyes. We shall see.

All of this is to say that since my Contact experiences, I have discovered that anything is possible and that Love is the glue that holds the Cosmos together. I have discovered that when I change the way I look at things, the things I look at begin to change. I used to believe that when everything falls into place I will find peace. Now I realize that when I find peace, everything falls into place. We can call the source of this wisdom 'God' or whatever you choose to call it, but most importantly, I would say that my most important learning has been that when fear knocks at the door and love answers – no one is there.

This is what it means to be a New Human being!"

Rev. Michael J. Carter, USA.

Michael, Interfaith minister, received his BA degree from the College of New Rochelle and Master of Divinity degree from Union Theological Seminary. While serving various Unitarian Universalist congregations in New York, Michael trained as an anti-racism trainer and presently serves as the minister of a Unitarian Universalist congregation in North Carolina. Michael has spoken at UFO Conferences and on radio and TV. A long-time UFO Experiencer, he lectures extensively on the topic of religion and UFOs. He appeared on the Sci-fi Channel's Steven Spielberg's production of *Abduction Diaries: The Real 4400*. Rev. Carter's books: *Alien Scriptures: Extraterrestrials In The Holy Bible*, and *A New World If You Can Take It: God, Extraterrestrials and The Evolution of Human Consciousness*.

A Christian Minister of over forty years, Jeff Schulte resides in Australia. Jeff generously and courageously shares his personal experiences, such as his extraterrestrial encounters and beliefs in reincarnation, due to his past life recall. These profound experiences have given him an innate and deep understanding of God. His dilemma was that some of these experiences were not in harmony with his Church.

The Subject of God and the Offworld Perspective by a Christian Minister with Over Forty Years in Ministry – Jeff Schulte.

It is only relatively recently that I have come to realize that I have been an Experiencer all of this incarnation, and probably in many of my previous incarnations. Already with these few words, most Christians reading this will recoil with: This minister believes in reincarnation?

It wasn't always the case, however. I was born with a previous life memory and because I was born into a devout Christian family, I quickly learned to justify that memory in any way possible that didn't include reincarnation! Unfortunately for those who were my tutors, I always felt that whatever justification was used it didn't quite hit the mark, so for most of my life there was a remaining question mark over this subject, which I managed to push into the background.

Another subject that never sat well with me was the doctrine of the nature of God, or rather 'Who or What' God is. Again, I was able to push it into the background until the last ten to fifteen years. You see, around that time I started having conscious and very real Contact experience with beings who, let me say, were not of the World! It was then that I started to think that I was losing my mind and sought out some help! My superiors were useless because all they knew was what they were told to believe, and teach. It was as if they were just mindless followers without any 'God-given' common sense to reason with! While most Christians just told me I was being possessed by demons. Mind you, I can't be too hard on them because for most of my ministerial life I was no better. At least not on the surface, and that made me a hypocrite as well. Then when the experiences started, I could no longer mindlessly teach what I was told to, without serious consideration to what I was teaching. This is when the subjects that I pushed into the background and stifled raised their heads again and I could no longer ignore them.

Reincarnation, I'll leave until later, for now, I will address the subject of what I have come to understand about the nature of 'Who or What' God is! When I first realized that what I had been taught and was teaching didn't add up, my life became very confused for about three years. Of course, it never did add up to me, but I was able to push it into the background and teach the accepted line each time it came up – so I was a hypocrite. But there came the time when I just couldn't do it anymore. Why? Well following the intense increase in my off-world visitor experiences, I began to get epiphany after epiphany! Why it took around three years to resolve itself, I'll probably never know, but when it did, it was like the scales fell from my eyes and everything made perfect sense to me.

At this point, I would like to say, for the sake of those who can't accept what I have to say or if you have a differing opinion to mine, then that's fine with me because your faith and relationship with your God are precious and sacrosanct to you and I in no way wish to disturb that.

What follows is as best as I can explain at this stage of my understanding of God following years of Contact with beings that were not of this world. Before this time I uncomfortably accepted what I was being told to believe, which is pretty much that God is the Creator and Supreme Being who is omnipotent, omniscient and omnipresent. Strangely, what I believe now is not that far from this teaching and, apart from the epiphanies which I believe were brought about by my Contacts, the Bible as the Christian Church has it today actually speaks of what I have come to understand.

So here it is:
The term God is relatively recent terminology from the past few millennia and has since been hijacked by controlling forces to manipulate and control the people.

- God is not a being but rather God is the Spirit or Energetic Force that we may call Unconditional Love. As such, God is the noblest and most beautiful of all spirits or energetic forces.
- God is not the Supreme Being. However, God is the Energizing Spirit that drives the highest and most noble of beings.
- God is not the Creator. However, God is the Spirit or Energizing Force, which may have inspired what we understand and call Creation.
- God is not the Universe or Multiverse or Ultraverse. However, of all of the energizing spirits that may have been found, God remains the Highest and Most

Noble of energizing spirits to be found across the full spectrum of universes.

- God does not speak, but the impulse of this Spirit directs the hearts of those who draw upon Its noble, energetic inspiration.
- God does not forgive, but is the very essence of Forgiveness.
- God does not punish, but those who reject or turn their back on this most noble spirit will always have to settle for less than Perfect Bliss.
- God does not Love, but is the very essence of Perfect Love.

So, God is in no way, shape or form a being, just as electricity is in no way, shape or form that toaster sitting on your bench. However, just like that toaster requires electricity to operate and fulfill its task, so does a being require a Spirit to drive it. If that Spirit is God, aka the Spirit of Unconditional Love, then such a being will rise through the levels of existence to the highest and most beautiful being ahead of those who are yet to discover its beauty and power.

So that's it in a nutshell. Oh, and by the way, I said that the Bible had helped in this understanding, so here I will cite the writings of John the apostle: 'God is Love, and he who dwells in Love dwells in God, and God in him.' (Paraphrased from 1 John, 4:6), and Jesus' discussion with the woman at the well: 'God is Spirit.' (from the Gospel of John, Chapter 4). Neither spirit nor love are beings, however, they are energizing forces that may drive the impulse within a being. At the time of this writing, I am still active in Christian ministry and I see zero 'clash' with the teachings of the one that we call Jesus the Christ.

Just a sub note Mary: We are all eternal beings who experience what we may say are physical incarnations or experiences. If we can accept that concept, then there is no 'One Being' who will be greater than the other. No One Being who is supreme as all will be equal. No One Being who is omnipotent. Omnipresence may be considered, and all would be omniscient at the Ultra-Eternal level. However, Spirit may be omnipotent in that it may be considered the highest form among other spirits, and omnipresent in that it is not bound by space and time. However, it wouldn't be omniscient, as Spirit, of itself, is pure energy and has no consciousness to speak of."

A Starseed in India Writes

Religion is the mainstay of Indian life. However, what is the Indian culture's interpretation regarding UFOs and extraterrestrials?

I was contacted by a young Indian man, Sourev. Sourev is convinced he is a starseed and his understanding has created many problems because it is so different to the beliefs of his Indian culture and the majority of his countrymen. Sourev struggled with the knowledge that, for the most part, his countrymen were still entrenched in different religions and belief in many different gods. Sourev interpreted the 'gods,' for the most part as extraterrestrials. However, they are perceived as Gods by the majority of his countrymen and this left him feeling isolated.

Sourev: "First of all, I want to thank you for replying to my mail and I want you to know that you will always be there in my heart for the work you have done."

I asked Sourev how his Indian culture interprets the extraterrestrial phenomenon?

Sourev: "Mary, people hardly know anything about ETs and UFO stuff here, the consciousness of people is very narrow (both city and villages) and they are very polarized in their outlook. The problem is that people are so much into the gods (there are at least a million gods here). There are at least a million temples of various gods, and thousands of temples of Sri Krishna. There are people who follow the teachings, but there are more people (majority) who simply worship instead of learning what these spiritual masters were teaching, or were here to teach them. They have a different notion of God in this country: they think God is Krishna or Shiva and so on. I think that idol worship was created in India to focus on one being but eventually, like Egypt, people found more interest in worshipping God in their own ways and a variety of gods emerged, but I think there has been manipulation to keep people worshipping deities.

There is another problem in India, that if any person shows abilities, like the Indigo children, these children end up being worshiped by the people.

If the people knew about the various dimensions, people could see various possibilities and live in a different way. I have relatives in the States, and when they were here I told them everything, and when I saw your video of your lecture at the Bases Project Conference, I thought to myself, "Mary and I think alike," because I had also told my relatives to observe the color of the body of Krishna.

Note: Krishna is blue, suggestive of blue extraterrestrials. See my lecture, *Awakening the New Human: Triggers of Consciousness* at the Bases Project conference, 2014; available on YouTube.

However, I am not ready to disclose myself because I must be ready with answers when they shoot questions, and I have not done my homework properly. When ready, the time will come when I am confident. But up to now, I have only conveyed this information to my parents and a few of my friends. I have been searching for ETs and information related to them all my life. It was natural to me. The Internet arrived around 2004 or 2005 here, and I saw Dr Steven Greer's *Disclosure Project* in 2004.

I personally had two accidents and was healed miraculously overnight. Once it took only twenty-four hours for me to heal my leg after an accident, and the second time it took only seven hours (a night's sleep) to heal completely from an accident; the second one was more severe than the first.

Apart from these, my personal experience was something which was very important to me and happened in my High School. I was in a dimension of Timelessness where I could feel a female energy or person who was very happy to see me and was elated when she felt me. I was changed, and became a different person entirely within a fraction of a moment when I was able to go inside her through her breath to her heart and felt her love – and I felt complete. Everything was happening so fast within a fraction of a second that my consciousness could not handle it. I could not come back to the present because whatever I felt had become my reality and this physical reality was no more. I wondered how it was even possible for me to feel such a thing, but I felt the same thing accurately five more times in my life, only to feel it more and more clearly, and all this was happening in a fraction of a second.

I was at peace when, last year, I learned about dimensions and read a book called *Am I A Child Of The Stars* by Enrique Barrios, and especially the chapter called *A Blue Princess*. It was the exact same experience for me. The only difference was the author could see whatever he felt and I could not see the face of the being because it was pure energy and not physical.

Please convey my regards to the Star Children you meet. I really felt a lot of affection for nine-year-old Cathy, who said 'Mary has big ears.' I could feel what she was feeling."

Sourav from Bhubaneswar, Odisha, India.
Ref: (Cathy – Chapter Two).

Note: I get a few inquiries from Indian individuals who seek support. The culture, for the most part, still precludes this phenomenon from being mainstream, even though so many images in their culture indicate the extraterrestrial hypotheses.

Core beliefs are certainly challenged after encounters and the consciousness shift is making us reappraise our reality and beliefs through such profound personal experience. If it has been so profound that previous beliefs fall short, it becomes a journey of trust in their personal resonance.

I think the Dalai Lama has a wonderful perspective in his statement of how to be with extraterrestrials below:

Buddhism

"If we receive some visitor from other Galaxies, it's the same as human being. They may be little different sort of shapes, but basically, they are the same. Furthermore, same sentient being, so respect them. Look at them as the same sentient being. We can immediately shake hands if they have some sort of similar hand: If we place too much emphasis on the strangeness and watchfulness, that creates anxiety and more fear."

Dalai Lama on how we should treat extraterrestrials.
https://www.youtube.com/watch?v=zKTu6VBhU2A

Researcher and author, Joe Lewels, PhD, in his excellent book *The God Hypothesis*, explores the reality of extraterrestrial life and its implications for science and religion. In the afterword (p. 312), Joe Lewels states that at a time when the theory of evolution is being challenged by mainstream scientists, theologians are behind the times in understanding the implications of leading-edge scientific thinking.

"More than ever before there is a sound scientific basis for understanding the human soul and the concept of God as embodied in a conscious and living universe. This is the message that the theologians should be pouncing on and conveying to the public."

Lewels concludes in his afterward, that the message of The God Hypotheses, is based on the scientific understanding that the universe is holographic in nature and all things in the universe are interconnected at the quantum level.

"This scientific/spiritual knowledge teaches us that physical reality is but an illusion that makes it appear we are separate from God and from all other things."

(p. 313) *The God Hypothesis.*

Zac (see Chapter Nineteen) explains his understanding of God when I asked him the question: "So the God many believe in, just like the version of the old man which is supreme. Is that God because we have believed in that form of God? What is your understanding of God or the Source, or Universal Consciousness? How do you understand this?"

Z: "My personal understanding is that God is everything. All that is because all that is, is one, so when we speak of God, we speak of an essence that is higher than us. And since energy itself cannot be higher or lower it is just separate frequencies. It's just how our limited, materialistic brain perceives the quantum energy."

M: "So when you have greater understanding you no longer need a particular form; you honor the fact we are a collective essence."

Z: "Yes, and it is why, as I said earlier, my spiritual guides are just another version of me."

What Do These Non-Human Intelligences Believe?

The information here is resourced from a whistleblower, former Army Sergeant Clifford Stone (USA), who has interfaced with some of these nonhuman intelligences in a very tangible way, and this information adds weight to the quote below, when the Christian Bible, when referring to the creation of humans, refers to God as plural. The question arises, who is God and who is 'Us'?

"Then God said, and now we will make human beings, they will be like us and resemble us."

Christian Bible. Genesis 1:26

Fifty-Seven Varieties of 'Us'

Former Army Sergeant, Clifford Stone (USA), has shared publicly his previous work, which was retrieving extraterrestrial craft and interfacing with some of the intelligences operating spacecraft. Stone stated that General Douglas MacArthur organized a group called the Interplanetary Phenomena Research Unit, in 1943, which continues to this day. Its function was to recover objects of unknown origin, particularly those that are of non-Earthly origin. Stone was part of the Extraterrestrial Retrieval Team who worked at NATO, and he has seen living and dead extraterrestrials in his official duties on the army team that retrieved crashed ET crafts. Stone stated that when he got out of the military in 1989, fifty-seven different varieties of alien beings had been cataloged. He acted as an 'interfacer,' face to face with these beings.

Stone: "I was involved in situations where we actually did recoveries of crashed saucers. There were bodies that were involved with some of these crashes. Also, some of these were alive. While we were doing this, we were telling the American public there was nothing to it. We were telling the world that there was nothing to it.

You have individuals that look very much like you and myself that could walk among us, and you wouldn't even notice the difference. These are living, breathing creatures, just as mortal as you and I. They had feelings; they had families. They had a cultural society. The one thing that they didn't have was hate, hostility. They had anger, but the anger, from what I observed, and I don't know how to explain it better than stating that it was an intellectual anger. They could not comprehend how a species such as us, that had such great potential to do such wonderful and marvelous things, could do such horrible, nightmarish things to one another.

I want people to understand that they're not hostile. They didn't come here to enslave us. Before Men had a language they could have enslaved us because they were there, then.

Do I believe in God? Yes! And they believe in God too, but our definition of divinity is probably in conflict with theirs, which doesn't mean that we have a different point of view. They could wipe out many religions if they attempted to better define the concept of God, and at the same time, they would get themselves killed before taking the lives of others. But they are also ready to defend themselves. I think they will continue to monitor us until we no longer constitute a threat, within the next thirty years. This is from a document taken from an intelligence memorandum, which was sent to the FBI.

They are not hostile. One sure, true case that they're not hostile is the fact that they have survived their own technological advances, and the only reason they did this is because of their spiritual growth.

Our technology is not on par with theirs, but then very subtly, a much more sophisticated, technologically superior race would intercede on our behalf, neutralizing a threat.

They wanted us to understand how futile going to a nuclear war could be and how easily they could stop it. Most are not hostile. If they were, they would have destroyed us long ago."

Former Army Sgt Clifford Stone, author of *Eyes Only*.

Stone thinks that the extraterrestrials will not permit us to explore the depths of outer space until we've learned to grow spiritually, and that they will make themselves known soon, if we don't first acknowledge their presence.

I hope this chapter will assist those who are in the process of exploring their core religious beliefs with an expanded perspective. The Encounter Experience is a challenge to all we have been conditioned to believe. However, I believe this challenge can also be a freedom to learn more about ourselves and how we interpret our human experiences, and to learn to trust what we truly feel within.

Chapter Nineteen

SHAMANIC HEALER

"I am here to wake people up!"

Dr. Maree Batchelor M.D.

Synchronicity

I was nearing completion of this book and I had a strong feeling to re- connect with Dr. Maree Batchelor. I first met Dr. Batchelor six months ago, after presenting my lecture *Triggers of Consciousness* at the Afterlife Explorers conference in Melbourne, 2016. After this lecture, Dr. Batchelor was very emotional, and her experiences related to the content of the lecture in a profound way. I also believed she would be interested in what we are doing with the FREE organization.

Dr. Batchelor: "As I received your email this morning and I was replying, I received this huge feeling of energy and knew this was good; the knowing this was meant to be. I always receive very big energy downloads when things are right and this energy shift today was confirmation this is where I am meant to be going. After the conversation with you on the phone, I was in this bubble. I felt it is all okay!

It has been very hard, as I keep waking up in a world that doesn't understand anything. When I heard you speak at the afterlife conference lecture I felt what you brought in was so high, it was the most expansive information I had received in a long time. It was what you understood, and what you opened up to. I felt that this was, for me, the highest truth. People don't realize the matrix is galactic. Many don't understand that the 'gods' of the old religions, the Great Beings and Ascended Masters that people are going to temples and bowing to, are really multidimensional galactic beings."

Your Lecture Propelled me Into Another Realm

"The lecture was an absolute catalyst and it put pieces of the puzzle together and catapulted something enormous in me. After all my research, I just felt 'I know all this', and hearing that other people started to know this too was just amazing."

Grief – A 'Wake-Up' Call!

"My awakening journey began in June, 2008, with a tragedy. My son William was only four when he died. Often he would say to me, 'I love YOU more than you Mum.' I didn't understand until after his death; it was the capital YOU he was referring to. I felt he was very special. He was seriously injured in a freak accident and as I was on my way to the hospital to see him I saw this bright light, directly in front of my eyes, and I thought I was having a migraine from all the horrendous stress. However, at that precise time my son was in theater, and unbeknown to me, they were doing open-chest cardiac massage and he actually died on the operating table. Although they managed to revive him, he finally died eleven days later. Soon after, I realized that when my son was having open-chest cardiac massage surgery and died, it was at the same time the bright light had come to me. A week later, I went to where he had been injured, and this same bright light came out of the exact site where the accident happened. I was immersed in it and I got the feeling 'It's all okay; it's all going to the plan.' I couldn't understand why I would feel like that. It was insane. How, on any human level, could I feel this was okay! I was in deep grief and would say to God 'You have to help me,' but I wasn't religious at all. Here was I, an un-awakened, 3D, highly successful woman calling out to God! But what I got back was 'You must be still.' It was soon after my son died that I knew I was getting downloads; something big was guiding me."

My Awakening Continued – India

"I began to explore my spirituality by visiting an ashram in Melbourne, which in turn led me to the spiritual village of Ganeshpuri, India. It was at the Hindu temple there where this special Great Being Bhagawan Nityananda was buried. The temple was filled with hundreds of people, and I felt this incredible energy zapped me on the head. I felt it was galactic. I suddenly had this recognition, and an unbelievable connection with a Braham Priest, Abhi, who was not even dressed as a priest at the time. The connection was confusing; it felt like a soul connection. It made no sense but I felt I knew Abhi from a past life. When I left to return to Australia I felt this huge loss at leaving him, similar to leaving a part of me behind. I wasn't consciously looking for any of this; I was still living very comfortably in the 3D world. I just knew of my connection to this Braham Priest and I was downloaded with the information. I had this divine job to do, and to work with him connecting India to Australia and other countries; to break down normal 3D paradigms for the young, the old, the black, the white.

I realized from hearing your lecture that this Great Being, Bhagawan Nityananda, an Ascended Master was, in fact, a Galactic Being. I also knew that Abhi, the Brahman Priest, was a being from my star family. I wanted to get him to Australia because I wanted my husband to join me on this spiritual journey. We managed to get a visa for Abhi to stay with us. I felt that he and I were activating each other for a greater purpose. At this point, my husband did not understand; he thought I was crazy and told me to leave. This was so painful, but on some level I had to trust this was all meant to happen. I believed that I was now in training and I had important work to do. I felt this somehow had been set up.

I live in Mount Eliza, which is a small outer suburb of Melbourne. Previous to all of this, we were well-known and respected. The surgeon and the GP with four amazing children and then – boom – suddenly, I am in Cosmic Consciousness and the whole town thinks I am a 'nutcase.' They couldn't understand what had happened to me. I think they believe I had a breakdown after my son died, but now more people have come to realize that I am okay. The feedback from my patients has been positive and I am getting a good following. I still make sure I do all the usual things in my community with my children, so people can see I am okay. It's like I am not the 'crazy person' my husband had said of me.

I started working in a holistic healing center, but although I was in a place with more awakened people, I still felt they didn't really 'get me.' At this time, I felt very alone, isolated and misunderstood; sometimes I felt I could have disappeared; it was so extreme at times. I know I am here to help people who experience what I have experienced and I believe some would jump off the cliff unless they are helped, they are so disorientated and confused. This information is vital. We also need to recognize the health systems aren't working; we have more youth suicide, obesity, cancer, depression, and they need us. I have a job to do. But I am finding my voice. I am finding my power, and now I am feeling so connected.

I get given 'knowings' and then I receive confirmation. I would say to my clients 'I know I am in the DNA I am in your cells, I am unwinding DNA.' I would be saying this, wondering how I knew it, but I just knew – I knew. Patients would say to me 'I am 'tingling,'' and things would leave their body and they would feel things lifting off. I pieced it together and realized this was so deep in our physicality. I would clean up the vessel. It became obvious this was what I was doing. I realized, as I started this work, this whole energy zone would come in around me. I realized it was a galactic zone and I would be up in a galactic realm of what I felt was a higher aspect of me, and I am just a conduit for it and I just know that is my role.

Note: This description is similar to how former Israeli Computer Scientist, Adrian Dvir, spoke of his healing with extraterrestrials. Ref: ACERN DVD, *Expressions of ET Contact: A Communication and Healing Blueprint?* and *Healing Entities and Aliens* by Adrian Dvir, 2003.

A few of my core patients seem to have 'awakened' very quickly and act as feedback loops for me, and they will give me information. One eighteen-year-old had her third eye activated, and now she sees many beings around me. She told me one of the spiritual beings she saw me connected to in India was in me. Other people have seen other beings in me, including a Native American Indian, even a Chinese being. How much people perceive depends on how aware and awake they are. It depends on their third eye activation; some are seeing multiple beings in front of them. I feel that the more I expand I am retrieving aspects of me from past lives. It feels like time has collapsed and there is no time, and they are all me. They are doing the work with me. I get amazing downloads for people and get precisely what they need to be told. I know exactly what I am meant to do and when I am meant to do it. When my patients come into the room I sometimes need to say to them, 'Your brain is not going to comprehend, this but you will feel it.' Even if they don't get the concepts of what I am telling them, they get the vibration and that's enough, which is fantastic. I have also developed the ability to speak and transmit light language. Initially I would be thinking to myself 'Is this for real?' but then I would see it working. The language was a vibration to upgrade people."

M: "So you bring in codes with the activations?"

Dr. B: "I don't see a lot, but just know I am. I can feel them coming in. Occasionally I see a symbol, but really I just know and feed them in, and it's like things peel away from people and transformations happen. I am here to wake people up. Activate new programs and activate their DNA and clean off the programming, the receivers and densities which are keeping them and controlling them in the matrix. The matrix has become more palpable and more observable, and I just know I have to get people out of this slumber/slavery; this robotic, suppressed, joyless, addicted, materialistic world that we are in. There is big work ahead, as we need to make sure we don't get hooked back into the old ways. If we are not at our best it is because something is being activated/hooked in again; it's not our natural state; we are not meant to feel that suppressed, that bogged down.

The shape-shifting that's happening to me with my patients is incredible. Some of the people seeing this are not always 'awake' (multi-dimensionally aware), but they are seeing this too. They are astounded by it. Even University students, disconnected and troubled by their lives, admit something's happening with my work on them because of the relief they feel after the first session. They can become very emotional and say they feel they are themselves for the first time. I know what I am doing is off the charts for people."

M: "When you say you are shape-shifting, what are they seeing? Do you know what you shapeshift into, or who is coming in?"

Dr. B: "The shape-shifting happens when I move into a higher vibration. These beings, I believe, are past-life aspects of me that come in. They are the wisdom teachers I was in the past.

I feel portals are opening up for me where I am living and meditating and where I work. A cylinder comes up, and I am connected to a galactic support crew.

As well as galactic help, I believe we can all benefit from human support and help on our journey.

There have been a few people who have been vital on my journey; one who I saw at one of my lowest points. I quite miraculously had this download, that I was to go and see Caroline Hales, an integrated energy healer who I had first met some years prior. Her bodywork is amazing and she helped me to ground myself. The second person is Dr. Gretha Zahar, a radiation chemist and scientist. I attended her clinic in Jakarta and still use her tools to detox.

The third person was Sue Waters. She is a wonderful and talented intuitive and clairvoyant. We met by some amazing synchronicities. Sue already knew you (Mary). We had a similar story and, just like me, we have both been plucked out of our normal lives and thrust forward into this work. We have both experienced Contact and received huge downloads. Sue previously worked as a scientist in the pharmaceutical industry. I first contacted Sue by phone. After our phone call, she said she had received enormous information for me. She had never had so many downloads about a client. She recognized we had a big connection from previous lives and on the craft. Sue said that I had been on craft many times and been transformed, given information. After the session in person, we both felt we had been taken on craft for a discussion. This is similar to when I have patients; sometimes we feel like we are in another dimension, and with the more aware it's almost like we are bi-locating during the session. "

Shamanic Awakening

"I also did a session for Sue. We had this revelation: she was actually seeing the matrix and how the programming controls us. How entities are high- jacking people, and there is an integration of implants and negative entities within a person for control. In subsequent sessions she saw I was actually working with DNA, splicing and removing segments, taking out the old and inserting in new. The new DNA looked golden. As this is inserted, the rest of the DNA lights up for abilities!"

Note: "It was interesting to hear Dr. Batchelor mention 'Golden DNA' as that information was similar that referred to by another client of mine some years ago. This client, 'T', told me that in her recall she was shown two types of DNA strands in humans: double helix and then another strand coiling around it. This third strand of DNA was golden and white. She felt that the DNA was being changed and balanced by an extraterrestrial being.

"On one of my visits, the ET in charge was showing me some DNA strands. It was in a laboratory again and he (the being) was explaining the upgrading being done to human DNA. It was projected in the room above the console I was in front of, as a hologram. The DNA was being coated in gold (perhaps monatomic gold), and I could see how it swirled upwards through the DNA strands. I asked 'Would I get that done to me?' and was told I had already had it applied to me. The ET I was with wasn't bad or manipulative, he was helping us to move forward so I think it can be interpreted differently by each individual.

T (Experiencer).

Dr. B: "I had even more feedback from Sue after that session when I worked on her, however."

S: "OMG! I can see the matrix, what has happened to the codes, all the transmissions, the Aliens in disguise; everyone is being programmed. Is this supposed to happen? OMG! I am like Lucy in the movie! It is so clear. We are in a matrix. I can see a craft; its overhead and transmitting frequencies into the people, and little drone spheres are coming out of the craft. It looks like everyone is a robot. I see codes, like barcodes, being put into their heads. This has changed my life. I knew it; now I see it. I see everyone is programmed. I see the programs coming in. It's unbelievable, but I needed to see it, although it's a shock. It's all different now; I see things differently. It's inter-dimensional."

Ref: Movie – *Lucy*

(In the movie, Lucy accidentally absorbs huge amounts of a specific new drug which opens up her DNA progressively, and more and more of her DNA gets switched on and she becomes super-aware, with amazing abilities, and can see the matrix/ holographic nature of reality).

Dr. B: "I told Sue not to worry, just observe and it will be integrated. After the next session with her, she told me what she perceived. She saw me splicing DNA, using the energy and the frequency to splice off old parts and remove inorganic segments of implanted technologies. I protected and activated the DNA to shield the original DNA blueprint, to create a more crystalline DNA. I feel strongly that we all need to get rid of the programming. We need our DNA to be cleared, as it were, from our family lineage and karma, etc., which blocks us with our experiences in this lifetime.

I feel like I just work on what is needed, whether it is past life imprints, present life issues, programs or implants from the matrix, or from the family lineage, such as generational programs, either father's or mother's inherited programs, which continue because of the behaviors of the family unit that keep it so locked in. These behaviors and programs can also skip generations. It is interesting that Sue is able to articulate and draw what I am doing, and that it is work in higher dimensions and how I am bringing this into the human. Her understanding and work are amazing.

What I am aware of is that I am somehow getting into the DNA. I feel it's actually subatomic, the atoms. What keeps coming up, intuitively, is the feeling that we are changing from carbon-based to crystalline. It has to be a process because we have to change this physicality. I am removing the karmic patterning that keeps us running to the old programs, which stop us from being what we can be."

M: "How did you explain this work and understand what is going on when you are working this way?"

"I feel I have become a modern Shaman, and who better than one trained in 3D."
Dr. B: "I call myself a doctor for holistic counseling, spirituality, and meditation. I call this an energetic healing process. From a disease perspective, we really have to get this understood. I believe Western medicine is going down the wrong track. I feel many who are starting to actually wake up sense something is wrong and they get depressed. They then go to the doctor and get an antidepressant and this shuts them down again, with little hope of them waking up. It is clear to me that we, as doctors, are on some level trained by the pharmaceutical industry. It doesn't mean the doctors are bad; they just are unaware this is going on. They are busily prescribing the very thing that shuts people down and puts them back into this programmed matrix.

When someone says to me 'Oh yes, I hear you have gone spiritual.' I respond 'Actually, this is reality.' It is quantum reality; it's science. We are talking science."

Junk DNA or Shut Down?

"My understanding with the DNA is that we all have been shut down; I believe purposely, to be kept as a kind of slave species. It stops us having the life we should have, which I believe is one of peace, joy, love, and happiness, rather than life being a grind with just moments of that. I feel even with NDE, yes, they have been activated, but I don't believe they are all given the highest they can have. I believe there is a great deal of manipulation going on at a number of levels. I also believe manipulation, dumbing down is helped by chemtrails, electronic devices, mercury in the teeth, etc. This information was downloaded to me.

Sue has confirmed to me the same information. Sue has also seen me shapeshift through multiple lifetimes. During a session, she has said, 'You are not you now; you have become an ancient Chinese healer.' We have both experienced, when speaking on the phone together, that we have been taken onto the craft and things are being done to us in a positive way. I feel all my Contact is amazing, beautiful and positive. I don't believe the beings that are around me are allowing me to have the level of manipulation I see in others. Although it appears people around me can be manipulated to create challenges for me, however. But I see this as situations to make me grow."

My Understanding of How it Works

"DNA is changed by frequency. I bring this in through my hands, my being; through my voice and through the light language I use. I also play mantra, which expands the frequencies and makes it even more powerful to clean people up. Some patients actually see things leaving their body and light going into certain parts. Frozen shoulders will start to move as I am unlocking in their bodies the trauma and the illness that sits there. This is the way of healing; this is the way to go. Illnesses are just that we have moved too far away from the truth of who we are. Sometimes after a session, my patients will have a cathartic process, some need to sleep, some feel fantastic, or they may also have a download. One of my patients recently said to me 'Get ready. It's time for you to talk. It's going to be big.' Then they say 'Oh, I don't know why I said that'."

M: "Do you get a sense of the greater aspect of you; what form or origin?"

Dr. B: "I just know I have done healing work for many lifetimes. I also feel that in some lifetimes I was killed because of it. I feel, however, this time, people are ready to accept and the people are coming to me because it's not working out there. They will come so shut down, not knowing what's going on, I will work on them and the light comes back in their eyes. It's like I switch them on and they feel connected to something. My receptionist said we ought to do pre and post shots of them coming in because they come in so shut down and leave looking younger, brighter and lighter. I do feel I need to get my message out and tell the medical people this – we need to be waking up the doctors. I feel things are changing rapidly now.

I have a clear idea how far I can go with each person. I am really very open and I say to them 'Your mind will not understand this but you will feel it.' I had one patient who was very 3D and he said: 'I don't believe ninety-five percent of what you say but I feel it one hundred percent, and my life has changed and I feel so much better.' My work is about feeling it: do you feel better or not! And at the end of the session because they have felt it, or gone out-of-body, and feel lighter, then they say they feel more peaceful.

I was asked how I would describe myself, and I said that I think I am a galactic DNA re-wirer. That's what I am doing: DNA upgrades and activation through galactic connection."

M: "As regards this galactic connection, do you have a sense of who these beings are or your connection to them?"

Dr. B: "I think I am a vessel for these galactic beings that work through me, but I also know that for them to work through me more powerfully, the more I am clear of my old programs the more I can activate the blueprint of my DNA. These galactic beings put something through me that changes my frequencies to bring in the healing. I also know that there are others that assist; when I put my hands on a patient I can call forth a galactic 'team' to also put hands on, to activate more energy to enhance the healing. I get assistance and I know there is also a power that comes through me.

I have not taken any drug or sleeping tablet since the death of my son and I live in peace and harmony. I am visited by Light Beings that definitely support me as part of my work. My physical body has changed as I have upgraded, for example, I feel that my hunched shoulders I had all my life are now straight. I feel there is physical rewiring. It's a process, as you can't hold these frequencies unless you are clean; you can blow circuits. I do feel this crystalline structure is coming in that matches the planetary crystalline grid line. As a cleaner vessel, I have become a conduit of this light."

It is About Helping to Bring in the New Human

"Fortunately, with the new children, they are already activated. I believe that their frequency will be so high they won't be able to shut them down as we have been. They just need to trust the feeling, what is okay and what is not; it's a visceral discernment. I recall one patient, a ten-year-old boy who was staring at me, (this was some months before the shapeshifting had fully started). He said: 'How is your face feeling on the blue being of you sitting on your right shoulder, and how is the face feeling on the purple being on your left? There is another golden one on your head. They are all you, but with a different-shaped face on each.' I thought this was amazing and this was just a kid that had come in to see me with his mum. It is amazing how these kids are aware of so much. To be able to support them is just wonderful. We are evolving at a rapid rate; we clearly needed to be catapulted into it so we could help others."

Afterword

Dr. Batchelor, M.D., comments on DNA in Chapter Fourteen, which explores the possibility that human DNA is now being activated for humanity to evolve.

"After reading the chapter on DNA, I got a deep sense, a real knowing, that this information is bringing together pieces of the puzzle that start to form a picture of our highest truth.

In each of us we have this knowing, but for some, it is yet inaccessible by the very DNA programming that has created us and is then sustained by the dense manipulation of the matrix we live in. This information is here to activate and awaken our truth. I felt I was surrounded by a bubble of energy and by high-frequency beings as I read the information in Chapter Fourteen. This indicated to me that this information is true and vital for humanity. I agree with the information that a number of off-world/alien beings has artificially modified our genetics. Some, not so benevolent, wanting humanity to remain enslaved in a limited, lower 3D reality without knowledge and connection to our divine gifts and source energy.

However, some of us have already started to have our DNA activated to overcome some of the modifications. We could be called the 'first wavers', on the leading edge of the awakening movement. We, as these 'first wavers' have already been switched on at a DNA level (as mentioned by others in this chapter), to remember our mission to embody a higher truth about humanity and to help bring in the frequencies to subsequently trigger awareness in others.

The DNA in its current state of the sleeping individual is causing disease, disharmony, dissatisfaction, and separation. This has created a mindset of greed and violence, which has led to global unrest with planetary environmental destruction and a propensity for war. The individual behavior and thinking are thus affecting us globally. This keeps us in fear and chaos and easily controlled by powerful beings (both human and off-world) with negative agendas.

The Solution: we need to awaken individuals at a DNA level by activating and upgrading our Divine DNA blueprint to bring individual harmony, leading to global peace and Universal balance. The good news is that the DNA is changing – the DNA chapter gives evidence of this. It is happening at birth for some children, to increase their consciousness and override dominant patterns and conditioning that the rest of us are subjected to. Others of us may not have received this upgrade at birth but have been switched on and activated later in life. This switching on occurs by increasing frequencies. We live in a time where increased photonic light packages from the sun, combined with benevolent galactic higher-dimensional input, has commenced the process of awakening the individual. The DNA that is being activated holds some further keys to awakening. We need to understand, as others have stated in the chapter, that some of the alien DNA that has been engineered into the human is blocking this process. This inorganic DNA acts as a receiver to further negative influences and ensures control by non-benevolent beings.

In addition, we have been tricked into carrying forward fear-based DNA patterning and programming from past life Karma and family lineage inheritance. This is further enhanced by cultural and societal influences geared towards individuals striving for acceptance and therefore sustaining the sleeping status quo. To complete the picture, we also need to be aware that there are biological, environmental and energetic negative manipulations e.g. Chemtrails, toxins, electromagnetic, low-level frequencies (EMFs) subliminal hypnotic symbolism, and much more, all ensuring we stay asleep, keeping the DNA blocked, making it harder to activate, clean and clear.

To state this more plainly, the non-benevolent manipulators of our DNA continue to influence and control us by keeping us in fear, asleep and separate, with less hope of DNA activation to a more evolved human being. The work of those of us that have overcome some of this DNA manipulation i.e., have already been activated to some extent, is to remove the negative alien influences at a DNA level and to clean off additional receivers and the additional fear-based programs.

The DNA needs to be activated. Cleaning, clearing splicing out the inorganic negative alien aspects, removing inherited patterns and negative karmic influences along with additional influences of the matrix. Upgrading the DNA to its original Divine Blueprint for innate abilities. This would allow an elevated level of joy, peace, and love, the ability to self-heal, and heal others, increased intuition and connectedness, development of higher senses like clairvoyance and clairaudience and an increased connection to a higher power, with greater wisdom and expanded awareness and knowledge, and more. A connection to the truth of who we were originally meant to be!

The DNA activation, as suggested in Chapter Fourteen, is brought about by frequency. The first wave of individuals, including the new children and the light workers already activated on the planet, can help bring in the necessary frequencies. The DNA can be altered by frequencies held in symbols, sacred geometry, artwork, music, mantras, light language and by transmission through high-vibrational counseling, information and touch. All of this is becoming available by those of us capable of embodying higher frequencies and acting as conduits of this high-frequency galactic light.

We also need to be aware of the negative side of some of these modalities. Lower vibrational forms (e.g. symbols, art, music, entertainment, media) are used purposely to keep us asleep. Working in 3D and in higher dimensions, the DNA can be upgraded. As mentioned, pieces of the inorganic alien DNA, additional receivers (toxins and parasites, etc.) and inherited DNA imprints (both individual karmic and family patterning) can be cleared and upgraded. This clears the physical, emotional and energetic body, bringing forth the New Awakened Human. The newly awakened human, as a collective, can provide the tipping point towards the restoration of the planetary balance and harmony and subsequent survival of the human species on the Earth. The benevolent galactic beings supporting this movement toward awakening are working very hard on a DNA level to assist humanity with this."

The Book *Awakening*

"I also wanted to say about your book *Awakening*. As I read it, I received further activations, symbols and some of my techniques got downloaded to me. I would read *Awakening*, and close my eyes and get downloaded symbols I now use over people. I also picked up techniques where I should be tapping some part of the body. This all happened while I closed my eyes while I was reading something in *Awakening*. Your first book *Awakening* was definitely an 'activator.' Some really clear information came through. I also recommend it to my patients. I feel that if it is too 'out there', that's okay, I am planting a seed. I feel obliged to get this out. My patients need to become open and be able to cope with reading your book. This is real – this is what we are talking about.

I am on your team. I have things to say because it's time to step up."

Dr. Maree Batchelor worked in mainstream medicine as a GP (family doctor) for over twenty years. As well as her medical degree, she has a Diploma of Obstetrics and Gynaecology and is a Fellow of the Royal Australian College of General Practitioners.

She is also a mother of five children. After the tragic death of her son in 2008, she experienced an awakening and went on to study and practice with a holistic approach to her patients. Spiritual counseling, meditative self-inquiry, and energy healing formed the basis of her practice.

A further profound experience in India, in 2014, propelled her even deeper into the realms of energy medicine and the holographic field. Now, using embodied light frequencies, she removes behavioral triggers and energetic blocks from a patient's physical, emotional and energetic body. Working as deeply as the DNA level to clean, clear and activate full potential. This releases past life karma and trauma, dysfunctional family lineage patterns and the effects of the conditioned matrix we all live in today. Her work is multidimensional and consists of energetic counseling and hands-on healing. The relief from her sessions, both in person and by Skype, is life changing.

Postscript

I believe what Dr. Batchelor describes of her work is similar to what is described by indigenous people as a form of shamanic healing.

In my YouTube presentations, I share the numerous strategies these non-human intelligences work with to bring in the frequencies, which appear to be instrumental in the activation of our DNA. These frequencies may be in the form of artwork, 'star languages', scripts, music, symbols, etc., and new models of 'intuitive energy' work. The sound frequencies have the ability to heal, according to the many accounts by those working with a shamanic model. There are many similarities to Dr. Batchelor's description of her healing modality and how she understands her ability to bring in the energy and frequencies, with a specific focus on the activation and healing of the DNA.

The parallels to Dr. Batchelor's work can be viewed in the ACERN DVD *Expressions of ET Contact: A Communication and Healing Blueprint?* (2004.) Experiencers share their stories. For example, Rochelle D' Elia speaks about her model of healing and the frequencies she believes she brings through with her star language (Light language), with specific movements. She states, 'I act as an ET surgeon, I work to 're-tune. I bring in the frequencies most needed at the time and as I see the problem in the energy field, I bring in sound, color, and symbols, as we are multidimensional in nature.' This DVD also shares some of Adrian D'Vir's stories of his experiences working with extraterrestrials in a multidimensional space, similar to Dr. Batchelor's understanding.

I have mentioned in my presentations that what may be occurring in scientific terms through this process may be understood by Russian Research. In *Vernetzte Intelligenz* (Networked Intelligence), authors Von Grayzyna Fosar and Franz Bludorf show how scientists and linguists prove DNA can be influenced and re-programmed by words and frequencies without cutting out or replacing single genes. They have discovered DNA is like a holographic computer, and information can be transmitted by vibration and frequency called wave genetics. DNA causes disturbing patterns in a vacuum, producing magnetized wormholes, tunnel connections between entirely different areas of the Universe, through which information can be transmitted through space and time. DNA attracts information and passes it into our consciousness. This process of hyper-communication is most effective in a state of relaxation. The book offers a compelling scientific explanation to how results occur when a healer works with frequencies on the energetic and biological body.

Simon Harvey-Wilson, in his 2000 thesis *Shamanism and Abductions: A Comparative Study*, demonstrated the amazing parallels between Shamanic experiences and Abduction experiences, which appear to have identical outcomes, such as healing abilities, the ability to operate in multidimensional realities, transformation of the individual.

Ref: Simon Harvey Wilson – Edith Cowen University,

Shamanism and Abductions: A Comparative Study, Western Australia 2000.

The Holographic Universe

Researchers from a number of scientific disciplines within China's universities have studied unexplainable phenomena in a unique group of people with 'Exceptional Human Functions' (EHF).

"The results of the Chinese Teleportation experiments are explained as a human consciousness phenomenon that somehow acts to move or rotate test specimens through a 4th spacial dimension, so that specimens are able to penetrate the solid walls/barriers of their containers without physically breaching them."

Source: Eric Davis, PhD FBIS.
The Effects of 'QI Energy' On Plant DNA & Cellular Growth
http://alternativenewsproject.org/newsletter-rss/article/consciousness/scientists-witness-woman-with-exceptional-powers-rapidly-grow-a-plant-from-a-seed/

"Chulin Sun is a woman with exceptional powers (Shen and Sun, 1996, 1998; Sun, 1998). A member of the Chinese Somatic Science Research Institute, she is a practitioner of Waiqi. Waiqi is a type of qigong that teaches the practitioner to bring the qi energy of traditional Chinese medicine under the control of the mind. Chulin Sun can induce plant seeds to grow shoots and roots several cms long within twenty minutes using mentally projected qi energy. This has been demonstrated on one hundred and eighty different occasions at universities as well as science and research institutions in China (including Taiwan and Hong Kong), as well as other countries (e.g., Japan, Thailand, Malaysia, etc.) (Ge et al., 1998; Qin et al., 1998; Lee et al., 1999). 'We took part in and repeated the qi germination experiments seven times, and five of them succeeded' (Ge et al., 1998). This remarkable effect on seed development has drawn widespread attention (Tompkins and Bird, 1973; Lee, 1998)."

According to Danielle Graham, a founding editor and current Editor-in-Chief of *SuperConsciousness Magazine* (also an American Institute of Physics experimental researcher), those who study the physical effects of the EHFs mind-matter interface often collaborate on their findings. The researchers agree they are observing repeatable, hyper-time-space-non-linear macro phenomena that violate the classical and relativistic models in which the nature of physical matter is currently understood.

It is commonly understood by these scientists that an EHF's personal and individual evolution is directly linked to their individual skills; the greater their capacity to manipulate matter; the more spiritually evolved the EHF is considered to be. In China, those individuals with known EHF's are honored as heroes and celebrities; national treasures that are sought after as teachers, advisors, and consultants.

There is no doubt that the more evolved we, as a species, become, the more abilities and heightened awareness of our multidimensional reality we will develop and, it appears, our ability to manipulate it.

Chapter Twenty

INTER-DIMENSIONAL TRAVELERS

Out-of-body Multidimensional Journeys

Julia and Michael

Julia was born in Slovakia (lived in ex-USSR, Russia, and Germany) and is the author of *I Have Seen It Tomorrow* (*Videl Som to Zajtra*). This extraordinary book explores multidimensional out-of-body experiences. I believe her understanding and that of her husband, Michael, is an important perspective on understanding the range of human encounters with nonhuman intelligences. It is important, as many of those who experience encounters do so in an out-of-body state, not only physically. In FREE, recent surveys have shown that OBEs were prevalent in over eighty percent of extraterrestrial experiences. It highlights how this information is significant, and it is clear that if we are to explore the full range of multidimensional complexity in human encounters, then what is experienced in the out-of-body state is vital to this understanding. Julia and Michael have ongoing conscious recall of their out-of-body experiences, which offers us unique insight into the OBE. Their descriptions are of what it feels like and how they understand it. The communication with the Nonhuman Intelligences (NHIs) and the information they receive and discovered during these experiences is, I believe, profound and deserves attention. It offers a unique perspective in terms of the nature of reality, other worlds, dimensions and the nature of consciousness, which is fascinating.

I am delighted they have agreed to work with FREE in terms of this information as they offer intriguing perspectives on the holographic nature of reality, which will offer unique insight and assist research in the nature of human consciousness and reality itself.

It was compelling that some of Michael's OBEs were identical and corroborated information in some of the earlier chapters in this book.

Ref: *Videl Som To Zajtra* by Julia Sellers,
Slovakia, Ludoprint, a.s., 2015. www.juliasellers.sk

Julia: "I am currently a lecturer on OBEs in the Czech Republic and Slovakia. OBEs are the main topic of my expertise. I am a dual citizen (USA/Slovakia), currently living in Slovakia. Part of my family (including Michael), live currently in the USA.

I have experienced OBEs since 1995, and it first occurred when I was twenty-five. During this time, I believe it involved Contact with nonhuman intelligence guiding me in my dreams, and explaining to me different scientific theories, such as gravity, anti-gravity, or how a human body functions, to a point that they tried to transform/ transfigure my body on what I believe was a deeper molecular or atomic level.

My husband, Michael, has experienced OBEs for forty years. In fact, all the time I have known him; I have observed his out-of-body experiences. I was particularly interested because of my own OBEs, which began twenty years ago. However, Michael has had OBEs since birth, with a conscious birth recall of the prenatal stage in the uterus of his mother. It is important to say that Michael's OBEs occur not just in a sleep state, or lucid dreaming, hypnagogia, astral projection, REM micro sleep, etc., but are experienced with full consciousness. I also believe it is extraordinary that he can be out-of-body for half a day or more. It appears that Michael often finds it difficult to keep himself in his body or grounded, and sometimes it is hard for him to get back into his body afterward.

I can tell when Michael is out-of-body by his body movements and his eyes. When out-of-body, he moves like a robot and can lose his balance. Furthermore, when out-of-body he has a hard time writing, as his muscles are relaxed (to the point where it is hard for him to hold a pen). Plus, he has difficulty expressing himself. He can be out-of-body for many hours, even half the day. He is traveling through different dimensions, galaxies and he is able to perceive pictures and flashes from the past/ future of any person he focuses on. He is able to describe in a great detail how, for instance, a murder took place; he would see it in his mind, like a movie which is sometimes in black and white, sometimes in color. He is able to be out of his body and literally present at the scene while watching how everything happened.

Michael's abilities were accessed in 1998, by a 'government' to help to solve a murder. This is not remote viewing (RV), but a real out-of-body experience. However, he can remote view, communicate with animals, the deceased, toddlers, newborn and babies not yet born, still in their prenatal stage. He can retrieve information from walls, doors, woods, trees, and pieces of furniture, stones, crystals, and plants. In fact, any material that is not plastic."

Synaesthesia

Julia: "He also experiences synaesthesia. When he listens to music or any sound, he will perceive colors, as well as geometrical forms attached to it. He will perceive form in words, and each syllable has a form for him as well as color, and each letter has a different vibration. He can smell vibrations; different vibrations will smell different, just as different emotions smell differently. For example, anger smells very much different to joy."

The Mission and Contact with Nonhuman Intelligences (NHI)

Julia: "In my book, *I Have Seen It Tomorrow*, there are first-hand accounts of Michael's OBEs and inter-dimensional travel. I believe this ability has given him a unique insight into science theories behind the OBE phenomenon as well as detailed descriptions of what can be seen/perceived during those experiences; places one can visit, such as planets, the Moon, the core of Earth, etc. He recalls his past lives, natal and prenatal, and so-called 'conscious birth'. Since his birth, he has been in Contact with certain types of NHIs (Nonhuman Intelligences), which he believes sent him to Earth with an important mission. They have always directed his life and his mission here. The NHIs appear like plasma with different geometrical shapes and appear to be full of light. They have no physical form and their light has an audible and inaudible vibrational sound spectra attached.

Part of Michael's mission is to have three children because they would be carriers of special genes and they too will have special missions important for the future of Earth. Another part of Michael's mission is in regards to energy grid alignment in certain regions of the world (especially the Ukraine and surrounding area). Michael's traveling OBEs to the above-mentioned region achieve this, and the releasing of his energies into the ground, where it is picked up by the Earth grid directly."

Inter-Dimensions Past and Future

Julia: "When my husband is visiting a certain place or just passing or going through a certain place, he can go back in time and perceives whatever was happening at this place in the past.

For instance, when we were visiting a castle (during a sightseeing tour) he was able to see, both via RV and out-of-body state, what had taken place in a particular room in that castle a couple of hundred years ago. He is able to describe what the people looked like, what they wore, what they were doing, etc.

In 2000, Michael and I were going up the stairs in an old apartment building in Europe. While walking up the stairs, Michael behaved like he was trying to make space for people coming down the stairs near us; the staircase was very narrow. He moved towards the wall as if letting people walk past him. I asked him what he was doing, and he said he was making space for German SS officers in uniforms, heading down the stairs. He said that they were not able to see us; they passed straight through us, so to speak. This incident suggested that Michael went back in time and was able to perceive both the current time flow (which was us walking up the stairs) as well as the past event, which took place some time back during WWII when these German officers were coming down the stairs.

I have inquired about this building after this incident and I learned this building used to house German SS officers during WWII."

Michael Tells His Story

Michael: "I have had OBEs and paranormal experiences for as long as I can remember, even as a toddler. My OBEs occur every day; sometimes more often, sometimes less, depending on the weather, season or my emotional state. I even remember being in my mother's uterus, how it felt, the sounds, colors, and surroundings. I also remember many of my past lives, including one in Egypt.

When I am out-of-body and when I don't allow myself to fly away, so to speak, I would see my body below me, but there is no form attached to it. When you are out-of-body, it feels like being in the body, but the surroundings are very, very different. You can hear what is taking place behind walls; you can travel through walls or doors; you can see from all directions at once, and hear what is happening in the distance. When out-of-body, a part of your energy quantum extends out of the body and into space. When I felt like traveling, I would just leave my body and wander around. I can wander anywhere, such as different countries, dimensions, and galaxies. Basically, any place I want to explore I can go there. I have explored Mars and discovered that there was running water on Mars a long time ago. I learned this before NASA did; they only published the news about this a few years ago. There are also certain types of bugs on Mars.

I can perceive different beings, all the time, whether it is different apparitions filled with light or if they are pure light, or just colors, shapes, different sounds. I can communicate to color as well. I can see past and future all the time, not only mine but other people's. I see a far-distant past when the Earth was being created; the dinosaurs, volcanoes erupting, etc."

OBE and Remote Viewing

Michael: "When out of my body, it feels like I am physically present. I am part of the scene for real; it is multi-dimensional. I am not just an onlooker or an observer, but a participant. When I leave my body, I leave the 3D and exist in a quantum of energy, which is not dense like physical matter. This non-physical quantum of energy is able to pass through walls, doors or dense matter. It is far less dense than physical matter. Its oscillations change to vibration; EM waves, changing to scalar, electromagnetic longitudinal tone waves; cold plasma: direct vibrational cognition, which is made of the so-called standing waves. Everything is feeling-based at its core; feeling is sound-based. Vibration is feeling-based; oscillation is light-based. First, it was vibration (sound) and only out of sound, light was born. Light is an oscillation, so sound and light interchange always. But it is the feeling which is important. Sound is feeling and feeling is vibration and it is vibration that matters; it is feeling that matters; light comes later on. Light is an EM wave, so are thoughts and emotions. Emotions are not feelings; they are EM waves, while feelings are mechanical sound waves. So basically, if you want to get to the heart of the matter, you have to go through feelings (through sound, mostly infrasound and ultrasound). Emotions and thoughts are light-based (EM) and they are not real feelings, so to speak.

Remote Viewing (RV), however, does not involve real experiences in the way the OBE is experienced. RV is more like you are watching a movie; you are not present at the scene, and you watch it on the screen, as it were.

However, when you are out-of-body, you really know you are because the surroundings look very different, smell different, feel different, and your hearing sense is different. When you are out-of-body you feel the three-dimensionality, except it is more than 3D, it is multidimensional. You are able to perceive with three-hundred-and-fifty-degree vision and hear what is going on in the street, apartment or building simultaneously. It is like you expand into space; your quantum of energy or consciousness pours into the space around you.

When I have an OBE, I experience and live through everything that will happen in the near future. For instance, if my wife and I are in town and we haven't decided to have lunch, I know about it prior to it happening. I will have the lunch out-of-body fifteen minutes prior to the actual lunch in the physical body, which means I feel the taste of the food and experience it with my senses prior to physically eating it. So I actually live through the whole future event prior to it happening.

I discovered that the past, as such, is not fixed; it can be changed because it does not exist separately. It is a part of the present, as is the future, so both could be changed with intense feeling-based intention directed at whatever you wish to change. However, sometimes when the future passes over a certain color horizon (color being EM light), meaning a certain EM wavelength, the future becomes fixed and there is no way you can change it by directing your own vibrations (feeling-based) to the object or matter which you wish to change. If the situation, the thoughts and feelings involved in the situation, are vibrating above orange color (on the spectrum of the visible light EM oscillations) it is not possible to change the situation and/or your future, so to speak.

When out-of-body, you don't need physical eyes because you can see by touch, smell, taste. You can feel the shape of objects at a distance. For example, if something is round or square, you feel the shape at a distance while out-of-body; at the same time, you can taste whatever you are looking at; you can hear it too because every object has its own sound/vibration, whether it is a hum or whatever sound, including infra and ultra-vibrations. Basically, every object has its own internal vibration, a signature. At the same time, you can get a feeling of how dense the object may be that you are observing: whether it is soft or hard. You don't have to touch it; you can touch at a distance, as it were, so no matter how far away you are from the object when out-of-body, you can touch it at a distance, smell it at a distance, hear it at a distance, and feel its shape at a distance. Occasionally, I have problems with my eyes when I am here on Earth. I can't read through my eyes. I read through touch and feel and thought. I only am able to type through the shape of air and thought. When out-of-body, it is not a problem. When I come back to Earth I may walk into a wall because I am not sure what to do; my physical eyes become a problem for me.

Furthermore, when returning back to my body I have gone backward in time, so while out-of-body I am in the future, as it were. When returning back to my body, I am returning back to the present. All the time when out-of-body my aura extends into space and I don't have to physically see the object, I feel it with my extended aura or energy quantum. I don't have to see with physical eyes because I can see with my aura and energy, which does the touching, feeling, seeing, hearing and smelling for me. When you leave your body, your weight changes, as a quantum of energy leaves your body. When you are back to being physical, your weight changes again. Out-of-body your weight changes because the energy quantum extends behind the boundary of your body into space. Energy is weight; energy is mass and mass is energy, and the difference is in potential.

Sometimes, I have a difficult time coming back to my body. Sometimes, you can return to your body whenever you want to. Sometimes, if you are far away, it is harder somehow. It is being directed automatically. There appears to be some kind of self-regulated process when it comes to returning back to the body. If you go into the astral (lower dimensions, 4D or whatever) it is easy to go back. The higher you go, however, the deeper you go, the more complicated it gets. Sometimes, when on a mission, I am directed by beings of what I would call light and color, for the lack of better words. The higher you are, the less dense the matter gets, coming all the way to pure light and color and sound (in the form of waves).

Remote viewing feels totally different to the OBE. When out-of-body you experience everything for real. For example, if you are out-of-body watching someone being killed, if you are close enough to the person you can feel blood springing out of the dying person's body. After the person dies, you see his signatures leaving the body. It is the part of the energy quantum that does not die; it just gets out-of-body after death in a signature-like form; I think some people might call it a soul or a spirit."

Ref: *I Have Seen It Tomorrow* (*Videl Som To Zajtra*) (Excerpt).

Expansion of Michael's Description of His OBE Travels

Michael: "When I am out-of-body, my orientation relies solely on extrasensory perception. I orient myself through touching at a distance. It is similar to experiencing heightened vibrations of feeling. The energy quantum that leaves my body, or rather extends beyond its physical boundaries, spreads in the area, and with the help of feelings can describe at a distance any person or object observed. It's a principle similar to an animal, which does not see at night and yet can navigate its body. Vibratory oscillation energy, (which is a part of my body, but is, at the same time, extended into the broader space/time area), has the ability to cover my vision, touch, taste, hearing, feeling and the sense of smell. The physical eyes, ears, nose, tongue and skin don't have to be used when you achieve a particular vibrational-oscillation pulse within your body. You are suddenly hooked on a resonance, which helps you to enter a higher rhythm, which has the ability to uncover the world of extrasensory perception for you."

Multidimensional Communication, Symbols, and Geometric Forms

Michael: "I am able to reveal information on many topics. However, people do not know how to communicate with me at the level of my mind, which is telepathic. I could teach people a variety of new scientific theories as well as explain them. My problem, however, is that the regular words of my language can't convey the information easily. I am only able to express basic ideas or supporting points of the topic. I see all information in one indivisible whole unit via symbols, geometric shapes, colors, and radiation. What I perceive sometimes cannot sufficiently be expressed in terms of a language. The core ideas on certain topics that I have stored in my body, nobody can read or retrieve in any way. The information and knowledge are not being stored in the brain. The information I am downloading has nothing to do with the brain. It comes and is stored inside my body and in my spirit, my inner being. OBEs have been part of my life, even as a toddler. Sometimes, I will leave my body for extended periods, even days. Sometimes, I leave the body very quickly and easily. I leave at will. Occasionally, I may leave my body against my will. I am pulled out-of-body automatically and unexpectedly. Many times I am drawn out-of-body into situations I do not want to observe or know about. Those situations might include stressful, unwanted or graphic content.

Occasionally, I have a problem returning into my body, but at other times I get back into the body smoothly and automatically. It seems that returning back into the body is managed by some kind of mechanism. Sometimes, I clearly know I am back in the body, but it feels as if I did not return to it completely, for whatever reason. It feels as if a certain portion of quantum energy is left beyond the borders of the physical body. When this happens, I suffer from what I call a time-delay, in the amount of a couple of minutes. I see things happening on the nonphysical plane several minutes before they happen in the 3D physical reality. Sometimes, I see them happening many hours, days, years prior. Sometimes, I see situations from the past, which happened hours ago, days ago, years ago, even eons ago."

Space/Time

Michael: "In the OBE state, neither time nor space exists, information is instant telepathic thought via EM radiation, skin, internal organs, taste, auditory, olfactory receptors, or through different electrical twinges in different parts of my body, such as palms, chest, neck, etc., which can serve as 'yes' or 'no' answers if correctly interpreted. There are different types of extended states of consciousness, which include the following: deep meditation, lucid dreaming, hypnagogia, déjà vu, REM micro sleep, astral projection, OBE when sleeping, OBE under full consciousness. When in an expanded state of consciousness, you leave the time/space domain; you perceive on a higher quantum-holographic-level where everything is connected; observer and observed are the same. They are united into an inseparable whole. You are able to perceive the past, present, and future going on at the same time. You get into a realm where the effect comes prior to the cause. You don't use physical eyes, but perceive with your third eye: pituitary gland, or receive information via other means, such as channeling, direct vibrational cognition, skin, internal organs.

When having an OBE, the whole left part of the brain shuts down, while the right part, responsible for understanding symbols, intuition, and whole vision, so to speak, takes over. At a certain level of out-of-body, you view and perceive via your third eye (the inner vision); you enjoy the so-called three-hundred-and-sixty-degree vision; hear through walls. Even get info through skin receptors or taste, auditory and olfactory receptors within your body. Furthermore, the pineal gland, thalamus, pituitary gland and even thymus gland play a role in expanded states of consciousness. If you go deep enough and are able to enter a theta state of mindwaves as part of your expanded state of consciousness, you can not only remote view but also remote interact and remote influence. Connect to the level of quantum holography/nonlocality, and you can influence the past as well as the future via the present moment because, at this level, the past, future, and present become one."

Note: Remote influencing as well as remote interaction on other than a physical level is heavily misused by the secret services of the world powers.

Michael: "When in a state of expanded consciousness and out-of-body, you are unable to speak in words and language (the left part of the brain is responsible for this) and are only able to interpret in symbols, pictures and images. For example, when in this state of mind, information consisting of, say, ten pages, written in words, can be shortened into one symbol or picture. Also, when in this state of mind, intuitive and sensory abilities activate."

Note: This understanding is identical to those who draw the symbols. They explain that just one symbol contains compressed files of information.

Julia: "An international authority on the paranormal and altered states of consciousness stated the following about Michael's state of consciousness when remote viewing out-of-body."

"A lot of other things tell me that his limbic system is 'taking charge' or 'taking over' from the two brain hemispheres. He's still human, but beginning to operate better at a higher frequency than what is normal. It's almost as if Michael is becoming pure consciousness. I am certain the people you contacted will have their own opinions to offer after they have tested him. During those tests, have them really investigate how his limbic and reticular activating system is doing. Sounds to me like both have flipped into a totally different mode or frequency. Consciousness in the form of holographic standing waves (scalars) runs through the whole body, not just the brain."

Quantum Future Running the Dense 3D Present

Julia: "Michael experiences three levels of reality: The reality in a non-physical form, which happens prior to reality in the physical form, i.e., the dense matter form as we know it. This means that prior to physical reality, there exists the so-called non-matter, or quantum reality, which orchestrates the physical reality, the 3D world. The 3D world does not exist, according to Michael. It is a construct of our own mind; everything is flat, including all information.

Our present and the now moment is determined or run by the future, so to speak, or rather it is coming out of the future. This, however, violates the law of causality. Michael, in his everyday life, lives two different realities. First is the non-physical reality happening at a subconscious or future, quantum level. The second is the dense physical reality, and the same as the first non-physical reality, except it happens in the 3D structure, as perceived by the mind. Michael lives through and perceives the physical matter, the 3D structure, only after he first experiences it through the non-physical reality out-of-body state. He experiences the same events twice, as it were. First time on the non-physical level, and the second time in our physical reality 3D structure. In Michael's words, 'I live my life backward. I live it first in the future, then backward to the present.'

Michael is actually coming back to the present directly from the future. This is what Michael says about eating bread out-of-body in the future and then physically buying it in the shop while being in the physical body: 'I did not move anywhere. I simply ate the bread first out-of-body, then, later, I went to the shop and bought it'."

Time Does Not Exist in Space – Forward and Backward is Equal

Julia: "Michael, out-of-body, travels both in the past and the future. In effect, he lives in the future most of the time. While out of his body, he experiences what happens in the future and then when he returns to his body, he would repeat the experience in his physical, 3D reality. All out-of-body experiences are basically different levels of extended modes of consciousness. Our consciousness is made of scalar waves, which extend into outer space-time. Some individuals can go out-of-body fully awake, and can function out-of-body and also perform other activities in real time. Michael visits his future in the out-of-body state. When he comes back into real time, he will live the 3D reality he had perceived in his out-of-body state."

Communication with Nonhuman Intelligences (NHI)

Julia: "Michael talks about being in touch with three beings of light/color. He calls them ITS. The colors he perceives are golden, turquoise, and violet.

These nonhuman intelligences do not have physical bodies or contours but are forms of energy, neither male nor female. The beings of light are geometric forms with different sound/vibration, either audible or inaudible. Light and color are basically made of electromagnetic waves. Certain frequencies or wavelengths of electromagnetic radiation appear to the human eye as colors. But there are many colors the human eye cannot perceive, although Michael can perceive them; wavelengths may appear as a single color.

The ITS appear like moving, shimmering, bright colors of geometry, similar to plasma spider-web substance, also like bubbles or amorphous shapes without contour: a type of plasma, vibrating in different sacred geometric shapes that are a form of direct consciousness. The being that Michael communicates with the most looks magenta purple with shades of red and yellow in its center. Sometimes, he communicates with a being of white with shades of silver gray in its middle.

Since the beings have colors that do not exist on Earth, it's difficult for Michael to describe them. They communicate telepathically, and the information spreads out of the time-framework. When communicating with them, Michael feels he is part of them and they are part of him. The beings think and experience at the same moment, as does Michael with them. There is no boundary of time or space; they are united and Michael says there are no words to describe this communion.

These beings do not have names, only a specific energy signature. A name is based on waves of energy. Any energy form, wave or frequency has its own signature; it possesses its own form and shape. Its frequency gives off a specific form. Out of form, different names arise. The name is a form of language and has its own function; the form cannot be separated from its function. For example, a form of a hexagon has a different function than the pentagon. The forms of hexagon and tetrahedron cure, reunite and add balance and harmony. The pentagon, for example, has an important role in the process of materialization (creation or the emergence of mass from antimatter). The Universe has its own architecture, orchestrated by high-dimensional entities composed of shades of color, light, and audible and inaudible sound vibration, and higher forms of intelligence. Different entities govern and are responsible for, different aspects of the overall architecture of the Universe. The nonhuman intelligences transmit information and instructions to selected people on Earth, with respect to the future processes of our planet, and solar system. This is done via meetings, where several hundred people from Earth, in an OBE state, participate. These are mandatory, as important topics are discussed there, relating to the future and development of Earth.

Michael's nonhuman friends send him in his OBE state, and sometimes physically, on missions to various places on the planet. The purpose is to transfer a specific energy frequency into a physical location: ground, and soil, as well as to specific people, to transfer constructive energy to change a situation for the better. For example, Michael was given an assignment in one unnamed country to go there physically and disseminate his energy in the Southern part of this region. By so doing, his energy will go further to reach the people the energy was intended for in the first place. Sometimes, Michael is sent on special missions, which involve collecting the energy of special stones."

Michael said: "I was working and collecting the energy of special stones. I am sucked of all my energy. I just managed to get home. Stones are a source of rare elements in the universe. Higher beings of light and sound feed off it."

Communication Through Color

Julia: "Purple is an excellent color for healing. Purple is the color associated with happiness and is a big, positive energy in the universe. Purple light contains sound; color is sound, the whole EM spectrum contains sound and, depending on the ratio of sound contained within the EM spectrum, we get different modes of light and EM radiation. Light and sound are intertwined; they are of the same nature; they are one, but in different modalities and even in places that sound does not travel, sound still exists.

You don't need a channel for sound to exist, but you need a channel for the sound to be detected as sound because sound, as vibration, is audible or inaudible, the vibrations are everywhere. Sound, without a channel, is in a frozen, still state.

Communication with NHI beings is through color and wind, not sound. Sound is for animals. Sound is magnetic. Wind (especially solar wind) is sound/vibration as well, but with an electric component in it. So basically, it is a color as well.

Sound in the form of communication is a lower level of communication. The higher levels of communication are color and intergalactic wind. Thought is instantaneous and is sound turned into light. Color/light is the primary channel for this communication. Time does not exist in space; forward and backward is an equal shape. Sometimes, communication which occurs with other human beings will not be in real time. The person may not have been born, but the energy form communication in the future or the past may exist before the person is born. It is possible to speak with a person and they are not born yet or have died many years ago.

Colors have different weight, although this is only a potential weight (mass). However, when you are out-of-body you can feel the potential weight of color as real mass, as mass experienced in 3D and the physical body. This means that if photons, which are EM waves, spin a certain way, a certain spin is required. They turn into denser matter. Those light photons will eventually become mass. On the other hand, if photons change their spin they can become subatomic particles, which can pass through matter. So when Michael is out-of-body, he can feel the potential mass of different colors of the EM spectrum as if it was real, as if he could weigh it in his hand. It is possible, through mind, to interact with colors to change them into another color. Therefore, mass and energy are one and the same at its core."

Consciousness, Intention and the Paranormal

Julia: "Matter comes into being through plasma standing waves, which become liquid light, ether, semi-ether, into denser structures of matter, all the way to the 3D matter as we know it in our dimension. Human consciousness can change the future under certain conditions. You can only achieve order out of chaos. Entropy is governed by syntropy (negates entropy), and it is syntropy which runs the initial conditions. We operate from the future. The future, which is the past, and similarly the beginning and end, starts at the same point; beginning and end are one and the same.

Solar activity, the phases of the Moon, have effects on any paranormal activities, such as remote viewing, out-of-body, lucid dreaming and astral travel, near death experience; even the weather: if it is cloudy, sunny, raining, thunder or lighting, and even seasons. Personal mood, feelings, the state of mind as well as of the people who are around, will affect the paranormal activity of others. This, combined with the state of mind as an observer, which can alter the outcome of what is observed. Intention, as well as attention, affects what you try to influence, remote view, manifest, de-manifest or observe. Your consciousness on a quantum level is entangled with what you observe, so the outcome depends on the level of intention, the amplitude of the standing wave you co-resonantly produce, with attention and the state of your mind.

Observer and observed is one and the same. You can use tension in muscles to predict the future. You can also use skin receptors to predict the future. There are certain receptors in your bones, in bone marrow, which are sensitive to specific vibration and can be used to predict future and other information. The same goes for tongue receptors, and smell and scent receptors; they can be used for drawing out information on a paper or directly into your mind. Furthermore, with the help of other receptors within your body, you can detect and decode various information with your nose, tongue, skin, blood, bone marrow, different internal organs or different parts of your body, such as palms, feet, chest, shoulders, lower abdominal, etc. Theta waves work the best for getting your mind into a state under which you can easily perform different paranormal activities. Theta waves are produced in half-dream states, lucid dreaming, hypnagogic states, REM micro sleep, and when out-of-body or near death. There are different levels of theta waves, from 4 to 7 Hz, but at a certain level of theta waves you can not only remote view, but also remote interact (remote influence) with objects and people at a distance, and by so doing change past as well as future.

Brainwaves are not only produced by the brain, but throughout the whole of the body. Consciousness spreads through the whole body and you can download information through your intestines, your palms, and certain other parts of your body, as indicated earlier. To induce a theta-level state in your body, the theta waves operate throughout the whole body. Natural empaths or psychics can be born with this ability and easily move between alpha or beta states into the theta state, and some even to delta-wave states. For example, Michael spends many hours a day in theta. The theta state gives you an opportunity to work on the quantum holographic level where everything is connected. When getting out-of-body by different techniques or technologies, or by using drugs, resulting in theta induction, you have to be cautious. Your light body, scalar-frequency body on a higher level is connected to your physical body and will be unprotected, as your OBE, theta state or other expanded mode of consciousness is artificially-induced by the above-mentioned technologies, and so it can make you vulnerable to astral attack."

Expanded Consciousness

Julia: "Human consciousness can be expanded naturally or artificially via drugs, and other techniques. The base-pulse rhythm of vibration behind an unnatural expansion of consciousness will feel very different when compared with the base-pulse rhythm produced by feelings of so-called, unconditional love. This is when the consciousness expands naturally, just by the production of feelings based on love, mercy, forgiveness, and gratitude. I believe that artificial expansion of consciousness can be detrimental. Spirits, entities, different frequencies around you are automatically attracted to your base-pulse rhythm. Each human being pulses on a different base-pulse rhythm. Sometimes, your frequencies can couple with frequencies around you and strange things can occur.

Energy takes different forms: visual, sound, infrasound and ultrasound included, as well as white noise, taste, smell or touch via skin detectors. All depends on the vibratory oscillation rate the energy pulses on. Sometimes, in expanded modes of consciousness, individuals are able not only to hear the sound, but also see the color of the sound, see the geometrical shape of the sound, smell and taste the sound. All depends on the frequency level your consciousness is able to work at. Each and every frequency has sound, color, shape, and smell. Some frequencies communicate via special detectors in the skin, which are directly connected to osteocytes in bones, which direct the functions of bone marrow and blood formation at the same time. Blood, for instance, is a gateway to antimatter, which in turns leads directly to the so-called dark matter. The dark matter runs the formation of the universe as well as our human body, based on the 'as above, so below' principle. It is undetectable by an artificial apparatus, but can be detected by human consciousness."

Blood as the Bridge Between the Realm of Physical Matter and the Spiritual Realm

Julia: "The blood is a bridge between physical matter and spirit. It is the boundary which, when crossed (providing you reach a certain vibrational frequency), your physical body will undergo certain physical, chemical, biological changes on a deep atomic and molecular level. If the vibrational pulsing of your physical body continues to vibrate higher and higher, loss of sexual desire will follow, you stop eating and finally becoming a breatharian (surviving on nothing but air). The last phase of transformation means the person no longer needs to sleep. These are not the only changes your body undergoes when changes take place in your in blood chemistry based on co-resonant vibration, strengthened by feelings of peace, unity, love, etc. If you attain this level, then, suddenly, you will be able to tune into the vibrational field of knowledge and information, which was not previously available, such as information on the future. You, basically, just request information in your mind and the information is instantly available. Information is based on vibrations of sound/ feelings, as opposed to oscillations which are light-based. Living consciousness is associated with love in its purity; love in its perfection, in its eternity, which has

341

nothing to do with our earthly physical love

Pure love is connected to feelings, not emotion. Feelings are vibration-based, and emotions are electromagnetically-based. At the core of inner feeling there is vibration, and if the vibrations are audible, there is sound. So, inner feelings, including love, are vibration/sound-based. This means vibration mixed with electrical sound, which is a longitudinal standing spherical, non-Hertzian, nonlinear compression (sine) wave, which constitutes direct cognition/visions of the future, based on vibrational-resonance information, rather than EM-light information. Love is the living consciousness and each human being has the ability to become unconditional love, because the human body is able to vibrate the same characteristics/imprints that love enjoys, when understood from the perspective of physics. It is a standing wave, which operates via resonance, which means it never ends vibrating; it continues manifesting and de-manifesting (pushing and pulling). Better yet, it vibrates in direct pulses or quanta. If you become this wave called love, you can materialize and dematerialize at will and transfigure the cells in your body, which involves cell cytoplasm and the cytoskeleton acting on, and directly affecting, the DNA in the cell, which, under this influence, is able to transform on the molecular level, as well as the atomic level and beyond. The cytoskeleton of the cell, under certain conditions, is influenced by your inner feelings and gravity. So you can influence your own DNA and influence gravity directly, by producing certain vibrations. The feelings of unconditional love/unity/ universal connection can transcend gravity and the body can levitate. You will have access to future events by tapping into this vibrational field of information where past, present and future blends together."

Intention is Key

Julia: "If human intention is magnetically intense enough, it can cause transformation of one form of energy into another and materialization occurs. It is all about the depth of a feeling-based intention. If this is high enough, part of your consciousness automatically crosses over the speed of light and materialization, or dematerialization occurs. If the intensity of your intention, the vibration oscillatory rate based on resonance your cell cytoplasm produces, is not high enough, no materialization occurs and your intention will stay on the level of thought.

It is the intensity of your feelings which changes the base-pulse rhythm, as well as the angular spin rotation of particles/waves. So, basically, you are what you feel. Only then you become what you think. Feeling is first and out of those feelings, thought arises. All feelings generate a certain frequency which has amplitude (aka intensity) as well as wavelength. Yoga practitioners meditate to the point where they feel a universal connection to everything. When you experience this kind of feeling, which some people might call feelings of unconditional love, you are able to perceive yourself both as an individual part of a whole as well as the whole itself. So, basically, you are both the part as well as the whole at the same time. You become the observer as well as the observed, and their unification. When your feelings are intense enough, they might negate gravity and this is when anti-gravity occurs and people can levitate. There are numerous accounts of levitation, yoga practitioners and even levitating nuns.

The feelings of universal connection might be artificially produced by certain sound/vibration, both ultrasounds and infrasounds involved, but also under binaural sound conditions. That is when the right and left parts of the brain are connected and work as whole rather than individual parts. When feelings, vibrations of universal connection or unconditional love, are generated at the physical level, the waves your body produces are moving back in time. A process of implosion and/or fusion is taking place. Your EM waves are changing to vibrational longitudinal waves; oscillations, electromagnetically, can change into vibration, which is longitudinal but retains the transverse electrical component. At a certain point, when hitting certain vibrational frequencies produced by meditation, feelings of love, the waves in your body change to longitudinal scalar standing waves, produced by cavities in the body such as the lungs, skull or the belly. In a process called cavity resonance, you are able to hit the vacuum field (ZPE field, etheric field, electrostatic potential of dielectric field), a mode which has to do with direct cognition based on vibration. This cognition is based on vibration or feelings produced by your own body. In this mode, you experience premonition, visions of the future, the past, have an OBE or can remote view with better results than achieved by precognition, which is electromagnetically thought-based. Basically, in a state of the so-called expanded consciousness, your body resonates with oscillation vibrational pulses which go beyond liquid EM light. You can reach plasma level.

To my knowledge, consciousness is made of standing waves, which, being scalar in their nature, are constantly pulsating in and out of creation. So the scalars are pulse or quanta-based. If humans learned the nature of implosion (cold fusion) and explosion within their own bodies, they'd be able to connect into the ZPE. The (for now) yet undiscovered human senses of each human body are feeling-based, which in turn is (audible/inaudible) sound-based, which in turn is vibration-based. It is our feelings that change reality. You are what you feel, not what you think. Each human can produce torsion waves or standing scalars under certain circumstances, such as the coupling of heart and brain. Furthermore, scalar standing waves, being pure potential, have no polarity; they are positive, negative and neutral at the same time. Certain ducts in the human body, which science has not yet discovered, can produce these. For example, there is one located on the right side of your body, close to the hip bone.

However, a more subtle energy than torsion and/or scalar energy exists at a deeper level. It is the so-called cold plasma, which to a certain degree can be accessible by bone marrow as well as blood and skin. If you want to improve your precognition and intuition you have to access feeling-based vibrations rather than EM-based oscillations within your body. So, sound works better than light, so to speak, for improving your precognition. It is the ability to produce standing waves in your body, via co-vibrational feeling-based resonance, that will improve your precognition. If your body can attain a level of non-resistance psychologically, the uniting force of resonance will take over. You must be able to tune into the field which is based on electrosound (tonal) vibration, rather than electromagnetic oscillation, or you will not be able to access the kind of cognition which is direct, instantaneous and vibrational. If you want to levitate, then turn your mind and body into a huge standing wave, which will go back in time by implosion until you hit vibrational co-resonance levels, which negate gravity. This is when your body starts levitating. It is not the brain; rather it is skin, bone marrow as well as blood cells, which are responsible for yet undiscovered and unidentified senses of each human being."

On Past, Future, Present, Gravity, and Unconditional Love

Julia: "Whatever leaves the body during out-of-body experience might be called consciousness: energetic quantum of vibration oscillation pulsation, etheric energy, dark matter energy. Consciousness is the link or the substance through which materialization takes place. Consciousness is fundamental.

The higher intensity, the higher amplitude, and the higher resonance give the optimum chance for materialization of your intention to occur and the ability to change the course of the future. The present comes from the future; syntropy rules and entropy is the servant. There is no past or future. There is only the eternal now. By generating certain feelings a certain way here and now, you can change both your past and your future. When you change your past, you automatically change your future as well. Past and future cannot be separated and are connected via eternal now. The present moment changes both past and future. Past and future unite into one inseparable whole in eternal now if your body emits certain frequencies. The past and future can be altered in one moment, when you try to change your past by feeling a certain way. These feelings automatically change your future, as there are no boundaries between time and space once you reach a certain vibrational frequency. So when you try to change your future by feeling a certain way, again, you automatically change your past. The now moment is the key. Feeling now and feeling a certain way, and/or producing a certain frequency in order to change both your past and your future, is how it occurs. Everything is sound and vibration, so everything is pulse/wave based; there are no particles only waves. These, however, are only pulses or quanta created by the pressure of vibration. Everything is energy, and energy and matter are the same, or rather the opposite sides of the coin: we say that energy and matter are the same, just different modes of one united whole.

We only perceive things as matter because our consciousness is located at a certain frequency dimension. If we go to a higher frequency mode, we would not perceive matter, but something which looks like matter but less dense. If your body were able to run certain higher frequencies, the physical would be perceived as less dense, as light, waves, shimmering colors, different geometrical forms, and plasma. Michael sees this all the time just because his consciousness is working at higher frequencies than the consciousness of other people. Sound creates light. 'In the beginning was the Word,' says the Christian Bible. Word is a mechanical, longitudinal, sound-based, vibrational wave. Light came out of sound. Light is a transverse electromagnetic wave. There is a third kind of wave which unites the two in a spiral, like geometry, creating a circle, sphere, ball, or orb and these include both longitudinal as well as transverse modes of wave propagation. The human body can negate gravity if you vibrate at certain frequency reached by contemplation, meditation, emitting feelings of unconditional love or other methods of altering consciousness. There are numerous accounts of yogis and nuns or monks levitating when meditating or in a state of the so-called contemplated bliss."

Rocks and Minerals

Michael: "Rocks, minerals, crystals, semi-crystals, sand, and walls can communicate. Diamonds, for instance, are very special as they contain a unique lattice which is able to emit special, high-frequency vibrational oscillations, which can heal and include properties which, when fully functioning, defy classical physics. It is this high frequency with which crystals communicate to people via instant thoughts. It is my understanding that energy from stones serves as food to many ET entities, as well as NHIs."

Note: Michael said one of his many tasks out-of-body is collecting this special energy from the stones.

Michael: "Water, as we know it, H_2O, isn't real water because real water has helium in it and the human body is able to produce it under certain conditions. It was shown to me that bone marrow, the part called osteocytes, organize our blood and the DNA. Osteocytes operate through feelings, such as feelings of love or hate. So feelings can make osteocytes react a certain way. They, in turn, create the red blood cells, which, in turn, release hormones. Hormones are the chemicals that operate the body, so the body is operated by feelings. When we produce feelings of love, the body tends to be healthy. DNA is also controlled by feelings."

Direct Knowing

Michael: "I can download information with my eyes closed and using automatic writing. I put down thoughts coming from within. It looks like I pull information through the chakras in the middle of my palms and also my feet. The vibrations feel strong there and you can reply to questions on different topics of interest just by listening to the vibrations felt within. Direct knowing does exist and is vibrational in nature. It should not be confused with channeling. In channeling, the downloaded information is via light waves, which are electromagnetic waves. However, with direct knowing you get information via vibrational waves, which are mechanically compressed, longitudinal waves of, what I would call, electrical sound/tone, audible as well as inaudible, rather than EM in nature. It is your heart that is in charge of the body, not the brain."

Zero-point Energy (ZPE) – You Are What You Feel

Julia: "ZPE entangles all things. When consciousness interacts with the ZPE, materialization takes place, providing a sufficient intensity of a feeling-based intention, as well as specific wave angle/phase, is emitted by an observer/creator. Materialization is explosion out of the ZPE. Dematerialization is implosion back into ZPE. Depending on what level your own consciousness is stationed at, you perceive an object either as something physical in 3D or just contours of geometrical form of higher dimensions, or waves of light, color or just pure sound/vibrations in higher dimensions. So basically, what you see as an apple in 3D, is something else in 4D, something different again in 6D, changing from physical matter into geometrical forms into light: liquid light, ether or sound/vibration; feeling-based scalars. All levels of dimensions to any object and or human being exist simultaneously. Every living object is physical matter, a crystal lattice, light (EM waves), liquid light, sound (mechanical, compressed, vibration waves) and plasma; at the same time creating a sound/light continuum. It is sound changing into light and light changing back into sound, forever and ever in a wild dance, so to speak.

There is no duality; there are waves only, which are the same as matter, by the way. Waves are perceived as different things, depending on which spin, angle, wave, phase, level or dimension they are perceived from. You can change the angle of perception by your feelings; the more intense the feeling, the higher pressure they produce. The mechanical, compressed sound vibrations produced by such feelings react with microtubules in our cells and change reality around you. They can even agitate DNA from within, resulting in a DNA upgrade. You are what you feel, not what you think, and perception is holographic."

Feelings Are Not Emotions

Julia: "People are correct that emotions are important, however, feelings are even more important, and they are different from emotions. Everything is feeling-based at its core. Feeling is sound/vibration-based. Vibration is feeling-based; oscillation is light-based. First, there was vibration (sound) and only out of sound was light born. At the beginning, there was Logos: the word, the sound, the vibration. Light is oscillation. So sound and light are interchangeable. However, it is feeling which is important. Sound is feeling and feeling is vibration and it is that vibration which really matters; light comes later. Light is an EM wave, so are thoughts and emotions. Emotions are not feelings; they are EM waves, while feelings are mechanical sound waves. If you want to get to the heart of the matter, it's through feelings, sound, infrasound and ultrasound. Emotions and thoughts are light-based (EM), and so they are of a different nature to feelings. You need feeling, sound or vibration to heighten your intuition and RV skills.

If you want to RV you have to do it through feelings, not emotions, and go time-reversed, or undergo the so-called implosion. It is called the 'phase conjugate mirror principle.' If you are able to get back in time all the way to the core vibration, sound/

feeling, you will get yourself into the realm of pure vibrational cognition. In this realm, you can RV, heal, review the future, communicate with spirits, access information; it is the realm of creation, materialization, and dematerialization.

When I use the term feeling, I mean inner feelings, such as love, as opposed to physical feelings of touch or temperature of a physical nature. Feeling is vibration, a longitudinal wave in nature. Longitudinal means that it moves away from the source and back to the source as opposed to up and down oscillations, which constitute emotions or thoughts, which are of EM nature. Any EM wave has a transverse movement, which is oscillation. So, during the RV session, if you are able to get into a certain mood or state of inner feeling, which has to be of vibrational (sound nature) close to a state of bliss or rapture, you are able to hook up, via resonance, into a field from where you can draw information via direct resonance, versus getting the info via EM waves, which is light.

When having an OBE, you can hear through walls, hear people on the street speaking. I see with three-hundred-and-sixty-degree-vision and pick up feelings of other people. I can smell different aromas and taste different tastes, even if I am not eating anything. When out-of-body you are in a vibrational state; your consciousness functions in a vibrational state, and the body is able to emit standing waves, which are of a scalar nature and are able, via resonant cavity, to hook up on the ZPE. In workshops, I refer to longitudinal, mechanical, scalar, spherical-sinusoidal, non-Hertzian nonlinear wave. A longitudinal wave is a vibrational wave, the opposite of a transverse wave. A mechanical wave is a wave which requires a medium to transfer; a typical mechanical wave is sound. A scalar wave is a standing wave, which is in a potential state. There is no vector attached to it; no actual gradient or magnitude. A sinusoidal wave is a wave which takes on specific geometry; it is basically what you call a sine wave which, compared to other waves, moves in a harmonic manner. To my knowledge, a sinusoidal wave is a spherical wave, and vice versa. Non-Hertzian waves are waves which don't require wires in order to move, so wireless movement of waves is typical for non-Hertzian waves, and Tesla talks about this.

Nonlinear waves, in lay language, means that output and input are not identical, meaning that at a certain point, a wave will get much higher amplitudes although it did not receive any outside energy. The additional energy comes via resonance from the ZPE. For instance, a bone contains certain receptors, which can be regulated by feelings of unconditional love. Those receptors, in turn, regulate the formation of the bone marrow and this regulates the formation of red blood cells, which regulate the function of the whole body.

By emitting feelings of unconditional love, you regulate your health and the ways your body functions. If you vibrate at a certain frequency, which has a certain intensity/amplitude, wavelength, and this frequency is what I term unconditional love, you can connect to the ZPE.

The term 'unconditional love' might have different meanings for different people. What is meant by the unconditional love frequency is the frequency produced by the 'longitudinal, mechanical, scalar, spherical sinusoidal, non-Hertzian, nonlinear wave'.

For some people, emitting unconditional love vibrations means merging with nature or objects around them, so they become both themselves and the objects they merged with. They lose the ability to vocalize; they only understand what they see in symbols, or can draw it, but are not able to use any words to describe what they see. They undergo intense feelings of unity, oneness, and rapture. Some hear music in the background or have blurry or wavy visions, etc. It is hard to get into this state, however, some use meditation, contemplation or other techniques.

It is not the brain, but the heart that organizes the body; the brain just decodes EM waves for the most part. The other type of decoding happens on the cellular level throughout all your body. The consciousness is sound/vibration-based. It is a hologram. The whole body is a hologram. It has sound/vibration at its core, which can be audible or inaudible. Vibrations start in the vacuum, which is not empty at all. So the consciousness spreads through the whole body. It is intimately connected to cytokinesis in the cell, or rather; it is connected to microtubules and microfilaments in your cells, which can be influenced by your feelings: love preferably. Your feelings can tell microtubules and microfilaments how to stretch or pull in the cell, and by so doing, the cell directly gives a signal to hormonal and duct systems to produce the correct hormones. You can run your hormones through inner feelings. The sound on the level of your body is the feeling. Melanin in your skin is able to receive sounds from the outside and those sounds then couple, via resonance within your body cells, and produce feelings of love, fear, etc. Sound/vibration connects directly to feelings.

Tesla waves are defined as EM waves mostly, but they are described as not regular EM waves, rather scalar-potential-EM waves, which can perform the so-called wireless transfer. Some call them longitudinal EM waves or E-gravity waves, which others reject as they maintain that an EM wave cannot function in a longitudinal mode. To my knowledge, the Tesla waves are connected to dielectric static electricity discharges, where dielectricity plays an important role. Furthermore, the outer sound is a fluctuation or pressure-based displacement of air particles, so you cannot compare a sound wave to a regular EM-based particle. But the inner sound/vibration that comes from within and is created within your cells at the deepest levels, to my knowledge, consists of virtual particles existing in the vacuum, which is not void but full of potential particles.

In some cases, the human body can, via resonance, create a strong vibrational shaking, such as a shamanic dance, which can cause cold fusion in your body and agitate your DNA, resulting in transformation, transfiguration, etc. Nerve impulses are electrochemical in their nature. Certain receptors in the brain can communicate with EM waves directly. Although scalar waves have not been demonstrated in a lab experiment, this does not mean they don't exist. They can only be detected by the device which is called human consciousness, and can be detected by the skin, for example, via melanin.

Using skin, you can predict the future. I know that scientists will come to this conclusion in the future. The perception is really very specific for each and everyone. I would also add that there are many dimensions people can perceive, so what one sees in one dimension as, say, an apple, the other, who is vibrating at different frequencies, might see the same apple as a geometrical form shimmering with different lights, yet others can see the same apple as a blob or just a pure sound/vibration. Given the nature of physical reality, people perceive the same thing differently, as reality is one big hologram and we perceive it holographically."

Music and Sound

Michael: "Sound has vibration at its core, when directed and received by different parts of the body. Vibration, in the form of sound, couples with vibrations of the organs, flesh, muscles, bones, etc. By coupling, it becomes the so-called co-vibrational resonance, which is enhanced by the process of cavity resonance in the body. The resonance, at a certain frequency, intensity, and pitch, is able to connect the body to the zero-point and draw free energy from deep within the etheric levels. Musical instruments tuned to 432 Hz and 421/422 Hz and (to my knowledge) 424.96 Hz, are able to produce resonance within your body and connect directly into the zero-point energy. To my knowledge, the 440 Hz-tuned instruments are not able to do this.

The vibration within your body awakens when listening to certain sounds. This is what is happening when you are getting into a certain mode of feeling; it is more or less the Kundalini awakening, so to speak. The most productive and safe way of enabling such vibration starts within when your body is producing feelings of unconditional love and is organic and natural. The resonant frequency starts the phase conjugation within the body and they produce standing waves, which, in turn, influence the spin of particles on an atomic level, which, in turn, influence the amount of ether, scalar energy, zero-point energy coming into the nucleus (atom).

The human being is able to influence, via feelings, which are vibration (it works best with standing scalar waves), the amount of ether entering into your body via atoms. Using feelings, every human is able to affect the blood and hormonal systems. Basically, the whole body is affected by feelings of love, so to speak. The blood is a bridge between physical matter and non-physical matter. It is the boundary that is crossed if certain vibrations are reached in the body and the molecules transform; the physical body changes and so does the chemistry, as well as the biology of the body. The last phase of the transformation makes you a breatharian, living off air and sun energy. When certain changes take place in your blood chemistry, based on co-resonant vibrations, strengthened by feelings of peace, unity, love etc., then you are able to tune into a vibrational field which contains information, which was not available before."

Information

Michael: "Information is non-local. It cannot be created or destroyed, just like energy as well as matter because one turns into the other. However, information can be altered by reacting to waves (pulses) of consciousness. Information is self-organizing and follows the principle of syntropy/entropy complementary pair of opposites. Information is not solely carried by light, as light only represents a small portion of the EM spectrum, but also by other parts of the EM spectrum as well as the sound spectrum: the audible and inaudible. Individuals can decode information by relating to it in the form of light and other forms. When waves of consciousness are emitted from the body, based on the principle of the hologram, they react with waves around us, which contain information. Depending on the phase, frequency, intensity, wavelengths, amplitude, angle of angular rotation, and spin of particles (sub-particles, quasi-particles), we are able to decode the information. This also depends on how the light, which contains information, is broken, bent, reflected, diffracted, refracted; whether there is an implosion wave, going-back-in-time wave or an explosion wave that we are able to fully retrieve, (channel, download, downstream, direct, vibrationally cognate) or if we receive just partial information contained in the quantum of information. By the way, information is released in pulses or flashes of quanta.

The best light-harvesting device, I believe, is the human skin, as it contains melanin, which can harvest the sunlight. With the help of NaCl (sodium chloride) when your body is submerged in the sea water, melanin starts a certain reaction in your body and with the help and by a process called Photolysis, similar to photosynthesis in plants, and with silica playing a central part, helium is produced by cold fusion under room temperature in a process which involves cavital-resonant nuclear transmutation, based on resonant standing waves acting like a phase conjugate mirror.

The spin of waves is directed by the Universal consciousness. This is made up of standing scalars and functions best via what I call co-vibrational resonance of frequency, based on feelings of unconditional love. Spin changes, depending on the pressure of the flow of the ether. Human consciousness can directly navigate and direct the pressure of the ether. The angular rotation of spin changes when our feelings or our mood change and when it is intense enough to reach a certain frequency. Feelings based on pure love, which are scalars themselves, run the hormones, neurotransmitters and proteins in the body as well as the formation of red cells in the bone marrow and intestines. That is why certain sensitive people can download feelings directly from the bones and intestines and turn them into information. Furthermore, certain types of standing waves (resonant, longitudinal, spherical and/or sine scalars, when run on the so-called phase conjugation principle/mode), can regulate the flow of ether into and out of atoms, and when this is the case, gravity and anti-gravity can be regulated at will. Moreover, standing waves can be produced and emitted by each human body under certain conditions. The human body functions on the universal-consciousness principle, which means it is self-regulated, self-sustained, self-organized, self-regenerated. It runs on harmony or self-balancing of two opposite forces, aka fusion/fission, expansion/contraction, male/female, plus/minus, yin/yang, complementary opposites, and by so doing creates the perpetual cycle, the never-ending motion of perpetual mobile technology.

Consciousness was never created and will never be destroyed; it just is, and spreads itself through the vacuum, which itself is not empty but full of potential. Nothing but vacuum exists. There is no time, no space. Nothing is impossible for the human mind. We are the true co-creators. We can change the way light behaves by directly interacting with it via our consciousness when we consciously direct feelings (electromagnetic, tonal, vibrational longitudinal standing waves) of a certain frequency at light waves so they interact together. The frequency is the frequency of pure love. Love is a special frequency of certain waves, which have a specific wavelength, amplitude, intensity, phase, spin, angular rotation, and should be taken seriously by the mainstream science. This frequency does not show any voltage and cannot be detected by artificial gadgets, but by human feelings alone.

Activities and occurrences such as teleportation, poltergeists, telekinesis, ETs, NHIs, OBEs, NDEs, STEs, Deja vu, hypnagogia, astral travel, astral projection, interdimensional travel, levitation, orb travel, RV, ARV, scrying, ghosts, channeling, direct vibrational cognition, telepathy, synchronicities, crop circles, clairvoyance, prophecy, ESP, spontaneous healing, etc., can be attributed to a unique model of our universe (and the human consciousness is a part of it), which runs as homonymic/ holographic self-sustaining structure based on standing longitudinal, non-Hertzian, scalar-spherical (sinusoidal) waves, which themselves pulse into and out of existence, so to speak, and by so doing, through the mode of a complimentary opposite, the universe runs forever in ever-repeating cycles of perpetual motion."

OBE Meetings – Moon and Mars

Julia: "Michael told me he takes part in regular meetings out-of-body, with hundreds of other people from Earth, who can also function in an out-of-body mode. They are briefed on different topics of interest and importance, as well as the latest developments and future direction of Earth."

Michael: "We meet out-of-body and talk about different things and are lectured by other important people who used to live on Earth. We are also updated by different beings that are not of Earth.

Once, I talked to a person who was also out-of-body, but this person was not among the living and could have been of non-Earth origin. He told me that there was a lot of gold under the surface on Mars. The being knew the exact location of the gold deposits on Mars. There are huge gold deposits on Mars, and that might be a reason why, in the future, different factions will fight over Mars. There were once functioning pyramids on Mars, and some of them remained there, but they are not functioning now. These pyramids were built by different ET civilizations, in order to obtain energy. In the future, there will be official (not secret, as now) expeditions launched from Earth to Mars, for the purpose of researching to what extent the conditions on Mars allow for the building of colonies and towns for future resettlement on Mars. Some of it is actually happening right now, however, it is kept secret from the public.

Many visitors from other planets and ET systems and civilizations visit Mars. The main reason for these visits is/was to search Mars for a variety of different raw materials.

I believe that, in the future, people from Earth will settle on Mars. There will be people living there for the purpose of research and work. There has been, and will be in the future, mining for gold and some precious metals that we lack on Earth. Those metals have other characteristics and properties compared to Earth metals. The atmosphere on Mars is similar to ours because there are people moving around without oxygen masks, although most people wear oxygen masks outside. The US government has buildings on the Moon, but this information is hidden from the public. Inside these, people can move freely without oxygen masks. Also, there is flowing water on Mars; some lakes are quite large. Whole seas and oceans used to exist on Mars. There are also fish, small lizards and various insects living on Mars. I saw running water on Mars in 1998, and NASA announced the same fact, only two years ago, in September 2014. In the future, many pharmaceutical plants will be built on the Moon for the processing and manufacture of medicinal products, and some of this has already begun."

Pyramids Built with Help of ETs

Michael: "The pyramids in Egypt were built by Egyptians with the help of extra-terrestrial civilizations through laser technologies and levitation techniques. There are many pyramids on the ocean floor as well as on Mars. There are energetic grids in Egypt connected to other dimensions, which mean you can travel in time and different dimensions from certain locations in Egypt.

Pyramids are power plants. They generate energy and can be used for space travel. The capstone of the Great Pyramid of Giza was deliberately taken away by the Egyptians, and hidden in the ground. An archaeologist found it, but it was stolen by an unnamed secret service organization. A pyramid is not able to function without the capstone.

Aliens visited Egypt and enslaved the Egyptian people in the past. They used humans to process pure gold, found underground. The energy from the pyramids was used in this process.

These ETs and NHIs came to Egypt to get resources. After the aliens did not need the Egyptians, they killed them because they did not want the Egyptians to use the sophisticated technologies, which the aliens introduced. The Egyptians believed the aliens were gods. Michael recalls a past life when he used to mine the gold, and remembers the pyramids and how they were built. Some of the aliens were robots; some of them part-robotic. Some had four legs; this can be seen in the hieroglyphs on pyramid walls. Aliens used lasers to dig holes into the ground so that Egyptians could find the gold more easily. Egyptians used power plants and a special machine which produced food. There are many pyramids all over the world and hidden underground."

Portals and 'Gates' in Space

Michael: "Doorways, 'gates' exist in many places in the Universe. The woman's uterus is a gate: a tunnel through which universal (cosmic) energy flows and through which the so-called soul enters a human fetus. Sometimes, the uterus gate opens and a woman can get pregnant without having sexual intercourse. The energy, which later becomes a fetus, will be flown into the uterus via the uterus gate, which is able, under certain circumstances, to open via resonance, and receive the energy needed for the creation of a child.

Gates also exist in special places in different parts of Earth, and sometimes a boat/ship traveling to these special places in the ocean will travel in time. You can travel in space too. Gates exist in special places in the solar system. Sometimes, the sun creates entrances/gates because the colors of light open the portal. If you are near a gate, you get drawn inside it automatically and can't return through the same door, but can only return through a different door. Temperature, colors of light and gravity open doors or close them. Often these gates do not change locations, but they do close or open sometimes, but they are not static."

Nature

Michael: "Trees are special energy forms, which mostly live about 2000 years on Earth. They emit very blue and green aura. It is a special energy. They are people and animals in past lives. It is offensive to break a tree or attack it in violent ways. It might cause pain to this tree. When this happens, the tree is very sad and upset. It cries and becomes depressed because part of the energy pattern of the tree is broken – ripped. I know it because I can feel its pain when touching such a tree."

Michael was telepathically interacting with a small fish in a jar (aquarium). The fish said he likes it when someone sticks fingers into the jar to play with it. The fish was complaining about being lonely and wanted another fish to join it. The fish felt lonely. Fish experience feelings such as sadness and or happiness. The fish also asked to be moved to a different location of the room, as it did not like where the water tank was situated.

Near-Death States (NDE)

Michael: "I once experienced traveling through a tunnel, and it was not part of a near death experience. It was a part of my regular out-of-body experiences. I concluded that while the tunnel phenomenon happens mostly in NDE, it is also part of a regular out-of-body experience. The out-of-body experiences are of different levels and are an inherent part of each near-death experience."

What Happens When We Die

Michael: "For most people, they go to a new body. A few people can suffer pain from past lives after they die. For your information, a person is not dead until he is reborn. Just because their body died here, on Earth, does not mean they are dead. Often, they are waiting for their next journey back to Earth. So, it is either a new body or a higher level for some people. Some people will suffer from illness or trauma, even after their body has died here. It does not matter at all. Until they are reborn, they might still feel pain. I know it one-hundred percent because I witness it many times.

People might or might not affect the date and circumstances of their own death. It depends on the color of light (or the wavelength) their light (energy) body vibrates at. After you hit a certain frequency (color of the EM spectrum) you cannot change the future, present or past, nor can you change the date of your own death."

The Soul and DNA

Julia: "Are the parents of children pre-destined? What is it that chooses the parents and kids? Is it the right constellation of solar energy around the time when the baby is made?"

Michael: "Yes, mostly, but not all. DNA is important, but a small factor is intelligence. The baby is not there for a while after the egg and sperm unite and it flies inside several weeks after you get pregnant. It is only cells and no real baby-consciousness. The so-called solar wind, i.e., solar energy, ions, have a big effect on a fetus. DNA is important, but not the most important. DNA is not DNA, as we know it. It is a code of colors and color patterns."

Michael and Julia Respond

Chapter 8, The New Human

E: "The kids at the bases; what they are learning versus what the public learns is so different. There are schools on the ocean floor, in underground bases and offplanet."

Julia: "I can confirm the schools in underground bases and offplanet. Both my son and Michael have mentioned it to me."

E: "There is being made a 'new moon'. There are a lot of moons that are artificial, like around Saturn and Jupiter and other places, and they affect some people. When this New Moon is built, we will all be controlled, with no way to stop it. It's is for mind-controlling brainwaves."

Julia: "I can confirm this. Michael travels often to the moons of Jupiter. There is life there. Yes, I can confirm the Moon controls the mind, as there is the magnetic, sound-vibrational part to the scalar waves which do the control. The electric component does not have it. Must be magnetic, which is the Moon."

E: "He showed me with his hands the level the mind control device worked at and the level his mind frequency was, which was way above this device."

Julia: "Michael told me there is a device that can control your mind and blank-slate your memory. I think this was done to Michael directly as a MILAB victim. He does not want to talk about it yet. He said he has suppressed this memory."

Father: "Are you saying that they monitor frequencies and they can tell when you are in a certain place?"

E: "Yes."

Julia: "Can confirm; Michael does that too. He can tell you which group you belong to, which planet, this or another galaxy. He does it based on the colors of the frequencies he sees around people, especially their heads, chest, palms, and feet, and there is also energy he sees coming from your ears, nose, eyes and sexual organs."

E: "Basically, they target people who are special, and they stop them going higher than the machine. So they are trying to affect my consciousness and me."

Julia: "I can confirm this."

E: "Skin color: well, some are blue, some are gray. Mostly blue. Some of the Grays are good; some of the Grays are bad. Some of the Blues are good; some of the Blues are bad. It's like a personality split, and some of the Grays are like a cyborg, others are clones. Some Grays are tall and some are short, and some don't have a nose. A group of them is connected to a group here doing some of the not-fun stuff."

Julia: "I can confirm this, based on Michael's information to me. It is my understanding that Michael talks to Nikola Tesla, out-of-body. Tesla used to telepathically interact with his pigeon; it was his pet."

E: "I brought in information about the pyramids and water. Water is the power-source energy and the pyramids equal portals when water is near. Portal is when you are near energy."

M: "So a pyramid, with water near it, can create a portal?"

E: "Yes. When water is completely pure it is a source of energy. It's pretty endless. Water powers portals and other dimensions; it powers it up, basically."

Julia: "I am shocked. This is exactly what I heard from Michael. Michael says water can power a human being too. It can open portals, chakras in your body. But the water has to be pure, like a mineral spring from nature. Water holds the complete energetic signature of objects and can receive information, store information and later act on the information in the form of a frequency, which can affect human consciousness, and human consciousness can retrieve it from the water."

E: "By a special frequency. How you create it is actually very simple: you go into your mind and 'tune' it. You tune to the frequency; not sure how to explain using words."

Julia: "I can confirm this. The frequency starts in your thymus, goes to your coccyx, to the spleen, to the hypothalamus, the pituitary, the pineal, then hits the fontanel on top of your skull and goes back to the thymus, ending the whole circle. Michael travels through portals."

E: "I need to go to the Great Pyramid in Egypt because there is Orion energy in there. It's hooked up to Orion and Sirius. I need to go into a room because of the frequencies there, and it will activate the last bit of information in me and cause everything to speed up because that's the technology. It's portal access to everything on this planet."

Julia: "I can confirm. I have goose bumps right now, all over. I don't understand how the information from E and Michael is just identical; it's incredible. It is a download from one source."

E: "There are places with underground bases, where some people's souls are not really from there. Some people's actual bodies are from there, here and there, it is just a mixture, a whole other breed, a whole civilization."

Julia: "I can confirm. My son told me about a civilization or a group of people living underground. They have advanced technologies and taught things to my son when he was in Contact with NHIs. He told me, back in 2010, that he was taught the basics of materialization and dematerialization techniques, with some instrument which looked like a wand. He told me that people down there communicated telepathically. My husband had six DNA strands opened in 2010 and the highest amount of strands opened currently on Earth was eight (in 2010). Some monks in the Himalayas have this number open too. I had four strands opened in 2010, according to my son, and he has five strands open at the time."

Father: "E was telling me today that a lot of moons out there are artificial; they are old and used for different things."

Julia: "Michael has a special interest in moons. He often travels to Jupiter's moon. He also told me that the Moon affects the female, magnetic part of a human being while the Sun affects the electrical part. The Sun rules over the Moon and it is the solar flares and energy from the Sun that decide on the personality of the newborn; the genetic part and DNA only play a small role in it."

Father: "E told me about things put in the food, chemtrails, radio waves and water. The pollution re fluoride in the water. E said it makes you dumb, makes you stupid like you can't think, and so you go along with it."

Julia: "I can definitely confirm this word-by-word, exactly. Michael feels, sees and smells the chemicals in the GM food and can observe what it does in the body, frequency-wise."

E: "I was shown that the old grid was information control for energy and consciousness, which some call the morphological grid, and the consciousness mindset that was religion. So, information control for the mind and money for the heart, which are both energy currencies."

Julia: "I can confirm this. I really am shocked, as this is exactly what Michael said to me. E and Michael even use the exact same words. I am speechless."

E: "To keep them (people) in their box (left brain 3D), which is the twisted Saturnian energy that can't scale up through the emotions to the heart: the right brain, which some would say is the divine feminine."

Julia: "Confirmed. However, it is not emotions, it is feelings. Emotions are EM-based; feelings are vibration-and-sound-based and out of feelings, emotions come. The heart, as an organ, is feeling-based. There is vibration, sound, compression, longitudinal-mode of waves, versus the transverse-mode of EM waves that run the brain. The heart is run by feelings (inner vibration), while EM is outer oscillation."

Father: "It's a frequency war, a consciousness war, and because they can't stop the awakening they are trying to seal it. E was basically talking about targeted individuals and energy weapons. It's like a roaming AI supercomputer, to see where people's scalar waves are at; their brainwaves. When you go unconscious, it tracks that automatically and makes up a profile of who you are, where you are, and your history. I prefer to talk about better stuff."

Julia: "Correct."

About the Water

Father: "E spoke about water too, to purify it then energize it. He said that if they do this and drink this, it will help them in this process. Water can help the person, as water is multidimensional. It scales the dimensions and gets you to a place where you can go further."

Julia: "Confirmed. I began to have massive downloads in 2007. I suddenly started to drink from ten to twelve liters of water, which for a small person at forty-five kilograms was too much. A friend, who is a doctor, ran tests for why I drank so much water. The tests were fine, but I was told there might be a problem with my hypothalamus or pituitary gland, which is responsible for intake and regulation of water in the body. I was told it might function differently from the rest of people, but I know I used water for downloading and decoding information I received. When I have downloads, my eyes are closed and I either speak or write whatever is coming from my mind; this is when I need water. I have bottles of water everywhere, in each room; I take them with me everywhere. Water has a certain signature that can react with the frequencies of your body. It not only obtains information from human feelings, emotions and thoughts, it can react to them and interact with them.

Blood is the same, but a little higher degree than water, given that there is water in the blood. You can put your thought into water and have someone drink the water. That someone, then can get the frequencies of the thoughts into his own system and act according to the thoughts."

Questions

Dr. Rudy Schild 2016

Dr. Schild is Executive Director of FREE and an Emeritus research astronomer at the Harvard/Smithsonian Center for Astrophysics, following an extensive career studying Dark Matter, Black Holes and the fluid mechanical origins of Cosmic Structure. Because of his long association with Dr. John Mack, he has become interested in the formulation of a coherent understanding of the nature of space-time in the Universe. Editor-in-Chief of *Journal of Cosmology*, he has attempted to broaden the scope of scientific inquiry to include the nature of consciousness and the Universe of Universes. Dr. Rudy Schild was a close friend of the late Dr. Edgar Mitchell and is a co-founder of FREE.

Dr. Schild is now collaborating with Michael, to learn what he understands of NHIs, ETs, Space, planets, inter-dimensions, galaxies, etc. Michael was able to gather information based on more than forty years of experiences traveling out-of-body. Dr. Schild has commented that Michael's views are consistent with his own research on astrophysics for over forty years.

The following are paraphrased research questions (replies included) pertaining to topics of interest in astrophysics, addressed to Michael in July 2016, by Dr. Rudy Schild.

Yes or No Questions and Replies

Dr. Schild: "In your out-of-body experiences, do you ever explore the cold, dim, planet-like objects everywhere in the vast spaces between the stars? Yes or No?"

M: "Definitely, yes."

Dr. Schild: "I have detected their gravitational signature and call them 'rogue planets'. They should have masses and solid cores with atmospheric gases and weather effects much like our Earth, even with no nearby sun to warm them. On Earth, we have life forms occupying the oddest places, like sulfurous ocean vents and freezing-cold regions; on Earth, we call these life forms extremophiles."

M: "Yes, it has weather and yes, solid cores."

Dr. Schild: "There is one planet beyond the planet Pluto?"

M: "Yes, it has weather, but harsh. This planet has no CO_2 ocean."

Dr. Schild: "Do you know if the rogue planets (or other planets) everywhere host primitive life forms like our terrestrial extremophiles, such as in sulfurous ocean vents and freezing-cold regions; Yes or No?"

M: "Definitely yes. I talk only about the rogue planet beyond the planet Pluto. It is a damp planet. People must accept it supports life."

Dr. Schild: "Do these rogue planets and have roles in life-formation throughout the Universe? Yes or No?"

M: "Definitely, yes."

Out-of-body experience has been identified as one of the core experiences of extra-terrestrial encounters. The survey demonstrated that eighty percent of those with extraterrestrial encounters experience OBEs.

I believe the information in this chapter offers a broad and detailed understanding of the OBE, as it is experienced by Julia and Michael. The extraordinary detail of the OBEs; the feeling, sensing with the multidimensional perspective, I found very illuminating and extremely intriguing.

With eighty percent of those with Encounters experiencing the OBE state, I believe this information can be enormously helpful on many levels, both in the validation of their personal OBE, and understanding.

I believe the information will enable us to have a broader grasp of the nature of reality and how the awareness of the individual is expanded in the out-of-body state. It offers glimpses of what is possible for us to experience and learn in terms of the nature of personal reality and consciousness itself.

Note: The knowledge explored in this chapter is fully explained in Julia's book, which she is translating into English, and through her workshops on the OBE.

Julia Sellers – Lecturer, Author, and Coach

Born in Banovce nad Bebravou, in Western Slovakia (former Czechoslovakia), Julia experienced her first out-of-body experience in 1995. Since that time, she devotes her free time to the study of OBEs. She is interested in quantum physics, free energy, anomalous cognition, near-death experiences and topics of merging science and religion. Julia has three degrees. She studied in the former USSR, USA, and Slovakia. Majors studied: law, journalism, Russian Area Studies, Management, Phytopathology,

Fluent in four languages, she has dual American and Slovak citizenship. She is a translator-interpreter; a lecturer in the English and Russian language and an English teacher at the first private school in the Slovak Republic focused on the behavioral problems of children with learning disabilities and emotional problems. Executive Manager and head of the international section of the presidential election campaign, (Slovakia), she is the foreign relations adviser to the ex-Prime Minister of the Slovak Republic, an analyst for the Department of International Relations, deputy manager of the central election campaign, a foreign correspondent accredited to the US Department of State and a freelance writer and lobbyist. She also worked for the Fund for Constitutional Government.

Julia currently lectures on out-of-body experiences in Slovakia, the Czech Republic.

Conclusion

AWAKENING TO THE MULTIDIMENSIONAL NATURE OF HUMAN EXPERIENCE

"As the collective resonance of today's civilizations peaks, there will be a collapse of that once programmed into the collective. This will bring about a global awakening. There are so many forms that are seen, and these forms again are to be accepted as representations of consciousness and are meant as 'triggers' to crack the foundations of human thinking. It is happening already with children that are born without programs and have come directly (in essence) from other star systems and from various places in the spectrum of life's vibrating realms."

Tracey Taylor, 2000.

Shifting Paradigms!

I had very little idea twenty years ago when I met my first client with extraterrestrial encounters that it would change my life and my understanding of reality. I would never have been able to write a book such as this because it would have seemed too incredible. After all, it's not until you are exposed to this reality or the encounter experience itself that one can one grasp how limited and limiting our programming into a 3D reality can be.

As I explored the panorama of encounter experiences with my clients, I became aware of how it challenged and changed them. I too was challenged and changed by what they told me. I am thankful my training as a counselor taught me to be honoring and non-judgmental because otherwise, I would have struggled because what I learned from them challenged almost everything I had ever believed to be true. The process of integration to this expanded version of reality was both fascinating and confronting. It was because the individual came to me for support, that I was privileged to accompany them on their journey to new understanding, for which I am truly grateful. However, it is a journey, which meant I must question everything

I had been educated and programmed to believe. It became increasingly obvious to me, how much of what we are taught is distorted, and very often inaccurate. It comes with 3D-reality prejudices co-existing within the essential truth. I believe my awakening began when I acknowledged that much of what I had been programmed to accept was limited, and in some instances totally false.

I began to re-appraise my core beliefs and for a time I experienced a void, not really knowing what to accept as truth. This was extremely unsettling. However, this situation gave me time to process and reframe my reality parameters to a far broader, more inclusive one. This was extremely important if I was to gain a similar perspective alongside those of my clients. I realized that I must trust my personal resonance to truth and also release my need for certainty, as each new step I took led me further down the proverbial 'rabbit hole'. I acknowledged I didn't know what I didn't know. The strategy which encapsulated this process by which I could explore without limits was articulated beautifully in Thomas Kuhn's book *The Structure of Scientific Revolutions* (1962).

"Just observe, drop all your preconceived categories as best you can, and just collect raw information. Don't even use words like happened or didn't happen, exist or doesn't exist, inside, outside, real or unreal – just put that all aside and collect the raw data."

Ref: *The Structure of Scientific Revolutions* (1962).

Thomas Kuhn in this statement offered a useful strategy, which guided me to explore the complexity of this phenomenon in a way that was both logical and open. To collect 'raw data' for patterns and corroboration is an open-minded approach, which does not equate to gullibility. It acknowledges 'we don't know what we don't know'. If research into this phenomenon has taught me anything, it was the importance of not being hidebound to a particular conclusion or hypotheses. I learned quickly that a new piece of data could change all I had previously believed. Albert Einstein was my reminder in this statement:

"Whoever sets himself up as judge in the field of truth and knowledge is ship-wrecked by the laughter of the Gods."

Albert Einstein.

The Many Ways to Perceive the ET 'Elephant'

Thomas Kuhn's model of an open-minded approach to all data, even when I am unable to understand its relevance at the time, was important for another reason. This phenomenon is so complex it is possible to throw the 'baby out with the bath-water', especially when data confronts our worldview. Also, the encounter experience is so multifaceted and complex and relies to an extent on how the experience is expressed subjectively, and is also dependent on the level of awareness of the individual. This means the Encounter experience, perceived through the window of individual awareness, can be relevant for some, but not for others, who may be in a different stage of their awakening process. This doesn't necessarily make their information invalid, it just means as individuals we can focus on different parts of this complex ET elephant. This is why I believe, no one, no matter how informed or aware he or she may believe him or herself to be, has a mandate on this phenomenon, or the nature of reality. It seems to me that however many years I have explored this phenomenon, it makes me very aware how little I know. It has also made me very mindful that just because some data may not make sense to me at a particular time does not necessarily make this information invalid. Experience has taught me that data could well be crucial to my understanding at a later date.

I believe human programming and conditioning is far more powerful than many of us realize. Personal understanding and perception will strongly echo our personal 3D editing, as left-brain logic attempts to dominate. I believe one of the main outcomes of multidimensional experience is to act as a catalyst to break down this core conditioning to offer us the freedom to develop within ourselves a more open questioning of our reality window. The challenge for us is to trust and accept what this heightened intuitive awareness conveys. However, the stronger the individual conditioning, such as long exposure to higher education, science or religious beliefs, the more problematic it may be for the individual to cope with or accept the information from this source.

In modern western society, we are also conditioned to think before we speak; however, in multidimensional awareness, the reverse is often true. Operating multidimensionally, we can often receive information before we consciously think of it, a sense or knowing which comes without conscious thought. To access this, we have to learn to change the way we accept and process information and trust data from our intuition and body resonance and not just information from our left brain cognition and analysis. The idea, I believe, is to use both left and right brain in balance and harmony with each other, so that we can make sense of our 3D reality but also operate healthily in our multidimensional one. This process allows the individual access to information on all levels of awareness to better understand their expanded reality.

However, the reality 'lens' from which we interpret information is unique to each of us and what we perceive and interpret, will also depend on our attitude to these experiences as well as our conditioning. It is no wonder the perceptions and understanding of the Encounter experience are so diverse. Its interpretation depends on what part of the ET elephant we are exposed to, or what we decide to focus on or how easily we release core beliefs. Unfortunately, the older we are, the more probable that we are entrenched in this conditioning. This is why I believe it's important to explore through the eyes of the less programmed and less conditioned: the children and youth because they are not yet programmed or conditioned 'out of their light', as nine-year-old Cathy commented.

"At school, the children are 'programmed out of their light'."

Cathy, 9 years, Europe.

Information from Source

"Sit down before fact like a little child, and be prepared to give up every preconceived notion – follow humbly wherever and whatever abyss nature leads or you shall learn nothing."

T.H. Huxley.

It is because the older generations of humans have 'programming baggage' I have particularly focused on the understanding and perspective of the new generations of children and the youth. I believe they share their understanding with an openness often denied to their parents and I believe what they share has a unique integrity. The parents, in their wisdom, have listened to their children and realized what their child shares is important. For those who have concerns about the veracity of information, I believe the parents also know their child better than anyone, and they know the difference when their child is sharing an imaginary story or a real event. The way a child articulates their experiences or understanding is extremely important, and that is why I have been sensitive to the way a child or adult has shared and articulated it. Even when it may occasionally be difficult to follow, I felt this was important to keep the authenticity and flow of their experience. With this in mind, for the most part, the children, parents or young adults tell their own story in their own way. My primary input was references and supportive data. I have not altered language other than to clarify their experience and understanding of it.

For some readers, these accounts may resonate and will echo their own experiences, but for others, it may well challenge their core beliefs and reality matrix as too extraordinary, even impossible to accept. However, my mandate in writing this book was to be open to what I don't know and to what others may not know or be aware of. I learned that for me at least, if some information challenges me, I believe that I am being tasked to look to my inner resonance to explore why. The information may highlight something I have yet to explore or remind me of my conditioning. Do I mistrust information just because I have not yet accessed understanding to explain it?

"The day science begins to study the non-physical phenomenon, it will make more progress in one decade than all the previous centuries of existence."

Nicola Tesla.

Western society, in its arrogance, created a standard of what constitutes 'acceptable' personal reality. There are groups of individuals who impose this reality mandate with what I believe is a ridiculous notion: 'one box fits all'. It is interesting to note this is not present in the indigenous societies, who are all the wiser and mentally healthier for it. However, for the individuals living in western society and experiencing non-physical reality, it can be a recipe for disaster for their mental health if they accept such limited parameters. Especially when we know that, realistically, we all have the ability to have multidimensional experiences.

Dr. John Mack – Former Professor of Psychiatry at Harvard University

"We needed to create a new psychological model of reality."

"What we seem to have no place for – or we have lost the place for – is phenomena that can begin in the unseen realm and cross over, manifest and show up in our literal physical world. Immersion in the domain of extraordinary encounters may well presage the shamanism of humanity."

Dr. John Mack, author of *Abduction and Passport to the Cosmos*.

It is my belief that so-called modern society has lost its connection to its spiritual heart and what it is to be a fully-conscious human, due to the focus on materialism and science. I concur with Dr. Mack's statement when he explains that we need to create a new psychological model of reality. It is distressing that the 3D psychological model has a growing list of (what is considered) psychological dysfunctional. Psychological parameters, which arbitrarily dismiss human intuitive abilities, paranormal insights, and communication with spirits or non-human intelligences, all interpreted as psychological aberrations. Unfortunately, this has created a psychological 'straight jacket', and individuals awakening to their multidimensional nature are driven to mask their multidimensional abilities and conform to these limited parameters of experience to prevent the pigeonholing as weird, strange, or even more frightening, psychologically ill. A consequence of the 3D psychological prison means that anyone with multidimensional experiences is fearful for their sanity and may shut down this aspect of their consciousness. This means they also shut down the very thing that could nurture them and offer them access to a broader understanding. The loss of connection to their spiritual nature may (and does, I believe) become the cause of depression and alienation. Without this connection to the source of their higher awareness, the human journey may make little sense.

"The (Extraterrestrial) phenomenon stretches us or asks us to open to realities that are not simply the literal, physical world, but to extend the possibility that there are unseen realities from which our consciousness, our, if you will, learning processes over the past several hundred years has closed us off."

Dr. John Mack, Psychological Academic Model.
Ref: Interview with Nova, http://www.pbs.org/wgbh/nova/aliens/johnmack.html

The Reality Dysfunction

What makes something real? This is the central question asked by the Experiencer when they try to make sense of their expanding reality matrix. In the past, Ufology has set its store on proving this reality through the so-called nuts and bolts evidence, such as photographs, changes in soil, multiple witnesses and conscious recall, etc. Primarily because it is evidence that can't be denied scientifically. However, it is only one aspect of this complex phenomenon because Contact occurs in both the physical and non-physical world, so a holistic approach makes far more sense. My professional focus, (initially at least,) is a therapeutic one; I seek to understand the psychological, emotional and spiritual effects of these experiences, the less quantifiable, the non-physical. The question to be asked must be just how do we quantify the reality of the experience from this multi-dimensional perspective? If this experience highlights anything, it is the 3D-reality dysfunction. We have no choice but to create a new framework with a broader mandate with the acknowledgment we exist in a multidimensional reality.

3D to Quantum Hologram

Is it possible to create a holistic model, which will allow us to explore the complexity of this phenomenon, and embrace both the physical and non-physical aspects of its nature? I believe this is not an impossible task if we accept the non-physical component of the experience is a valid area of study. The Dr. Edgar Mitchell Foundation for Research into Extraterrestrial Encounters (FREE) was founded to do exactly this.

The scientific arm of FREE was co-founded by attorney and Experiencer Reinerio (Rey) Hernandez, astronaut, the late Dr. Edgar Mitchell, astrophysicist, Dr. Rudy Schild PhD, and myself. For Attorney (Rey) Hernandez his first conscious Encounter was life-changing, (Ref: full story on FREE website: http://experiencer.org/) and similar to so many Experiencers, the focus of his life and family changed forever. Rey has become dedicated and tireless to the support and growth of FREE and its broad mandate, which is to provide education, support, and research to gain further understanding of the true nature of human consciousness. This is specifically through research into anomalous human experience, such as Encounters with non-human intelligences, (however they may be understood by the individual), Near Death Experiences (NDE), Out-of-body experiences (OBE), and non-ordinary states of consciousness. FREE's Associate Director, Astrophysicist Dr. Rudy Schild, explores the nature of human consciousness through the Quantum Hologram Theory model.

Dr. Rudy Schild: "My own personal approach is to develop an academically acceptable theoretical basis to bring this phenomenon into the academic community. The quantum hologram treatment of the nature of consciousness and space-time reality offers an acceptable approach. A similar approach was pioneered by the late scientist/astronaut, Dr. Edgar Mitchell. I am working with other scientists within FREE to develop an academically acceptable theoretical model by our FREE statistical surveys."

Dr. Rudy Schild, 2015.

FREE now has an impressive body of academics, scientists, psychologists, researchers, and Experiencers. They bring their skills and expertise to this groundbreaking endeavor. The Experiencer survey is co-facilitated by rretired Professor of Psychology Dr. Jon Klimo PhD, author of numerous books on the Paranormal, with over 40 years in the fields of Transpersonal Psychology and Parapsychology, and Dr. Robert Davis, B.A., M.A., PhD, Neuroscientist, retired Professor in audiology, neuroscience, and electrophysiology and author of *The UFO Phenomenon*.

Neuroscientist Dr. Davis Explains the Nature and Focus of FREE

"A Study on Individuals who Report UFO-related Contact Experiences with a Non-Human Intelligent Being."

Robert Davis, PhD

FREE is conducting the world's first comprehensive, academic, research study on individuals that have had UFO-related experiences with a Non-Human Intelligent Being (NHIB). Our research is correlating reported consciously-recalled UFO encounters, with psychological and physiological effects, among other reported events associated with the experience. The research objective is to extend the scientific method of investigation to include the subjective experience, to understand the nature and implications of the transformative experience associated with encounters with UFOs and NHIBs. To do so, FREE has employed a phenomenological research approach to evaluate the essence of the impact of this experience to understand the nature of the phenomenon and its relation to consciousness and theories in quantum physics.

Methods

Subject recruitment was obtained using public outreach approach to inform individuals, organizations, researchers, authors, radio stations and websites that might have knowledge of the diversity of Experiencers of UFO-related ET Contact: those that have had Abductions and those that have not, which by far are the majority. The FREE research study explores areas that have not been previously studied from a large database of subjects, who report to having conscious recall of UFO-related experiences with NHIBs. Using a quantitative survey and qualitative phenomenological approach, this study addresses several major topic areas which include:

a. Family history of Contact
b. Contact experience
c. Nature of the ETs
d. Information received by these ETs
e. The physical experiences resulting from this ET Contact
f. Psychological aspects of the Contact experience

Summary

"The suggestion that is emerging is that the known laws of physics only apply while one remains within space-time, but can be overridden by any being, human, alien, or otherwise, who can 'enter', or move his or her consciousness, into the other realm that so many of these writers refer to.

But how does one enter this other realm? Perhaps this is what mystics and yogis are learning to do when they venture deep within their consciousness during meditation. It has long been noted that these are the very people who most frequently develop paranormal abilities.

Furthermore, it seems that conscious access to this realm may facilitate what we could term a 'physics of the paranormal' whereby solid objects and sentient beings can materialize from that realm into space-time, and vice versa. If this is the case, then arguments about whether UFOs are real or all in the mind are absurd and do little more than delay constructive research. It also suggests that the average physicist or neuroscientist's understanding of the link between consciousness and matter is inadequate. Clearly, however, evidence to support non-locality must be reproduced by independent researchers, and must await new developments in science to definitively explain the force, which governs and regulates this phenomenon."

Excerpt – FREE Study: *A Study on Individuals who Report UFO-related Contact Experiences with Non-Human Intelligent Beings,* 2016

Ref: For full study analysis: www.experiencer.org

With thanks to Dr. Robert Davis.

Note: Dr. Robert Davis is presently completing his research on the afterlife, *Life After Death: Should I Believe?* Due Feb 2017, published by Schiffer.

https://theufophenomenon.com/

Expressions of ET Contact – Triggers to Awaken?

"It should be borne in mind that the nature of Extraterrestrial communications is, in a majority of instances, star visitors communicate with humans by telepathic transfer of mental images and concepts rather than by words and speech."

Marie /Experiencer.

One of the most puzzling and intriguing aspects of the Encounter phenomenon which doesn't get the attention I believe it deserves is the unusual creative 'Expressions' after encounter experiences. This is the spontaneous verbalizing of Star or Light languages, production of unusual scripts, symbols and artwork, images of the beings and other geometric artwork. Certainly, it would be helpful to have research specialists in linguistics and symbology for example. However, at this time because such expertise is unavailable, it is largely unexplored. I believe it should be taken seriously, not only because it is evidence something real has occurred, but to find out what it is conveying to us. However, until this expertise is available it's important to collate this data and listen to those Experiencers who feel they can decode or translate what is expressed in this way.

Connecting to the Quantum Hologram

Expressions of ET Contact: A Visual Blueprint is a DVD which has some of these unusual artwork symbols and language produced after encounters. The individuals who create these Expressions say they feel impelled to draw or create them, but they are not in trance. The Star languages are spontaneously vocalized either when relaxed or when working with healing energy. In recent research, some Experiencers have been known to speak these languages when they are sleeping as if they are having a conversation with some intelligence. I believe their understanding is extremely significant, even if we don't fully understand the mystery just yet. However, I do believe it is multidimensional Contact communication. This is a similar interpretation to the unusual geometric forms and symbols that are produced.

The Late Dana Redfield – Experiencer and Author

"It's like working mid-plane between human language and mathematics and the higher laws of communication and creation.

I think that many of our symbols and drawings are like crude writing, efforts to translate what we perceive mid-plane but cannot bring into the whole.... It seems we are tasked with un-puzzling a kind of art-linguistic-sacred geometry. I recognize the similarity to certain aspects of the Kabbalah relationship of the human body to the Cosmos."

Dana Redfield, author of *Summoned* and *The ET-Human Link*.

The complex Expressions produced after Contact are certainly evidence of Contact reality, alongside transformative psychological and spiritual shifts. However, without doubt, it has meaning, even if at this present time what it indicates is not fully understood. Certainly, John (Chapter Twelve) believes his art acts as a catalyst to shift human perceptions to a heightened level. Artist and Experiencer, Tracey Taylor agrees and suggests her artwork conveys multidimensional information from these intelligences as do the symbols and scripts she has drawn spontaneously. It is interesting to note that even some children, appear to have the ability to decode this creative expression, as observed in Chapter Six when a seven-year-old boy appears to decode Tracey Taylor's geometric art. There are some adults who appear to have this ability to decode also, and I have shared their understanding in my presentations.

Ref: *Triggers of Consciousness.*

From what I have been told, not all this type of Expression is translatable and able to be felt or sensed. Also, some of the data is similar to compressed files: far too complex to be understood in a linear fashion. However, there is no doubt some of these Expressions appear to be in the form of catalyst or trigger, which can activate multidimensional awareness and abilities or cause them to feel healing frequencies. I explore this concept in two ACERN DVDs.

Ref: *Expressions of ET Contact: A Visual Blueprint?* 2002.
Expressions of ET Contact: A Communication and Healing Blueprint? 2004.

Activation and Healing

In the last few years, the numbers of individuals speaking the Star or Light languages has grown. I can only postulate something is activating this ability. What does it mean? Is the light language or star language another catalyst or trigger, which activates recall of our ancient human origins, even our star ancestry? Is this a result of communication with the beings to reawaken/activate dormant DNA, as Zac believes (Chapter Nineteen)? Certainly, as some individuals hear these languages they can become extremely emotional: they tell me it's a language they recognize from their star origins. For others, it may be less clear, but they certainly feel a deep resonance, even healing. Dr. Batchelor M.D. believes this light language is both healing and activating dormant DNA.

Ref: Chapter Twenty.

Frequencies via light language to activate and trigger heightened awareness and dormant DNA may also be similar to frequencies present in the music and songs Arthur produces (see Chapter Seven), which he believes come through his connection to the nice beings that healed him on the spacecraft with similar frequencies. It is fascinating and compelling that Arthur knew what to name the pieces of music before he even played them. Certainly the unusual titles: one labeled *Decoding DNA* is a very significant and rather an odd title for an eleven-year- old to use. Does this mean this music has a frequency to decode human DNA, as this title suggests? How fascinating to find out what is occurring when someone listens to it. It certainly could suggest that music can be another catalyst to this awakening process; another extraterrestrial strategy to shift human consciousness.

Interpretation of these Expressions varies the consensus, such as it is. These Expressions provide more evidence that something profound has occurred in the individual. Are these multidimensional communications to trigger our sleeping consciousness or new software for the evolving human? I believe we have yet to understand this aspect of the phenomenon, but without doubt, it offers more intriguing data to research and explore as we grow in awareness and explore the nature of reality and human consciousness.

"Everything is energy. As you focus closer and closer on the structure of the atom you would see nothing; you would see a physical void. The atom has no physical structure; we have no physical structure and physical things don't have any physical structure. Atoms are made out of invisible energy, not tangible matter.

We need to accept the inarguable conclusion. The Universe is immaterial-mental and spiritual."

R.C. Henry, Professor of Physics and Astronomy, John Hopkins University. Ref. *The Influence Verdict Philosophy had on Nikola Tesla*, Arjun Walia, 2014.

Hypnosis – A Link to our Multidimensional Awareness

Hypnosis – 'looking inside'
"Who looks outside dreams, who looks inside wakes."

Dr. Carl Jung, the celebrated Swiss psychiatrist and psychotherapist, in this statement, offers an important key which may help us to gain more understanding of this phenomenon and our multidimensional nature. Meditation, relaxation, can be invaluable for seeking answers from our inner wisdom. However, for some, hypnosis is the tool of choice, especially if they find it difficult to trust their own process.

The late Dolores Cannon, author and hypnotherapist, was a dear friend and colleague. She was certainly a significant pioneer in the field of hypnosis and exploration of the nature of consciousness. Dolores authored many books, which contained the information revealed through hypnosis. Some of this information offered an understanding of the nature of our multi-verse that was extraordinary. It revealed the multidimensional nature of human consciousness, such as past life memories, the soul's existence after death, and the life-between-life state. The Convoluted Universe series, particularly, indicated human consciousness might be able to traverse space/time, indicated in the holographic model of reality.

Psychologist, Clinical Hypnotherapist, and author, Dr. Michael Newton, used hypnosis to focus on the soul's journey in life, between life states and the spirit/soul's journey into the afterlife. It was compelling that many hundreds of individuals, no matter what age, culture or core beliefs, revealed corroborating data in his books *Journey of Souls* and *Destiny of Souls*. Although initially a skeptic, Dr. Newton became convinced the information had veracity. Psychiatrist and author Dr. Brian Weiss, discovered similar information via hypnosis. Again, information that suggested the soul survives physical death and will meet up with others who shared incarnations. (Ref: *Many Lives, Many Masters*). There are a plethora of books on survival of consciousness from those who have experienced clinical near death experience (NDE) and discovered their consciousness was able to observe in a non-corporeal state everything that was happening to their physical body – some experiencing a tunnel ending in a bright light, and at the same time feeling enormous love and peace. Many were told telepathically it was not their time to die, and they returned to physical existence. The detailed descriptions while the individual's spirit is out-of-body, is fascinating and compelling. But even more, the transformative changes after these experiences is significant evidence to convey a reality.

The multidimensional nature of human consciousness is routinely utilized in Scientific Remote Viewing (SRV), which can be so accurate that it is practiced by the military to glean information from other locations as well as through space-time. It appears that human consciousness can travel to a location when directed by simple co-ordinates. Conscious astral traveling, which is spontaneous in twenty percent of the population, but can also be taught. In this case, it appears the soul/spirit travels out-of-body to other locations, such as on Earth and other planets and dimensions, directed by the individual consciousness.

Subconscious exploration via hypnosis appears to confirm how extraordinary our quantum reality may be. Although there are misconceptions about the veracity of this information due to the fact the information can be so extraordinary, for some at least, it is easier and more comforting to believe the individual is creating scenes from an over-active imagination. However, I believe the reverse is true. The individual will often admit that not even in their wildest imaginings could they have come up with some of the concepts vocalized during hypnosis.

I personally have facilitated many hundreds of regression sessions. The complexity and depth of information revealed in this way often has profound spiritual content and the information can be so extraordinary and complex, the individual is often stunned by what they have articulated and the information that is revealed this way suggests we live in a multidimensional Universe. There is no doubt some of the concepts revealed in hypnosis are confronting, even bizarre, but in most instances, it seems to resonate on some level with the individual and can answer many of their questions. It can also be accompanied with deep emotion and result in healing on many levels. The individual may question some of the information because it may be very strange or very different from what they expected. However, this response in itself indicates the source of the information was not stemming from their conscious mind, where they would seek to control what is revealed. The 'high strangeness' offers confirmation they have activated another part of their awareness. I have no doubt that hypnosis offers a significant window into our multidimensional nature and our inner world, and is a valuable tool in exploring this phenomenon, both as a source of information about the Encounter experience and the nature of human consciousness.

The Children

However, for this book, I have endeavored to minimize information from hypnotic regression, although I have no doubts about its value. I have chosen to collate most of the information from conscious recall, as this is a source of information less likely to be dismissed. This is especially true when it is complex information from young children who have no way of knowing such data in normal circumstances. Their clarity and detail are incredibly compelling, and in some ways remind us of what we may have lost, but what still could be.

"Human beings have no idea how amazing they are, but to find out, they have to believe it first."

Cathy, 9 years.

Transformation

According to the groundbreaking studies by FREE, the outcomes from Contact in terms of changes to the individual, both physically, emotionally psychologically and spiritually, is compelling. It is clear that eighty-five percent had undergone a major transformation for the positive. They had become more spiritual, compassionate, loving, psychic, with a better understanding of themselves and their purpose in life. They have become less egocentric with more concern for the environment and less concern for monetary values. This is extremely significant and profound information. It demonstrates that for the most part, our interactions with the non-human intelligences (however we may interpret them) ultimately become a catalyst for positive change.

It is also clear from these significant studies by the FREE research team, these transformative changes do not occur from fantasy or hallucination. This research implies that through the Contact experiences we gain a deeper sense of who we are, our relationship and connection to the multiverse and each other.

"Something of great importance is going to happen on this Earth – not in your lifetime, but in mine. It will affect all units of consciousness, whether they are Mineral, Vegetable, Animal or Man. It is to do with global consciousness; a vast change of consciousness, and that is why I am here at this time, to experience this change."

Mike Oram, *Does it Rain in Other Dimensions?*.

In the early 1950s, at just four years old, Mike Oram, Experiencer and author, was told by the Light Beings that there was going to be a vast shift in human consciousness that will affect us all. I believe this statement from Mike Oram is stunningly prophetic. The shift in human consciousness has already begun, and we are all awakening to our Cosmic Heritage and the truth of who we are.

Excerpt from *Life After Death: Should I Believe*

Theories developed from studies in quantum physics, a branch of physics concerned with processes, and a series of equations which describe the behavior of sub-atomic particles, may provide the foundation to eventually explain the relationship between scientific principles, paranormal events, and even the concept of an afterlife. Developments in quantum theory, aiming to unify all physical processes, have opened the door to a profoundly new vision of reality, where observer, observed, and the act of observation are interlocked. The observation, for instance, that our conscious perception compels an electron to assume a definite position, acknowledges that we create our own reality (i.e., the observer effect). Taking this a step further, many physicists conclude on this basis that the universe is a 'mental' construction and that the interconnectedness of everything is particularly evident in the non-local interactions of the quantum universe.[1]

Theoretical physicist, Fred Alan Wolf, sums up this view:

"There is evidence (i.e., quantum physics) that suggests the existence of a non-material, non-physical universe that has a reality even though it might not as yet be clearly perceptible to our senses and scientific instrumentation. When we consider out-of-body experiences, shamanic journeys and lucid dream states, though they cannot be replicated in the true scientific sense, they also point to the existence of non-material dimensions of reality" [2].

© Copyright Dr. Bob Davis 2016

Scientists such as D. Bohm, K. Wilber, B. Greene, and K. Pribram consider that biological and physical phenomena associated with theories of consciousness may also be explained by quantum theory. A related viewpoint is that brain activity may also be based on holographic principles. K. Pribram, for instance, considers that memory is facilitated by such principles to mathematically convert energy received by the senses into our perceptions. This theoretical, holistic view of reality (i.e., a whole system being more than just the sum of its parts), of quantum consciousness, termed the holonomic brain theory, has gained increasing support among neurophysiologists like Jeremy Hayward, who emphasized that "Some scientists belonging to the scientific mainstream frankly say that consciousness next to space, time, matter and energy could be one of the basic elements of the world"[3]. But don't interpret this perspective too literally just yet since it stands in sharp contrast to the founder of the general theory of relativity, Dr. A. Einstein, who believed that quantum mechanics is "Not a complete or holistic science" [4]. In support of Einstein's viewpoint, physicist Richard Feynman said "No one understands it," and that quantum mechanic explanations of reality are "Marred with multiple unresolved paradoxes" [4]. And so the debate rages on.

The most significant theoretical consideration of the QH theory is that of mathematician, Walter Shempp, and former astronaut and scientist, Edgar Mitchell, [5, 6, 7, 8] who proposed that at the subatomic scale of matter everything in the universe is interconnected; all objects in the universe retain evidence of each event that has occurred to them and that this information is stored in this holographic form. They contend that this information can be retrieved by the mind when it attends to an object. Furthermore, the QH theory allows for distinctions that occur in our consciousness and those that can manifest on a physical scale to possibly better understand the relationship between consciousness and the brain. This may explain the reason how many things interact with one another such as thoughts in telepathic experiments. For example, if a person's consciousness is shared with another in the QH field and they are in close contact throughout space-time, telepathy may occur, i.e., it is not confined to the location of the person or object and is non-local.

Quantum physics has shown that such particles are not really objects and do not exist at definite spatial locations and times. Instead, they seem to show "tendencies to exist," forming a world of potentialities. The case for the mechanism that enables consciousness to extend beyond the physical brain arises from quantum physics. At the quantum level, all subatomic particles are entangled through quantum correlation and non-locality. This suggests a mechanism for a type of awareness that interrelates with matter and energy. Quantum physics was described by theoretical physicist Amit Goswami, as follows:

"Quantum physics is a new paradigm of science based on the primacy of consciousness...The new paradigm resolves many paradoxes of the old paradigm and explains much anomalous data" [9].

According to the QH theory, consciousness is an essential component of the universe, and all matter possesses subjective characteristics of consciousness (i.e., the foundation of everything). Thus, consciousness may be non-local in the same sense that quantum objects behave in a non-local manner. If true, the QH has potentially significant implications for understanding death. That is, when we die, we may no longer exist in space-time but instead behave outside the constraints of our 3-D time-space world continuum. However, many questions have yet to be answered about how the information of the QH is transmitted and how resonance occurs over vast distances. Nobel Prize physicist, Eugene Wigner, among other physicists, are realizing the implications of quantum mechanics for possibly explaining the nature of life after death and anomalous events. According to Wigner, quantum mechanics "proves the existence of 'God' or some form of cosmic consciousness. Similarly, another leading physicist and brain researcher, Christian Hellwig, concluded that consciousness has a quantum state, and that "Our thoughts, our will, our consciousness and our feelings show properties that could be referred to as spiritual properties..." [10] Support for this complex notion may be evidenced by reported ESP experiments which tend to illustrate that telepathy is not affected by distance (outside space), and precognition provides information of future events (outside time). The analogy from such evidence is that when we die, a characteristic of consciousness may operate beyond the space-time continuum and remain unaffected by death.

The theories and associated experiments in quantum physics (e.g., law of entanglement, double-slit, non-locality, and the observer effect), concomitant with unexplained anecdotal evidence from studies in NDE, OBE, mediumship, past-life recall, apparitions, super-psi, among other phenomena, lend indirect evidence to support the concept that our consciousness may influence and give rise to various phenomena that seem to exist in the physical world. The NDE may be critical for understanding the relationship between the brain and consciousness. Although our current medical and scientific concepts are inadequate to explain all aspects of the NDE, research suggests that aspects of an NDE correspond with, or are analogous to, some of the basic principles of quantum theory, such as non-locality and entanglement or interconnectedness, and instantaneous information exchange in a timeless and placeless dimension. The perplexing aspect of the NDE and OBE, concomitant with the experimental results in nonlocal intuition addressed previously, if proven valid, also suggests that our consciousness may be separate from our physical body and capable of affecting events remote from our body. That is if sensory information processing is in fact "nonlocal" it may explain the reported perception and the life review and images often described as a dimension without time and space, as reported by those who have had an NDE and OBE.

Consistent with the QH theory, physicist, C. Swanson postulated that the Zero Point Field (ZPF) (i.e., the lowest possible energy of a quantum mechanical physical system) offers much promise if we are to understand paranormal phenomena [11]. A fundamental property of this theory is that it incorporates the interactions of particles over long distances (i.e., non-locality). It shows that many strange anomalous events such as ESP, apparitions, reincarnation, and OBE and NDE, among others, may be explained by Swanson's proposed Synchronized Universe Model (SUM). This model which assumes that photons created by "distant matter," which contains almost all the matter of the universe, interact with one another. Therefore, every "zig and zag of a local electron is really a communication between it and the distant matter" [11]. If valid, the synchronous interaction of particles across great distances and times may explain ESP, i.e., "The sender can cause energy or information to refocus at some other point in space-time using the 4-D holographic principle." (Claude Swanson). This model, which proposes that our consciousness may leave the body and travel in space and time, may also serve as a basis to understand the NDE and OBE, in which the Experiencer describes the event from where his consciousness is, not where his body is. According to C. Swanson, the SUM may serve as a foundation to explain life after death and paranormal phenomena. He states:

"It can be used to explain how paranormal effects can be seemingly immune to time and space displacements. It may help us understand how two minds can be linked when separated by vast distances of space and time. And it offers a way to connect paranormal effects to changes in quantum noise, which is one of the central mysteries facing the new physics."

An extension of this interpretation may also explain the reported connection between one's own consciousness and that of other living persons or deceased relatives. This relationship has drawn the attention of several well-respected scientists, including Rudy Schild, research astronomer at the Harvard/Smithsonian Center for Astro-Physics, who proposed that:

"Consciousness exists in our space-time and constrains our waking perception," and that during sleep, we once again 'awaken' to full consciousness, only to discover that we never left that unitary state to begin with. After death we are awake, only to realize yet again, that when we are focused into a physical body with a finite time scale, that is when we are in fact, dreaming." [12]

A similar perspective held by cardiologist, Pin Van Lommel, is as follows:

"It seems to be possible to have a nonlocal connection with other people's consciousness as well as with thoughts and feelings of deceased friends and family and to communicate with them by way of thought transfer." [13]

Some researchers even consider that our brains may function as a hologram and construct physical reality by interpreting frequencies from another dimension which transcends time and space[14, 15]. Some paranormal phenomena may even have holographic characteristics. Bohm and Pribram, for instance, noted that phenomena such as ESP may be explained by this model which allows for individual brains to be interconnected parts of the greater hologram (i.e., information is exchanged between minds regardless of distance and stored non-locally in the ZPF). In other words, the brain's holographic structure may enable it to both send and receive holographic wave patterns as represented in thoughts. Evidence to support this possibility is supported by the behavior of light in a hologram. For example, if one observes the radiation flowing into and out of it, "the light is coming from the past, flowing through the image and then on out into space where it is absorbed in the future." [11] In fact, the DNA molecule may generate waves which can do this. Evidence to support this theory was provided by biophysicist, Pjotr Garjajev and his colleagues, who studied the vibrational behavior of DNA. Based on their findings, they concluded that:

"Living chromosomes function just like a holographic computer using endogenous DNA laser radiation. This means that they managed, for example, to modulate certain frequency patterns (sound) onto a laser-like ray which influenced DNA frequency and thus the genetic information itself."[11]

This concept provokes speculation about phenomena like past-life recall. In fact, Professor of Pedagogy, Andrzej Szyszko-Bohusz, has proposed a theory of genetic immortality in which parental consciousness and hereditary information is transmitted to children [16]. Based on studies in children who have memories of past lives, psychiatrist, Jim Tucker, advanced the concept that the science of reincarnation indicates that consciousness requires no physical binding to pass on through the generations. He believes that quantum physics suggests that since consciousness creates our physical world, consciousness doesn't require a brain to exist. He states:

"I understand the leap it takes to conclude there is something beyond what we can see and touch. But there is this evidence here that needs to be accounted for, and when we look at these cases carefully, some sort of carry-over of memories often makes the most sense." [16]

It has been demonstrated that experiences necessary for the survival of a species are learned and that this knowledge is passed on to subsequent generations. All organisms, for example, learn survival skills and pass these on. But what other kinds of experiences might be saved in our DNA over the many thousands of years when our ancestors were born, lived and died? Maybe it is possible that within your DNA memory your ancestors had life-changing negative experiences that were possibly encoded in the DNA and passed on to future generations, which can be accessed by us now? The question remains if memories are inherited by DNA, or if there is some other mechanism responsible for past-life recall yet to be determined.

Quantum mechanics postulates that each of the approximately eighty-seven-billion neurons in the brain, of which one-hundred times as many microtubules (i.e., forms the cytoskeleton in neurons and helps maintain the structure of the cell) exist in every neuron, either contains, or supports consciousness. Physicist H. P. Stapp's viewpoint [17] that the brain operates in accordance with the uncertainty principle of quantum mechanics is supported by physicist's Roger Penrose's theory that "microtubules," which exist both within and between brain cells, may be sites of quantum effects enabling entanglement (i.e. the quantum state of each particle cannot be described independently). Penrose teamed with anesthesiologist, Stuart Hameroff, to formulate the controversial "orchestrated objective-reduction" (Orch-OR) theory, which states that brain neurons behave as "quantum computers." They considered every synapse, which is where two nerves come together and do their "decision making," as a quantum system and the source of information computation. Accordingly, quantum activity within the neuron interact non-locally with other neurons and, along with the quantum hologram, facilitate a "conscious event." In fact, Penrose and Hameroff believe that the Orch-OR theory serves as the foundation for the human soul, NDEs, and OBEs, and may account for one's perception of reality after physical death. [15, 16]

Hameroff wrote:

"The connection to space–time geometry also raises the intriguing possibility that

Orch-OR allows consciousness apart from the brain and body, distributed and entangled in space–time geometry," and that "quantum information can exist outside the body, perhaps indefinitely, as a soul."

Related to this concept, physicists, John McFadden and Jim Al-Khalili, proposed that the brain's electromagnetic field may couple to quantum-coherent (i.e., entanglement) ions moving through microtubules, enabling the "binding" of cortical processes, and the emergence of consciousness [18]. Similarly, physicist Danah Zohar contends that biological quantum coherence serves as an organizing principle which may explain a "quantum relationship between consciousness and the body." Similarly, physicist William Tiller advanced the idea that the holographic properties of space are key to understanding the effects of consciousness and how ESP can take place in single living cells. C. Swanson supports this position as follows:

"These large-scale, coherent, resonant processes, where trillions of molecules in the body are in communication with one another and can function in resonance, brings up a new possibility: Maybe the body is a macroscopic quantum system, with a set of coherent quantum states all vibrating in step? If so, then some of the weird phenomena we have called "paranormal" might really be just quantum mechanics working its strange magic on the large scale of everyday life." [11]

Indirect support for the Orch-OR theory comes from evidence by computer scientist, Simon Berkovitch, who calculated that the brain has an "inadequate capacity to produce and store all the informational processes of our memories." He concluded that we would need "1024 operations per second, which is absolutely impossible for our neurons" [19]. Neurobiologist, Herms Romijn, came to the same conclusion. [20] He wrote:

"One should conclude that the brain has not enough computing capacity to store all the memories with associative thoughts from one's life, has not enough retrieval abilities, and seems not to be able to elicit consciousness."

The great challenge for science is to determine whether or not consciousness is distinct from the brain and can perceive a form of reality beyond the limited space-time continuum of our physical world when the body ceases to function. It is very difficult, if not impossible; to develop this concept into testable hypotheses since current scientific principles and associated methodology don't apply and are out of the domain of science to solve. The answer may have to be based more on one's personal viewpoints developed from teachings, experiences, and possibly a touch of "gut feeling." Consequently, there exists a need to dramatically alter the way, if at all possible, to best evaluate the many diverse aspects of the paranormal. As theories in physics, neuroscience, and psychology evolve, our increased understanding of the brain, consciousness, and physical universe, combined with the associated application of newly-developed, multidisciplinary research models, may offer greater potential to adequately test many unanswered questions of our world and beyond.

References (*Life After Death: Should I Believe*)

1. Menas Kafatos, Ph.D., Rudolph E. Tanzi, Ph.D., and Deepak Chopra, M.D. 'How Consciousness Becomes the Physical Universe.' *Journal of Cosmology*, 2011, Vol. 14.

2. Fred Alan Wolf. *The Spiritual Universe: One Physicists Vision of Spirit, Soul, Matter, and Self.* Portsmouth, NH: Moment Point Press. 1998.

3. Kauffman, S. 'God enough.' Interview of Stuart Kauffman by Steve Paulson: www.salon.com/env/atoms_eden/w008/11/19/stuart_kauffman/index1.html.

4. https://www.goodreads.com/author/quotes/1429989.Richard_Feynman

5. Hameroff, S. 2005. The Quantum Mind of Stuart Hameroff. http://dailygrail.com/Interviews/2005/1/Quantum-Mind-Stuart-Hameroff.

6. http://www.williamjames.com/Theory/PHYSICS.htm

7. Marcer, P. & Mitchell, E. 2001. *What is Consciousness?*, In Loockvane, P. (ed.), *The Physical Nature of Consciousness*, John Benjamins, Amsterdam–Philadelphia, pp.145–174.

8. Mitchell, E. (2000) *Nature's Mind: The Quantum Hologram, International Journal of Computing Anticipatory Systems*, vol 7, 295-312.

9. http//www.word-gems/mind.html

10. http://www.outerplaces.com/science/item/4518/physicists-claim-that-consciousness-lives-in-quantum-state-after-death *Physicists Claim that Consciousness Lives in Quantum State After Death*, Janey Tracey, Tuesday, 17 June 2014.

11. Claude Swanson. 2003. *The Synchronized Universe: New Science of the Paranormal*, Poseidia Press.

12. Schild, R. & Leiter, D. J. 2010. 'Black hole or MECO?: Decided by a thin luminous ring structure deep within Quasar Q0957+561,' *Journal of Cosmology* 6: 1400-1437 http://journalofcosmology.com/SchildLeiter1.pdf

13. Van Lommel, Pim. 2010. *Consciousness Beyond Life: The Science of the Near-death Experience.* New York: HarperOne: 130

14. Penrose, R. 1989. *The Emporer's New Mind*, Oxford Press, NY.

15. Penrose, R., and Hameroff, S. 1995. 'What gaps? Reply to Grush and Churchland,' *Journal of Consciousness Studies*, Vol. 2, No.2, pp. 98-111

16. http://reset.me/story/science-proving-memories-passed-ancestors/

17. Stapp, H.P. 2007. *The Mindful Universe: Quantum Mechanics and the Participating Observer*, Heidelberg: Springer-Verlag.

18. http://bigthink.com/words-of-wisdom/max-planck-i-regard-consciousness-as-fundamental

19. Berkovich S.Y. 1993. 'On the Information Processing Capabilities of the Brain: Shifting the Paradigm', *Nanobiology*, v. 2, pp. 99-107.

20. Romijn H. 1997. About the origin of consciousness. A new, multidisciplinary perspective on the relationship between brain and mind. Proc Kon Ned Akad v Wetensch; 100(1-2): 181-267.

Note: With much appreciation and thanks to Dr. Robert Davis, *Life After Death: Should I Believe*, for the excerpt below from his soon-to-be-published book.

Ref: Preliminary Results, Dr. Robert Davis, *A study on Individuals who Report UFO-related Contact Experiences with Non-Human Intelligent Beings.* 2016.

The following are some of the initial findings derived from reported Experiencers of Contact with UFOs and NIHBs. Collectively, there appears to be a very strong relationship between NDEs and UFO-related Contact. This includes OBEs and telepathic communication with human-looking beings. Both groups experience numerous physical and psychic changes such as increased ESP skills, ability to see energy fields, effects on electrical devices, medical healings, Spirit World connections and many other similarities.

Insights of this phenomenon from the survey results relate to the possible objectives of NHIB-type of communication, effect on consciousness, NDEs, and life-changing transformations, among others, as follows:

a. Over seventy-five percent of Experiencers have viewed their experiences as positive.

b. Eighty-five percent have undergone major transformations for the positive: more spiritual, compassionate, loving, psychic, understanding of oneself and purpose in life; less egotistical, more concern for the environment, less concern for monetary values, etc.

c. Four hundred and fifty individuals have had 'conscious' memories of being aboard a craft.

d. Eighty percent have had an Out-of-body Experience.

e. Fifty percent have reported a medical healing by a non-human intelligent being (NHIB).

f. Fifty-five percent have had 'missing time'.

g. Sixty-six percent have received telepathic messages.

h. The majority of Experiencers have seen a non-human intelligent being (NHIB) more than ten times.

i. Three hundred and ninety-five individuals have stated that they believe that they have been involved in what is commonly called an 'Alien Breeding Program.'

j. Thirty-five percent have had a Near Death Experience.

k. Eighty-three percent of Experiencers believe that the non-human intelligent beings (NHIBs) are somehow related to the Spirit World.

l. Ninety-five percent of Experiencers have had some type of 'paranormal' experience.

Survey results from two thousand three hundred Experiencers indicate similar behavioral/consciousness outcomes to those reported in NDEs as indicated in the responses to specific questions below:

a. Was your consciousness separated from your body at the time of the ET experience?
Yes: Sixty-seven percent.

b. While in this Matrix-like type of reality, did you feel separated from your body? For example, 'I lost awareness of my body,' 'I clearly left my body and existed outside it.'
Yes: Fifty-four percent.

c. While in this Matrix-like type of reality, did you seem to encounter a mystical being or presence, or hear an unidentifiable voice?
I sensed their presence: Thirty-six percent.
I actually saw this being: Forty percent.

d. What method of communication was used?
Two-way conversation using telepathy (ET present): Forty-one percent.
Non-physical thought/voice download from an ET to a human (ET not present): Thirty-seven percent.

e. While in this Matrix-like type of reality, did you seem to enter some other, unearthly world?
Some unfamiliar and strange place: Twenty-nine percent.
A clearly mystical or unearthly realm: Forty percent.

f. While in this Matrix-like type of reality, did you feel a sense of harmony or unity with the universe?
I felt united or one with the world: Fifty-four percent.

g. While in this Matrix-like type of reality, did you suddenly seem to understand everything?
Everything about the universe: Thirty-seven percent.
Everything about myself or others: Twenty percent.

h. While in this Matrix-like type of reality, did the reality of this multi-dimensional experience seem real to you? For example, as real or normal as you speaking with a family member:
Yes: Eighty-two percent.

i. Did you feel a sense of expanded consciousness in the presence of these ETs?
Yes: Seventy percent.

j. Have you ever had a Near Death Experience?
    Yes: Thirty-five percent.

k. If you could stop your ET Contact Experiences would you?
    No: Eighty-four percent.

l. Evolutionary forces are already at work, which will transform humanity into a more self-aware spiritually sensitive species, and the ETs have a role in this.
    Agree: Seventy-four percent.

m. I believe that my UFO experiences occurred to awaken me to the existence of larger cosmic forces which are affecting our lives and that the ETs have a role in this.
    Agree: Seventy-one percent.

In my opinion, the widespread occurrence of UFO experience is part of a larger plan to promote the evolution of Consciousness on a species-wide scale.

With thanks to Dr. Robert Davis author, FREE Study: *A Study on Individuals who Report UFO Related Contact Experiences with a Non-Human Intelligent Being.* 2016.

Encounters: www.experiencer.org and its in-depth surveys.

Certainly, one outcome that has become clear from the FREE surveys up to date, is that eighty-five percent experienced major transformation after extraterrestrial encounters. What does this indicate in terms of extraterrestrial agendas?

Note: FREE surveys are compiled anonymously.

To participate in FREE Surveys, read its findings or help with research go to www.experiencer.org

Cover Artist

The cover art for *The New Human,* by artist Lloyd Canning (UK), was commissioned after I met Lloyd in 2015, at the 7th Annual British Exopolitics Expo at Leeds University, UK. I was immediately drawn to his striking artwork. It became clear that Lloyd was expressing something that was very profound in his life. This book shares several accounts of how individuals having Contact may express their experiences through creativity. This was blindingly evident when I first saw Lloyd's art. I knew that he was the one to design the cover I needed for *The New Human.* What he has painted has fulfilled this objective and so much more. It is stunning!

Lloyd lives with his partner, Sharon, and his two children, Liam and Marley. Lloyd told me that his father, David Canning, is an artist, as was Lloyd's grandfather. Lloyd started painting at two to three years old and realized he could draw well as soon as he started school.

"My drawings and paintings would be put on the school walls, which was a real privilege. Art College was a massive disappointment. I just wanted to do my own thing so I decided to teach myself. I tried being a full-time artist, but after six months, I found myself doing commissions such as portraits and animals. I became a scaffolder, as it was the only way to earn my living and be free to paint for my own pleasure.

I began painting this subject because I have always been interested in UFOs and believed we were not 'alone.' In 2004, whilst driving my van, my friend was following behind me when, all of a sudden, what could only be described as a spaceship went right over the van, passing very low, about thirty feet. I saw the entire undercarriage,

Mary and Lloyd at the Exopolitics Conference, Leeds, UK, 2015.

which was metal. It was completely silent, which was weird. To be honest, it was one of the scariest things. I tried to scream, but nothing came out of my mouth. I was in a daze and totally spooked. I asked my mate if he saw it too, but he said he saw a small ball. If you ask him now, he says he saw nothing.

I have also seen a triangle UFO, a glowing red one, and some others. I realized this is real. The more I learn, the more I can paint on the subject. I feel I am on a mission and that is to tell this 'truth' through my art to show as many people as possible. I told a reporter my story for *The Mirror* newspaper, but they wrote an article which said I have been abducted six times in ten years, which is untrue. In response to that, I wrote on Facebook that this was incorrect. *The Daily Telegraph* wrote that I hoaxed it to get attention. I even got death threats from some people. On a positive note, I did get my art out there and now have followers in fifty countries and have sold pieces that have gone all over the world. So although I don't sell enough of them to make a living yet, I hope to one day. On YouTube, it states I am a channeling artist. That's quite a big statement to make but I can say I have had my face appear in one of my paintings. I have seen one ET during a meditation, which was eye-opening."

Email lloydcanning.lc@gmail.com

New Mind Records presents a range of relaxation and meditation CDs to suit everyone. Whether you're a novice or advanced, these CDs will enable you to reach a more relaxed and peaceful state of being. Combined with the latest audio technology, stunning music, subliminal positive affirmations and creative imagery, this is the whole package.

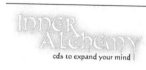

cds to expand your mind

Inner Alchemy is for those individuals who wish to expand their creative and intuitive abilities.

FOR HEALTHY MIND, BODY AND SPIRIT

Mind Medicine is created for stress-related illnesses, and changing old negative programs.

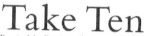

Take Ten
10 Minute Meditations for Busy People

Take Ten is designed for the busy person who wishes to refresh and re-balance with limited time.

Armchair journey is a virtual reality for the mind. Have fun as you explore your imagination.

Natural Mother

Natural Mother is a new way for women to approach relaxation and connect with their baby in pregnancy and motherhood.

Sound healing for those individuals who wish to try sound frequencies for mind, body, spirit healing.

New Mind Records | E contact@newmindrecords.com | **www.newmindrecords.com**

AWAKENING
How Extraterrestrial Contact Can Transform Your Life
MARY RODWELL

Many people around the world, from all walks of life, believe themselves to be in regular Contact with beings from outer-space.

Some people are aware of it, but many are completely in the dark, as ET encounters occur in numerous ways. The process of waking up to this multidimensional reality is not always easy, but the results are positively life-changing. Are you having encounters with non-human intelligences? How do you know? The first step is to be informed and Awakening to Contact is right here.

"Awakening: How Extraterrestrial Contact Can Transform Your Life. In my opinion, this book will become the bible of the Alien Abduction Phenomenon."

Dr. Roger Leir, author of *The Aliens and the Scalpel.*

"This isn't just a research book, it's much more, and written by a lady who has hands-on Contact with the people she writes about. Mary's professionalism shines through the pages, combined with concern and compassion for the people she is trying to help. This is a book about Experiencers that is an Experience in itself. Quality."

Kate Miller – UFO Mag (UK).

"*Awakening* has become one of my 'bibles' for witness support literature because of its unique focus on how to help oneself and other experiencers."

James Basil (UK).

"*Awakening* helped me enormously. I found these connections because of one keen and courageous woman; a professional. Awakening is a big Lantern book."

Author Dana Redfield (USA).

"Mary, your book is fantastic. I think it's the first truly comprehensive and accurate thing in print and you cover all with clarity and grace."

Ruth McKinley Hoover PhD (USA).

"I also wanted to say about your book *Awakening*. As I read it, I received further activations, symbols and some of my techniques got downloaded to me. I would read *Awakening*, and close my eyes and get downloaded symbols I now use over people. This all happened when I closed my eyes and while I was reading something in *Awakening*. Your first book *Awakening* is definitely an 'activator.' I also recommend it to my patients. This is real – this is what we are talking about."

Dr. M. Batchelor M.D. (Australia).

NEW MIND
PUBLISHERS

To order, go to **www.maryrodwell.com.au** or order direct by emailing Mary at **starline@iinet.net.au** or through Facebook **www.facebook.com/acern.com.au**. Also available through **Amazon.**

Maybe we are not who we think we are? As a species?

CPSIA information can be obtained
at www.ICGtesting.com
Printed in the USA
BVHW041615011218
534526BV00001B/81/P

9 780980 755510